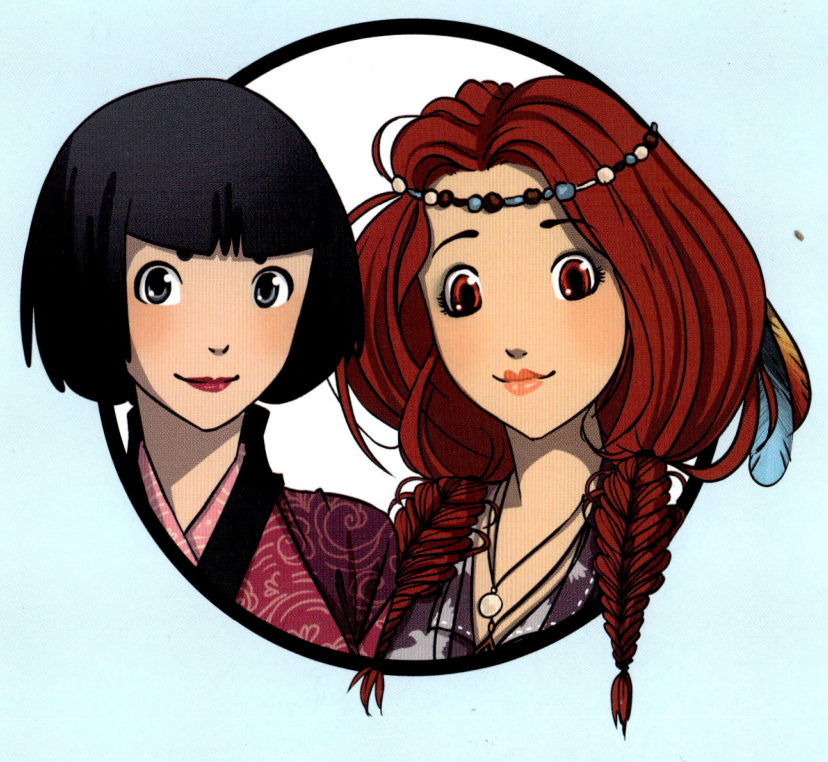

THE SHOUJO
MANGA FASHION
DRAWING BOOK

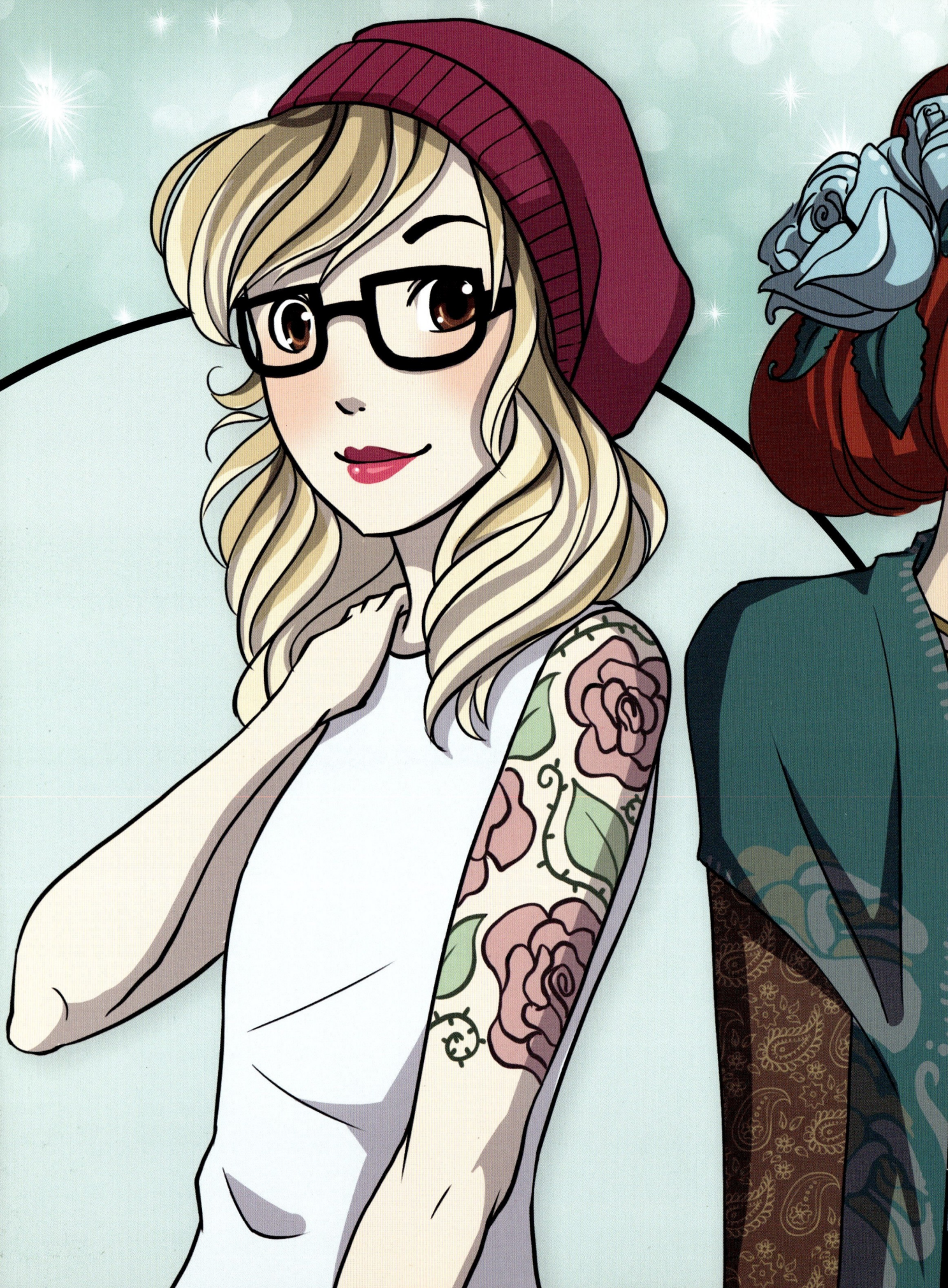

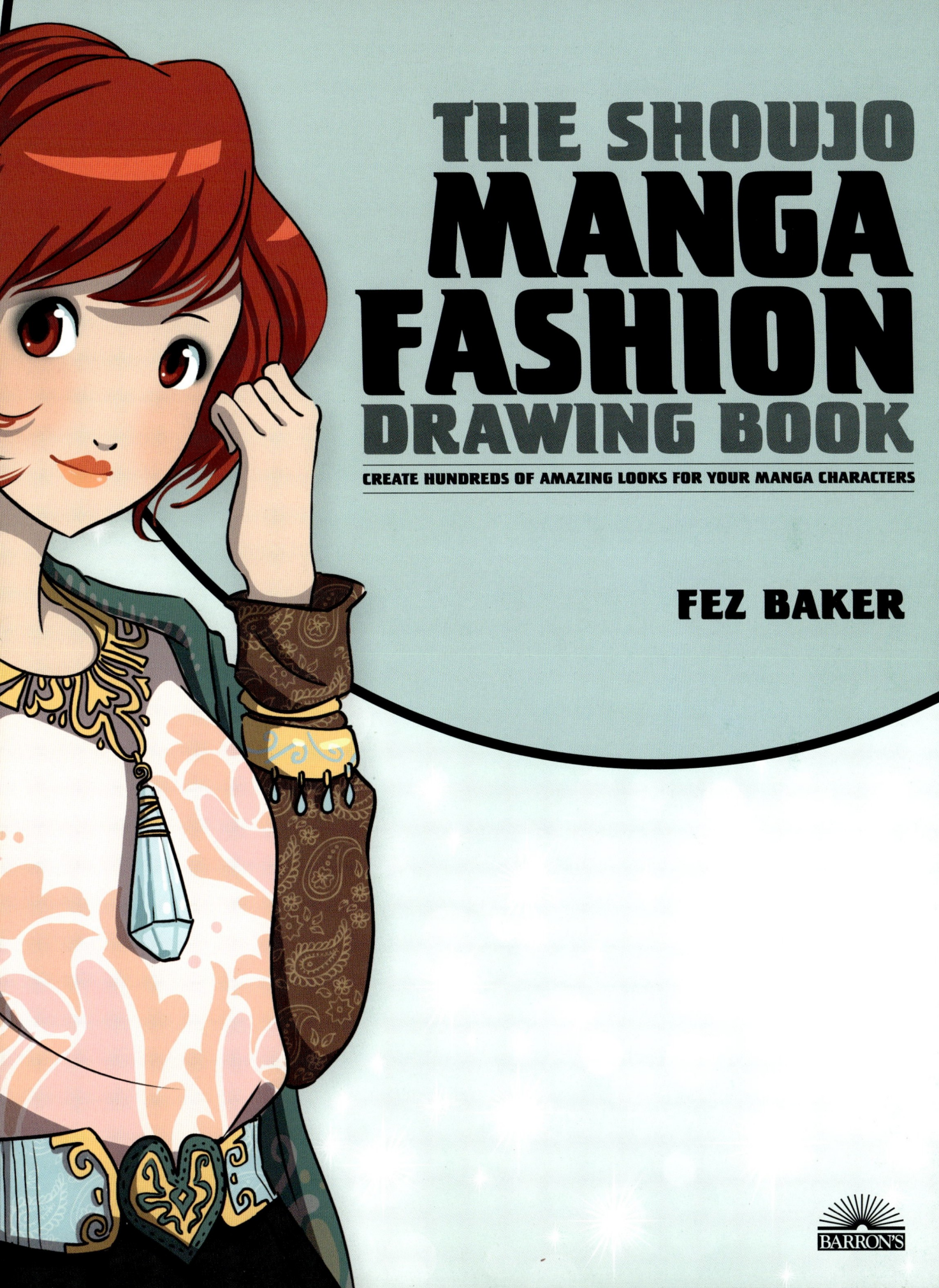

The Shoujo Manga Fashion Drawing Book

A Quarto book
Copyright © 2015 Quarto Inc.

First edition for North America published in 2015 by
Barron's Educational Series, Inc.

All rights reserved. No part of this publication may be reproduced or distributed in any form or by any means without the written permission of the copyright owner.

All inquiries should be addressed to:
Barron's Educational Series, Inc.
250 Wireless Boulevard
Hauppauge, New York 11788
www.barronseduc.com

ISBN: 978-1-4380-0658-1

Library of Congress Control No.: 2014948369

QUAR.MFDP
Conceived, designed, and produced by
Quarto Publishing plc
The Old Brewery
6 Blundell Street
London N7 9BH

Senior editor: Katie Crous
Senior art editor: Emma Clayton
Designer: Karin Skånberg
Copy editor: Liz Dalby
Picture researcher: Sarah Bell
Art director: Caroline Guest
Creative director: Moira Clinch
Publisher: Paul Carslake

Color separation in Hong Kong by Bright Arts Ltd
Printed in China by Hung Hing Off-set Printing Co. Ltd

9 8 7 6 5 4 3 2 1

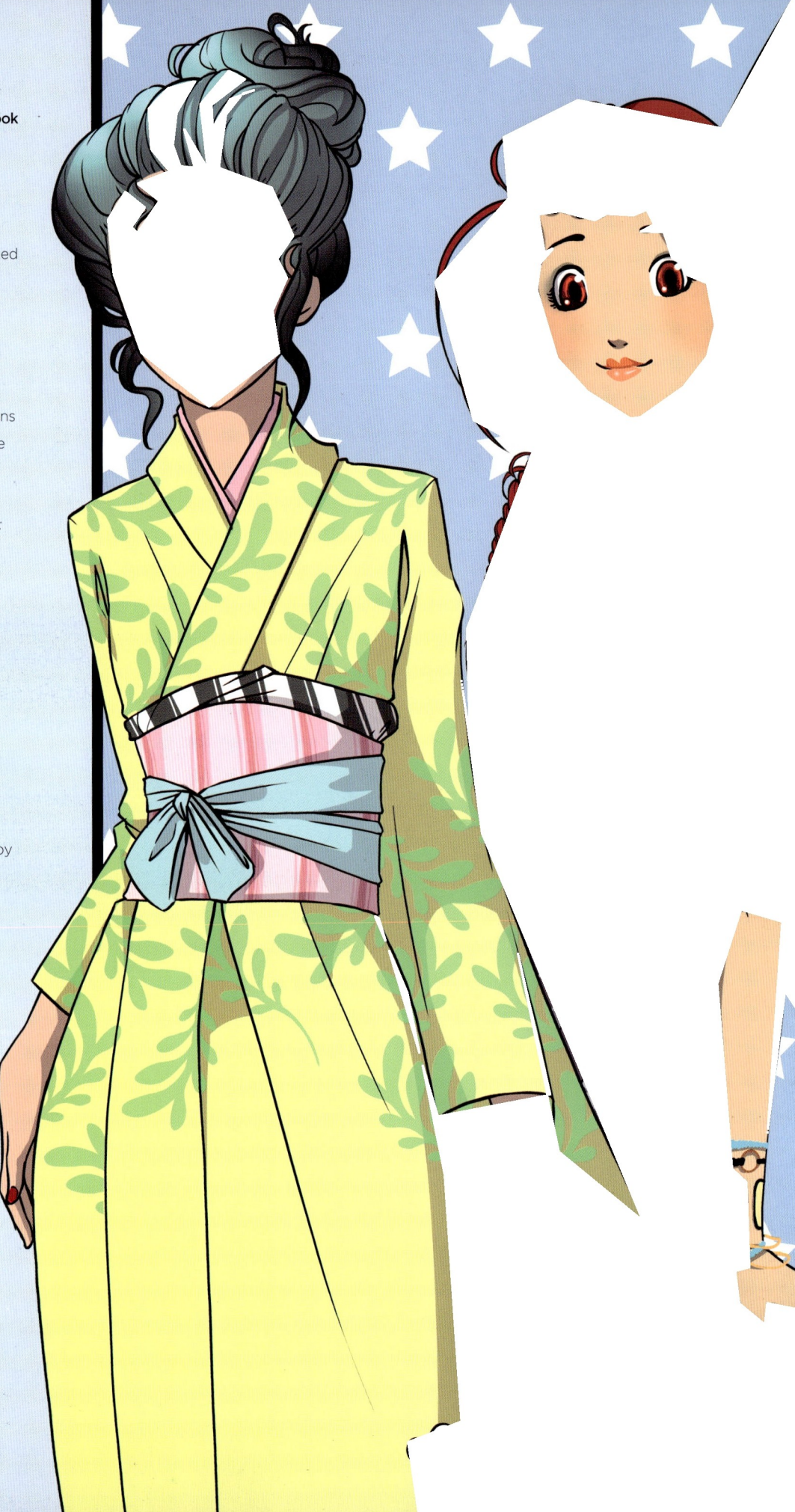

CONTENTS

| ABOUT THIS BOOK | 6 |
| COLLECTION SELECTOR | 8 |

CHAPTER 1 Drawing Basics — 12

ANATOMY	14
POSING	16
HEADS AND FACES	18
SKIN TONES	20
HAIR AND HAIRSTYLES	22
CLOTHING THE FIGURE	24
FABRIC TEXTURES	28
CREATING CLASSIC PATTERNS	30
CLASSIC CUTS	32
CREATIVE COLORING	38

CHAPTER 2 The Collections — 40

HARAJUKU STREET	42
PREPPY STYLE	46
BOHO CHIC	50
PUNK STYLE	54
HOLLYWOOD GLAM	58
ROCK ROYALTY	62
GOTHIC FASHION	66
CLASSIC LOLITA	70
SWEET LOLITA	72
GOTHIC LOLITA	74
GANGURO	76
HIPSTER	80
EMO AND SCENE	84
MIAMI BEACH	88
VINTAGE COLLECTION	92
DOLLY KEI	96
KIMONO STREET STYLE	98
CYBERPUNK	102
SUNDAY LOUNGEWEAR	106
WILDERNESS CHIC	110
MILITARY	114
WINTER KNITWEAR	118
ANDROGYNOUS	122
HIP-HOP	126
APOCALYPSE STYLE	130
SPORTSWEAR	134
BON CHIC BON GENRE	138

RESOURCES	142
INDEX	142
CREDITS	144

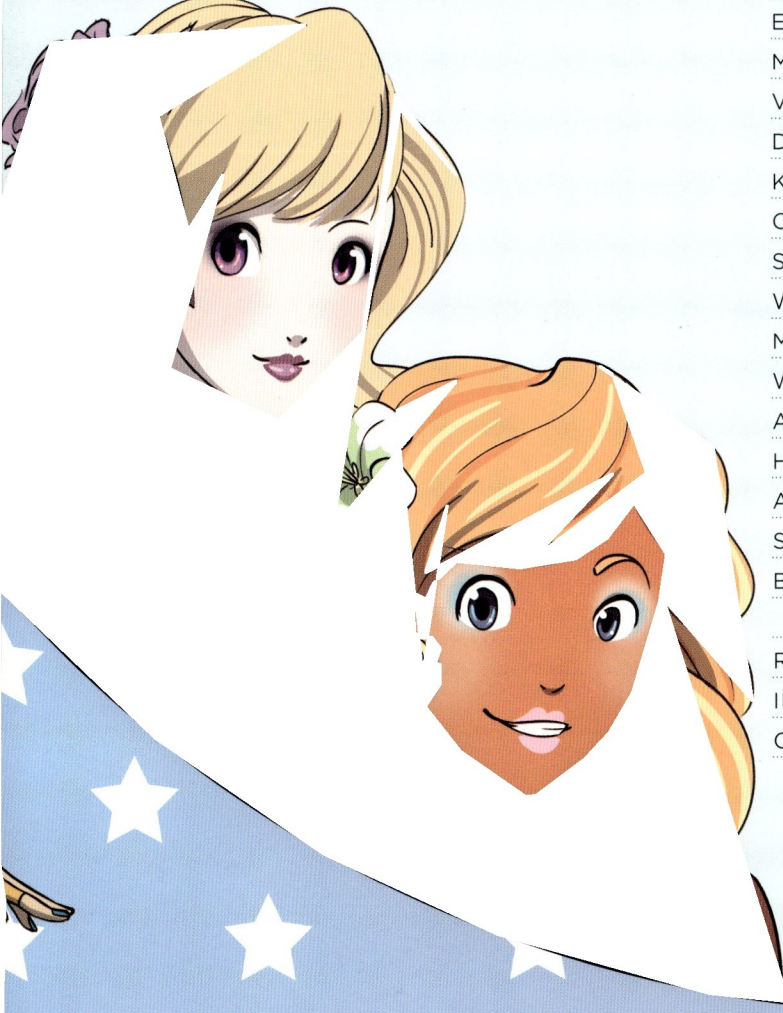

ABOUT THIS BOOK

DRAWING BASICS PAGES 12–39

This section takes you through the core principles of drawing, starting with the figure and ending with color theory. Referring to these pages first will make sure that your characters are suitably posed and styled—head to toe—for their chosen look. You'll also find sound advice on drawing different textiles and their patterns and textures, and a mini-directory of staple fashion cuts for key garments.

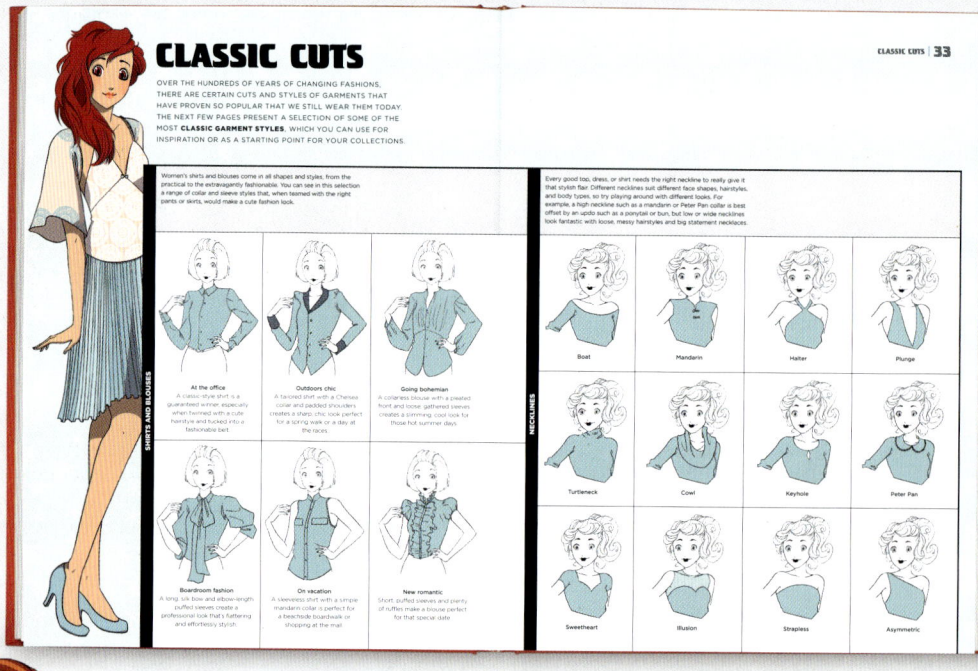

WELCOME ...

... to the catwalk, fashionista!

If you're anything like me, you've probably already realized that not only are manga characters super cute, but they get to wear some pretty amazing clothes, too. The girls and guys of the manga world are the stars of their own story, and they dress to impress.

Although we can't slip into a manga story ourselves, have you ever thought about how fun it would be to design their clothes yourself? With the tips and tutorials in this book, you'll be creating your own fashion collections in no time—perfect for dressing up your characters or building a portfolio of stylish manga clothing.

With contributions from two other talented artists—Emma Vieceli and Laura Watton-Davies—you'll find in here more than 25 different fashion looks, along with a whole bunch of useful tutorials, style notes, and step-by-step instructions. So get out your tablet, pens, or paints and start creating your fashion portfolio!

Fez Baker

ABOUT THIS BOOK

THE COLLECTIONS PAGES 40-141

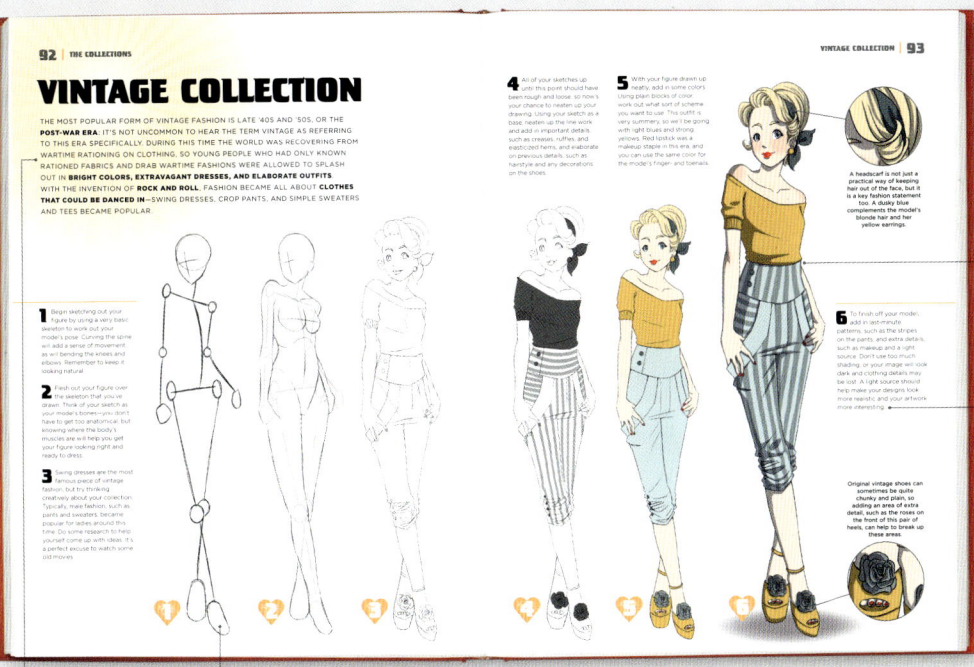

Choosing from more than 25 varying collections, this is your chance to become a manga fashion designer extraordinaire and clothe your characters in a way that expresses their personality and fits their lifestyle.

The final, fully clothed, styled, shaded, and colored character shows what you're aiming toward.

Clear and precise instructions accompany each illustration, providing detail on how to draw each step.

Starting with a sketched skeleton, see the process of how each step brings you closer to the fully clothed character.

A mixture of line work and finished colored items—designed to fit the featured models and their poses—offer plenty more inspiration for your character's closet, with helpful advice on how to replicate the piece and tweak it to suit your taste and/or purpose.

Each collection is introduced with background information and a summary of the distinguishing characteristics of the featured fashion style.

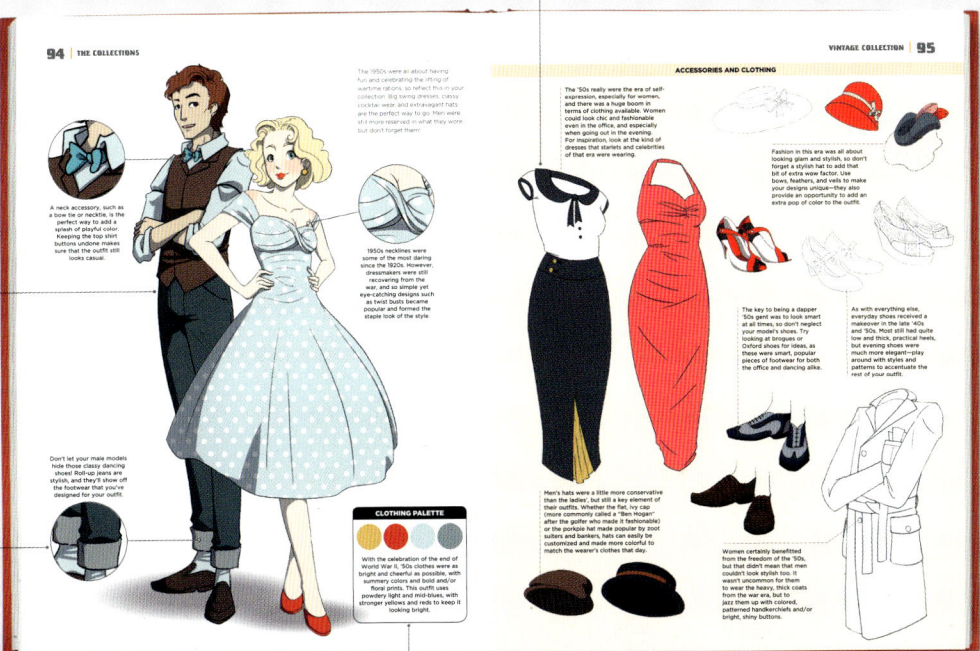

Two additional models showcase alternative outfits and poses, introducing you to further possibilities within the same look.

Defining features of the model and outfit are selected and magnified, allowing you to see the detail close-up.

A color palette provides a base from which to design and explains the main hues for the collection.

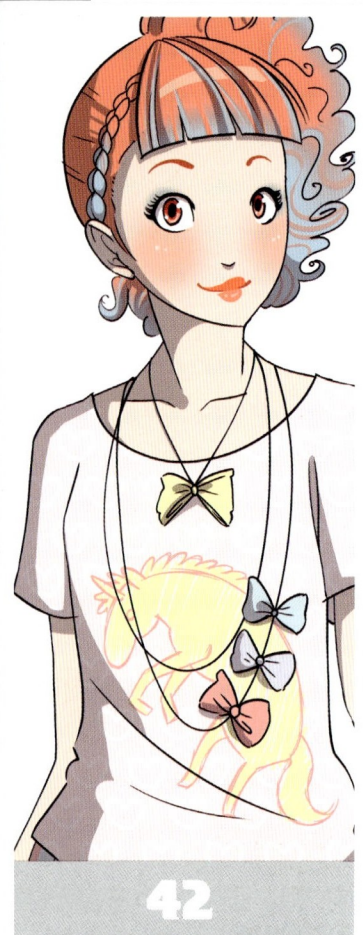

42
HARAJUKU STREET

46
PREPPY STYLE

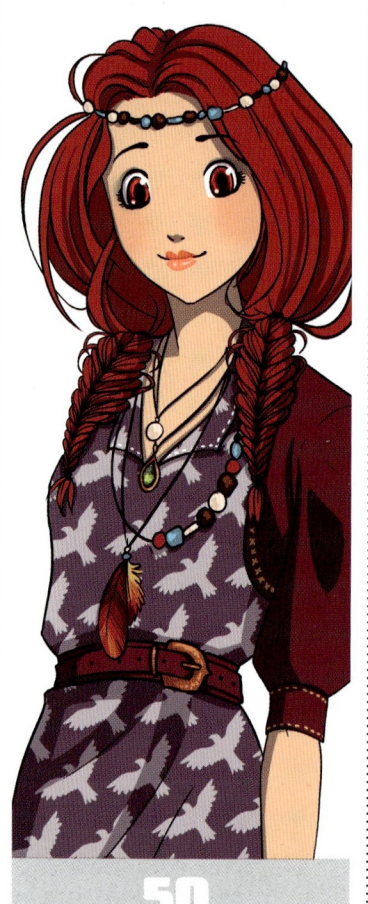

50
BOHO CHIC

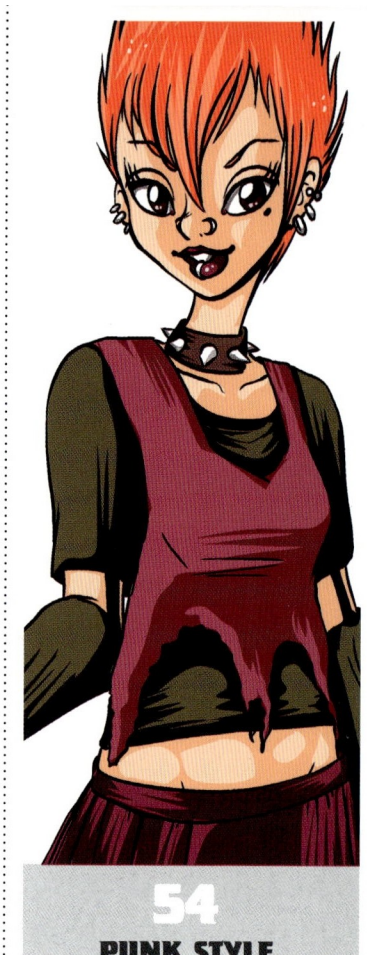

54
PUNK STYLE

62
ROCK ROYALTY

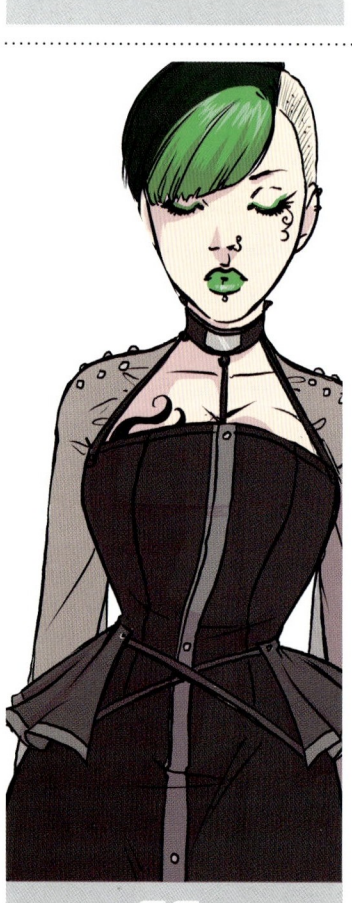

66
GOTHIC FASHION

70
CLASSIC LOLITA

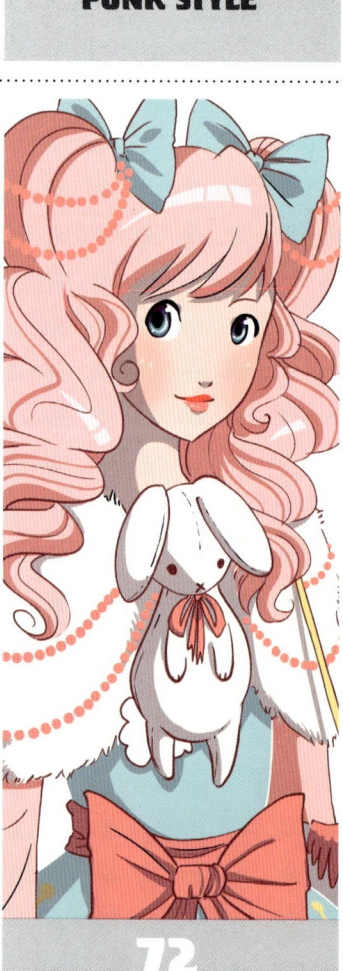

72
SWEET LOLITA

COLLECTION SELECTOR

Take your pick from the **FASHION PARADE** and use this quick-glance guide to all the collections in this book, treating your characters to a look that suits them completely. There is **SOMETHING FOR EVERY PERSONALITY**—from fun party girl to outspoken punk rocker, from trendy hipster to cute Lolita.

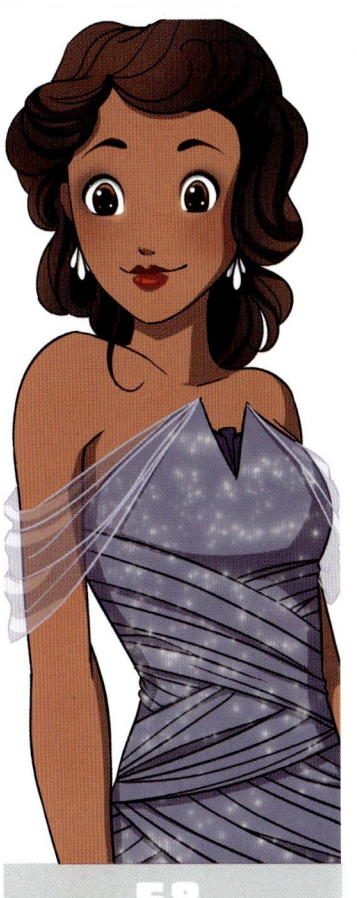

58
HOLLYWOOD GLAM

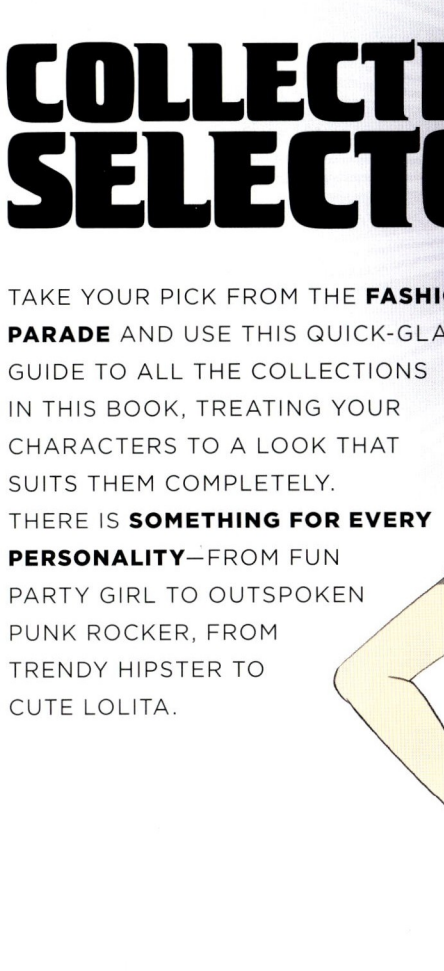

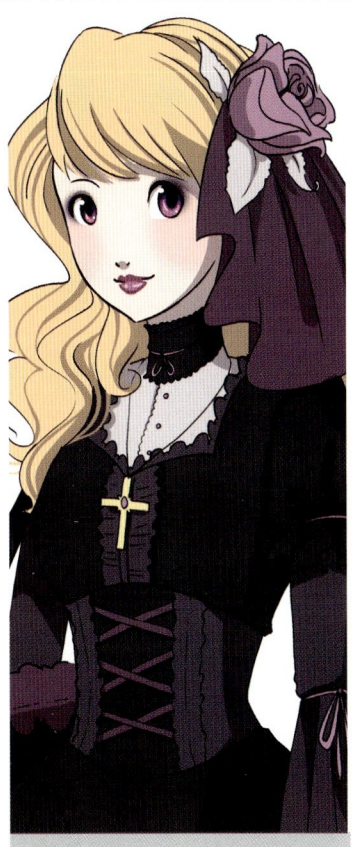

74
GOTHIC LOLITA

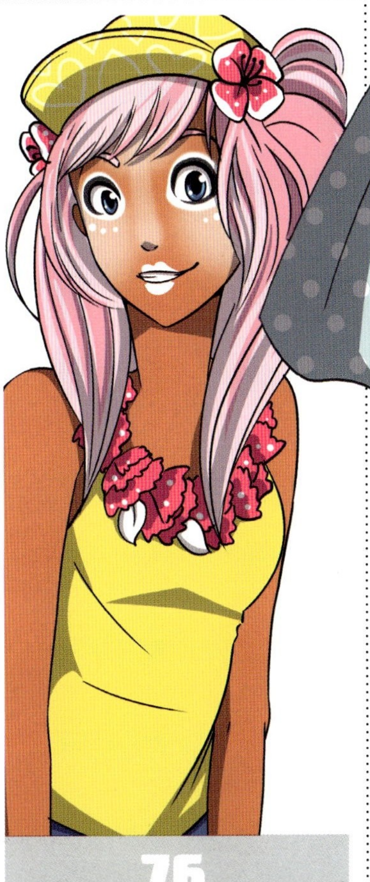

76
GANGURO

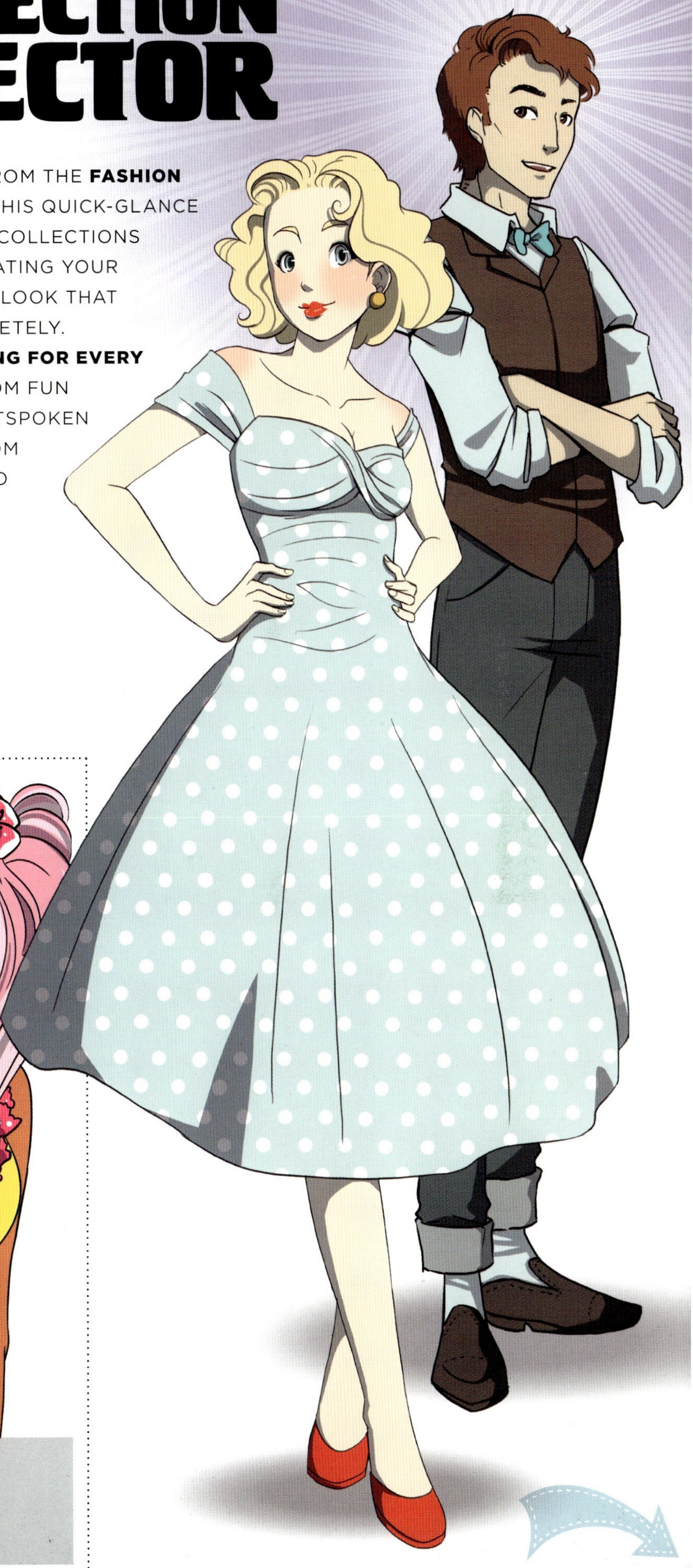

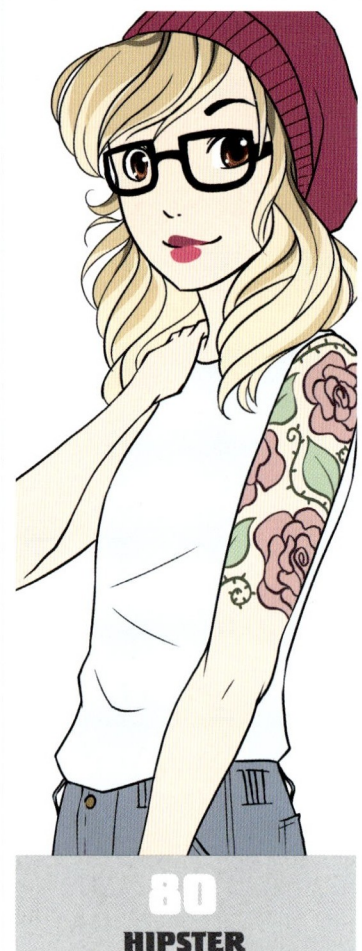

80
HIPSTER

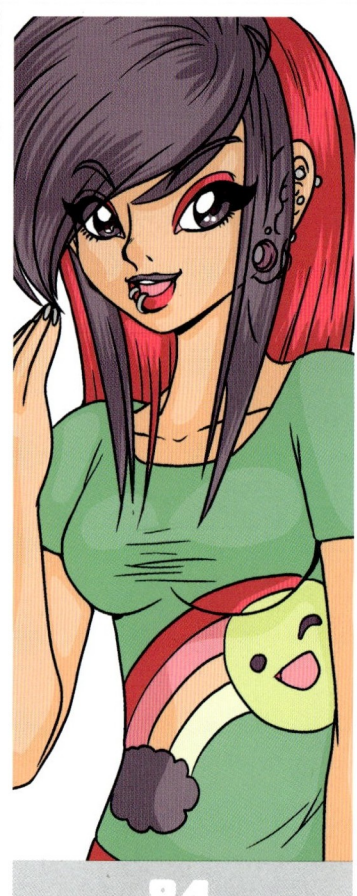

84
EMO AND SCENE

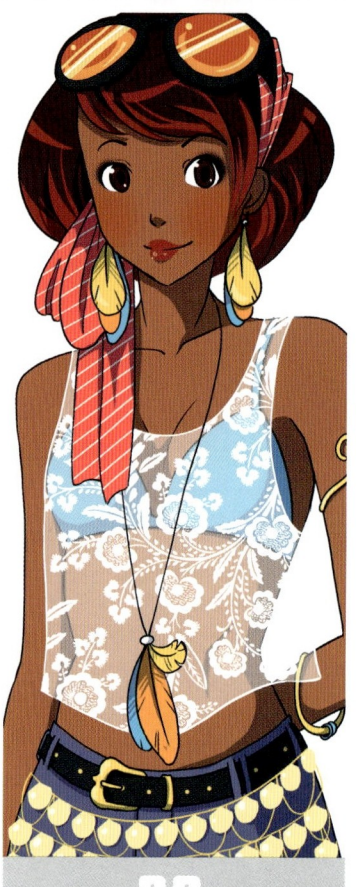

88
MIAMI BEACH

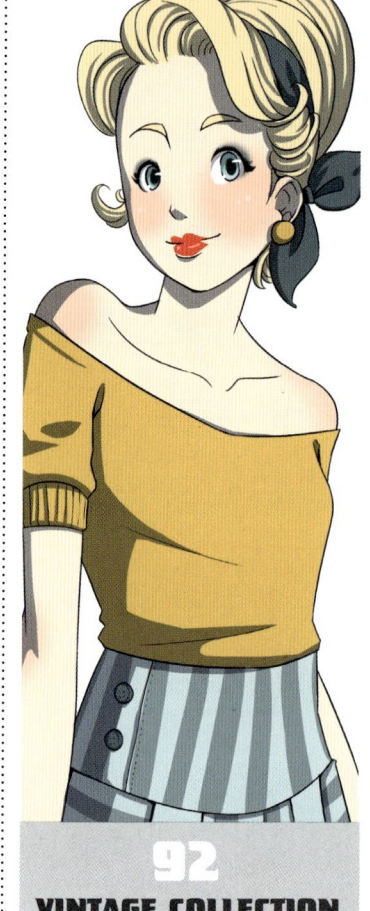

92
VINTAGE COLLECTION

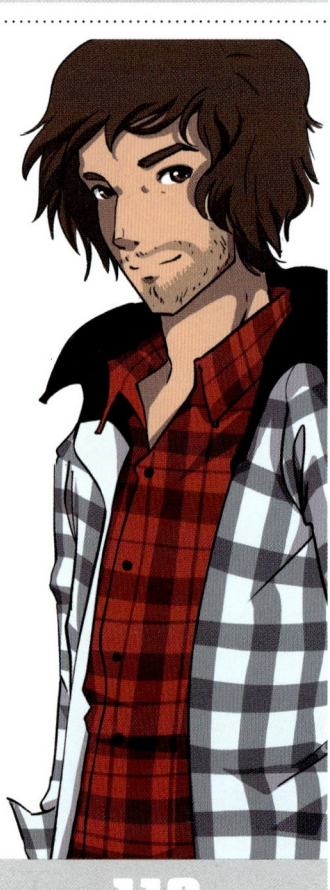

110
WILDERNESS CHIC

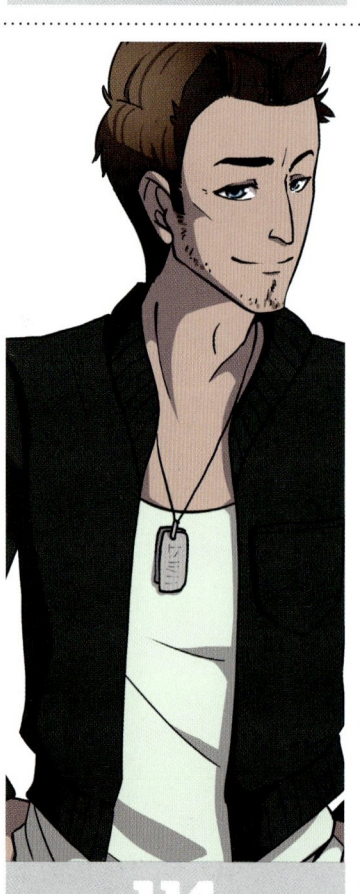

114
MILITARY

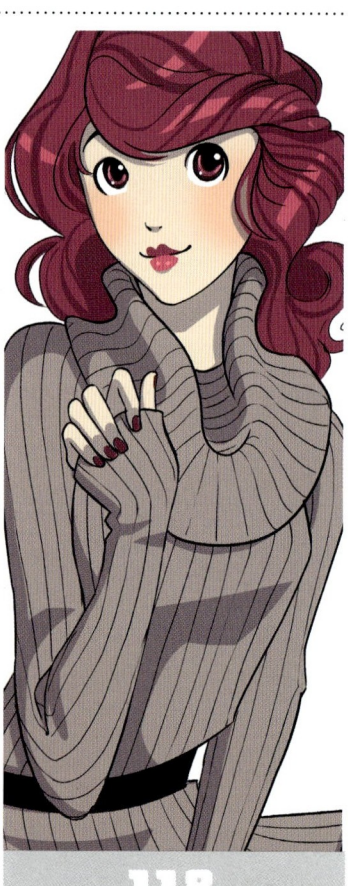

118
WINTER KNITWEAR

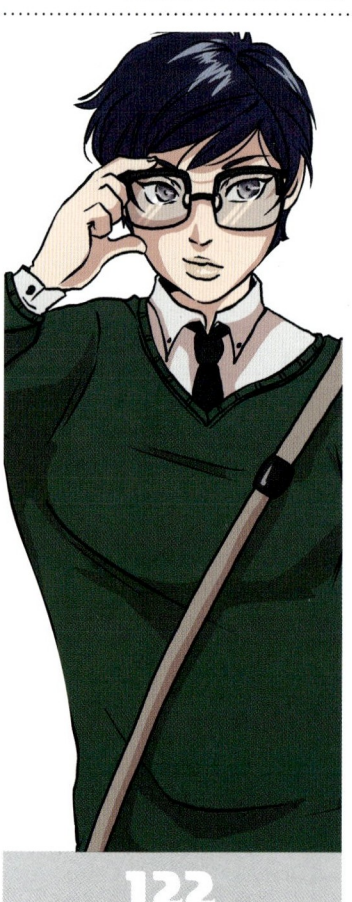

122
ANDROGYNOUS

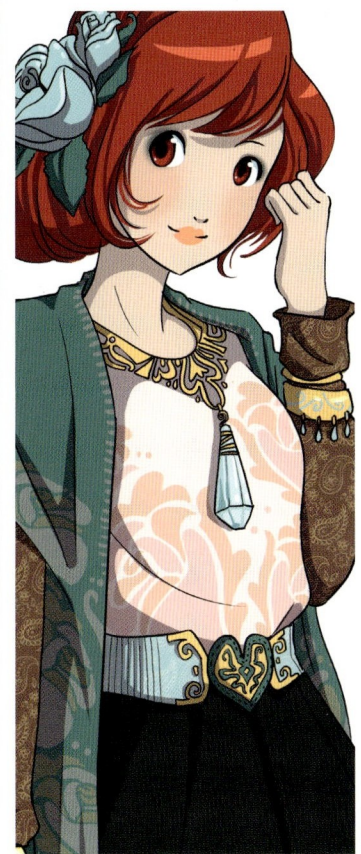

96
DOLLY KEI

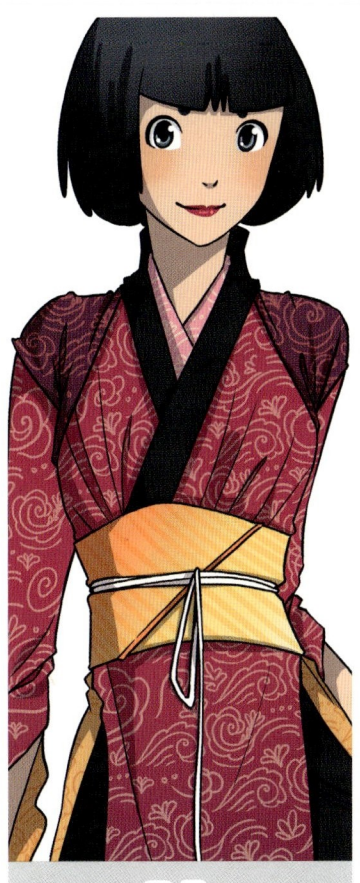

98
KIMONO STREET STYLE

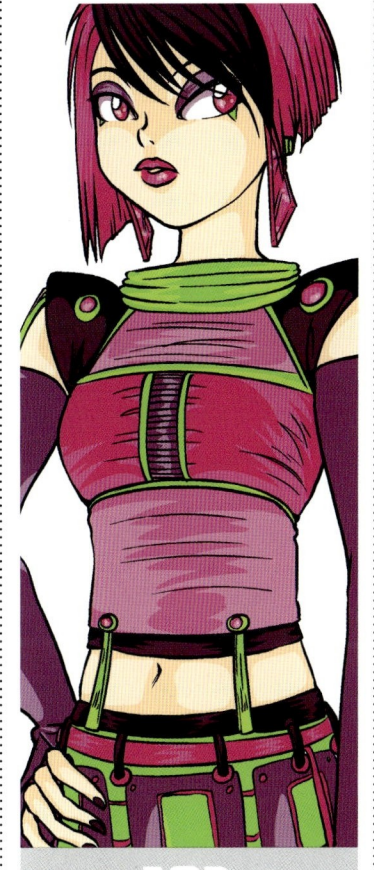

102
CYBERPUNK

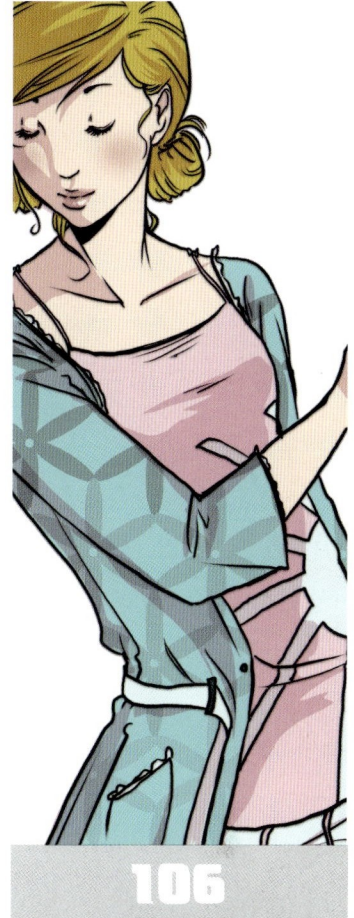

106
SUNDAY LOUNGEWEAR

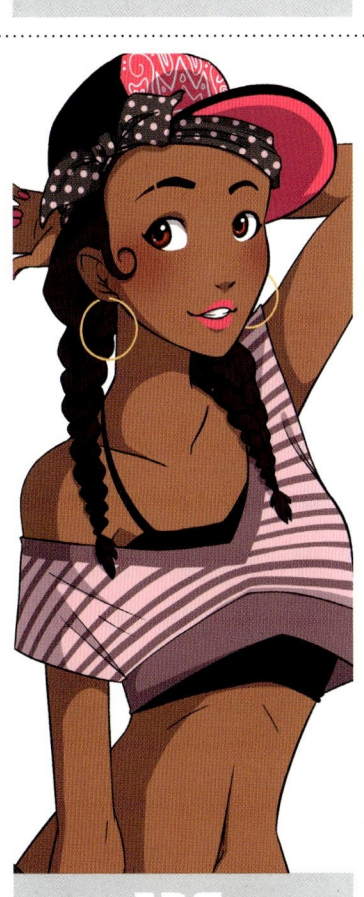

126
HIP-HOP

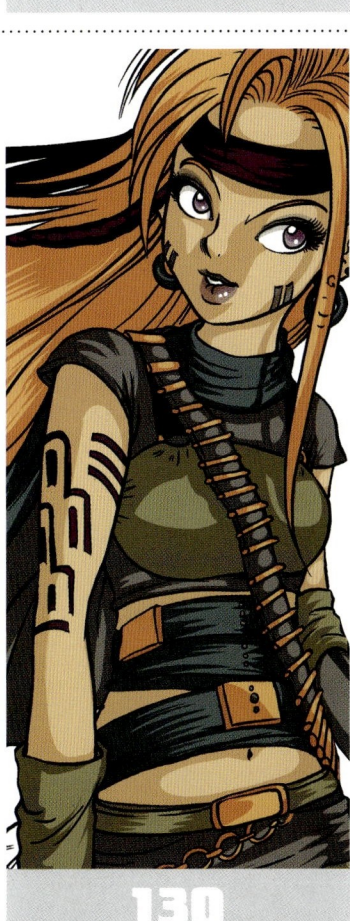

130
APOCALYPSE STYLE

134
SPORTSWEAR

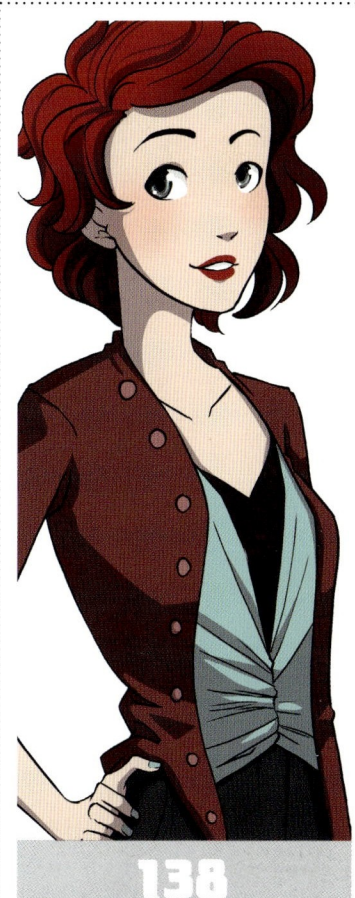

138
BON CHIC BON GENRE

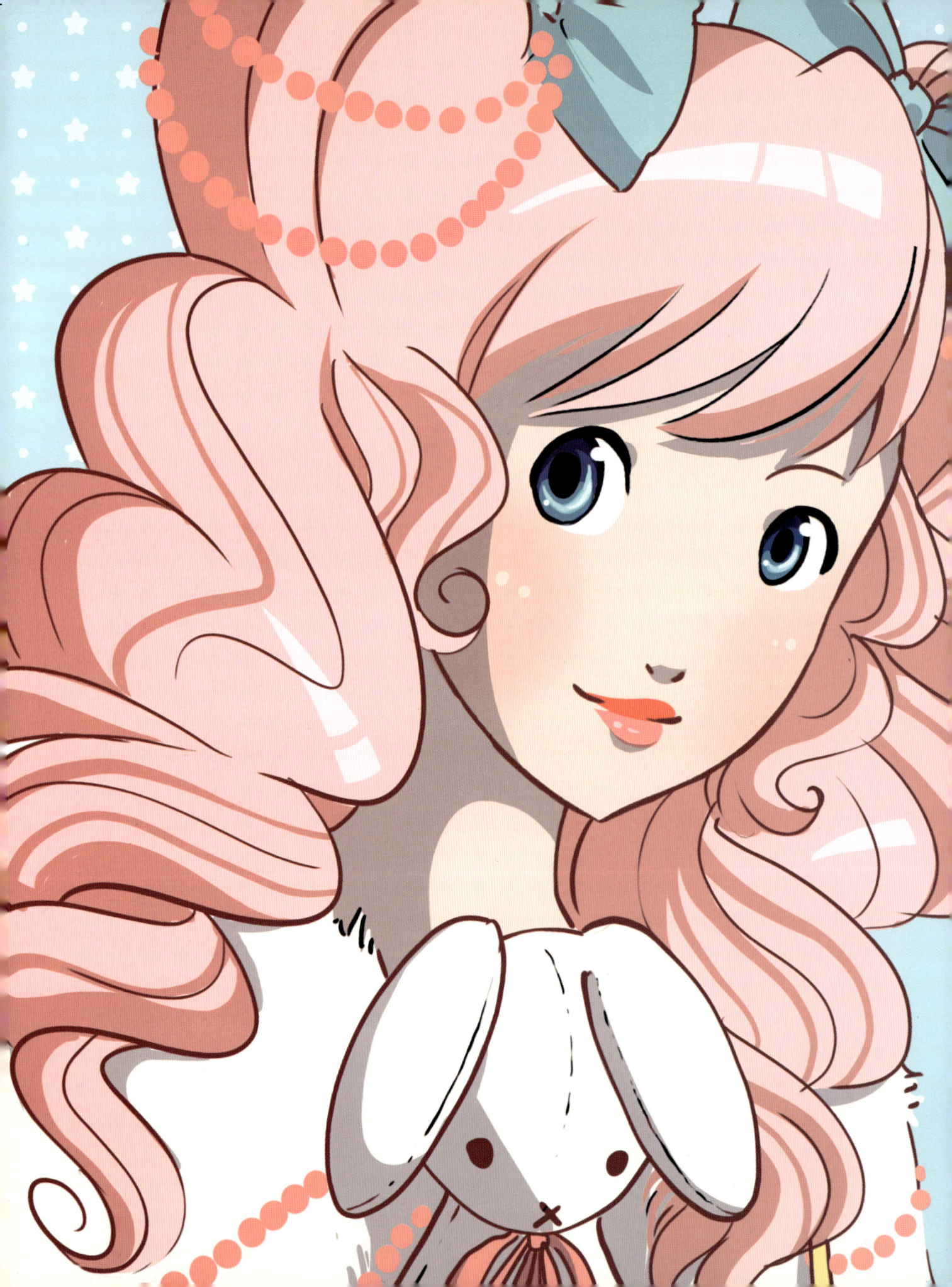

1 DRAWING BASICS

FASHION ISN'T ONLY ABOUT THE CLOTHES—IT'S ALSO ABOUT THE **POSE, EXPRESSION, AND HAIR**. UNDERSTANDING THE CORE PRINCIPLES OF DRAWING FIGURES, HEADS, AND FACES WILL GO A LONG WAY IN **MAKING YOUR CHARACTERS BELIEVABLE**, AND WILL GIVE YOU A **HEAD START IN CLOTHING THEM SUCCESSFULLY AND STYLISHLY**. AND WHEN IT COMES TO CLOTHING, FAMILIARITY WITH THE MAIN GARMENT CUTS—AND COLOR THEORY—WILL HELP YOU TO PUT YOUR OWN **DESIGNER TWIST** ON THE COLLECTIONS.

14 | DRAWING BASICS

ANATOMY

FEMALE

The average human being stands between seven and eight "heads" tall. This means that once you have drawn your model's head, you'll be able to measure how long the rest of the body should be.

- ● *Sternocleidomastoid*
- ● *Trapezius*
- ● *Deltoids*
- ● *Outer biceps*
- ● *Brachioradialis*
- ● *Flexor carpi ulnaris*
- ● *Pectorals*
- ● *Serratus anterior*
- ● *Abdominals*
- ● *Obliques*

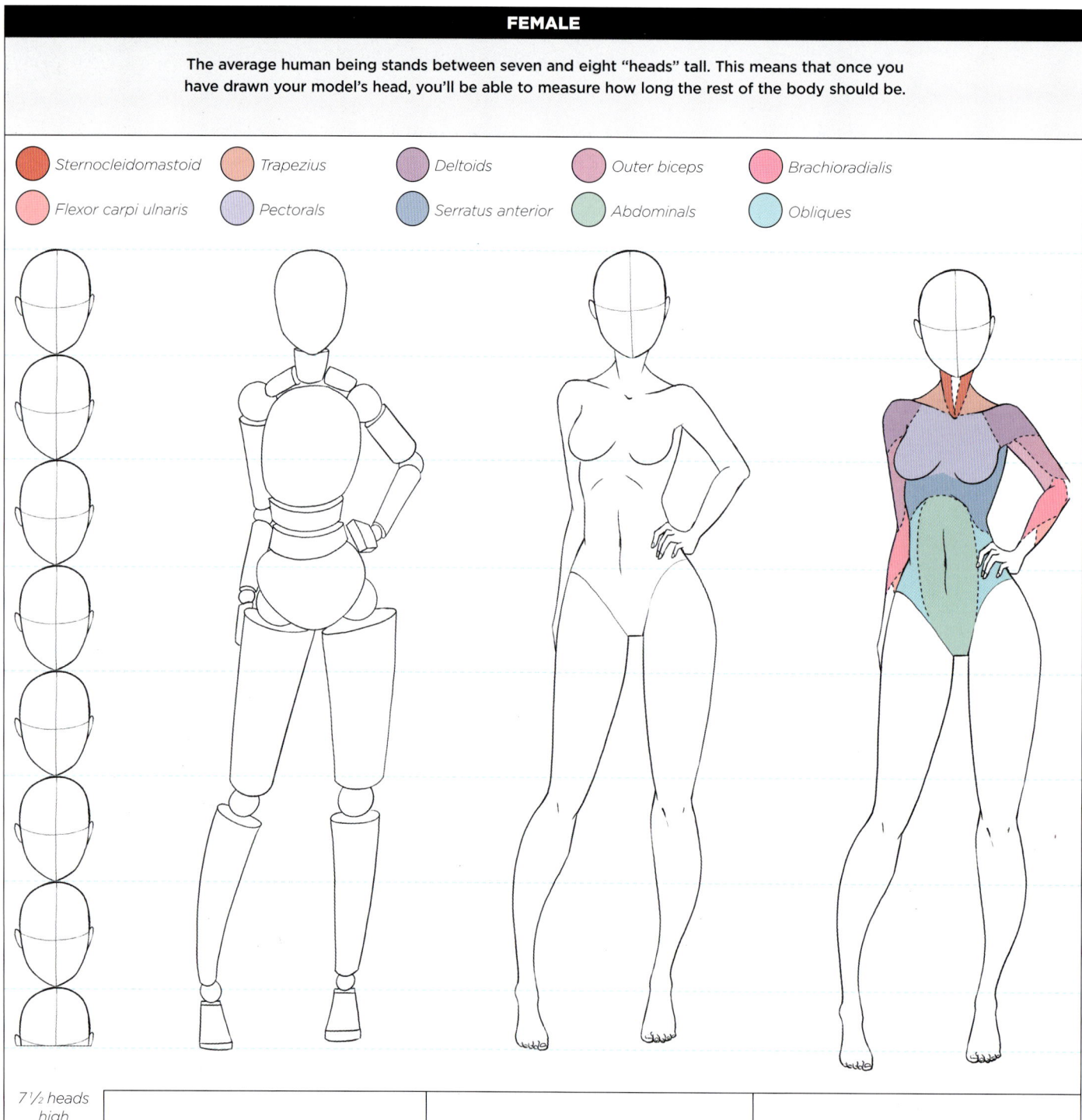

7 1/2 heads high

A great way to learn the basics of drawing people and anatomy is to break their bodies down into very basic shapes. Women naturally have a very soft, rounded shape; circles, cylinders, and rounded triangles all combine to create a basic figure.

Though every woman is a different shape, the classic body type that's often chosen for fashion models is the "hourglass" shape—this means the model's hips and shoulders are around the same width, and the waist tapers in the middle.

It's worth spending a little time studying the body's muscle structure. By understanding the principal muscles that comprise the arms and torso, you'll be better able to place features such as the belly button, abs, and ribs.

ANATOMY | **15**

YOU MAY WANT TO JUMP STRAIGHT INTO DESIGNING YOUR FASHION COLLECTIONS, BUT BEFORE YOU DO, IT'S IMPORTANT TO LEARN A FEW BASICS ABOUT DRAWING YOUR MODELS. WITH AN UNDERSTANDING OF **HOW THE HUMAN BODY WORKS**, YOU'LL BE ABLE TO DRAW **ACCURATE, APPEALING MODELS** TO SHOW OFF YOUR DESIGNS TO THEIR FULL POTENTIAL.

MALE

Typically, men are taller than women—though in the fashion world, there are some strikingly tall female models around. The male figure below is eight heads tall, whereas his female counterpart is seven and a half.

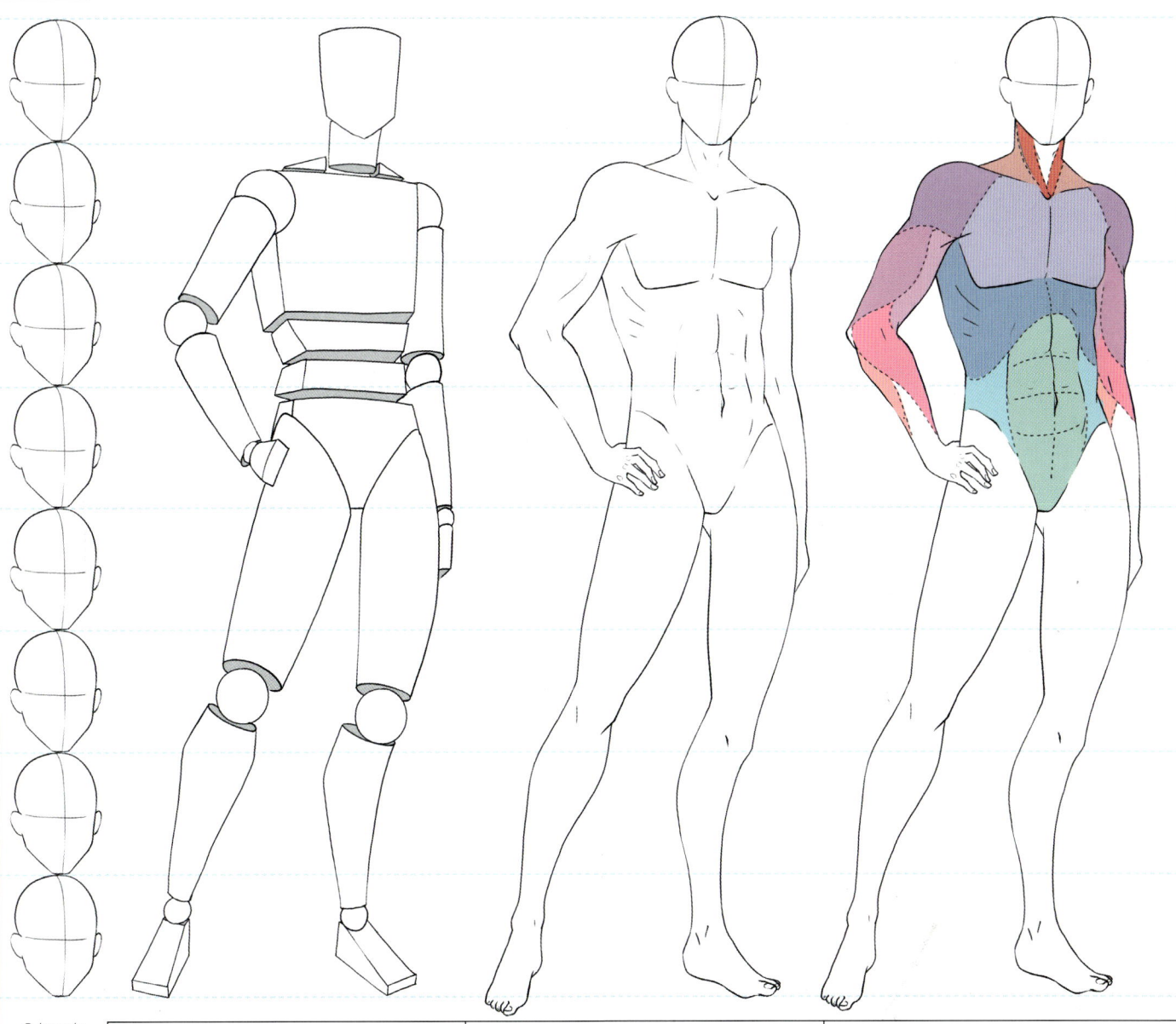

8 heads high

In contrast to women, men are traditionally very linear and blocky—their shoulders are very broad, and their bodies are made up of straight lines and sharp angles. Use squares and rectangles to create a strong, tall male figure.

In this figure, you can see how studying the muscles (see right) has helped to give the torso shape and definition. You can also see that this model has a very traditional male physique—his shoulders are broader than his hips, which gives his chest a classic "V" shape.

Though men and women are very different shapes, compare this diagram to the female figure's muscles, and you'll see that inside, they're very similar! Men's muscles have a tendency to be more pronounced, especially around the stomach and chest, so practice drawing these areas in particular.

16 | DRAWING BASICS

The poses below are perfect for showing off a collection of outfits. Remember to keep your models looking confident, sassy, and, most of all, like they're having fun!

POSING

NOW YOU'VE HAD A CHANCE TO PRACTICE THE BASICS OF ANATOMY, IT'S TIME TO LEARN A LITTLE ABOUT HOW TO POSE YOUR MODELS. IF YOUR MODELS HAVE **THE RIGHT ATTITUDE**, YOUR COLLECTIONS WILL LOOK SO MUCH BETTER—IT'S REALLY WORTH SPENDING TIME GOING OVER THE FOLLOWING TIPS.

POSING | 17

POSTURE

It's important to understand how a model's posture can change the way they come across to someone looking at your drawings. A model who is slouching, with hunched shoulders and her eyes fixed on the floor, comes across as uncertain and self-conscious; she clearly isn't comfortable in the clothes she's wearing. However, a model who is standing tall conveys a completely different image—by standing with her feet slightly apart, her spine curved, and her chin tilted back, she's showing off how much she loves her outfit. This is the perfect way to advertise your fashion collections.

WEARING HEELS

A good pair of heels is a must on the runway, but it's important to understand how wearing heels can change a model's posture beyond simply making her a little taller. As you can see, when a model is wearing flat shoes, her body has a very uniform alignment—the waist, hips, knees, and ankles are all balanced evenly. However, when wearing heels, these joints begin to tilt at pronounced angles—the higher the heel, the sharper the angle. This shift in angles makes the body's natural shape even more pronounced; the chest and buttocks are pushed out, and the knees bend slightly to maintain balance. For this reason, drawing a model with completely straight legs while she is wearing heels will look unnatural.

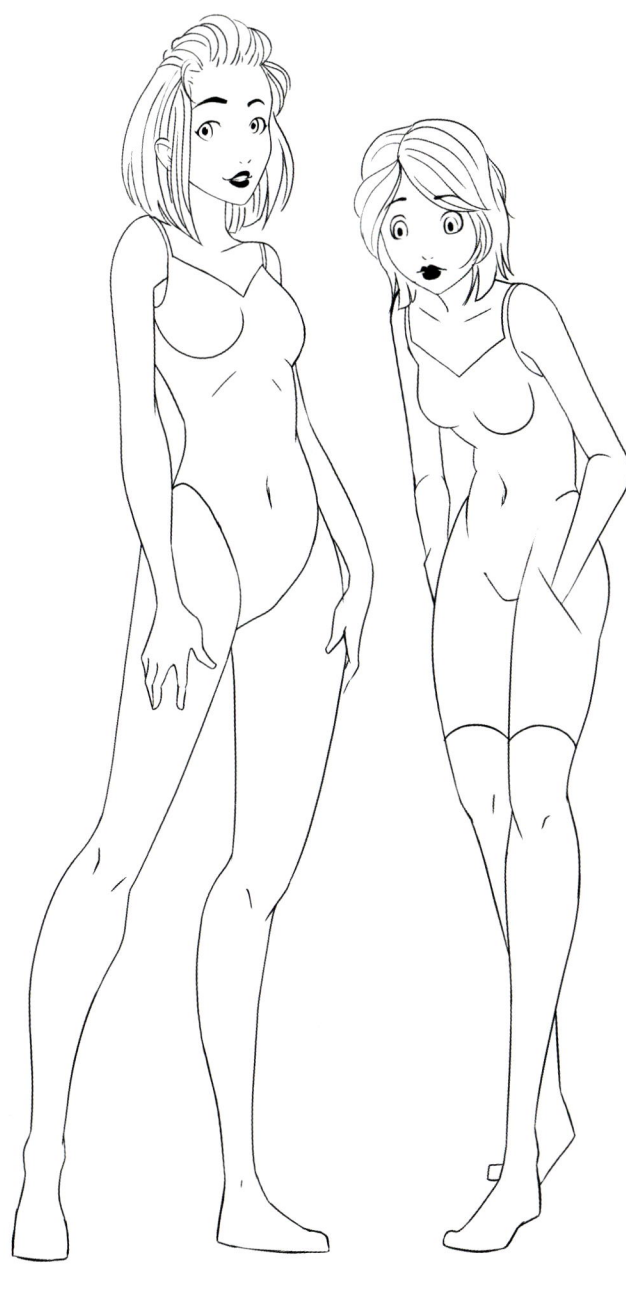

Posture has a huge impact on the way that people come across.

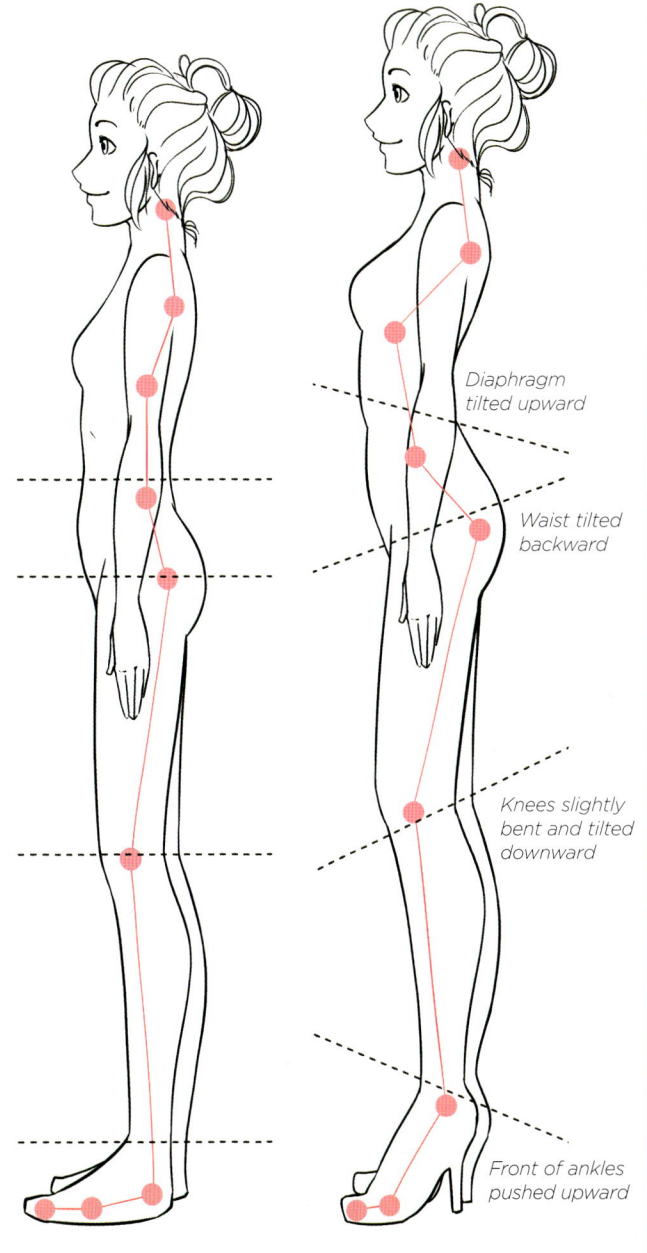

Diaphragm tilted upward

Waist tilted backward

Knees slightly bent and tilted downward

Front of ankles pushed upward

Wearing heels does more than just make a model taller; they change her posture too.

HEADS AND FACES

HEADS CAN BE ONE OF THE HARDEST THINGS TO DRAW: ANY MISTAKES IMMEDIATELY STAND OUT, AND THIS CAN BE FRUSTRATING FOR THE LEARNING ARTIST. HOWEVER, THESE SIMPLE TIPS SHOULD SOON HAVE YOU **DRAWING THEM WITH CONFIDENCE**.

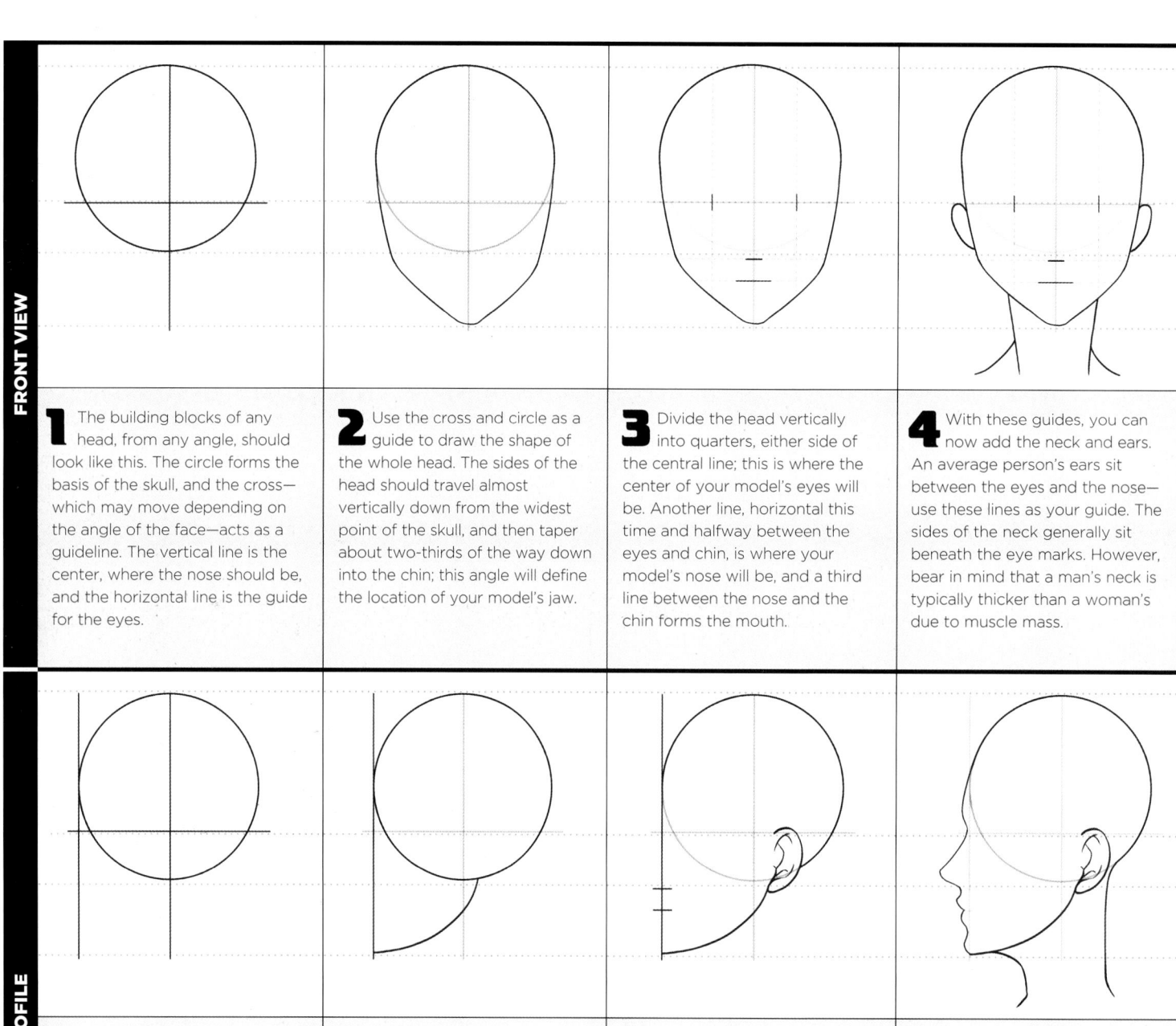

FRONT VIEW

1 The building blocks of any head, from any angle, should look like this. The circle forms the basis of the skull, and the cross—which may move depending on the angle of the face—acts as a guideline. The vertical line is the center, where the nose should be, and the horizontal line is the guide for the eyes.

2 Use the cross and circle as a guide to draw the shape of the whole head. The sides of the head should travel almost vertically down from the widest point of the skull, and then taper about two-thirds of the way down into the chin; this angle will define the location of your model's jaw.

3 Divide the head vertically into quarters, either side of the central line; this is where the center of your model's eyes will be. Another line, horizontal this time and halfway between the eyes and chin, is where your model's nose will be, and a third line between the nose and the chin forms the mouth.

4 With these guides, you can now add the neck and ears. An average person's ears sit between the eyes and the nose—use these lines as your guide. The sides of the neck generally sit beneath the eye marks. However, bear in mind that a man's neck is typically thicker than a woman's due to muscle mass.

PROFILE

1 As you can see, the same "circle and cross" method from above applies to side views of the face too. However, this time the center of the cross acts as a guide for where the end of the jaw should be; a second vertical line at the side of the circle forms the front of the face.

2 Using the central vertical line as a guide, draw in a curve from the tip of the chin to where the jaw ends; this should be where it comes into contact with the circle. The jaw extends just a little way past your central line.

3 As before, draw in a couple of lines at the halfway and three-quarter points between the eye line and the chin. Again, you can use these as a guide to draw in the ear as well; the highest point of the ear meets with the eye line, and the lowest point is on the same level as the nose.

4 Use these markers to help you draw the shape of the face. The forehead and brow come away from the line before curving back in to form the bridge of the nose. The nose comes back in to meet your nose mark, and the lips curve out before meeting again at the mouth mark.

HEADS AND FACES | **19**

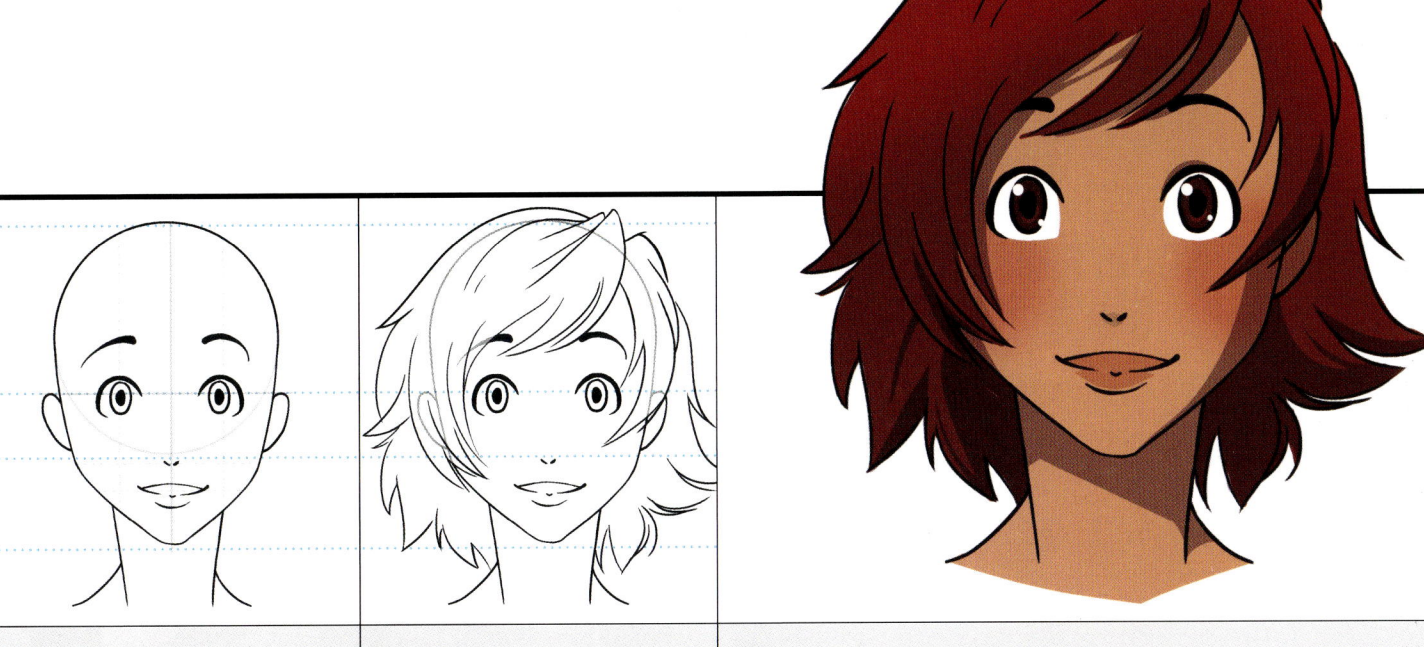

5 Here's where you'll see your lines starting to help out. Using your eye, nose, and mouth marks, draw in the model's basic features. The eyebrows will move around depending on your model's expression, but typically they should be placed about a third of the way between the eyes and the top of the skull.

6 Bear in mind the natural volume of the model's hair when drawing it in. It won't sit flush to the skull, otherwise the model's head may look too small or the hair may look thin and unappealing; draw it slightly away from the skull instead to give it lots of volume.

7 Even the most basic shading can help define the shape of your model's face. Choose a light source before you begin—in this image, the light comes from above and to the left. This means that there are shadows under the model's bangs, and also across the jaw and neck.

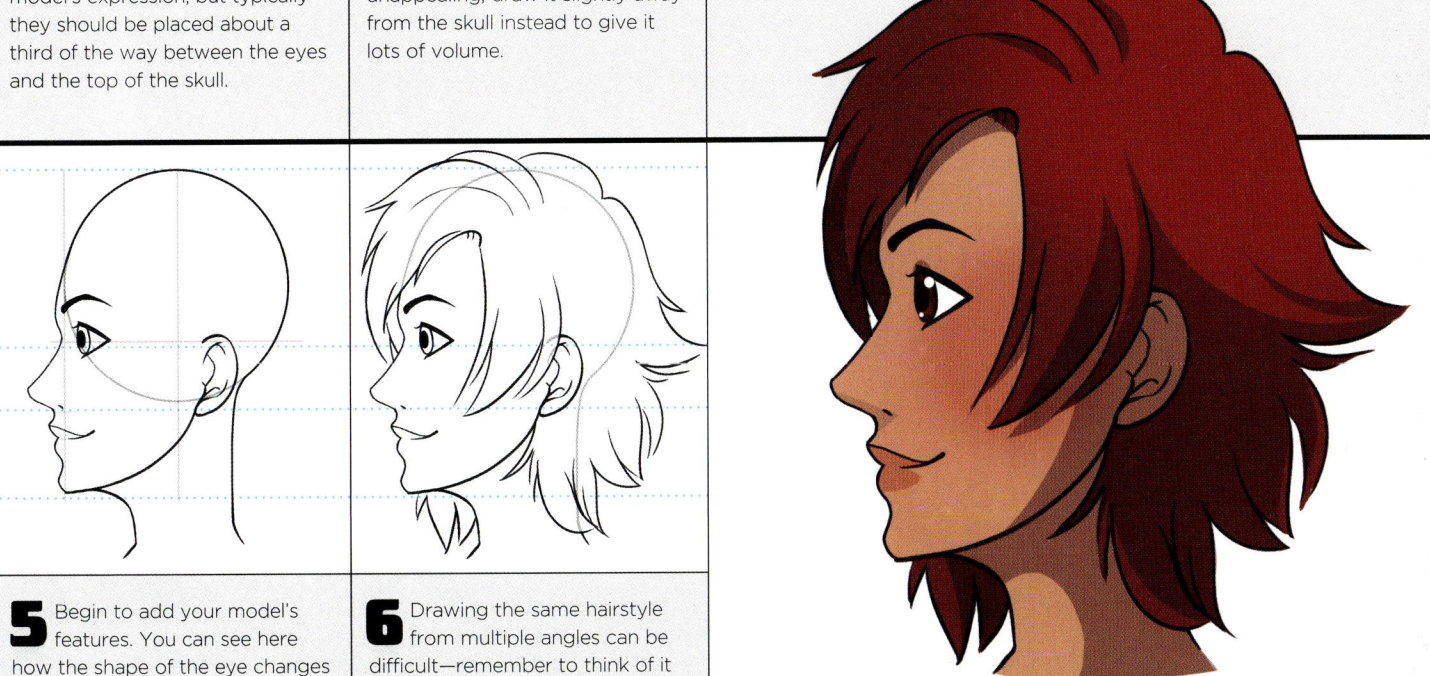

5 Begin to add your model's features. You can see here how the shape of the eye changes from the side in comparison to how it looked from the front. In a true profile view, like this one, the eye is set a little way back from the bridge of the nose; the inner corner of the eyebrow sits a little forward of it, as do the nostrils.

6 Drawing the same hairstyle from multiple angles can be difficult—remember to think of it as a three-dimensional object. Bear in mind the basic shapes that you drew when you first drew the face from the front—the length of the bangs, for example, and where the parting was. This will help you draw it from a different angle.

7 Basic shading will really help to bring out the shape. Bear in mind the parts of the face that are either overshadowed by others, or curve away from the light source; for example, the top of the neck is almost always shadowed, as well as the sides of the jaw and the underside of the nose.

20 | DRAWING BASICS

SKIN TONES

IT'S SURPRISINGLY EASY TO OVERLOOK A **MODEL'S ETHNICITY** WHEN YOU'RE BUSY DESIGNING CLOTHES, BUT IT'S A VERY IMPORTANT POINT TO REMEMBER. THE RIGHT MODEL CAN REALLY MAKE AN OUTFIT STAND OUT, ESPECIALLY IF YOU'RE DESIGNING CLOTHES INSPIRED BY A CERTAIN CULTURE.

EUROPEAN

Europe is a huge melting pot of ethnic cultures, due to trade and migration over hundreds of years, so there are many possible skin tones and colorations. However, each country still tends to have a typical "look" that's common. Here are a few examples.

SCANDINAVIAN | **GAELIC** | **POLISH** | **ROMANIAN**

ASIAN

Asia is a surprisingly large continent, and within it there are plenty of different skin tones too. Even someone from northern China will look very different from their southern Chinese cousin! The Japanese have always thought that pale skin is beautiful, and this look has been coveted for hundreds of years—but in contrast, Mongolians have very dark skin with red cheeks, and to them this is the ideal.

JAPANESE | **CHINESE** | **KOREAN** | **MONGOLIAN**

SKIN TONES | **21**

YELLOW TONES	WARM TONES	DARK: WARM TONES	DARK: COOL TONES

Black skin is beautiful and, like all of the previous examples, also hugely varied. People with black skin come from all over the world, from the Caribbean to Africa and Australia, and their beauty is as diverse as their cultures. By using different-colored undertones, such as warm or cool or even golden tones, you can vary black skin for equally striking effects.

BLACK

MEDITERRANEAN	EGYPTIAN	MESOAMERICAN	MELANESIAN

All of the examples on these pages show just a small percentage of the types of possible skin tones. There are so many beautiful cultures out there, from people with dark skin and blond hair to people with golden skin and gold hair; you might even find some inspiration for your outfits while learning about them.

OTHER ETHNICITIES

22 | DRAWING BASICS

HAIR AND HAIRSTYLES

YOUR FASHION COLLECTIONS MAY BE ALL ABOUT THE CLOTHES, BUT DON'T FORGET ANOTHER KEY ELEMENT—THE HAIR. **THE RIGHT HAIRSTYLE CAN MAKE OR BREAK A DESIGN**, AND KNOWING HOW TO DRAW ALL TYPES OF HAIR IS A GOOD GENERAL SKILL TO HAVE AS AN ARTIST.

CROWNS

The "crown" is the part of the skull from which hair naturally grows. Some people have crowns right at the front of their head, which means that their hair always has a voluminous, flyaway look, and some people have them at the back or the sides of their skulls. If you keep in mind where the crown is—or crowns are, in the case of multiple crowns—you'll find it much easier to calculate how your model's hair falls.

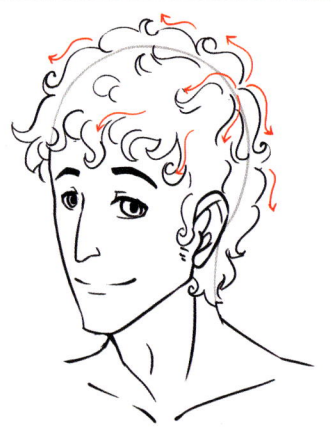

Back crowns
Push the hair forward and onto the forehead

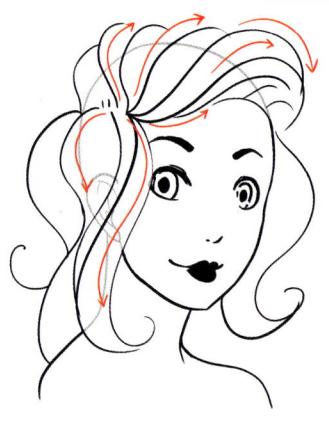

Side crown
Produces a natural sweep, which can be used to add volume

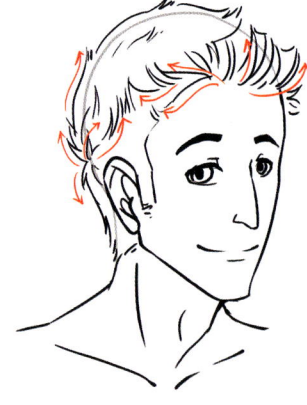

Multiple crowns
Give an appealingly "rough" look

HAIRLINES

As with crowns, people have different-shaped hairlines. This is the shape that the hair forms along the forehead and temples—and as you can see from these examples, there can be a lot of variation. Different hairstyles suit different shapes of hairline, so if you're having trouble trying to draw a specific style, try changing this small part—you'll be surprised how much of a difference it can make.

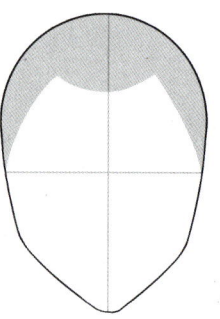

Typically male
Looks best with short hair or pushed-up bangs

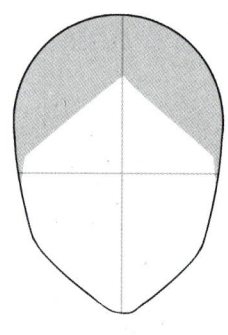

Peaked
Most flattering on round faces, as it makes them look longer

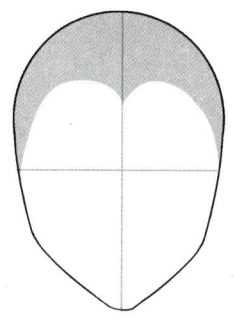

Heart-shaped
Works best on long faces, as it rounds off and makes it look more evenly proportioned

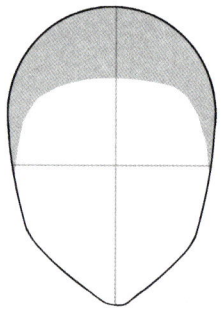

Curved
Looks best with hair pulled back from the face, as it rounds off the face nicely

CURLY HAIR

There are so many types of natural curly hair, from flowing waves to tight curls. Wavy and curly hair really make an impact on the runway, and, by remembering to draw with loose, curved lines and spirals, you should be able to replicate them with ease.

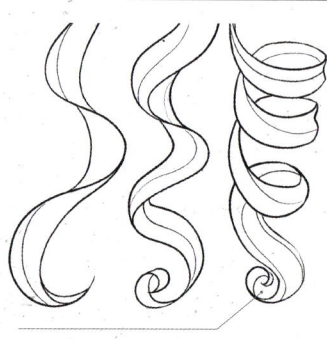

A simple "S"-shaped line dictates how wavy the hair will be.

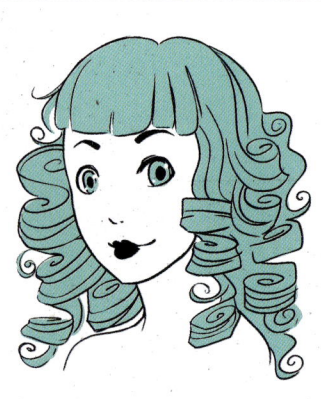

Styled ringlets

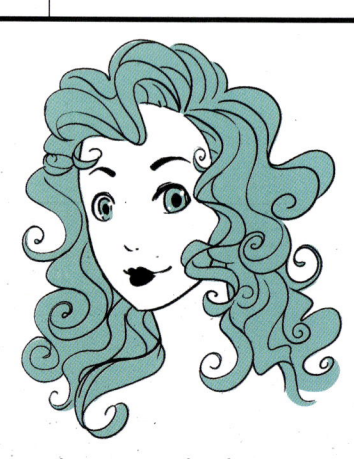

Loose, natural curls

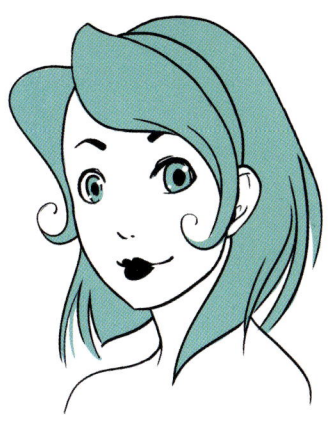	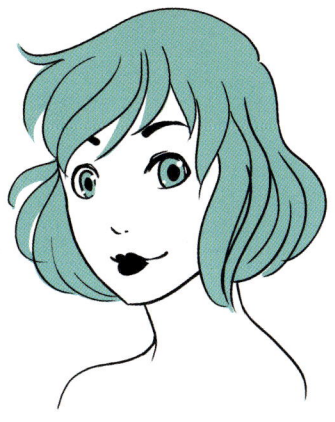	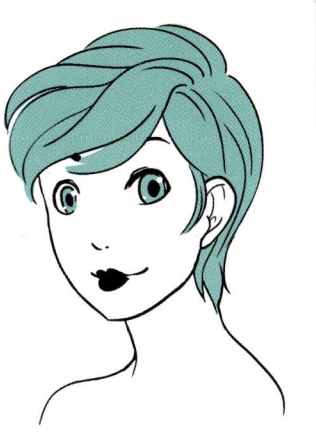	Short hair looks very stylish on women, and can be used to frame the features of your model. Using loose, curved lines keeps short hair from looking too flat or spiky, and short bangs help give it shape.
Straight, schoolgirl bob	Buoyant vintage bob	Pixie cut	
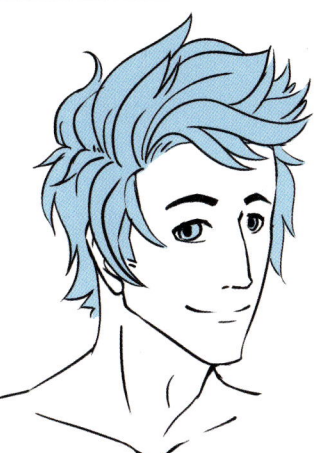	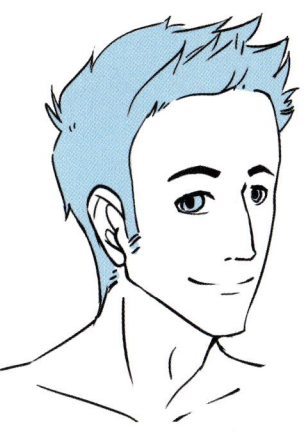	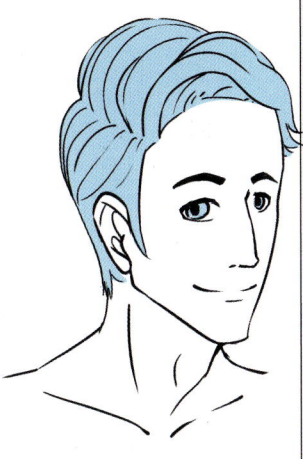	A lot of men wear their hair very short, and here you'll find it useful to keep in mind the previous pointers about crowns. By remembering which direction the hair is growing in, and where the model's parting is, you'll have no trouble drawing appealing short hairstyles.
Spiky hair with side parting	Crew cut with pushed-up bangs	Formal combed hair with side parting	
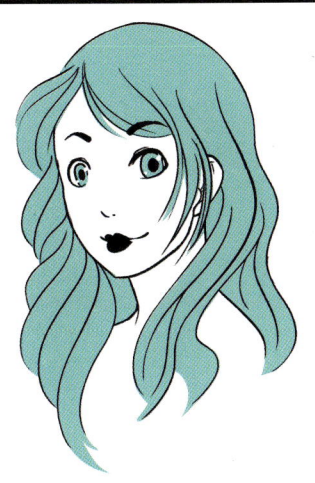	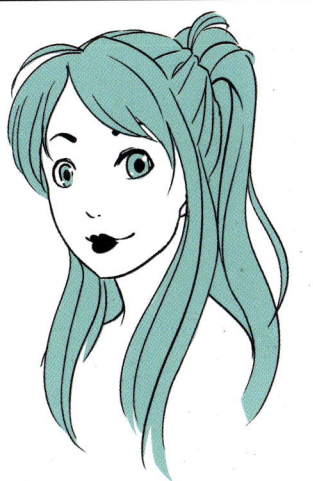	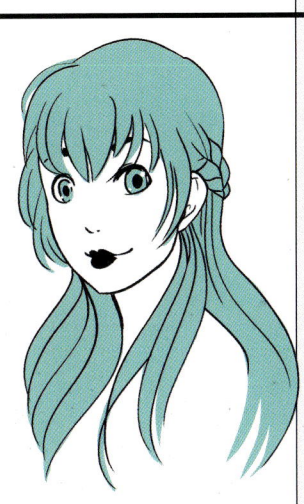	Long hair is a real head-turner, especially if it's twinned with plenty of volume and cute bangs. There's lots of potential for some really striking hairstyles, such as combining braids and ponytails for a more natural "half up, half down" look.
Loose and natural	High ponytail	Bangs and braid combination	
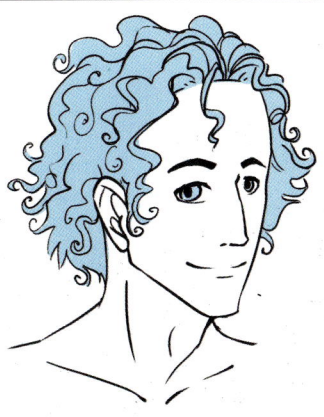	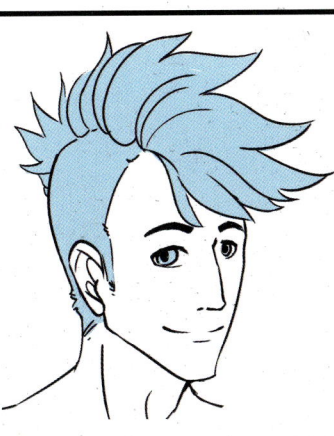	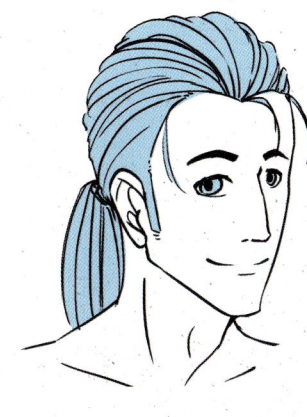	It's not just the girls who get to wear their hair long! Long hair on men is hugely popular in the fashion world, for the same reason that it's popular on women—it's striking, and has lots of potential for styling. From natural, Mediterranean curls to punky styles and ponytails, there's no limit to what you can come up with!
Loose, curly hair	Punk-rocker Mohawk	Long ponytail	

SHORT HAIR: FEMALE · **SHORT HAIR: MALE** · **LONG HAIR: FEMALE** · **LONG HAIR: MALE**

CLOTHING THE FIGURE

ONE OF THE MOST IMPORTANT THINGS TO LEARN WHEN DRAWING CLOTHING IS **THE WAY THAT IT DRAPES**. DIFFERENT FABRICS REACT IN DIFFERENT WAYS TO GRAVITY AND SHAPING, BUT THE FOLLOWING BASIC TIPS WILL APPLY TO ALMOST ALL GARMENTS, AND ARE KEY CONCEPTS FOR DRAWING FASHION DESIGNS. BEING ABLE TO DRAW YOUR OUTFITS CORRECTLY WILL REALLY **HELP YOUR COLLECTION SHINE**.

BASIC FOLDS

There are always two direct influences on the way that a garment looks—the effects of gravity, and the figure of the model beneath. Gravity will always tug a garment downward, causing bunching and folds. This downward pull is more obvious in thicker, heavier fabrics such as fleece or leather, and more subtle in lighter fabrics such as linen and chiffon.

The second, more important, influence on the fall of a garment is the model's body. Close-fitting and loose clothing sits differently when worn, but there are consistent areas where the fabric bunches and folds, as shown here.

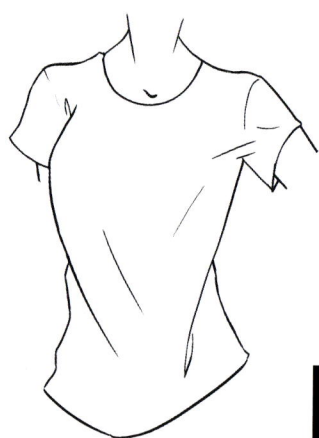

Close-fitting
Fabric is drawn tight and almost horizontal at all stress points, such as the bust, waist, and armpit.

Loose fit
Folds are more affected by gravity than the model's body; bust and waist folds hang downward.

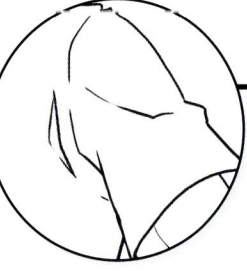

When the arm is resting or folded downward (see above), the garment creases where it gathers at the armpit; in contrast, when the arm is outstretched (see left) you can see horizontal creases where the fabric is being pulled outward.

Here you can see an example of gravity causing fabric to bunch and gather at the bottom of the torso. This is always more prominent when a garment is tucked into another beneath it, for example boots or pants. The arrows show the common areas where garments gather—you can see fabric gathering at the armpit, but also starting to create folds down the torso to where it bunches beneath. Where the torso travels around in a cylindrical shape, the downward folds will part in two ways, either traveling toward the central buttons of the garment or around the sides.

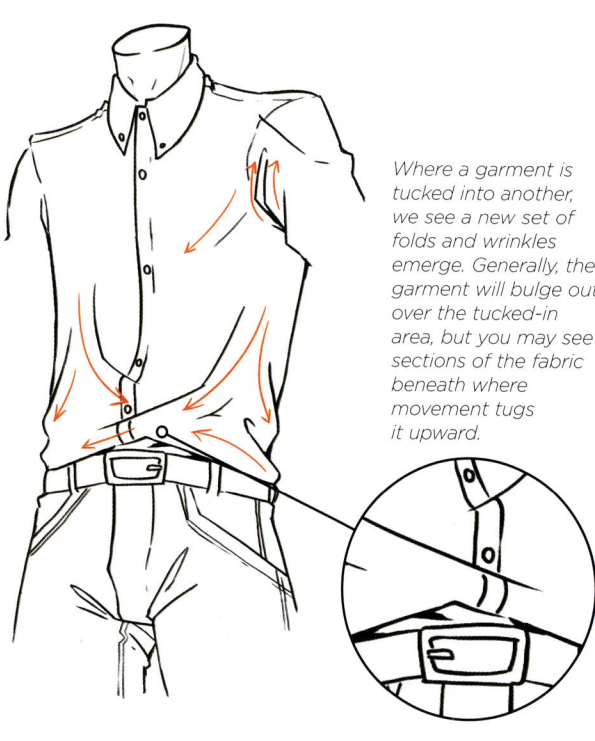

Where a garment is tucked into another, we see a new set of folds and wrinkles emerge. Generally, the garment will bulge out over the tucked-in area, but you may see sections of the fabric beneath where movement tugs it upward.

SLEEVES

The placement of creases and folds in sleeves can seem like an intimidating process for the artist, but they follow the same rules as every other garment. The majority of bunches sit at the arm's stress points—armpits, elbows, and wrists—and all folds along a sleeve radiate from this point.

1 Most notable in thick garments, you'll see two small bumps of fabric where the seam of the sleeve meets the main part of the clothing.

2 Folds at the top of the sleeve depend on the position of the arm, but you'll frequently see small creases coming downward from the hem where it bunches or pulls.

3 Fabric bunches or stretches at the armpit depending on the position of the arm (see the detail armpit panel above).

4 The most prominent creases in a sleeve are at the elbow. Fabric gathers in rolls, creased more noticeably toward the inside of

PANT CROTCH FOLDS

No matter what the type, pants have consistent folds that are important to memorize. Most important are the creases that emerge at the point where the thigh meets the pelvis; it will create a series of folds that extend out from the central point of the groin. These may even extend down the thighs as the fabric stretches across them. These lines often become more horizontal in appearance in looser garments, and longer and sharper in tight pants.

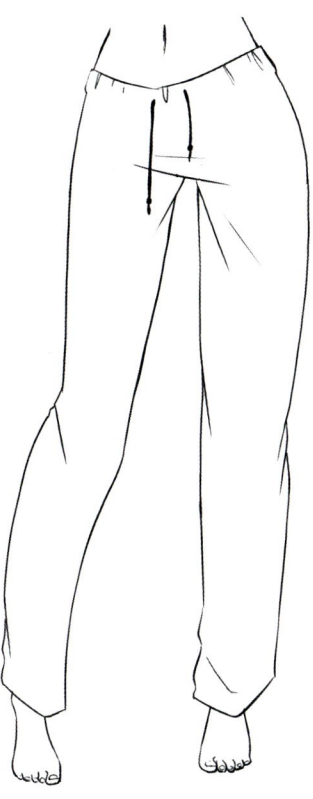

Casual pants
Folds at stress points are looser and travel downward.

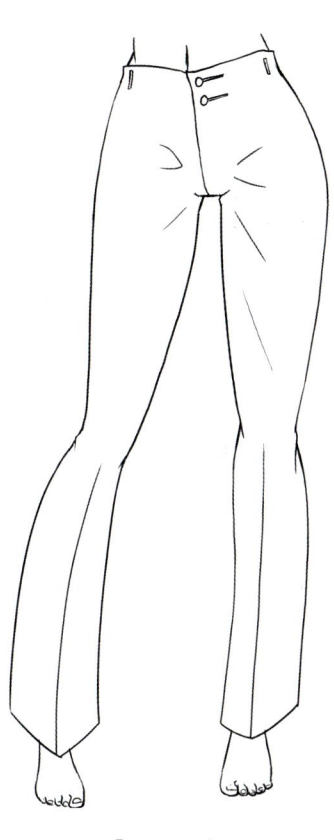

Dress pants
Tailoring minimizes creases around the crotch; crease down leg front gives a sharp, crisp look.

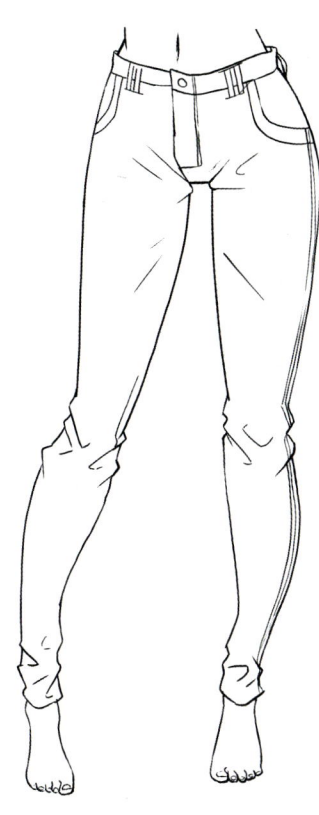

Skinny jeans
Stress points clearly defined; creases are pulled horizontally across the figure.

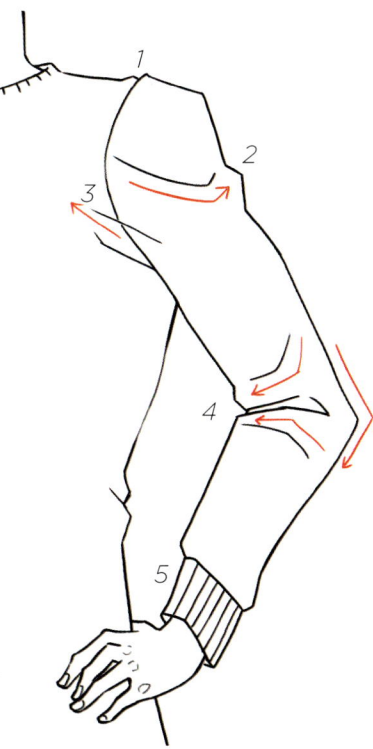

the elbow. It also stretches to a point on the outside of the elbow.

5 Where a garment has cuffs, it's common for fabric to bunch just above where the cuff starts. This is caused by extra length in the sleeve being pushed back by the wrist.

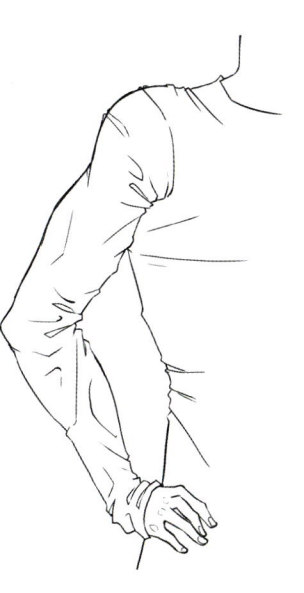

Tight shirt
With tight clothing you'll see stress points and folds appearing, but they'll be exaggerated and stretched by the model's figure. It helps to remember that the arm beneath the garment is a round object, so you can draw the folds around its shape.

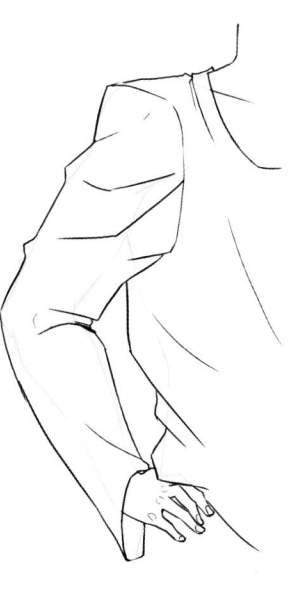

Loose shirt
A baggy garment has the added effect of gravity to change the way that it falls. You can see where it hangs by comparing it to the model's arm just visible underneath. The basic stress points still exist, but are pulled out of place by the garment's looseness.

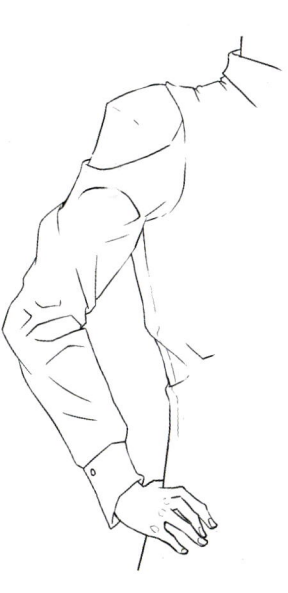

Thin fabric
Where a garment is made of thinner fabric, such as cotton or linen, it's common for it to crease more visibly than a thicker garment. However, you can still see all of the same stress points as outlined in the basic sleeve diagram.

MOVEMENT

As a model moves, a garment stretches and moves in different ways too. By imagining the hems and cuffs of a piece of clothing as simplified circles, you can visualize how the garment will change in different poses.

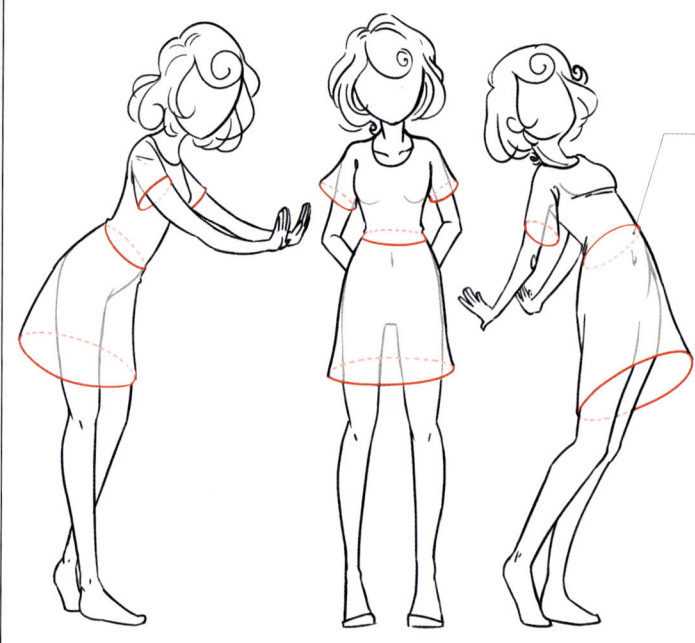

Skirt: As a general rule, the circle of the hem will behave in the same way as the "waist" circle, tilting and leaning backward and forward with the model.

Shorts: Because short shorts do not fall far, they will tend to stick out a little farther than longer or lighter garments. Picture the pinching of the fabric at the groin as the anchor point that holds the fabric still, while the rest moves with the body.

HATS AND HEADWEAR

1 In this tutorial we're drawing a baseball cap. Sketch in the shape of the skull beneath your model's hair, as well as a curved line across the head to show where the brim of the hat will sit.

2 Draw in a couple more lines—one over the center of the head so that you have a guide for the position of the center of the hat, and a second line just in front of the ear to mark where the brim will end.

3 Draw the front of the brim by sketching a smooth, curved line just above the eyes. As this model's head is at a three-quarter angle, the center of the cap should be off to one side as well.

4 Using the shape of the skull and the original curved line that you drew across the head, draw the rest of the hat. Remember that it won't sit completely flush to the skull—your model has to fit hair under there as well.

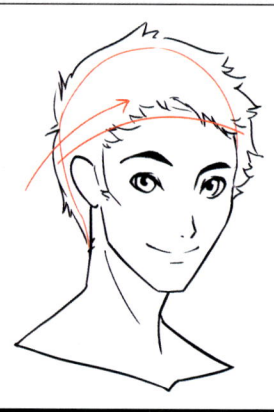 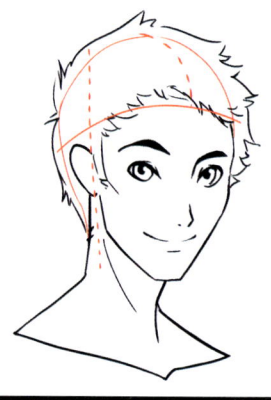 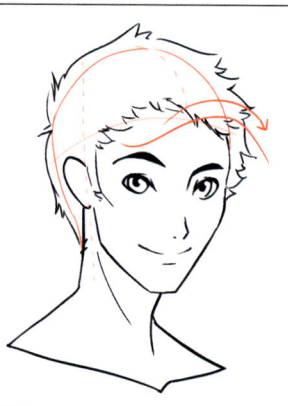 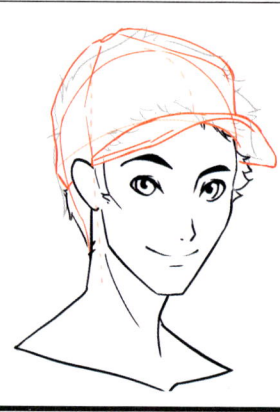

PLEATED SKIRT

1 Start by drawing two circles over your model's body—one at the waist, where the band of the skirt will sit, and one farther down where the skirt ends. If your skirt has a thick waistband like the one in this example, draw a third circle to mark where it ends.

2 Using smooth, curved lines, connect the circles together. A single, flowing line will make the fabric of a garment look lighter and more natural than if you use thick, jagged lines.

3 Draw several lines from the top of the skirt to the base to show where the fabric folds will lie. At the base of the skirt, draw a second, smaller circle inside of the first; the fabric will fold in toward this. Keep your pleats looking even and neat.

4 Between the outer and inner circles, draw a zigzag line all the way around. Then, join up the corners of these zigzags with the fabric above—don't forget to show where the fabric is visible between the creases.

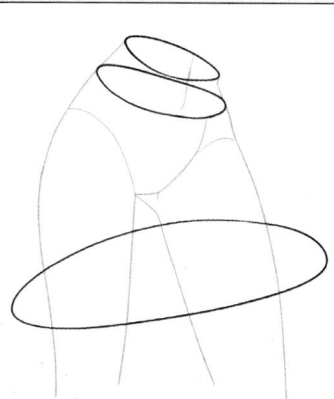 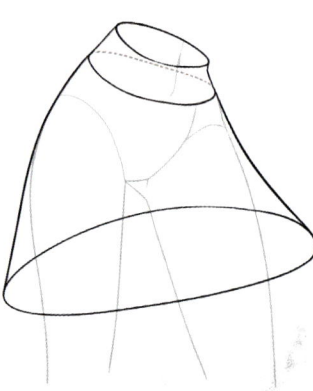 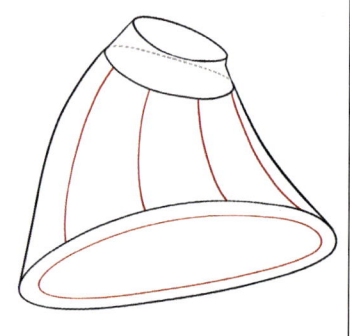 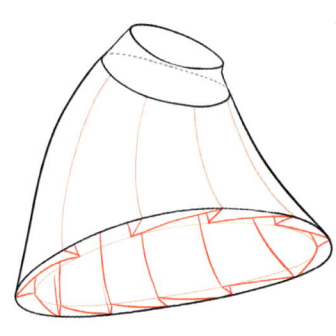

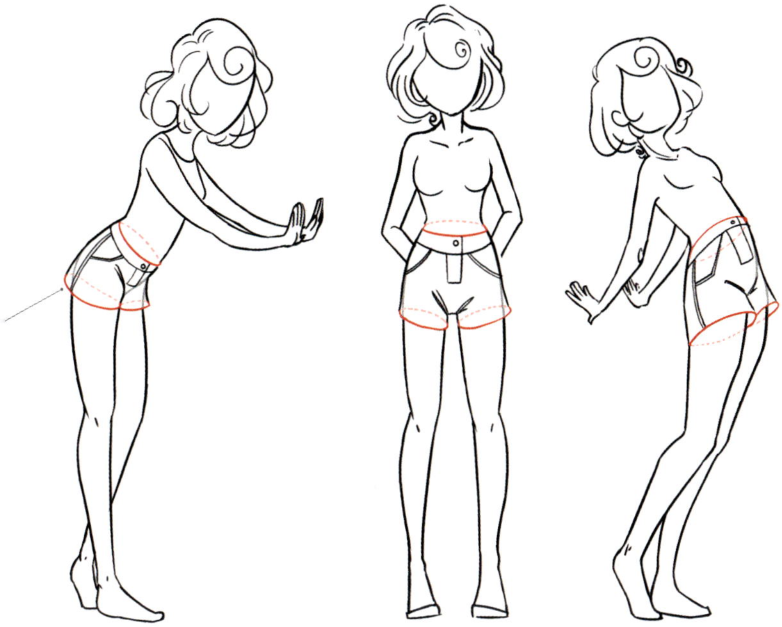

Pants: Acting slightly differently from shorts, the bend of the knees of pants will also affect their look. Unless the pants are made from a thick fabric, remember they will bulge slightly outward at the knee even when a model's legs are straight.

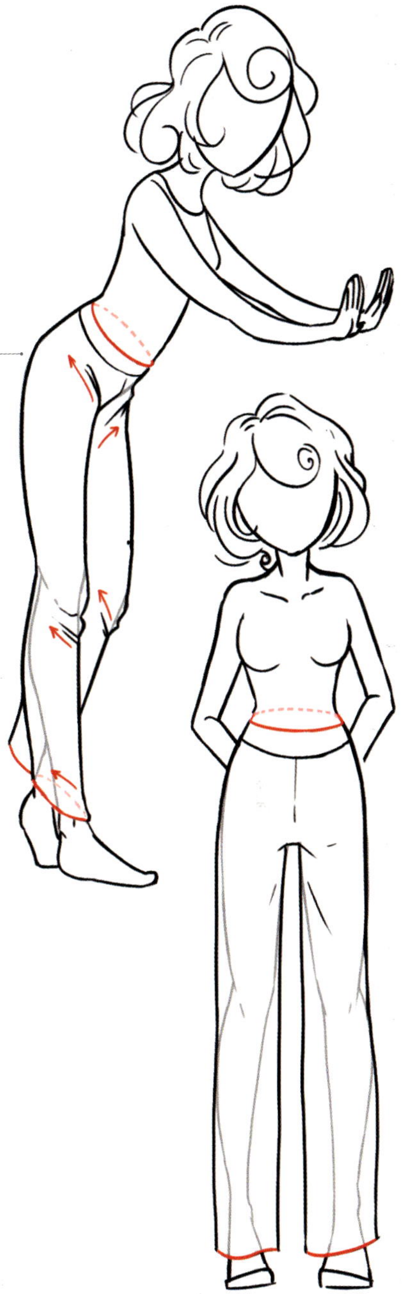

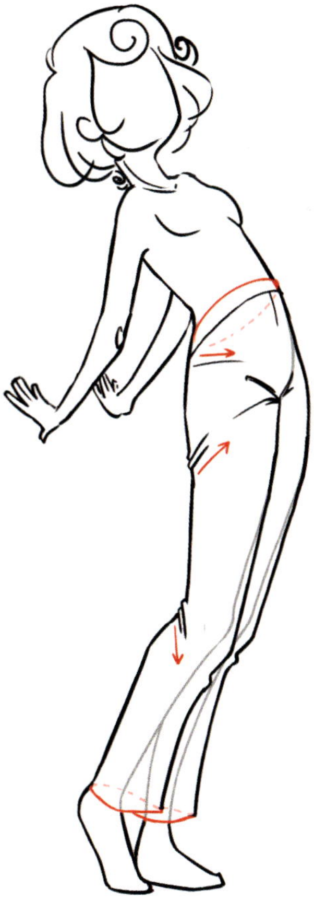

5 Clean up your sketch, double-checking that your hat looks as though it is sitting comfortably on the model's head.

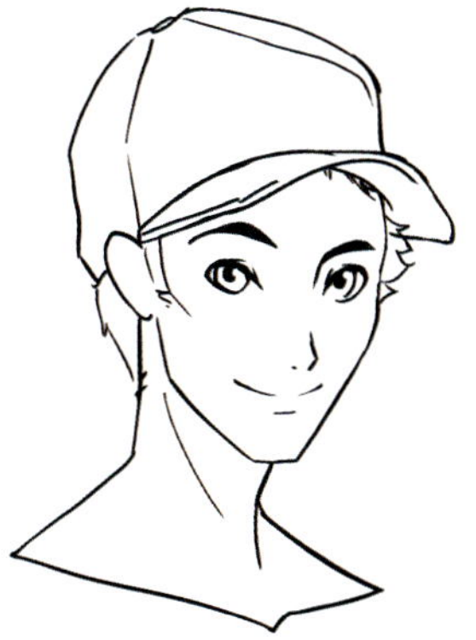

6 Any head accessory can be drawn using the steps below—try adding glasses, a headband, or cute hair ties.

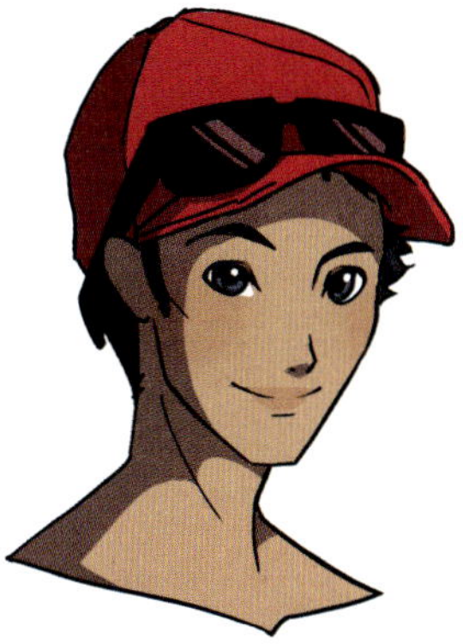

5 Using your sketches as a guide, clean up your lines. At this stage you'll be able to get a good idea of whether your pleats look natural or not—they can be tricky to draw, so don't feel disheartened if you need several practice runs.

6 Drawing a skirt flared outward from a model's waist and hips gives a sense of movement and liveliness to a drawing. When coloring, don't forget that patterns in the fabric should follow the curve of the skirt.

SKIRT SHAPE: FRONT AND BACK

The shape of a skirt is different at the front and the back. At the front, the fabric is relatively smooth; however, it can crease along the edge of the legs beneath and at the waist where the body tucks inward. On the back, the fabric is more stretched and formed by the shape of the buttocks and the thighs.

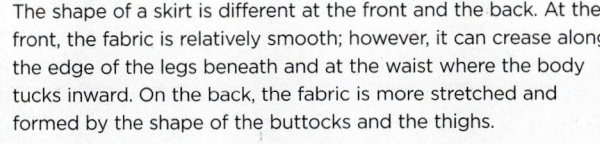

Front view *Back view*

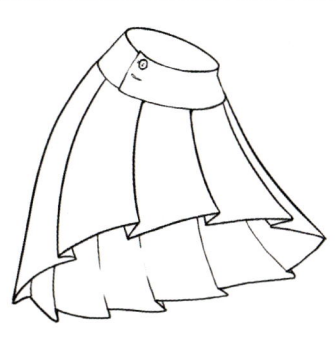
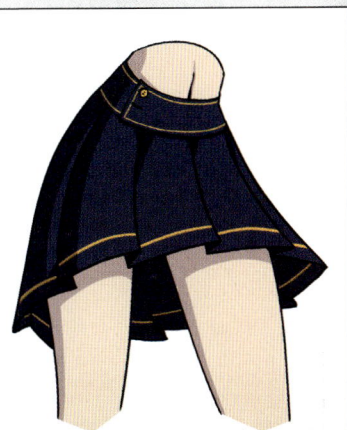
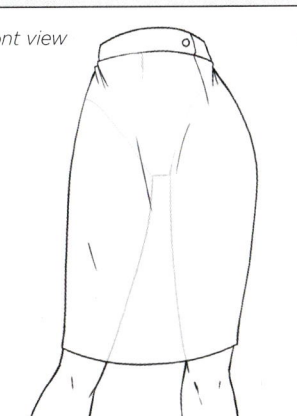
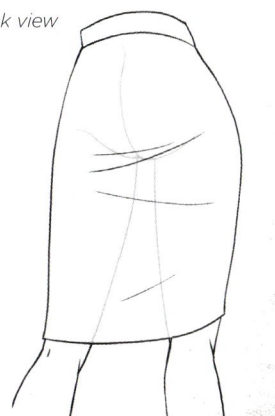

FABRIC TEXTURES

A WARDROBE FULL OF DIFFERENT FABRICS IS LIKE A TOYBOX TO A FASHION DESIGNER, AND THERE ARE SO MANY BEAUTIFUL MATERIALS OUT THERE. FROM USING FLOATY, SHEER FABRICS SUCH AS GOSSAMER AND SILK FOR A LIGHT, ANGELIC LOOK TO USING HEAVIER, BOLDER FABRICS SUCH AS LEATHER AND DENIM, **MOST FABRICS HAVE A PERSONALITY ALL OF THEIR OWN**. SPEND SOME TIME STUDYING THEM OR LEARNING THESE BASIC TIPS ABOUT HOW TO DRAW SOME OF THE MOST COMMON FABRICS, AND YOU'LL BE CONFIDENT IN MAKING **BOLD STATEMENTS** THROUGH YOUR FABRIC CHOICES.

DENIM

Denim is perhaps one of the most enduringly popular materials to be used in both couture and mass-market fashion. It's been around since the 1500s, but first became really popular in the 1870s—and it's been a firm favorite since! With its instantly recognizable style and ability to look right both in dressy and casual outfits, it's a must to know how to draw it.

Creasing
Because denim is a very thick fabric, it tends to crease only at points of the most movement, such as knees and elbows. Where it does crease, it creates thick, straight-lined folds that bunch together; in this example, you can see where the creases gather together at the knee.

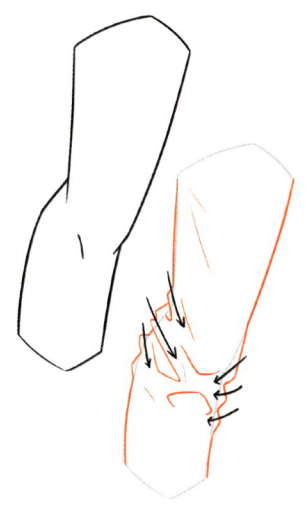

Seams
Another distinctive feature of denim—especially in jeans—is the flat-fell seam, which is the double-lined seam that you often see down the inside of the legs of jeans. Many designers have this sewn in a contrasting color to make it a feature. The dye in denim also tends to fade with wear, especially in areas where there is a lot of movement such as across the thigh and knee; some designers affect this fading on purpose to give their garments a loved, lived-in look.

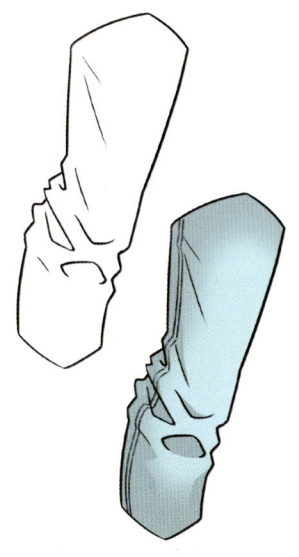

LEATHER

Leather is produced in many forms, from the softer suede and chamois leathers used in gloves and shoes to thicker leathers such as nubuck and patent that are popular choices for boots and jackets. Like denim, leather is popular for its versatility in both formal and casual garments, and is often favored for the appealing way it weathers with wear.

Natural creases
As a natural material, leather tends to hold its shape well and creases only at areas of great stress; in this glove, for example, it creases most visibly at the wrist and knuckles. A distinctive feature of gloves is the seams on the insides of the fingers, so don't forget to add these in too.

Aged leather
Leather ages well, and with wear develops an appealing, softer look. Creases and folds become more rounded, and the leather may sport lines and scratches that add extra character to a garment. In some leathers, areas that have been stretched with wear—such as across the knees, elbows, or wrists—may end up with a faded, aged look as well.

Patent leather
Leather that has been given a gloss finish, for a high-shine effect, is known as patent leather. Using heavy shading and select areas of light, you can replicate this look in your own designs.

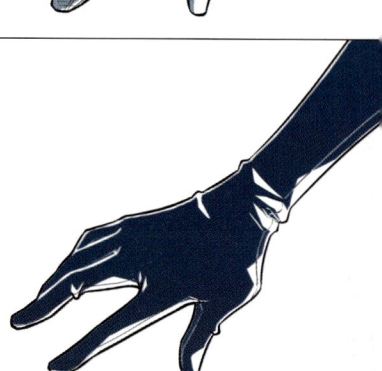

FUR

Faux fur has risen in popularity in recent years and is now so realistic that it can be passed off for the real thing—a perfect compromise for designers and animals alike.

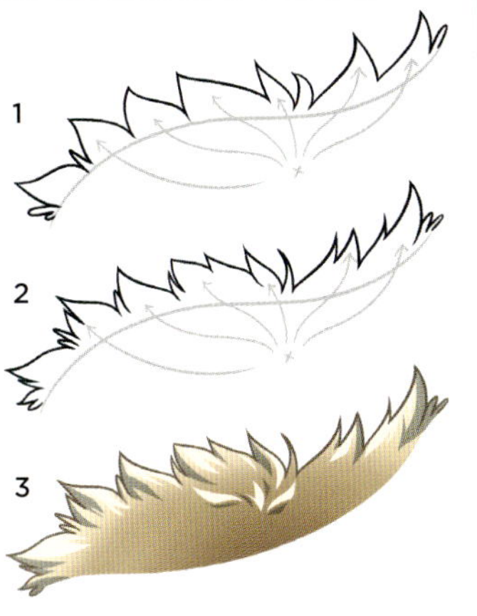

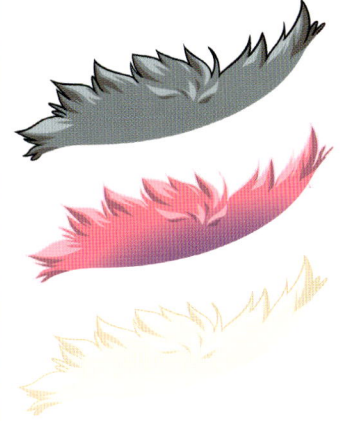

Drawing fur

As with drawing hair, drawing fur can be made much simpler by keeping in mind the direction of the fur. Drawing a central point for the fur to come from not only makes the act of drawing it easier, but it'll make it look more natural and plush as well. Start by drawing thick, simplified triangles of fur (**1**) and then adding more strands and detail (**2**), and finally the color (**3**).

Coloring fur

Fur comes in many beautiful, natural colors ... but that doesn't mean that you have to be restricted to just these. Natural tans, grays, and browns look great on bohemian or outdoor clothing; white fur adds luxury to evening coats and dresses. Alternately, using dyed furs in zany colors like bright pink and purple makes a statement all on its own—perfect for clubbing or streetwear.

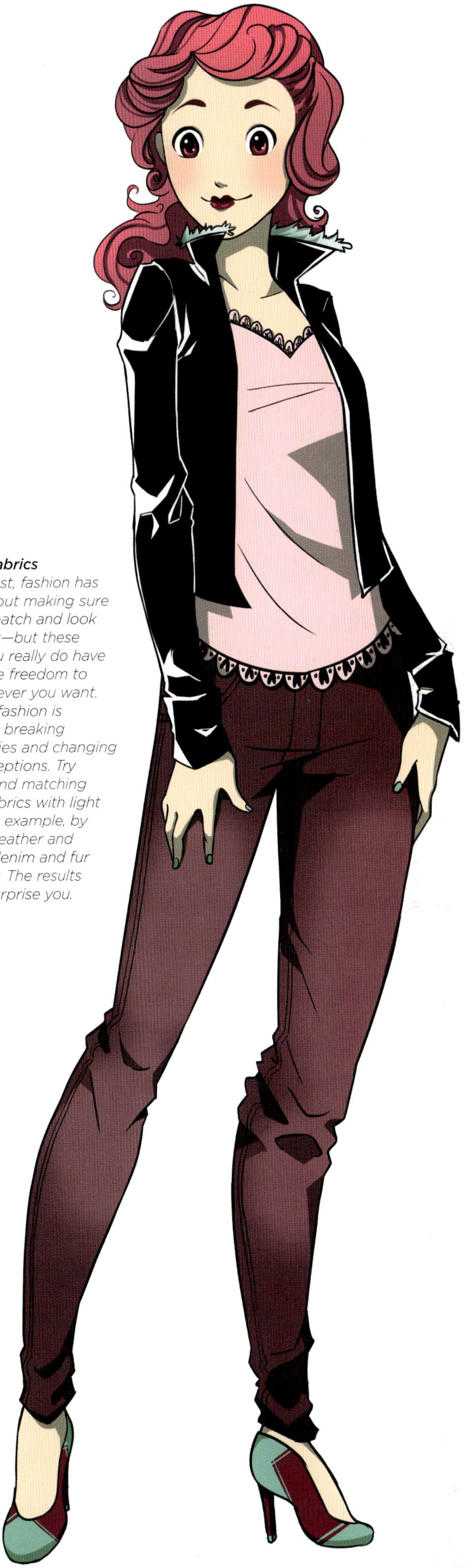

Mixing fabrics

In the past, fashion has been about making sure outfits match and look coherent—but these days, you really do have complete freedom to do whatever you want. Modern fashion is all about breaking boundaries and changing preconceptions. Try mixing and matching heavy fabrics with light ones, for example, by putting leather and lace or denim and fur together. The results might surprise you.

LACE

Lace comes in all forms, from rolls of lace fabric to trims and ribbons. It can also come in many patterns, from flowers to geometric patterns to folk designs, and this versatility is perhaps what has made it so popular over the years.

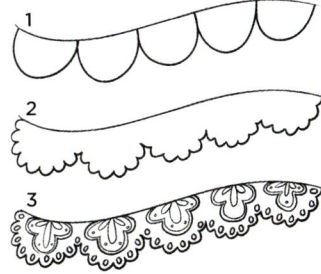
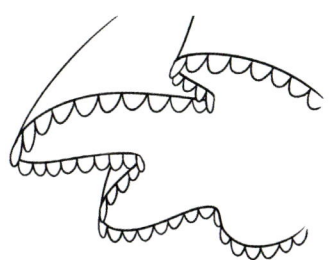

Drawing a lace trim

Start by sketching your desired shape (**1**). This trim uses a simple semicircle. Make the trim more elaborate by adding further, smaller semicircles to the edges (**2**). For the full lace effect, fill in the semicircles with plenty of cute, rounded details (**3**). Make sure that the details follow the semicircle shape.

Adding a trim

When adding a trim to a loose garment, such as a flowing skirt edge, simplify your shapes first so you can focus on making the trim look natural before you get caught up in drawing details. This trim has been simplified down to semicircles so that it can be drawn along the edge of the skirt; once this has been done, you can go in and draw the lace patterns.

CREATING CLASSIC PATTERNS

SOME CLASSIC TEXTILE PATTERNS NEVER GO OUT OF FASHION. WITH THESE SIMPLE TIPS, YOU'LL BE ABLE TO DRAW THREE OF THE MOST POPULAR—**TARTAN, ARGYLE, AND HOUNDSTOOTH**—IN NO TIME AT ALL.

CLASSIC TARTAN

Just as every English nobleman has a coat of arms to represent his family, the old clans of Scotland have a house tartan. Though these vary in color and number of stripes, all tartan fabric is created in the same way. Made popular by the punk movement in the 1980s, the most common tartan found in the fashion industry is the standard red, black, white, gold, and blue, known as the Royal Stewart tartan—the personal tartan of Queen Elizabeth II.

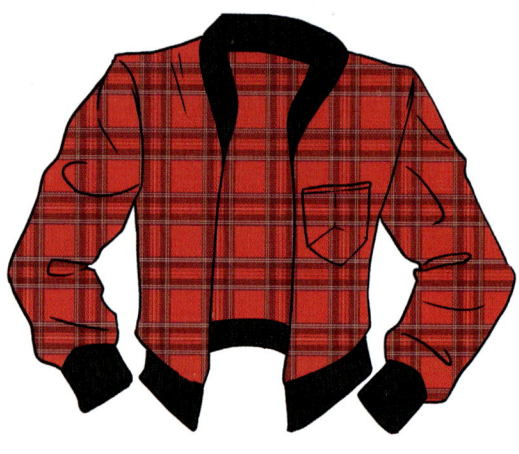

Royal Stewart tartan
Popular in both punk and outdoors fashion, this classic plaid pattern is recognized all over the world, and is perfect for making a statement.

HOUNDSTOOTH

Also originating in Scotland, houndstooth is a tessellating (interlocking) design that has been a regular feature in fashion collections since the 1880s. Unlike tartan, however, houndstooth is only ever presented in black and white; a smaller-scaled version of houndstooth is known as puppytooth.

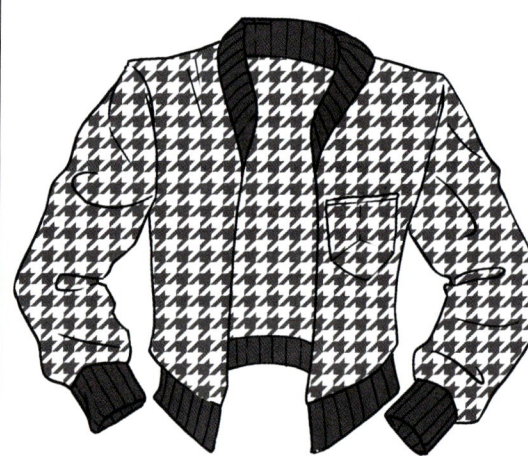

Houndstooth
The distinctive black-and-white shapes of houndstooth are a staple in evening and office wear. Distinctly feminine, it's not only classy but is also a sharp, crisp design.

ARGYLE

Argyle has been around since the seventeenth century, but became popular in the U.S. and the U.K. in the 1920s. Like the other patterns on this page, argyle was also created in Scotland. Not only were the Scots experts in weaving hundreds of years ago, but their traditional fashions have influenced designers such as Coco Chanel, and more modern names such as Christian Dior and Vivienne Westwood.

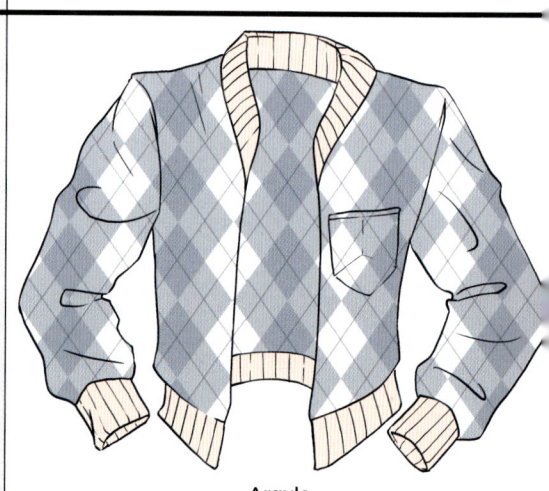

Argyle
Whether at the horse races, the golf course, or on the polo field, argyle is the aristocracy's pattern of choice.

CREATING CLASSIC PATTERNS | **31**

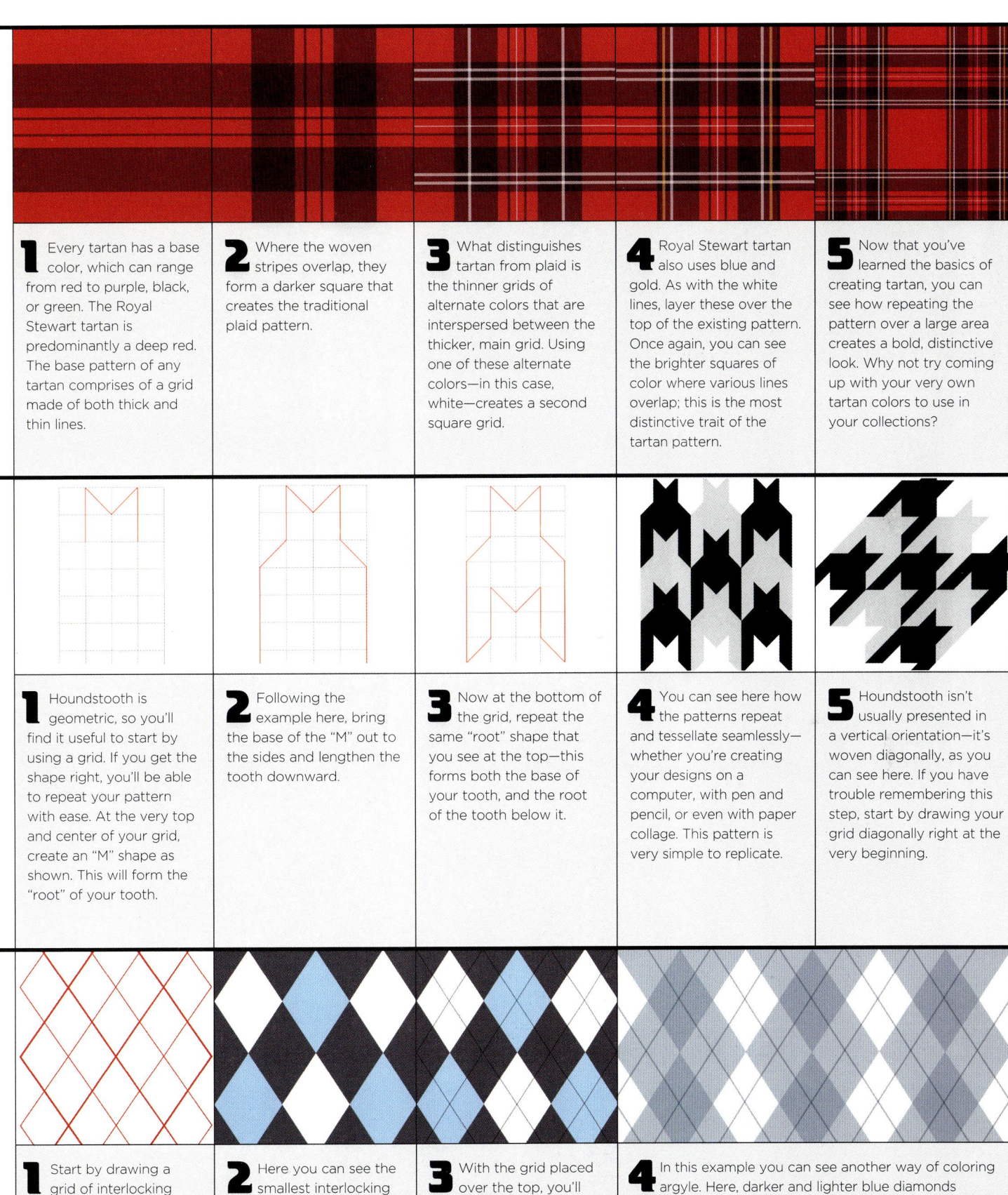

1 Every tartan has a base color, which can range from red to purple, black, or green. The Royal Stewart tartan is predominantly a deep red. The base pattern of any tartan comprises of a grid made of both thick and thin lines.

2 Where the woven stripes overlap, they form a darker square that creates the traditional plaid pattern.

3 What distinguishes tartan from plaid is the thinner grids of alternate colors that are interspersed between the thicker, main grid. Using one of these alternate colors—in this case, white—creates a second square grid.

4 Royal Stewart tartan also uses blue and gold. As with the white lines, layer these over the top of the existing pattern. Once again, you can see the brighter squares of color where various lines overlap; this is the most distinctive trait of the tartan pattern.

5 Now that you've learned the basics of creating tartan, you can see how repeating the pattern over a large area creates a bold, distinctive look. Why not try coming up with your very own tartan colors to use in your collections?

1 Houndstooth is geometric, so you'll find it useful to start by using a grid. If you get the shape right, you'll be able to repeat your pattern with ease. At the very top and center of your grid, create an "M" shape as shown. This will form the "root" of your tooth.

2 Following the example here, bring the base of the "M" out to the sides and lengthen the tooth downward.

3 Now at the bottom of the grid, repeat the same "root" shape that you see at the top—this forms both the base of your tooth, and the root of the tooth below it.

4 You can see here how the patterns repeat and tessellate seamlessly—whether you're creating your designs on a computer, with pen and pencil, or even with paper collage. This pattern is very simple to replicate.

5 Houndstooth isn't usually presented in a vertical orientation—it's woven diagonally, as you can see here. If you have trouble remembering this step, start by drawing your grid diagonally right at the very beginning.

1 Start by drawing a grid of interlocking diamonds—one large diamond placed over four smaller ones, with the edges of two larger diamonds placed over that.

2 Here you can see the smallest interlocking diamonds. The diamonds in argyle can be colored in many ways—this variation shows alternating colors (white and blue) placed over a gray background.

3 With the grid placed over the top, you'll end up with an effect of crosses passing through the center of your colored diamonds, for the traditional argyle look.

4 In this example you can see another way of coloring argyle. Here, darker and lighter blue diamonds arranged around each other over a white background give the impression of large, overlaid diamonds. The grid is still present over the top of them all.

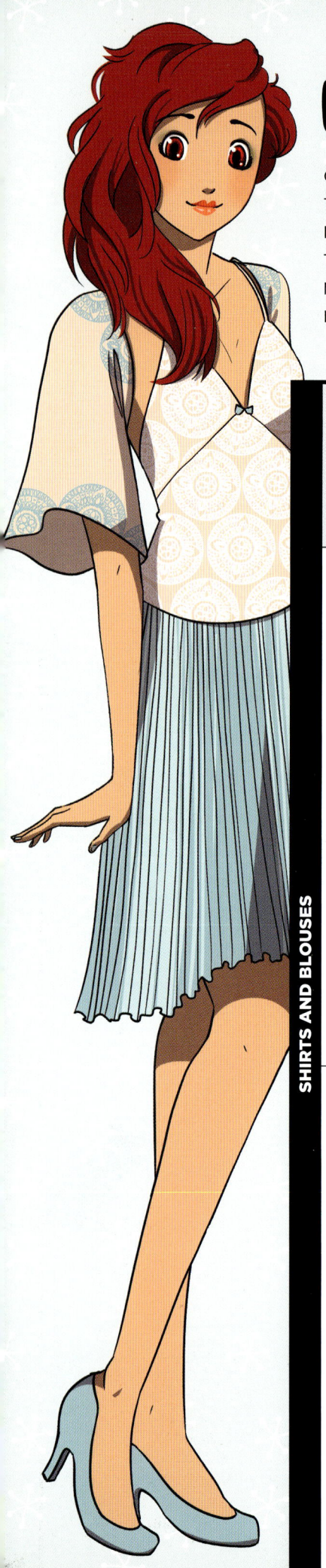

CLASSIC CUTS

OVER THE HUNDREDS OF YEARS OF CHANGING FASHIONS, THERE ARE CERTAIN CUTS AND STYLES OF GARMENTS THAT HAVE PROVEN SO POPULAR THAT WE STILL WEAR THEM TODAY. THE NEXT FEW PAGES PRESENT A SELECTION OF SOME OF THE MOST **CLASSIC GARMENT STYLES**, WHICH YOU CAN USE FOR INSPIRATION OR AS A STARTING POINT FOR YOUR COLLECTIONS.

Women's shirts and blouses come in all shapes and styles, from the practical to the extravagantly fashionable. You can see in this selection a range of collar and sleeve styles that, when teamed with the right pants or skirts, would make a cute fashion look.

SHIRTS AND BLOUSES

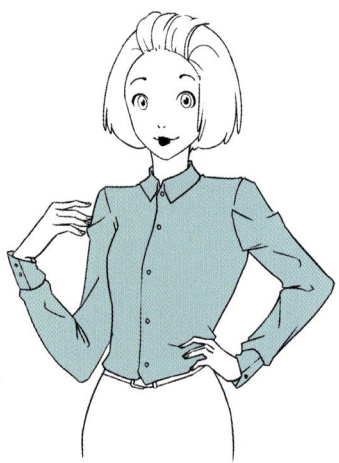

At the office
A classic-style shirt is a guaranteed winner, especially when twinned with a cute hairstyle and tucked into a fashionable belt.

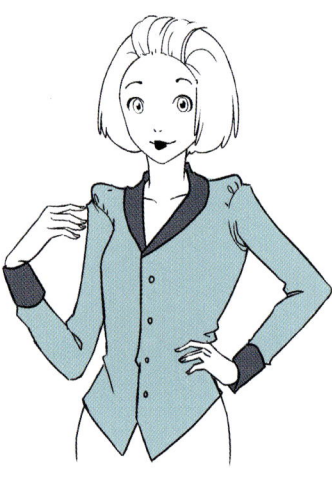

Outdoors chic
A tailored shirt with a Chelsea collar and padded shoulders creates a sharp, chic look perfect for a spring walk or a day at the races.

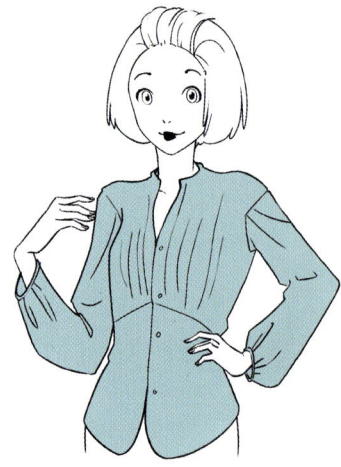

Going bohemian
A collarless blouse with a pleated front and loose, gathered sleeves creates a slimming, cool look for those hot summer days.

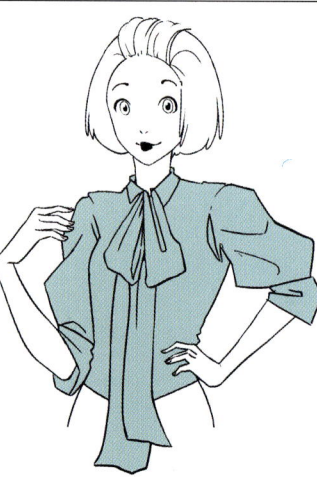

Boardroom fashion
A long, silk bow and elbow-length puffed sleeves create a professional look that's flattering and effortlessly stylish.

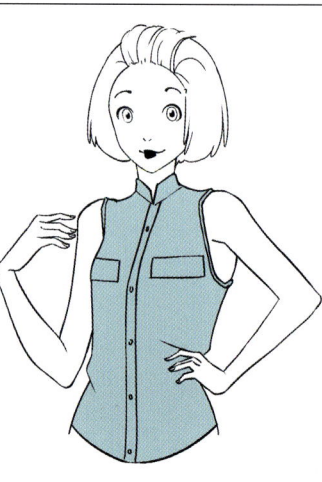

On vacation
A sleeveless shirt with a simple mandarin collar is perfect for a beachside boardwalk or shopping at the mall.

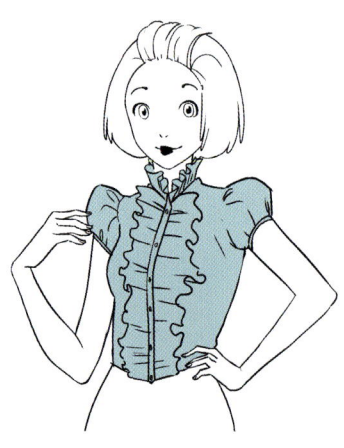

New romantic
Short, puffed sleeves and plenty of ruffles make a blouse perfect for that special date.

CLASSIC CUTS | 33

Every good top, dress, or shirt needs the right neckline to really give it that stylish flair. Different necklines suit different face shapes, hairstyles, and body types, so try playing around with different looks. For example, a high neckline such as a mandarin or Peter Pan collar is best offset by an updo such as a ponytail or bun, but low or wide necklines look fantastic with loose, messy hairstyles and big statement necklaces.

NECKLINES

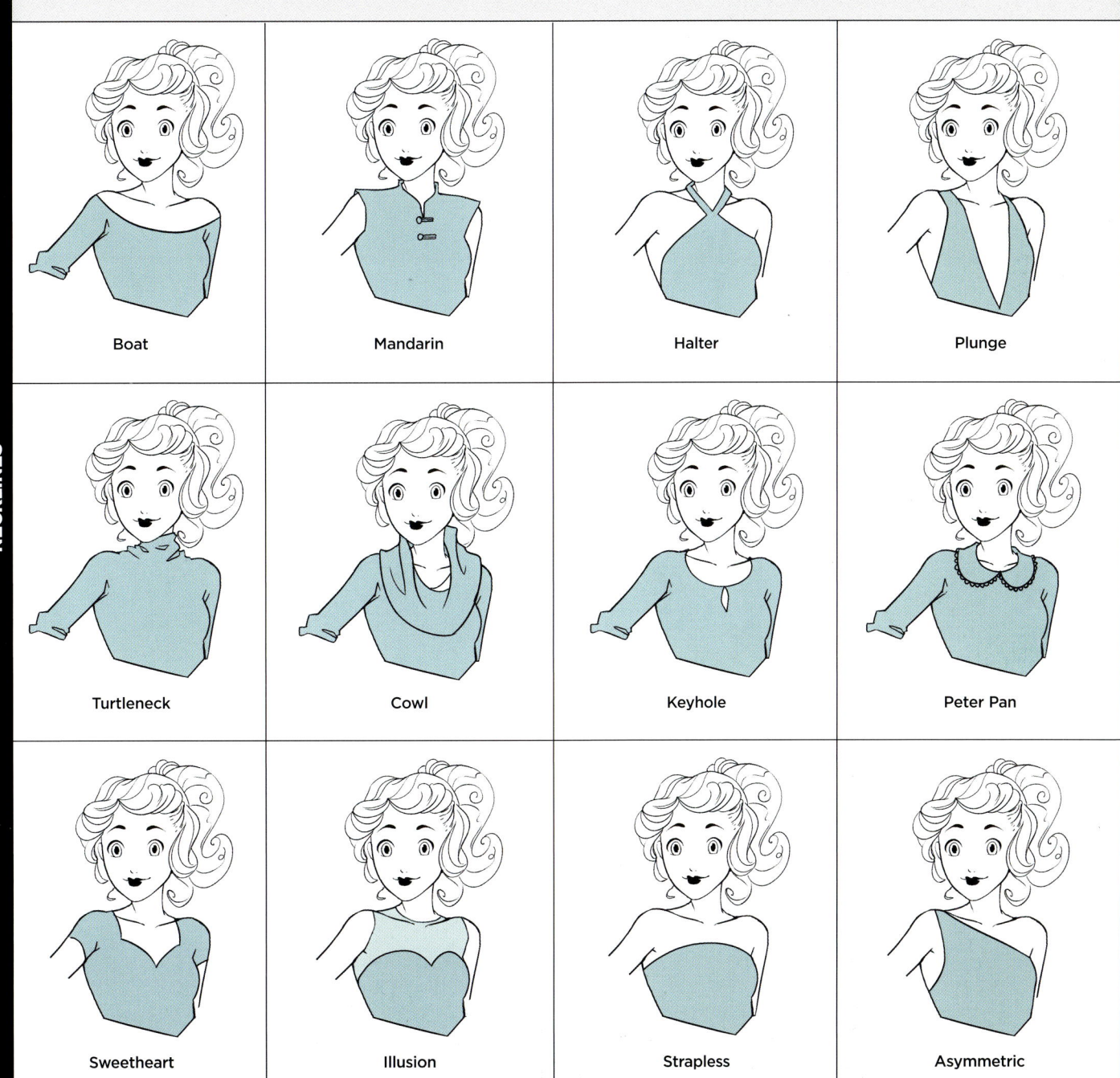

Boat	Mandarin	Halter	Plunge
Turtleneck	Cowl	Keyhole	Peter Pan
Sweetheart	Illusion	Strapless	Asymmetric

34 | DRAWING BASICS

SKIRTS

From daring miniskirts to long, flowing summer skirts, there are styles to suit every season and match any outfit combination. Start with a simple straight skirt: it follows the form of the legs. Draw the folds wider at the base and allow them to flow with gravity and motion. Then progress to trying the styles featured here. You can also adapt any of these skirt styles into dresses for some really cute looks.

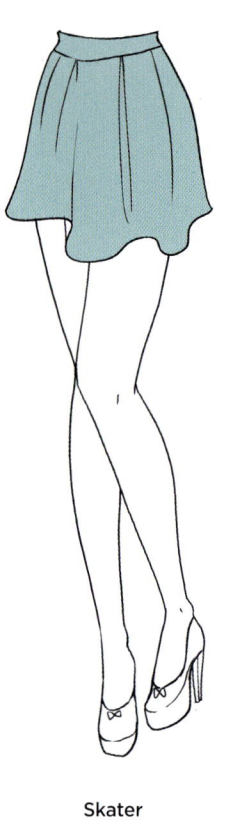
Skater

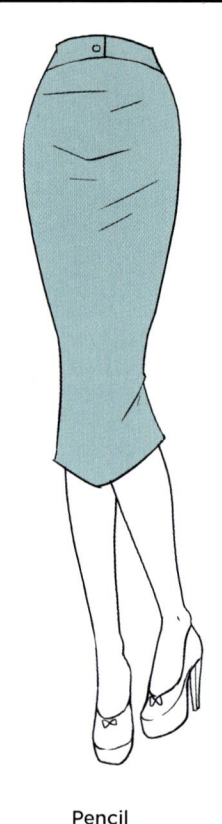
Pencil

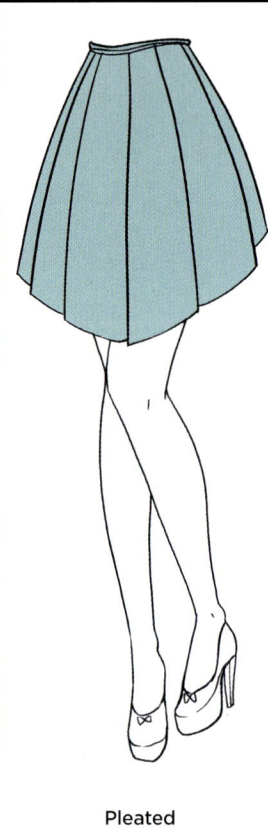
Pleated

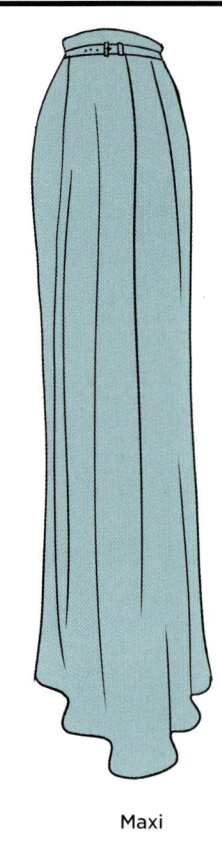
Maxi

PANTS

From loungewear and dancewear to casual and dress clothing, there are scores of classic pants styles to suit your collection. Fit the pants at the hip and construct them around the figure.

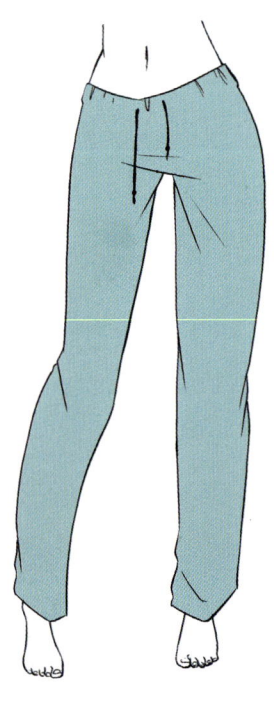

Lounge

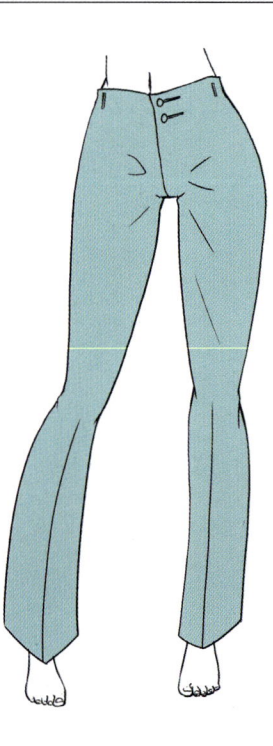
Dress

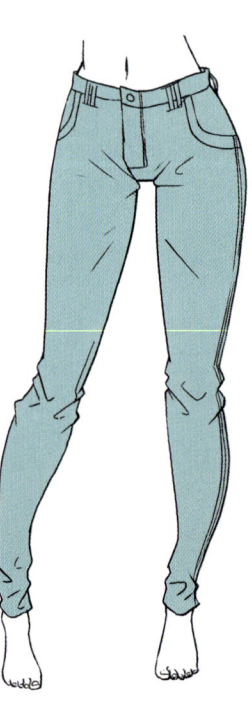
Skinny

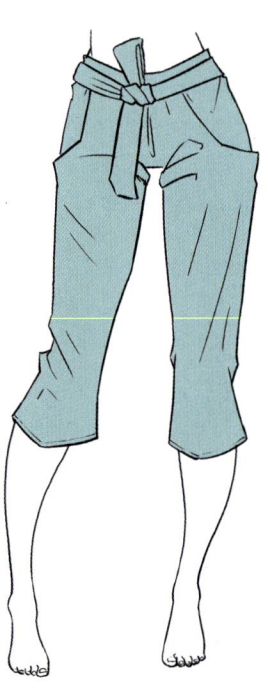
Cropped

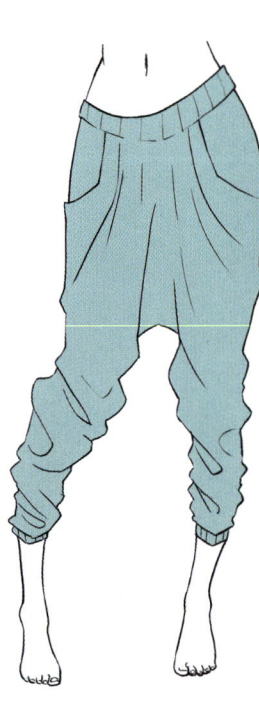
Harem

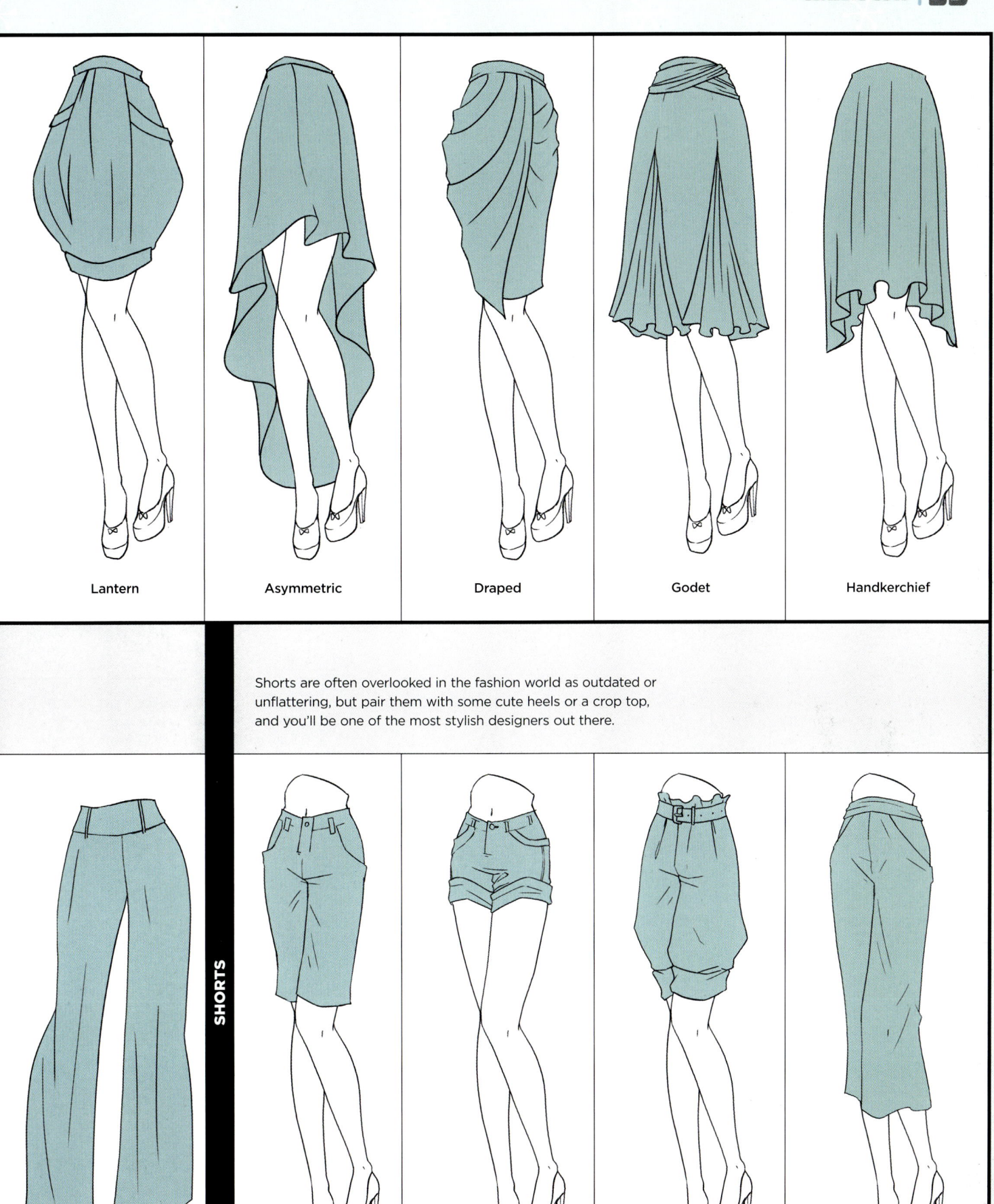

36 | DRAWING BASICS

Between the bridal market, evening events, and the red carpet, big dresses will never be out of style. From huge, fairytale-style dresses to elegant, slim-fitting pieces, a beautiful dress is guaranteed to make your fashion collections stand out.

A dress looks best with a simple pose so that the garment details are the main focus. For an evening gown, the legs may not show, so make sure the figure has the correct proportions.

DRESSES

Empire line
A flattering shape on almost all body types, as it conceals the waistline and hips, and accentuates the bust.

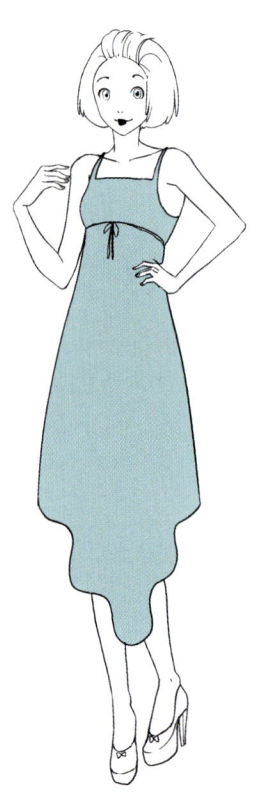

Basque
This dress style has a close-fitting, contoured bodice that flatters the waist and hips.

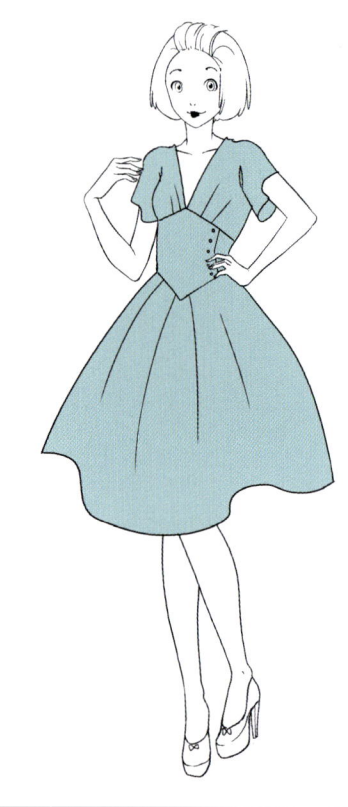

A-line
Traveling straight out and downward from the bust, this clean, classy look is popular for both bridal and formal collections.

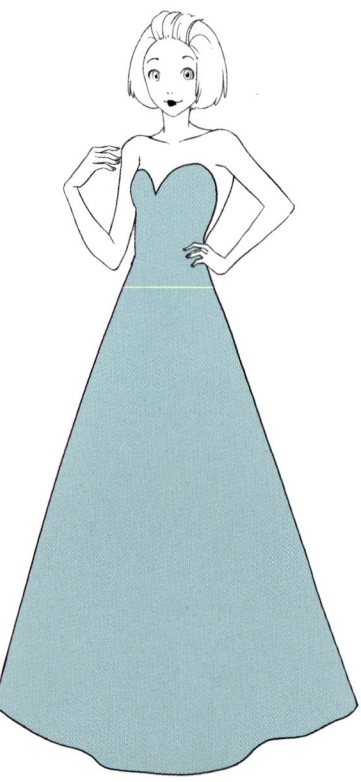

Mermaid skirt
Hugging the figure over the waist, hips, and legs before flaring outward just below the knee, the mermaid skirt creates a flattering hourglass silhouette, perfect for any red carpet.

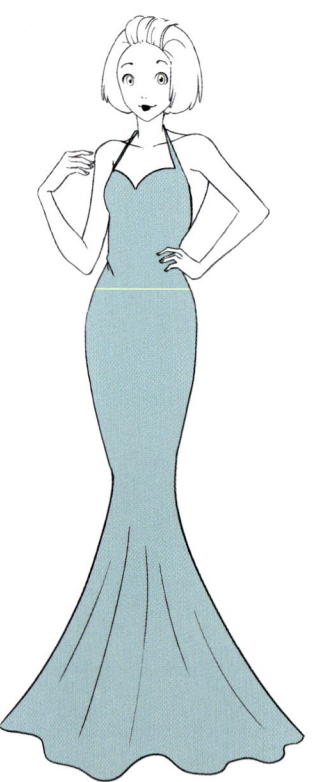

Ball gown
A large, circle-cut skirt is given volume with a half slip and a crinoline underneath, and often puffed out farther with layers of lace and overskirts over the top.

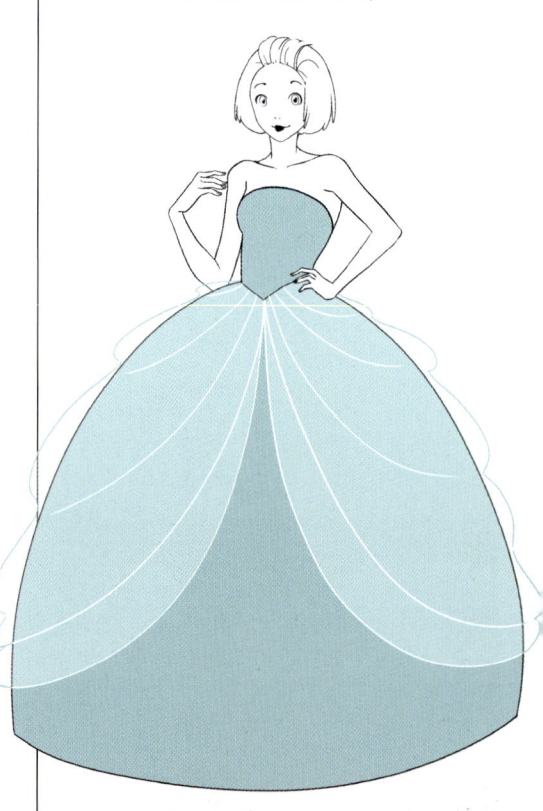

CLASSIC CUTS | 37

FOOTWEAR

A fashion collection isn't just about the clothing. As anyone could probably tell you, it's also about the shoes. From badass boots and cute clogs to hot heels and pretty pumps, the right footwear should complement an outfit perfectly as well as making a statement all of its own.

| Thigh-high boots | Riding boots | Cowboy boots |

| Stilettos | Kitten heels | Mules | Mary Jane | T-strap | Wedges | Platforms | Ankle boots |

HATS

Not all outfits require a hat, but the right headwear can certainly add a dash of character to a look. Knitted woolen or faux fur hats are perfect for casual outdoor collections, whereas a neat flat cap or trilby will add the perfect finishing touch to a men's eveningwear collection.

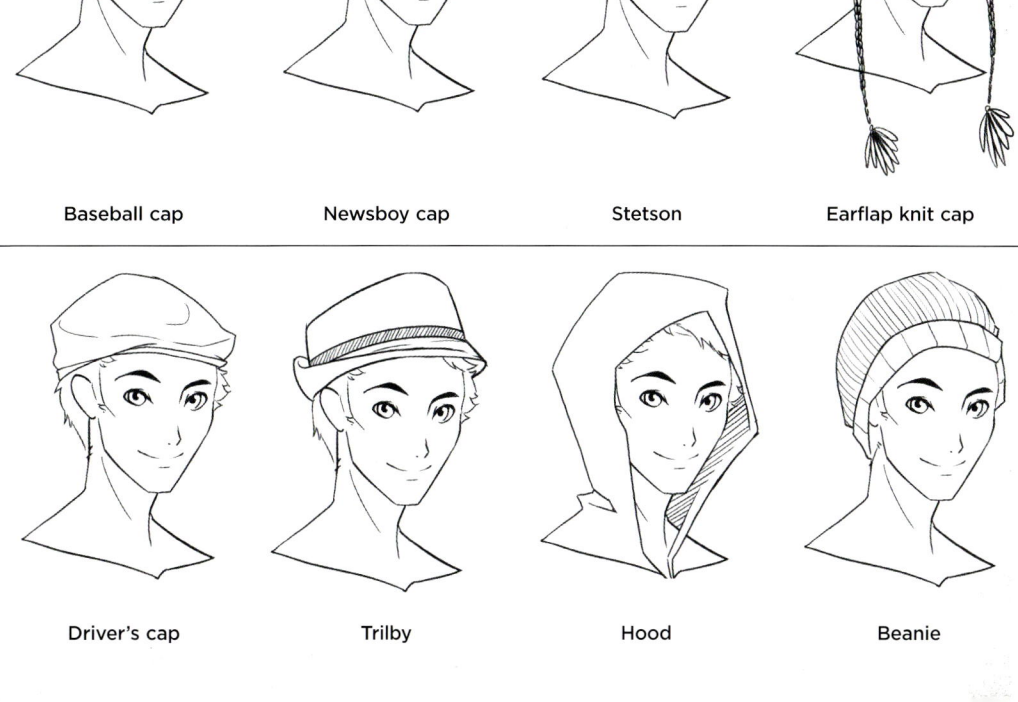

| Baseball cap | Newsboy cap | Stetson | Earflap knit cap |

| Driver's cap | Trilby | Hood | Beanie |

CREATIVE COLORING

THE USE OF THE RIGHT COLORS CAN REALLY MAKE A COLLECTION **A CUT ABOVE THE REST**. WITH CERTAIN TYPES OF CLOTHING, THERE WILL ALWAYS BE TRADITIONAL COLORS TO ADHERE TO—WHITE FOR BRIDALWEAR IN MANY CULTURES, FOR EXAMPLE—BUT EVEN BRIDAL GOWNS NEED A SPLASH OF COLOR HERE AND THERE. KNOWING COLOR THEORY SHOULD REALLY HELP YOU **HIT THE GROUND RUNNING** WHEN IT COMES TO YOUR DESIGNS.

THE COLOR WHEEL

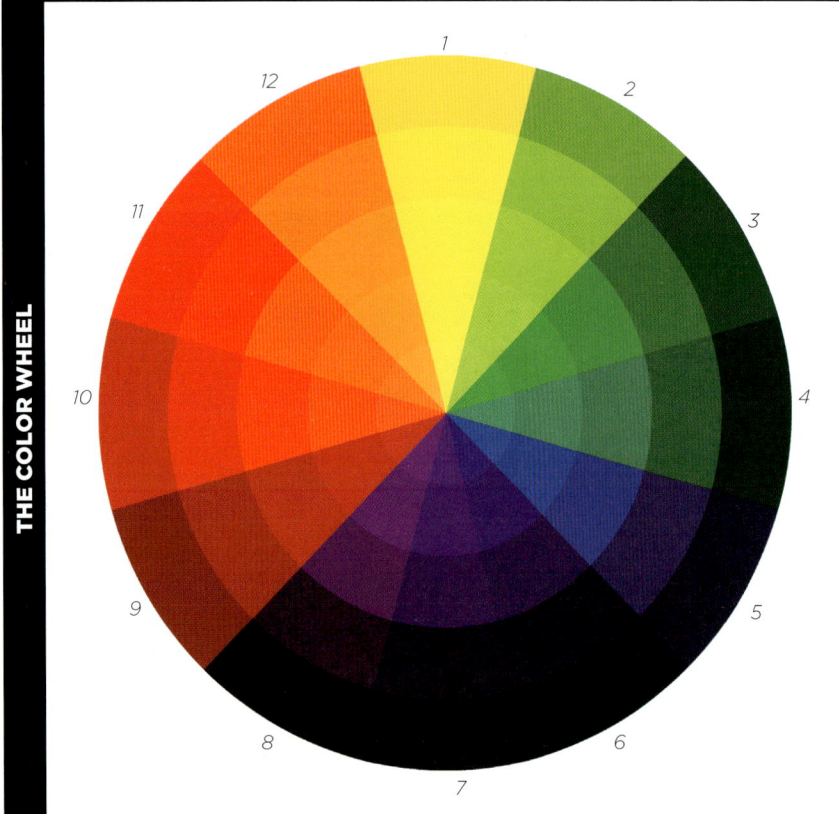

1 Yellow
2 Yellow-green
3 Green
4 Blue-green
5 Blue
6 Blue-violet
7 Violet
8 Red-violet
9 Red
10 Red-orange
11 Orange
12 Yellow-orange

Color theory is important for any artist—fashion designer or otherwise—to know. Because colors are so imbued with meanings and emotions, the right colors can really convey an outfit's mood or character. For example, people will generally see a man wearing red as strong and sturdy, and a woman wearing red as bold and confident; purple and gold convey a sense of royalty or wealth; while warm grays, browns, and pinks are comforting ... perfect for sleepwear. Take some time to look at the colors on this basic wheel and think about what colors you would choose for particular outfits.

PRIMARY, SECONDARY, AND TERTIARY

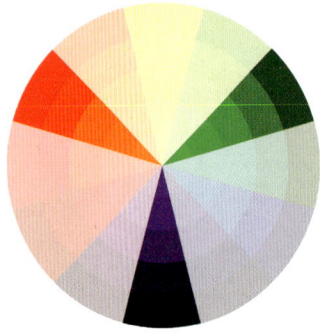

Primary
The three primary colors are yellow, blue, and red; these are the three colors that our eyes can process, and any other color that we see is formed from a combination of these.

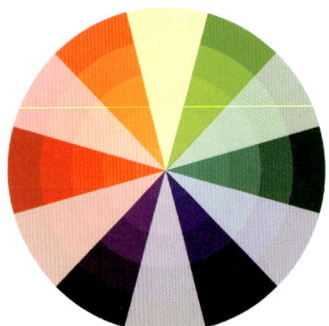

Secondary
Secondary colors are formed by mixing equal amounts of the primary colors; in the color wheel, these are green, violet, and orange.

Tertiary
The third color type is known as a tertiary; these are the colors that come between the primary and secondary colors, and have names such as red-violet and blue-green.

The colors in the wheel can be broken down into three distinct types: primary, secondary, and tertiary. It is useful to learn how these fit into the wheel, as they will teach you which colors are created when mixed together. They will also help you pick complementary colors quickly and easily. For example, if you have the wheel memorized then you will know that a blue–green sits opposite a red-orange, and so you can quickly choose colors that will sit next to each other attractively in an outfit or an illustration.

CREATIVE COLORING | 39

Once you know your way around the color wheel, you'll need to know how to combine two or more colors in an appealing way. Understanding complementary colors can be really quite useful—if you have an outfit that is too blue, for example, just add a small pop of orange and the whole design will immediately look better balanced.

COLOR COMBINATIONS

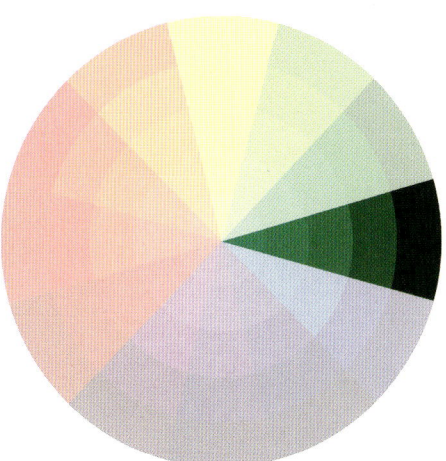

Monochrome
A monochromatic color scheme is one that consists of one color only. A perk of creating an outfit with this scheme is that it will appear uniform and consistent—however, with no secondary color to bring out details and shapes, it could also appear uninteresting.

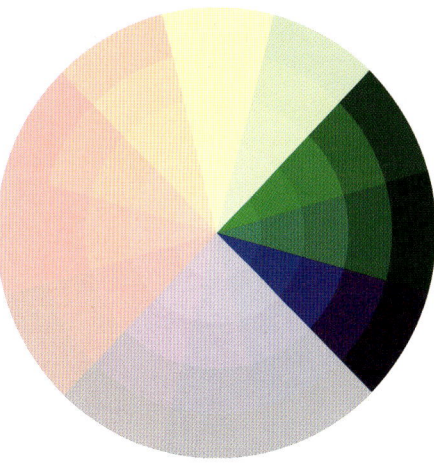

Analogous
Analogous colors are three colors that sit next to each other on the wheel; for example, green, blue-green, and blue. As well as being a useful color palette, they also help add depth to shading and highlights, which is especially useful when drawing a fabric that has more than one color in different lights. When shading this sort of fabric, you could color it a blue-green with blue shadows and a green highlight.

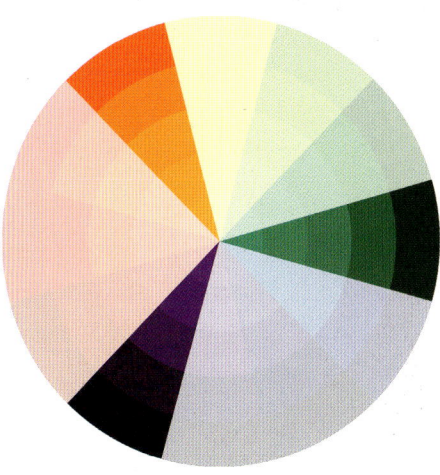

Triad
A triad of colors is three colors that sit evenly spaced around the wheel. For example, the primary colors create a triad; however, using just the primaries in an outfit can sometimes come across as too garish, so it might be worth experimenting with triads of other colors, such as this selection of yellow-orange, blue-green, and red-violet.

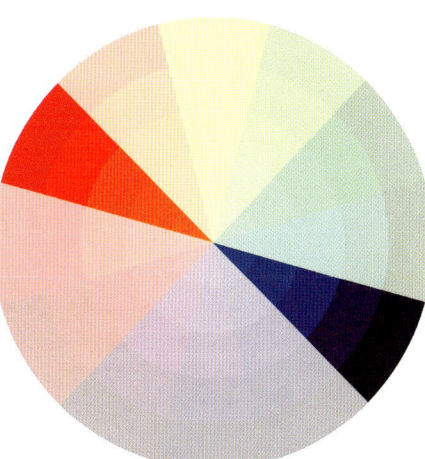

Complementary
To avoid an outfit looking too dull, a complementary color scheme will help to make sections of detail pop out. Complementary colors sit opposite each other on the wheel, such as blue and orange, or violet and yellow.

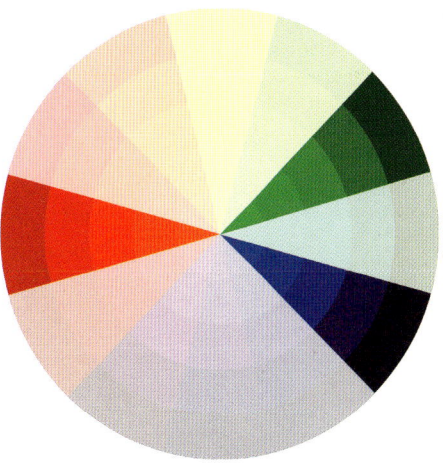

Split complementary
A split complementary color scheme is one that adds a third color to the traditional complementary colors. For example, instead of using red-orange and blue-green, bring in a slight variation by using the two colors either side of blue-green, in this case pure green and blue.

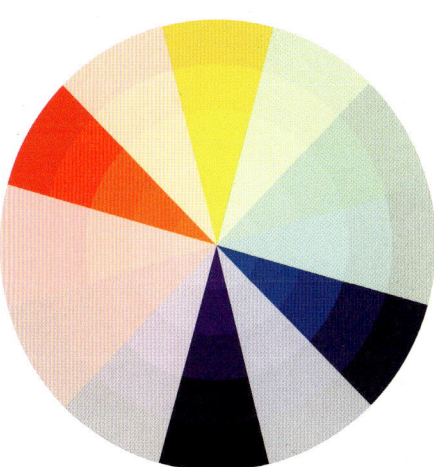

Double complementary
A little rarer in clothing design, double complementary color schemes can bring in too many colors and therefore make an outfit look too bright and over the top. However, you can avoid this by using two complementary colors that are close to each other on the wheel; this scheme introduces yellow and violet, and also blue and orange.

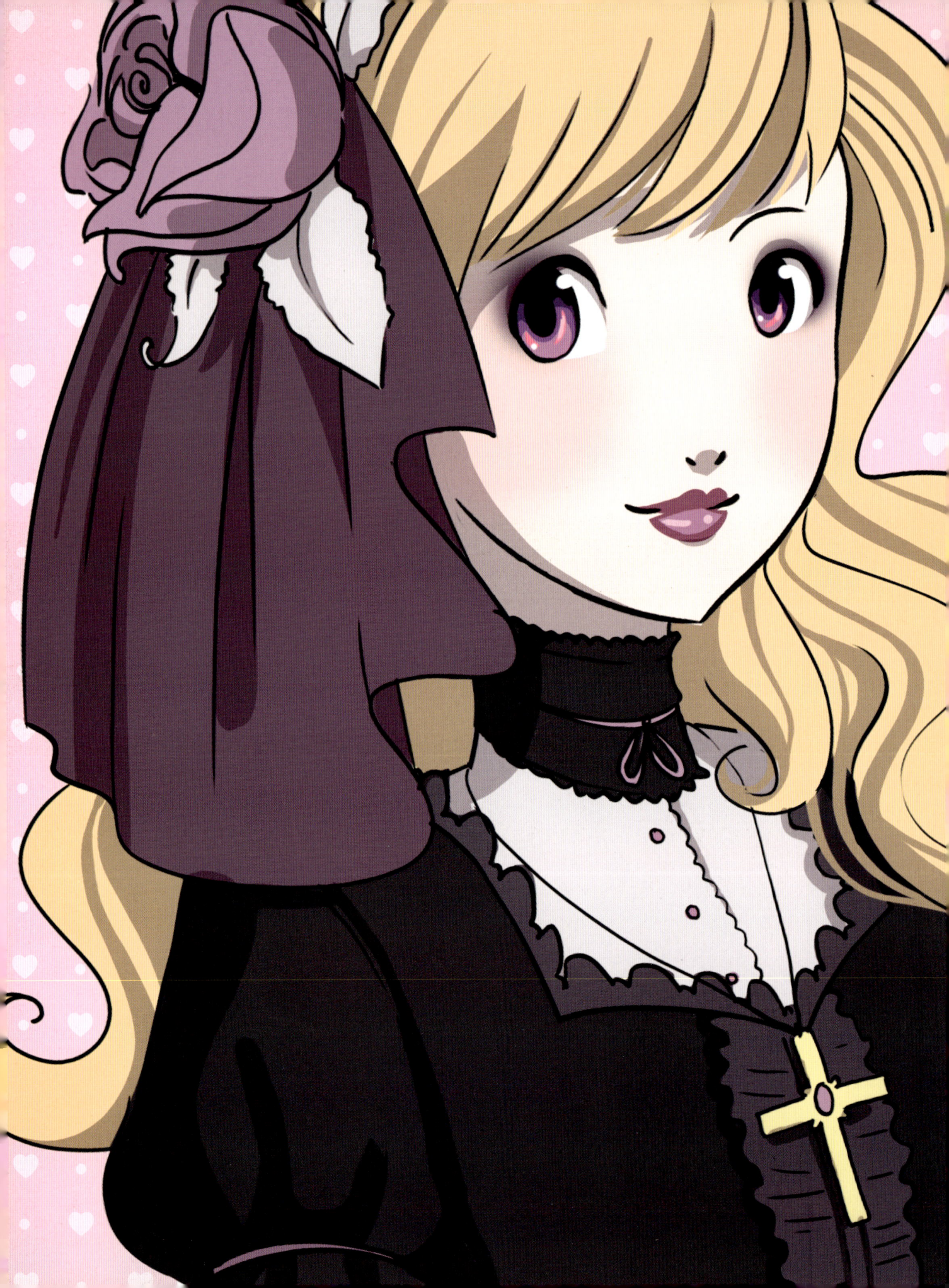

THE COLLECTIONS

FROM **JAPANESE STREETWEAR** TO **WESTERN POP CULTURE**, FROM **CLASSIC CLOTHING CUTS** TO **CATWALK FASHION**, FIND ALL THE INSPIRATION YOU NEED TO **EXPRESS YOUR MANGA CHARACTERS' PERSONALITIES**. CHOOSE FROM THE BRIGHT COLORS OF GANGURO, THE MUTED TONES OF EMO, OR THE COUTURE OF PARISIAN CHIC. **CLOTHING, MAKEUP, AND ACCESSORIES** ALL COMBINE TO CREATE A CHARACTER WHO'S FIT TO HIT THE STREETS, MALL, BEACH—OR EVEN THE FUTURE!

HARAJUKU STREET

JAPANESE STREET FASHION HAS BEEN PREDOMINANT IN TOKYO SINCE THE 1980S. A **FUSION OF MODERN WESTERN AND TRADITIONAL JAPANESE** CLOTHING, IT IS POPULAR WITH TEENS, AND OFTEN WEARERS GATHER IN THE **FASHION DISTRICTS OF TOKYO** TO SHOW OFF THEIR CREATIONS. THIS HAS LED TO VARIOUS STYLES BEING COMMONLY NAMED AFTER CITY DISTRICTS, SUCH AS HARAJUKU AND SHIBUYA.

1 Sketching the skeleton roughly will help you to work out a pose and see the basic body proportions before you get too caught up with details. Here, the model has her shoulders and hips twisted playfully, which is shown by her right hip and shoulder joints pointing inward toward each other.

2 Draw the basics of the body over the top of the skeleton. Remember which parts of the body curve outward and which tuck inward, and add in your model's facial features so that you end up with all of the basic elements drawn in. Now she's ready to be dressed.

3 Now that we've come to the fun part—dressing up—don't let worrying about keeping your sketching neat hold you back. You'll be neatening your drawings up in the next step, so keep your lines loose and focus on shapes and patterns. This girl is wearing a loose tee and skirt, so much of her figure is hidden beneath the clothing. There are lots of fabric folds and pleats to have fun sketching in.

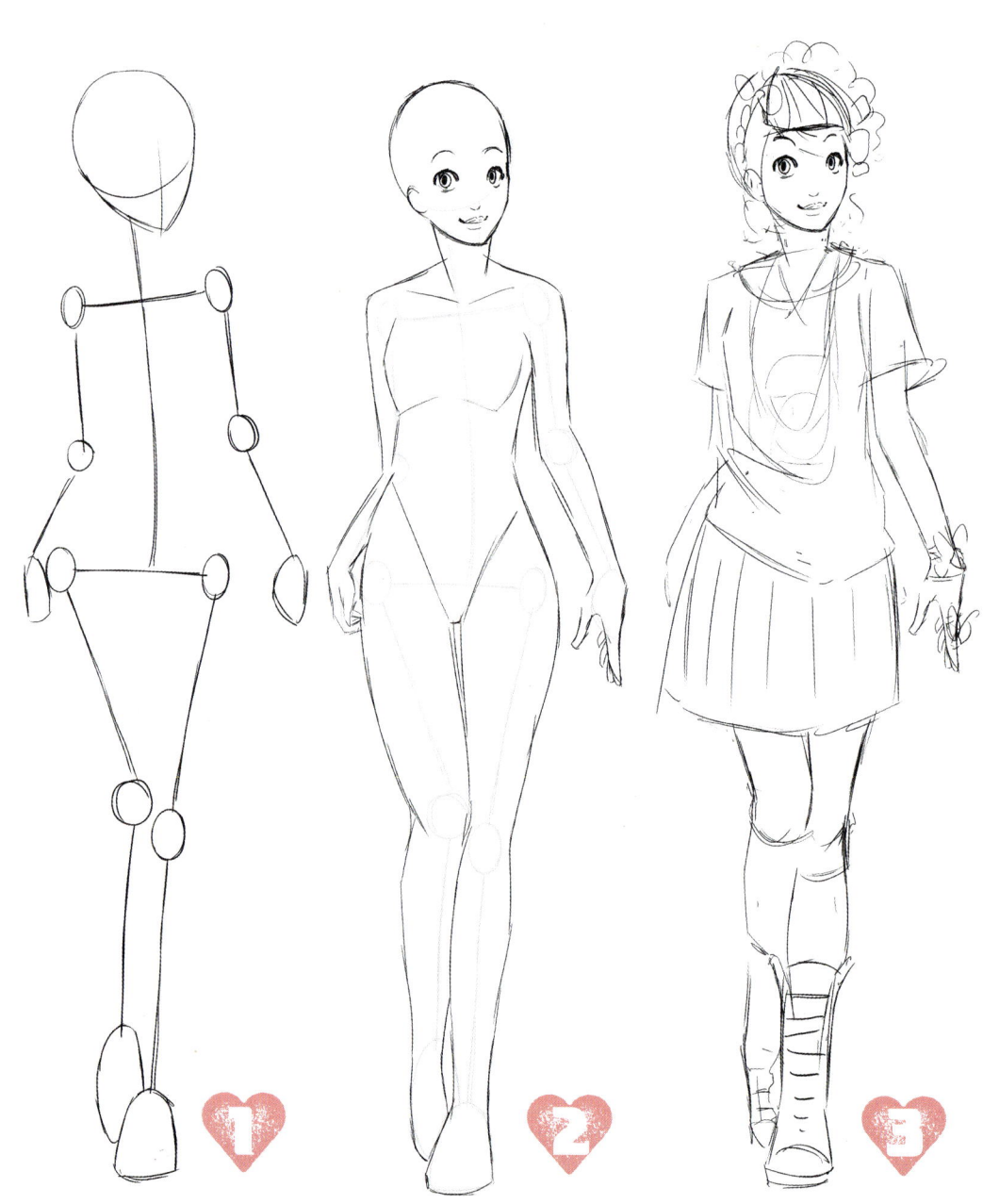

HARAJUKU STREET | **43**

4 It's time to clean up your sketch, and at the same time describe your model's outfit in more detail. Here, the outfit has a general theme of bows: street fashion is all about an excess of details, so add them in wherever you can—jewelry, hair, boots. Go wild!

5 For a fun, feminine outfit, we need a fun, feminine color palette: pinks and purples are always soft and girly, and perfect for this outfit. Add in pops of blue and gold to make elements of the outfit stand out. A lot of wearers of street fashion dye their hair: Why not add some color to your model's hair as well?

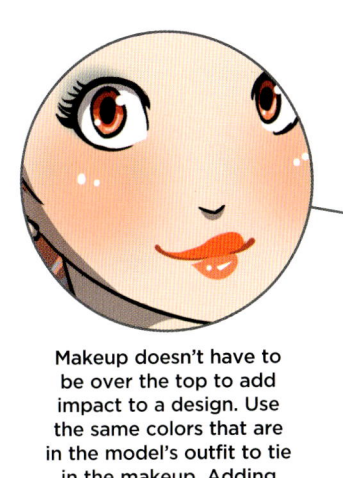

Makeup doesn't have to be over the top to add impact to a design. Use the same colors that are in the model's outfit to tie in the makeup. Adding extra details, such as white highlights to the cheeks and lips for extra shine, keeps the look bright and fresh.

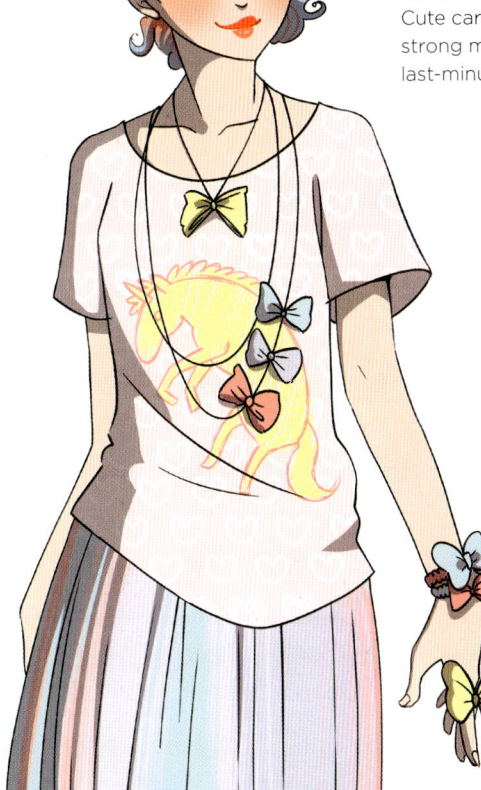

6 There's no such thing as "too much" in street fashion, so make sure to put in plenty of final details to finish off your design. Cute cartoons, bold stripes, and strong makeup add those perfect last-minute touches.

Light, airy fabrics complement the soft colors of this outfit. Multiple layers of colored tulle create a bright, voluminous skirt. Replicate the look by overlaying and fading colors together.

CLOTHING PALETTE

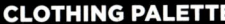

Street fashion has no uniform look across the whole style, but outfits should certainly be coordinating. Because this outfit has a light, soft look similar to the style of Sweet Lolita (see pages 72–73), we'll be sticking to pastels; soft gold, blues, and pinks create an appealing and cohesive palette.

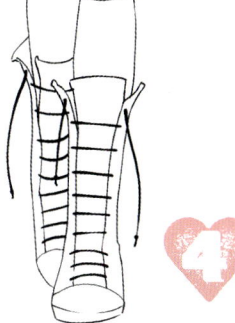
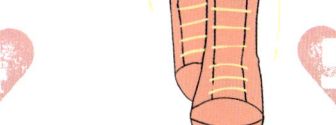

44 | THE COLLECTIONS

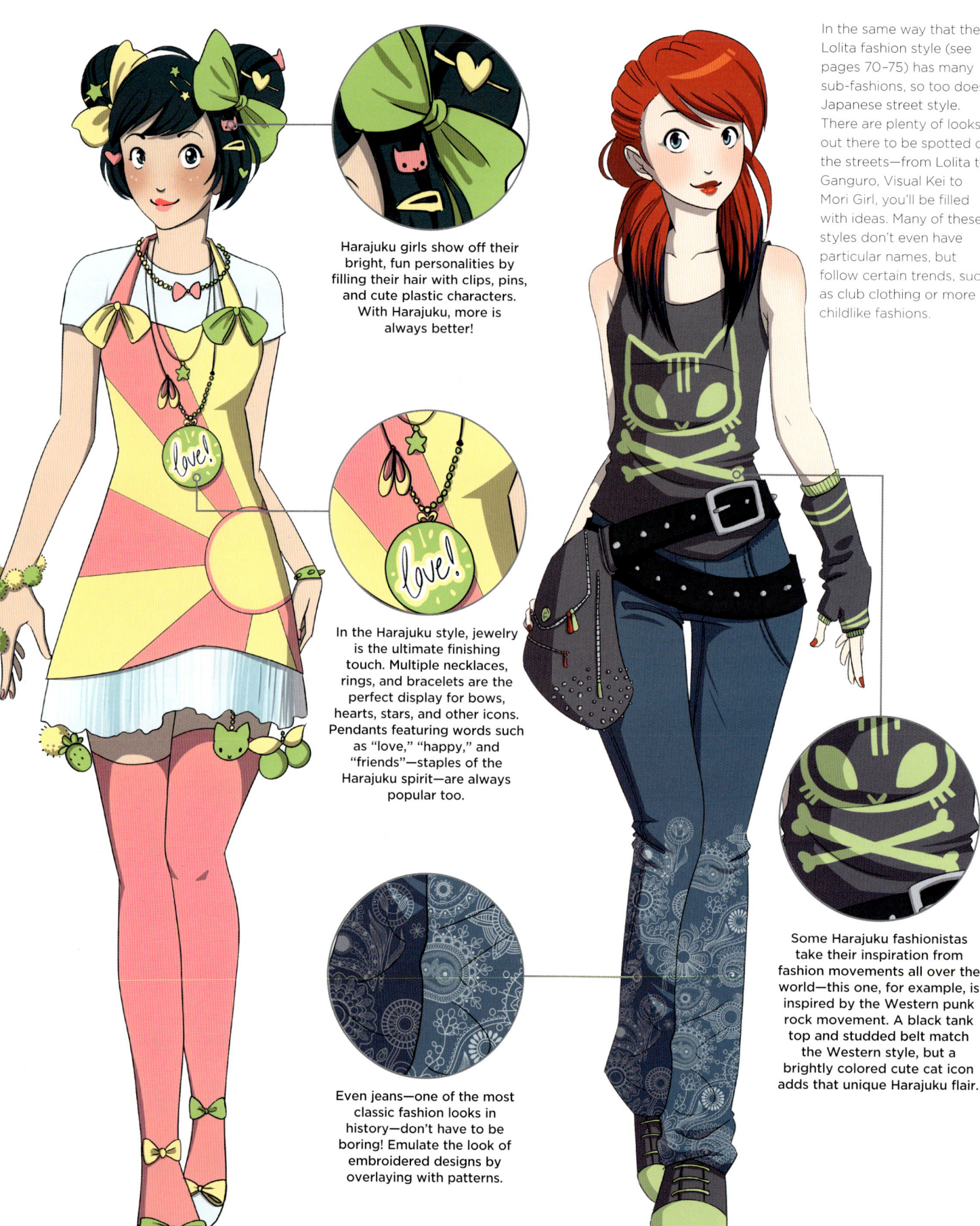

Harajuku girls show off their bright, fun personalities by filling their hair with clips, pins, and cute plastic characters. With Harajuku, more is always better!

In the same way that the Lolita fashion style (see pages 70–75) has many sub-fashions, so too does Japanese street style. There are plenty of looks out there to be spotted on the streets—from Lolita to Ganguro, Visual Kei to Mori Girl, you'll be filled with ideas. Many of these styles don't even have particular names, but follow certain trends, such as club clothing or more childlike fashions.

In the Harajuku style, jewelry is the ultimate finishing touch. Multiple necklaces, rings, and bracelets are the perfect display for bows, hearts, stars, and other icons. Pendants featuring words such as "love," "happy," and "friends"—staples of the Harajuku spirit—are always popular too.

Some Harajuku fashionistas take their inspiration from fashion movements all over the world—this one, for example, is inspired by the Western punk rock movement. A black tank top and studded belt match the Western style, but a brightly colored cute cat icon adds that unique Harajuku flair.

Even jeans—one of the most classic fashion looks in history—don't have to be boring! Emulate the look of embroidered designs by overlaying with patterns.

HARAJUKU STREET | 45

ACCESSORIES AND CLOTHING

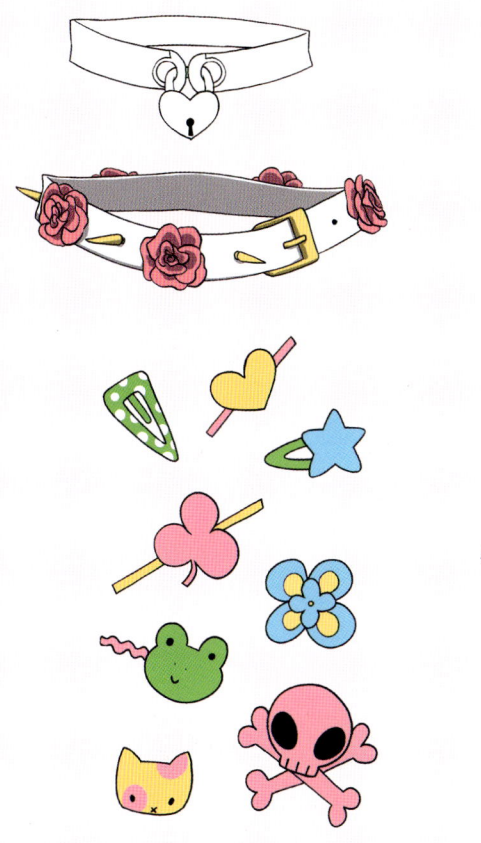

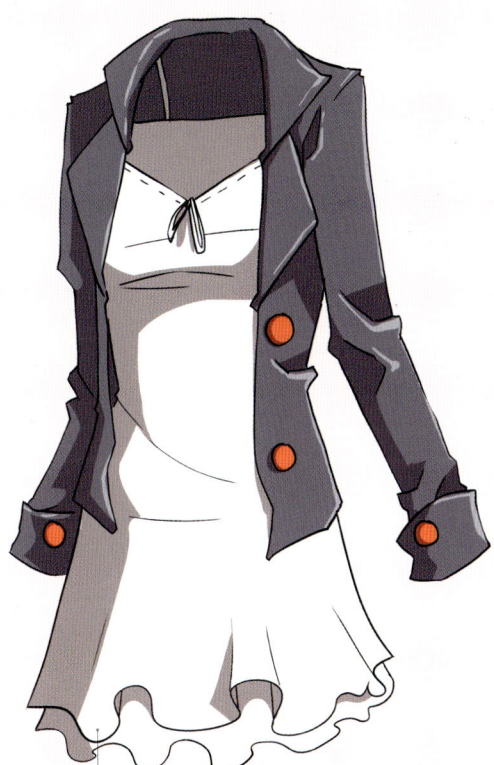

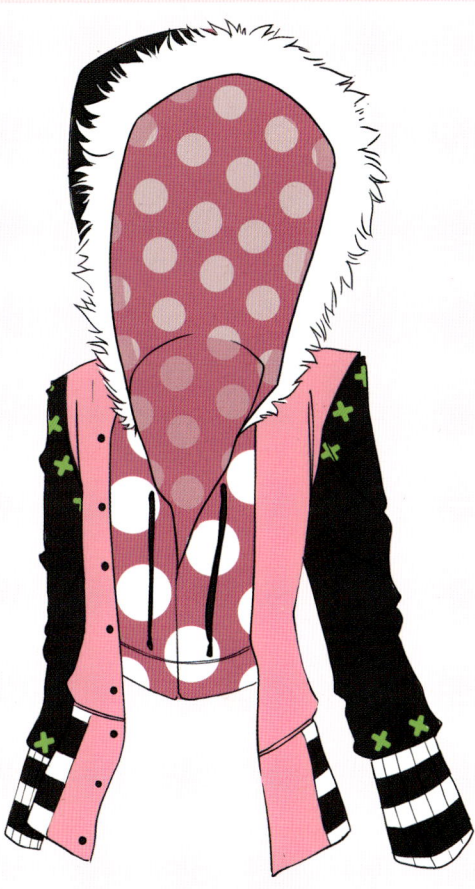

Try layering clothing for different looks. For example, a cute, lacy dress can create several different looks depending on whether it's teamed with a girly cardigan or a leather jacket. Combine styles and colors for a unique look.

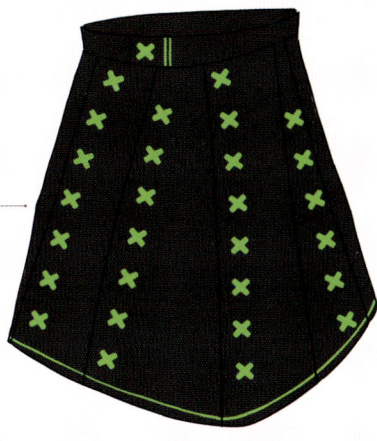

The Harajuku look is colorful, but you can still use gray, black, or brown. Add areas of detail—such as embroidery, iron-on patches, or chunky badges—in bright, bold colors to break up dark areas.

The more accessories your model can fit on her outfit, the better. Hair ties are always popular, as they can be clipped not just to hair but also to sleeves, collars, and bag straps, and with cute, bright characters on them, they're the perfect fashion accessory!

Shoes can be just as elaborate as the clothes—don't forget to add in cute accessories, decorative socks, or bright patterns to add that extra flair to your designs.

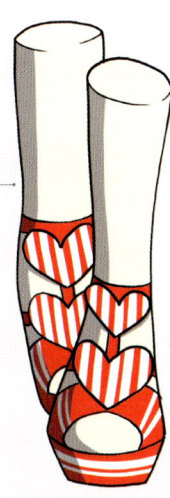
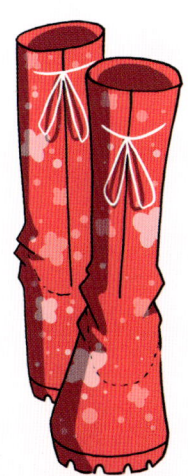
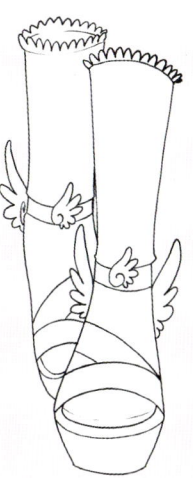
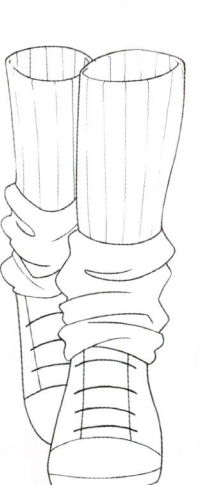
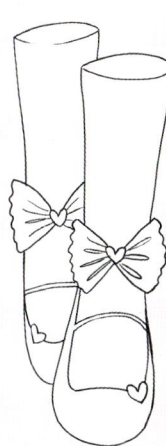

THE COLLECTIONS

PREPPY STYLE

PREP CLOTHING IS AN **AMERICAN FASHION STYLE AND SUBCULTURE** THAT ORIGINATED IN THE **EARLY 1900S** AND BECAME POPULAR THROUGH STYLE ICONS SUCH AS **AUDREY HEPBURN AND GRACE KELLY**. THE TERM DERIVES FROM ITS **ORIGINS IN UNIVERSITY PREPARATORY SCHOOLS**, AND SUGGESTS NOT JUST A PARTICULAR CLOTHING STYLE BUT ALSO A CERTAIN WAY OF **SPEAKING, MANNER, AND ETIQUETTE** PARTICULAR TO THE UPPER AND MIDDLE-UPPER CLASSES. THE STYLE IS PARTICULARLY INSPIRED BY **SCHOOL UNIFORMS**, AND PREDOMINANTLY FEATURES **CREWNECK SWEATERS, KNEE-HIGH SOCKS, AND SKIRTS**. PATTERNS SUCH AS **TARTAN AND ARGYLE** ARE POPULAR.

1 A smooth, curved line is a good starting point for any figure. This will form the figure's spine and help to give your image dynamism further down the line. Focus on the basic skeletal structure of the human body; don't get too caught up on details just yet.

2 Keeping in mind where muscles and other body parts should be, sketch the outline of your figure. Keep it simple: if you already know that your outfit will include pockets, take advantage of your preplanning and include elements of the pose that will interact with the clothing. Be prepared to tweak your drawing if necessary in the next step, though.

3 For girls, formal prep fashion is usually based on a tartan skirt and either a pullover or blazer. Think about the kind of shapes that you want to convey in your collection and base your choices on them—boots or shoes, heels or flats? A tie or a bow? A satchel or no bag at all? Look at existing fashion images to help you choose.

4 When cleaning up your sketch, use the opportunity to make any last changes—for example, this figure has lost any jewelry from the initial sketch that looked too fussy. Use slimmer lines to add extra details that will help describe the fabrics you're using—for example, a ribbed edge around the bottom of the pullover and the same again at the top of the socks suggests a woolen fabric, and stitching around the edges of the leather detailing on the shoes adds a point of interest.

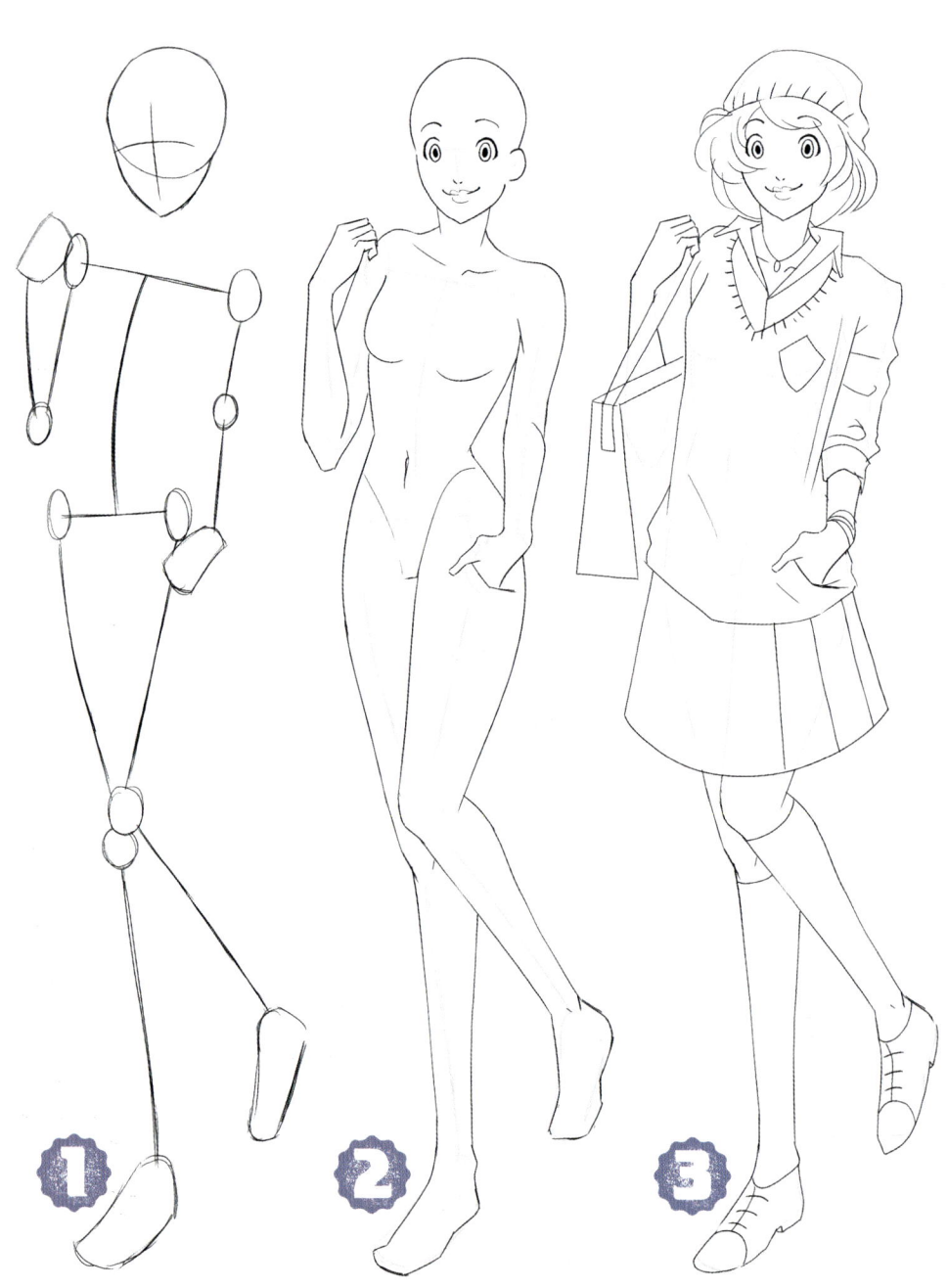

PREPPY STYLE | **47**

5 Using your chosen palette, add the colors for the outfit. Use the colors of the crest on the pullover as a basis, applying flashes of blue and gold throughout to give cohesion. Some of these colors might be too gaudy if used in large quantities, so use them in small pops instead, for example on the buttons of the shirt.

6 Add the patterns that make prep fashion so distinctive. See pages 30–31 for examples of some of the many different styles and colors of tartan available—try out a few before you make your final decision. Reflect the pattern elsewhere in the outfit for a uniform look; this figure is wearing a tartan hat, but you might want to also try tartan socks, a brooch, bag, or hair tie.

Tartan fabrics don't just use one or two colors; traditionally, three or four are used. Here's another chance to add some flashes of your chosen colors. Black and red are standard in tartan, but in the case of this model, we can use blue and gold as well.

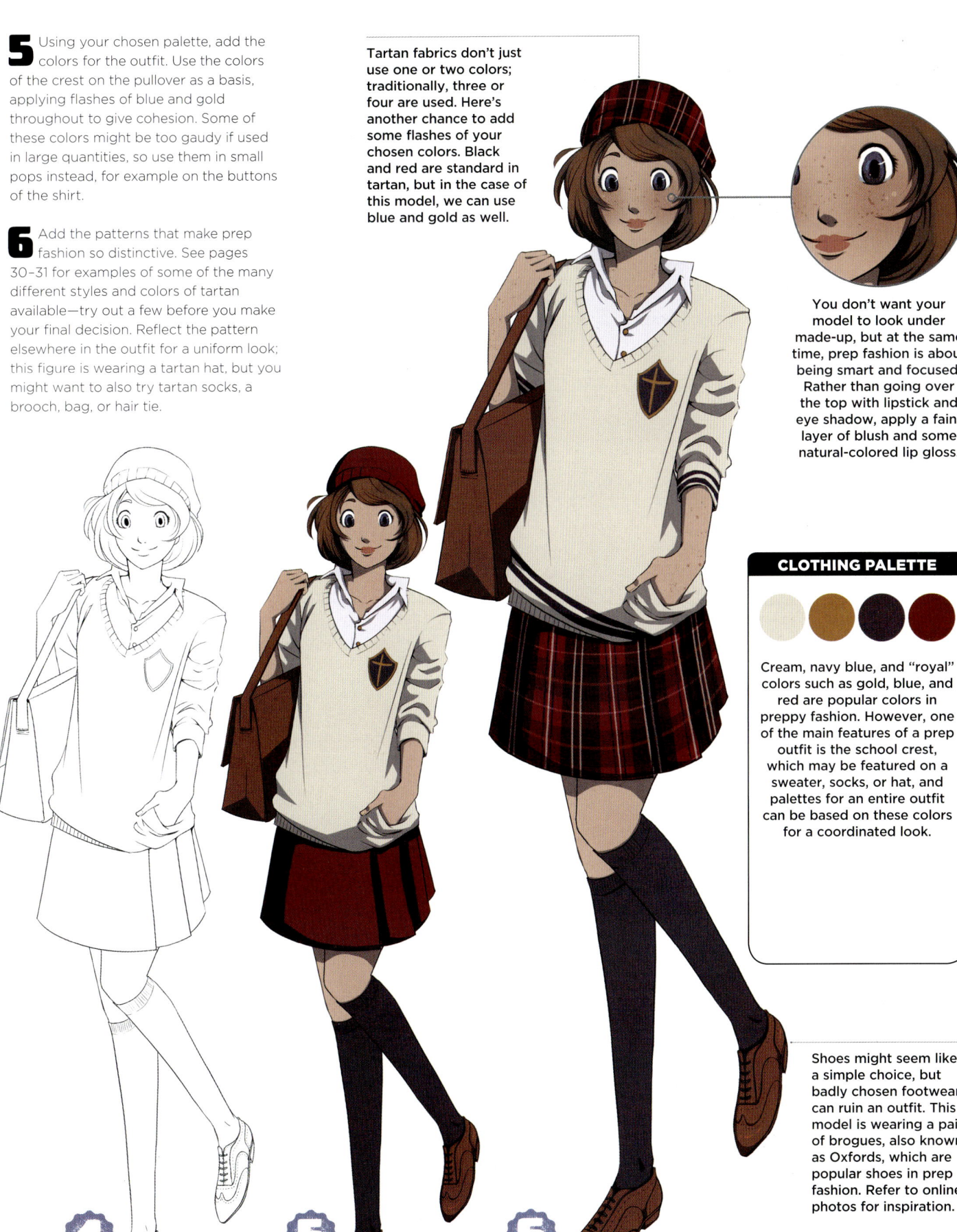

You don't want your model to look under made-up, but at the same time, prep fashion is about being smart and focused. Rather than going over the top with lipstick and eye shadow, apply a faint layer of blush and some natural-colored lip gloss.

CLOTHING PALETTE

Cream, navy blue, and "royal" colors such as gold, blue, and red are popular colors in preppy fashion. However, one of the main features of a prep outfit is the school crest, which may be featured on a sweater, socks, or hat, and palettes for an entire outfit can be based on these colors for a coordinated look.

Shoes might seem like a simple choice, but badly chosen footwear can ruin an outfit. This model is wearing a pair of brogues, also known as Oxfords, which are popular shoes in prep fashion. Refer to online photos for inspiration.

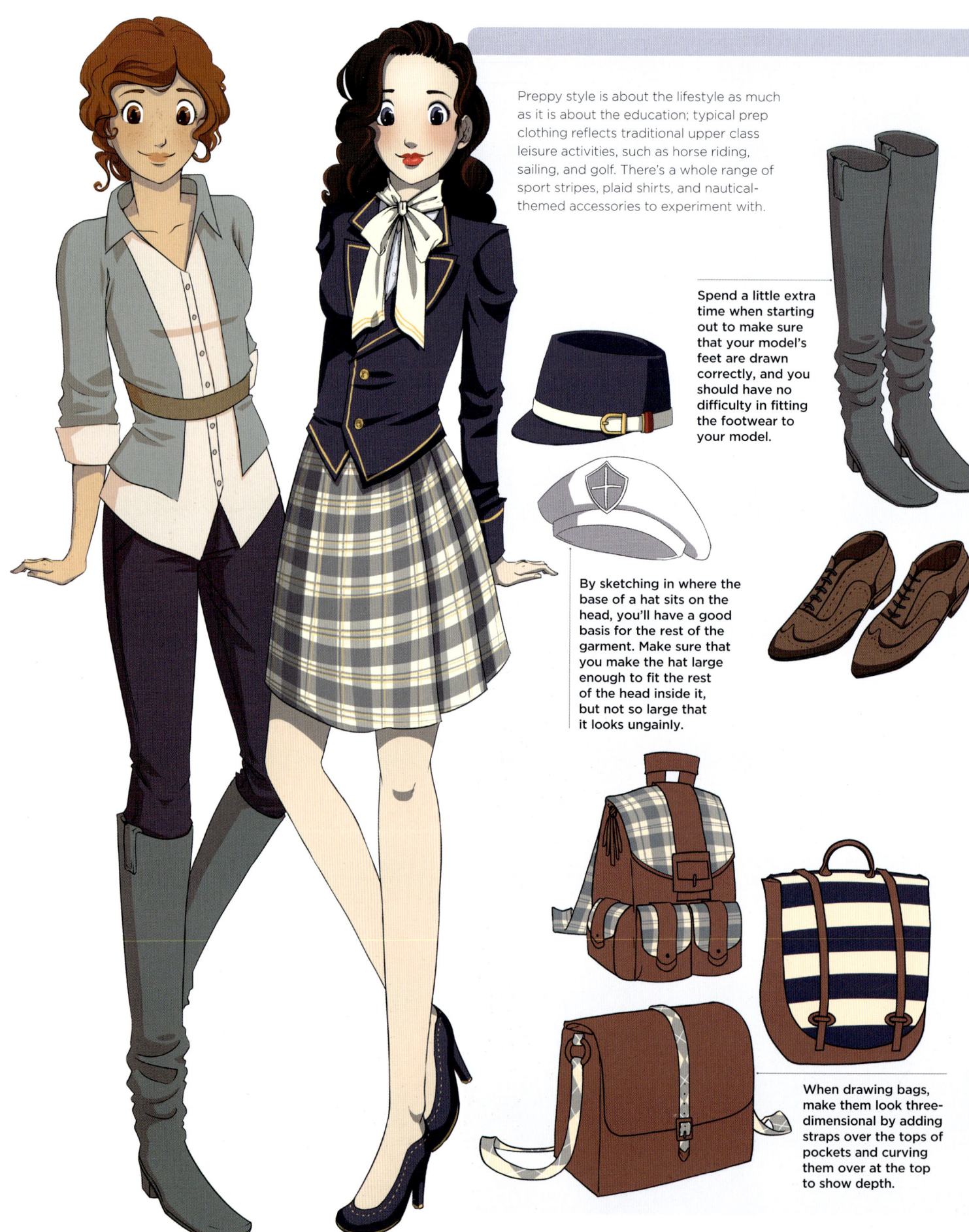

Preppy style is about the lifestyle as much as it is about the education; typical prep clothing reflects traditional upper class leisure activities, such as horse riding, sailing, and golf. There's a whole range of sport stripes, plaid shirts, and nautical-themed accessories to experiment with.

Spend a little extra time when starting out to make sure that your model's feet are drawn correctly, and you should have no difficulty in fitting the footwear to your model.

By sketching in where the base of a hat sits on the head, you'll have a good basis for the rest of the garment. Make sure that you make the hat large enough to fit the rest of the head inside it, but not so large that it looks ungainly.

When drawing bags, make them look three-dimensional by adding straps over the tops of pockets and curving them over at the top to show depth.

ACCESSORIES AND CLOTHING

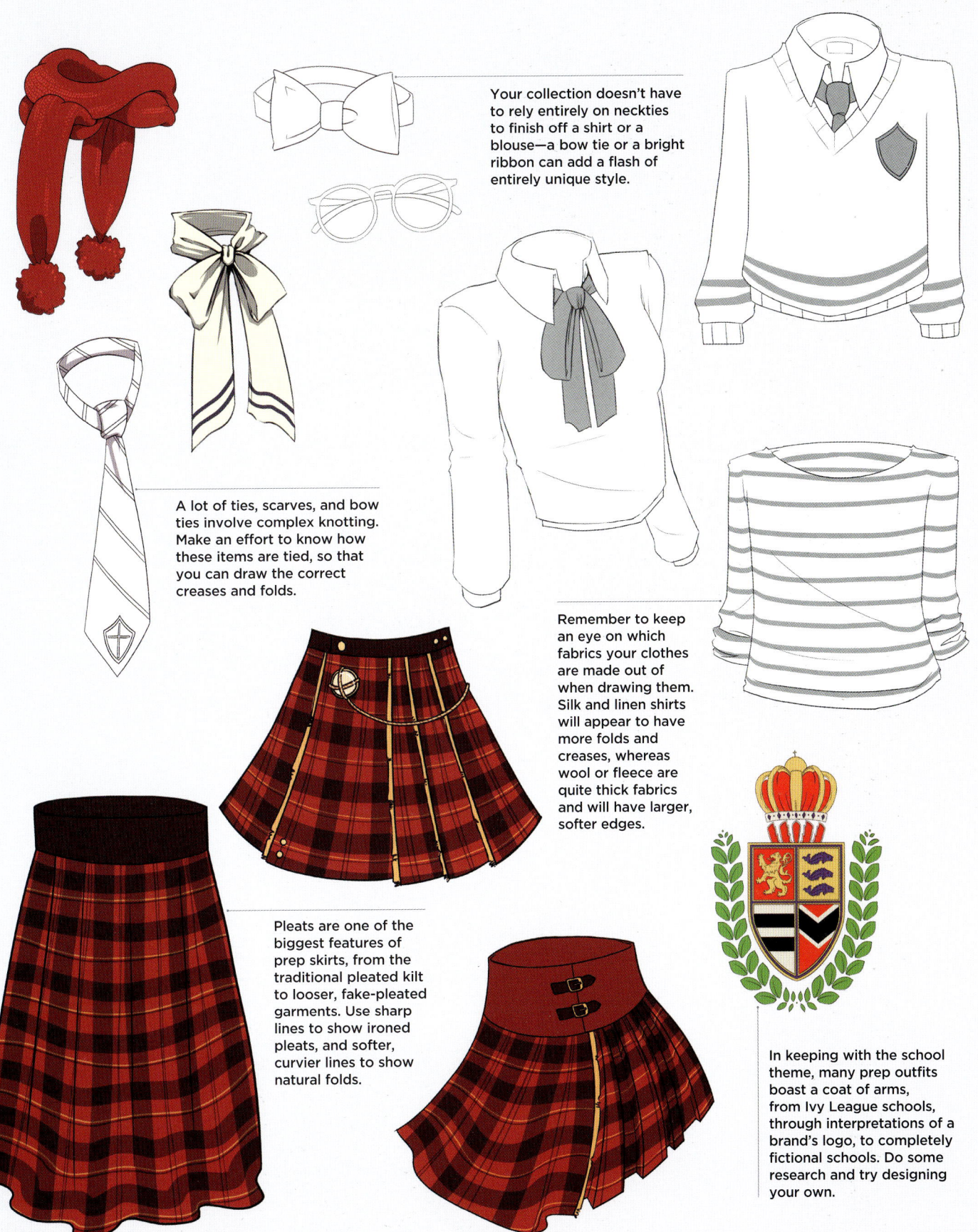

Your collection doesn't have to rely entirely on neckties to finish off a shirt or a blouse—a bow tie or a bright ribbon can add a flash of entirely unique style.

A lot of ties, scarves, and bow ties involve complex knotting. Make an effort to know how these items are tied, so that you can draw the correct creases and folds.

Remember to keep an eye on which fabrics your clothes are made out of when drawing them. Silk and linen shirts will appear to have more folds and creases, whereas wool or fleece are quite thick fabrics and will have larger, softer edges.

Pleats are one of the biggest features of prep skirts, from the traditional pleated kilt to looser, fake-pleated garments. Use sharp lines to show ironed pleats, and softer, curvier lines to show natural folds.

In keeping with the school theme, many prep outfits boast a coat of arms, from Ivy League schools, through interpretations of a brand's logo, to completely fictional schools. Do some research and try designing your own.

BOHO CHIC

THE **BOHEMIAN LOOK** HAS BEEN AROUND SINCE THE 1960S, BUT HAS SEEN A REVIVAL IN THE PAST TEN YEARS. MADE FASHIONABLE BY CELEBRITIES AND THE RISING POPULARITY OF FESTIVALS, IT IS A **COMBINATION OF HIPPIE AND FOLK CLOTHING**, AND KITSCH **1970S-STYLE DRESSES** AND **FLORAL FABRICS**. WITH AN ADDED SPLASH OF **FLOWER CROWNS, BANGLES, BIG HAIR, AND LACE**, IT'S PERFECT FOR ANY SUMMER EVENT.

CLOTHING PALETTE

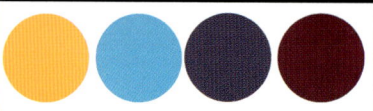

Boho fashion is all about natural colors—whether from undyed fabrics, or shades inspired by fruits, berries, and flowers. This outfit uses berry and plum purples as a base, with pops of gold and blue to make it stand out.

1 Using a very simple skeleton structure, plan your model's pose. The angle of the shoulders and hips should always tilt together at one side, to make the pose look natural and balanced. A curved spine adds a sense of relaxed movement.

2 Using the skeleton as a starting point, draw the rest of the model around it. Note how the curve in the spine has made her appear to be standing more comfortably—the bent knee and held-out hand make her look as though she is striking a cute pose, which helps to give her more personality.

3 Now for the fun part— designing your boho outfit. Long-sleeved, loose dresses are quite often paired with practical boots. Most important to the look, though, is the big hair— boho girls love to braid their hair, or accessorize it with headbands, feathers, and braids, so go wild!

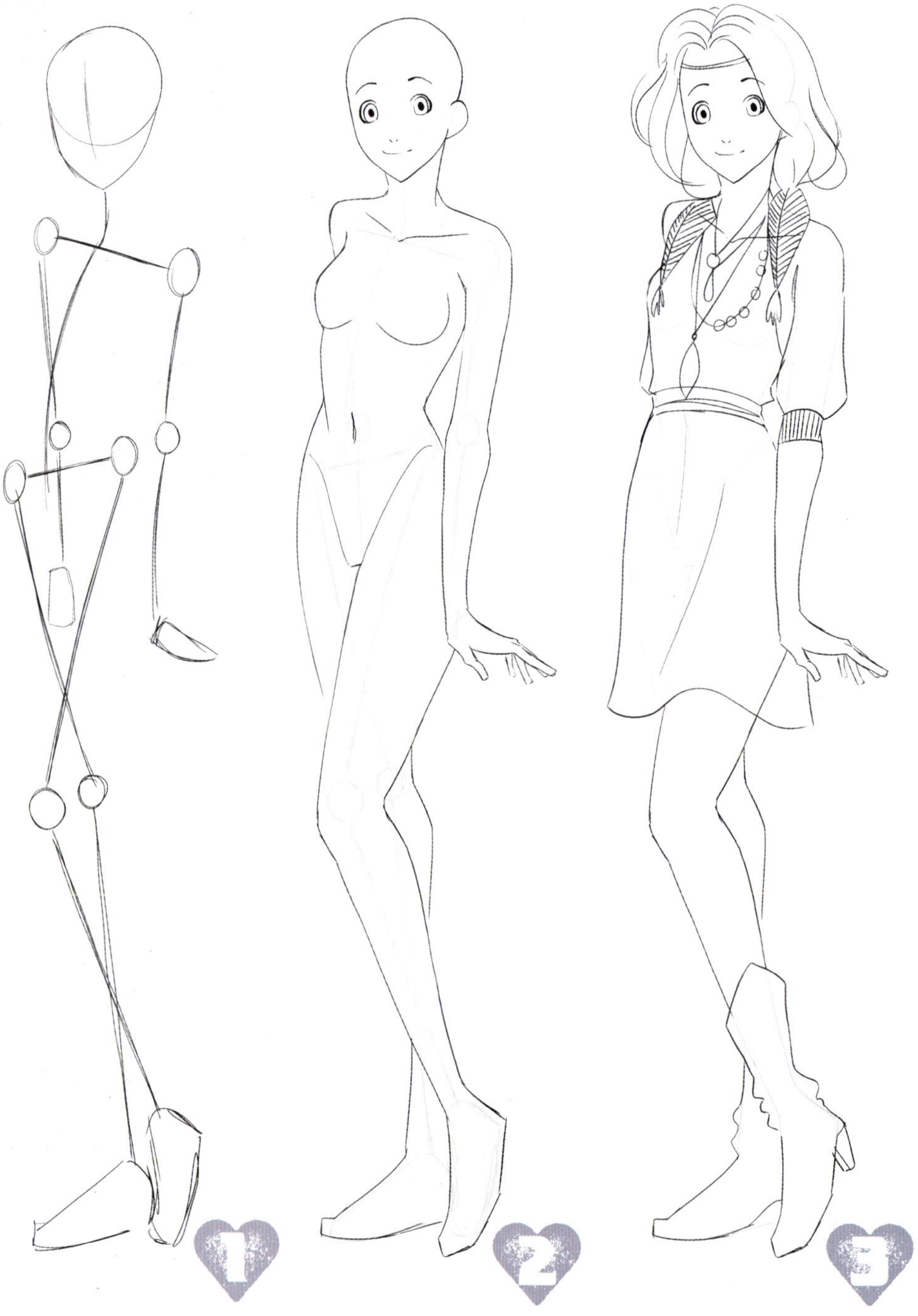

BOHO CHIC | 51

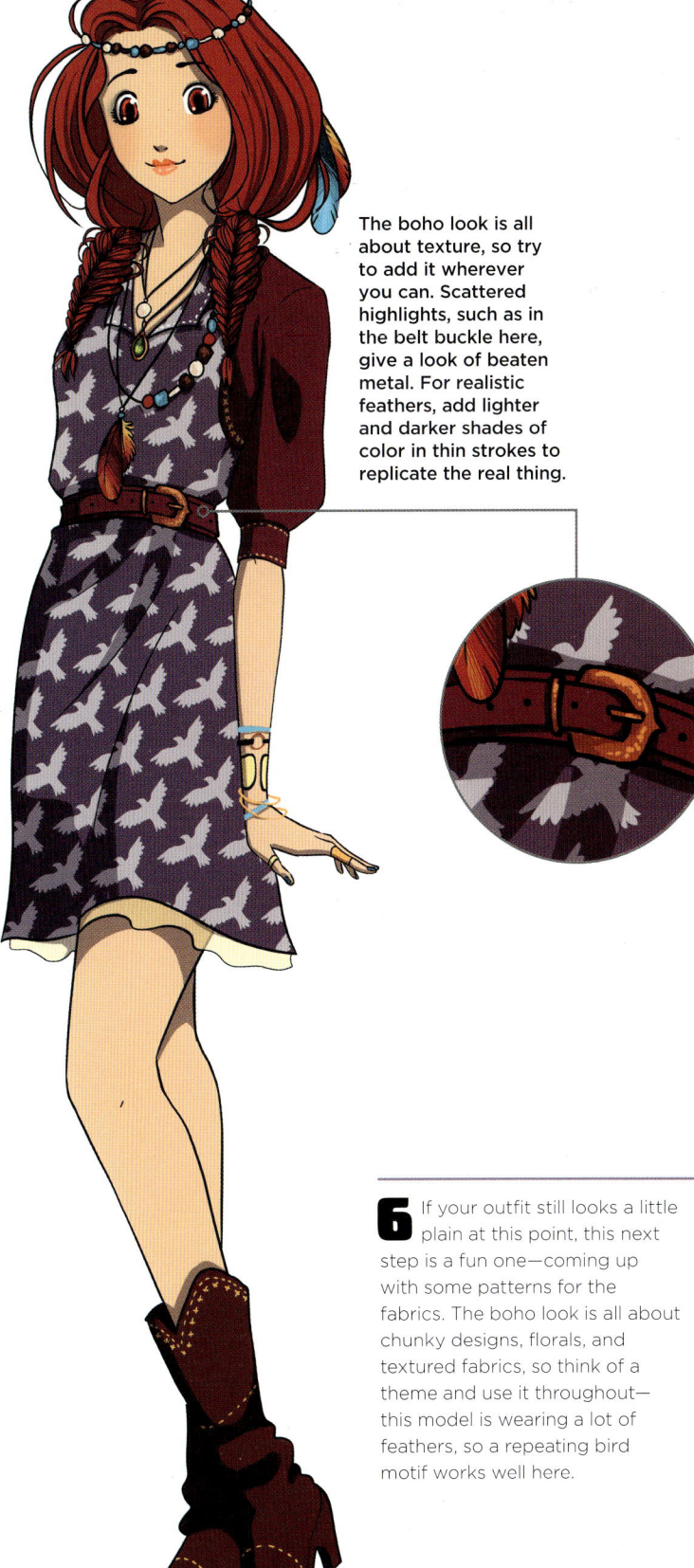

4 When cleaning up your sketch, you'll have plenty of opportunity to add extra details. Here, you can see chunky stitching in the jacket and boots, which gives that homey, folksy look—the model is also wearing a mix of different kinds of jewelry, from thick metal cuffs to beaded necklaces and chunky rings.

5 The Boho Chic look is very much a summer and fall style, so make sure to color your outfits with lots of warm, rich hues. The deep purples of the dress and jacket are brightened with some gold embroidery and brightly colored beads and feathers, and a layer of lace under the dress keeps the whole outfit looking feminine and delicate.

The boho look is all about texture, so try to add it wherever you can. Scattered highlights, such as in the belt buckle here, give a look of beaten metal. For realistic feathers, add lighter and darker shades of color in thin strokes to replicate the real thing.

6 If your outfit still looks a little plain at this point, this next step is a fun one—coming up with some patterns for the fabrics. The boho look is all about chunky designs, florals, and textured fabrics, so think of a theme and use it throughout—this model is wearing a lot of feathers, so a repeating bird motif works well here.

52 | THE COLLECTIONS

The boho look will serve you well both for relaxed, casual days out in the park and for trendy days out shopping. Cute, floaty skirts and tops will keep your collection looking fresh and summery, while layering fur vests, boots, and knitwear creates a chic fall look that's sure to turn heads.

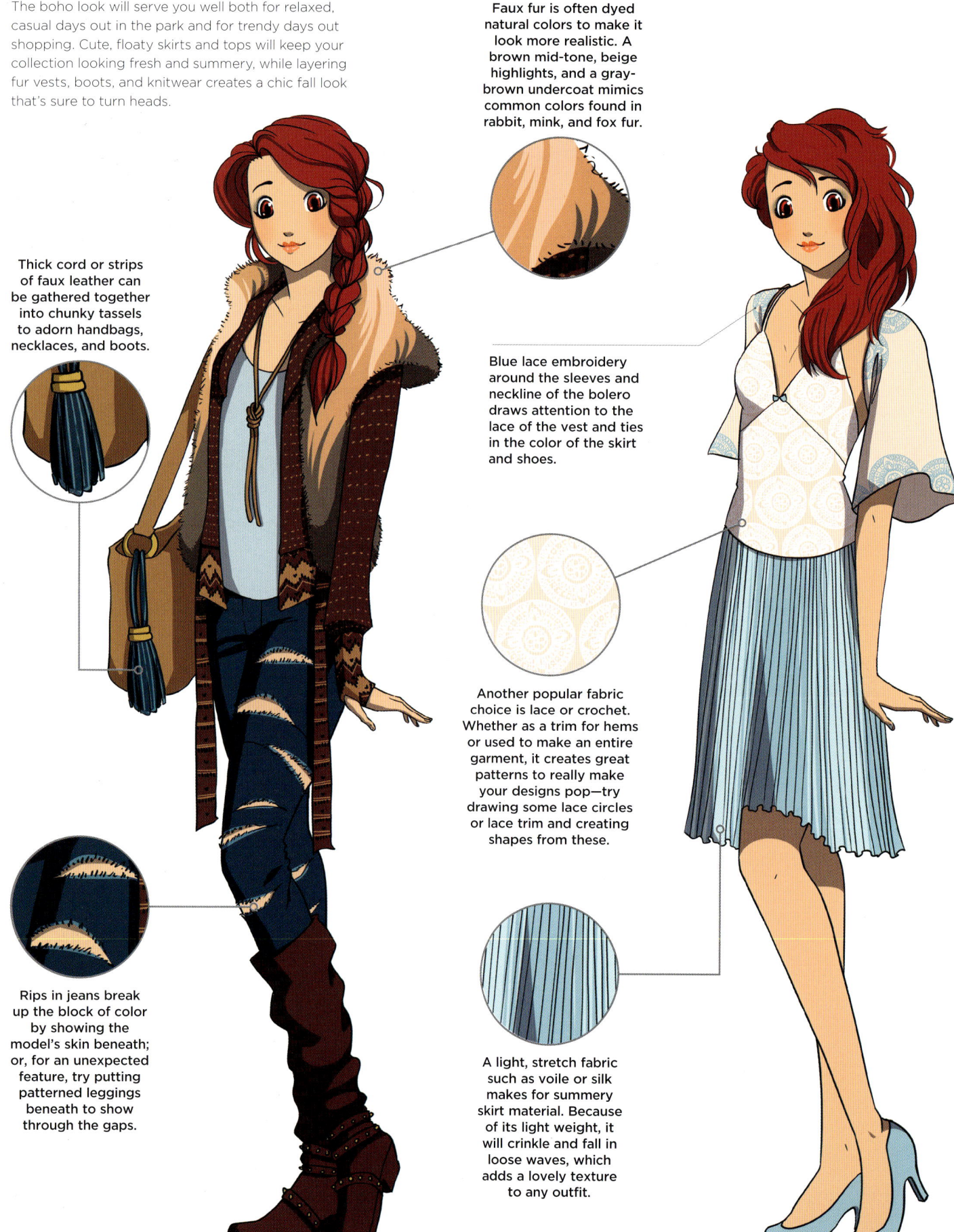

Faux fur is often dyed natural colors to make it look more realistic. A brown mid-tone, beige highlights, and a gray-brown undercoat mimics common colors found in rabbit, mink, and fox fur.

Thick cord or strips of faux leather can be gathered together into chunky tassels to adorn handbags, necklaces, and boots.

Blue lace embroidery around the sleeves and neckline of the bolero draws attention to the lace of the vest and ties in the color of the skirt and shoes.

Another popular fabric choice is lace or crochet. Whether as a trim for hems or used to make an entire garment, it creates great patterns to really make your designs pop—try drawing some lace circles or lace trim and creating shapes from these.

Rips in jeans break up the block of color by showing the model's skin beneath; or, for an unexpected feature, try putting patterned leggings beneath to show through the gaps.

A light, stretch fabric such as voile or silk makes for summery skirt material. Because of its light weight, it will crinkle and fall in loose waves, which adds a lovely texture to any outfit.

ACCESSORIES AND CLOTHING

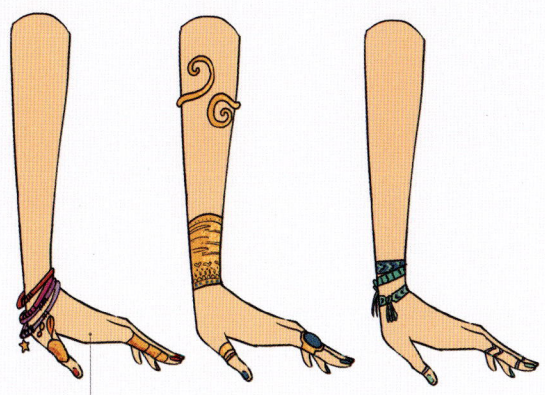

One main feature of the boho look is jewelry—and lots of it. Big chunky rings, stacks of bracelets, and armbands create amazing feature pieces for your models to wear. They don't have to be metal, either—woven bracelets provide a great splash of color, and you can even paint your model's nails in the same shade to make it all match.

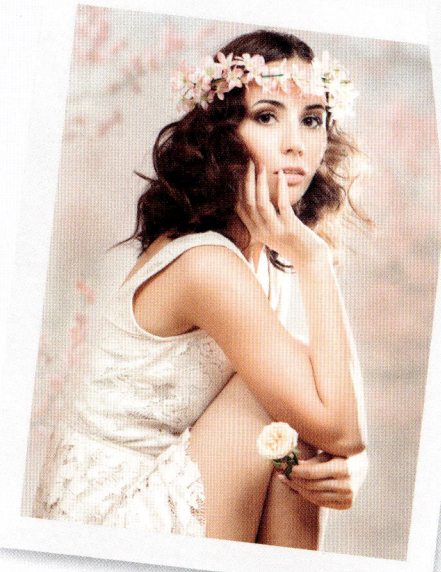

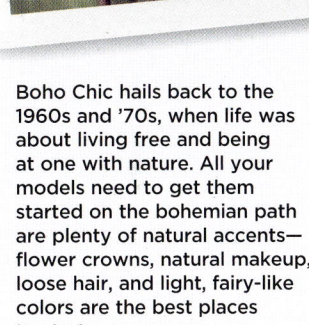

Boho Chic hails back to the 1960s and '70s, when life was about living free and being at one with nature. All your models need to get them started on the bohemian path are plenty of natural accents—flower crowns, natural makeup, loose hair, and light, fairy-like colors are the best places to start.

Boho Chic is all about the natural-and-folk look, so woven fabrics, beaded garments, and layers of lace are guaranteed winners. For summer, try designing some cute tea dresses and light, beaded capes; when the weather starts getting a little colder, a stylish cardigan will never go amiss.

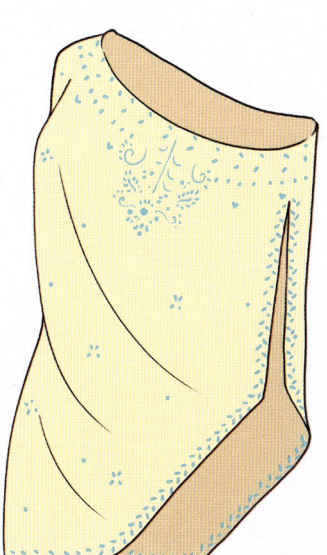

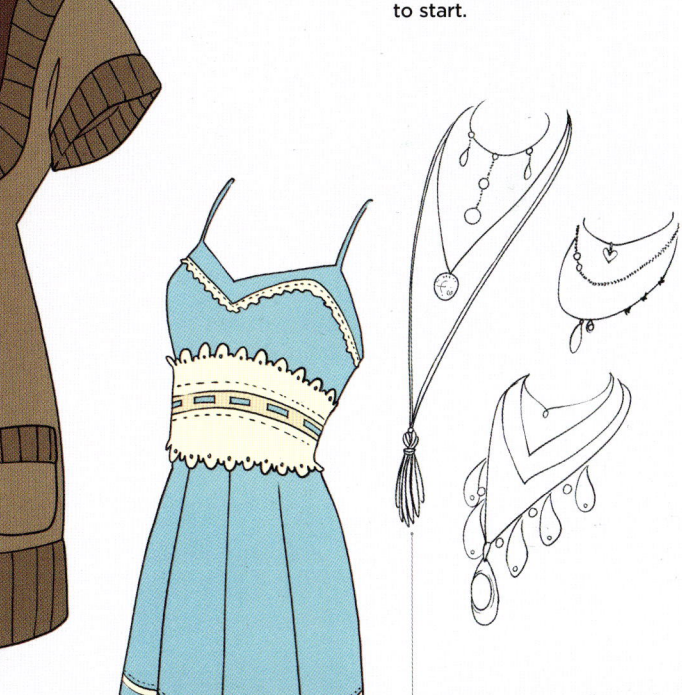

Don't forget to pile on the jewelry! Layered mixed necklaces will help to style up the neckline of any outfit; use chains of different lengths to create a cascade effect. Try creating necklaces out of found objects—old coins, vintage beads, even old tassels—for really showstopping looks.

PUNK STYLE

BY LAURA WATTON-DAVIES

REFLECTED IN THE WEARER'S CLOTHING, JEWELRY, AND HAIRSTYLES, THE **LOW-FI LOOK AND FEEL OF PUNK** IS THE OPPOSITE OF THE VALUES OF EXCESS FOUND IN OTHER MUSICAL STYLES. FEMALE PUNK STYLE IN PARTICULAR **REBELS AGAINST STEREOTYPES** BY MIXING UP **PRETTY CLOTHES WITH RIPPED GARMENTS AND CHUNKY JEWELRY AND FOOTWEAR**. PUNK STYLES GENERALLY INCORPORATE **CUSTOMIZABLE ROCKABILLY AESTHETICS**, ALONG WITH NEW WAVE, HARDCORE, AND ROCK ELEMENTS.

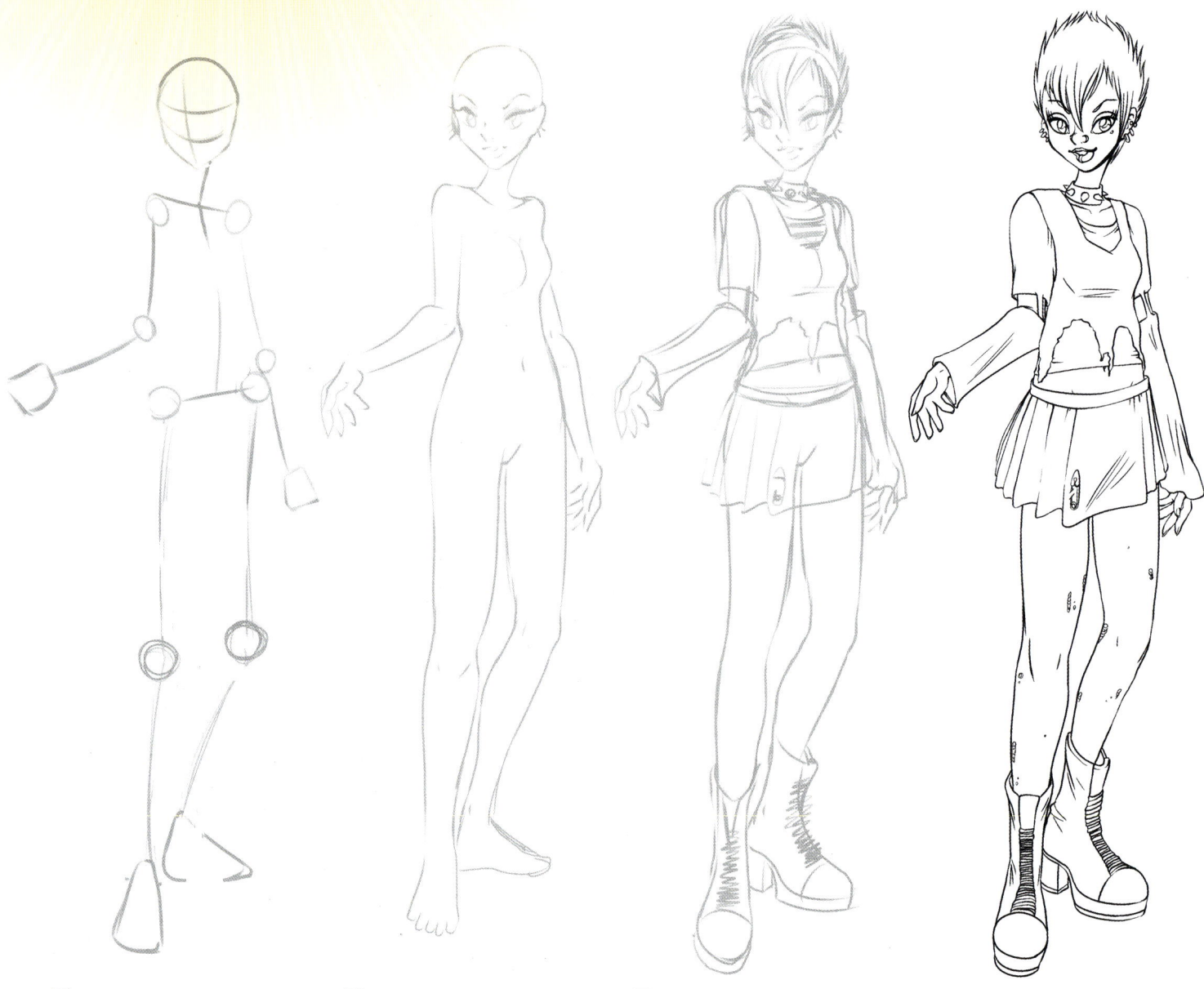

1 Draw body joints and lines with a light sketch. This defines the stance your character will take.

2 Use the knee and elbow circles and pose lines to help create your character and her body language with more definition.

3 Add some clothes that hang and drape by drawing drooping lines from a hanging point (for example, the shoulder). Let ragged garments hang freely at the bottom of the piece—for example, the waistline of a top, or the hem of a dress or skirt.

4 The hairstyle is a defining characteristic of punk and a chance to go wild. Here, a cropped hairstyle is drawn using short zigzag marks to create thin, spiked strands. To convey tattered material, ink using a curved, wobbly line.

PUNK STYLE | 55

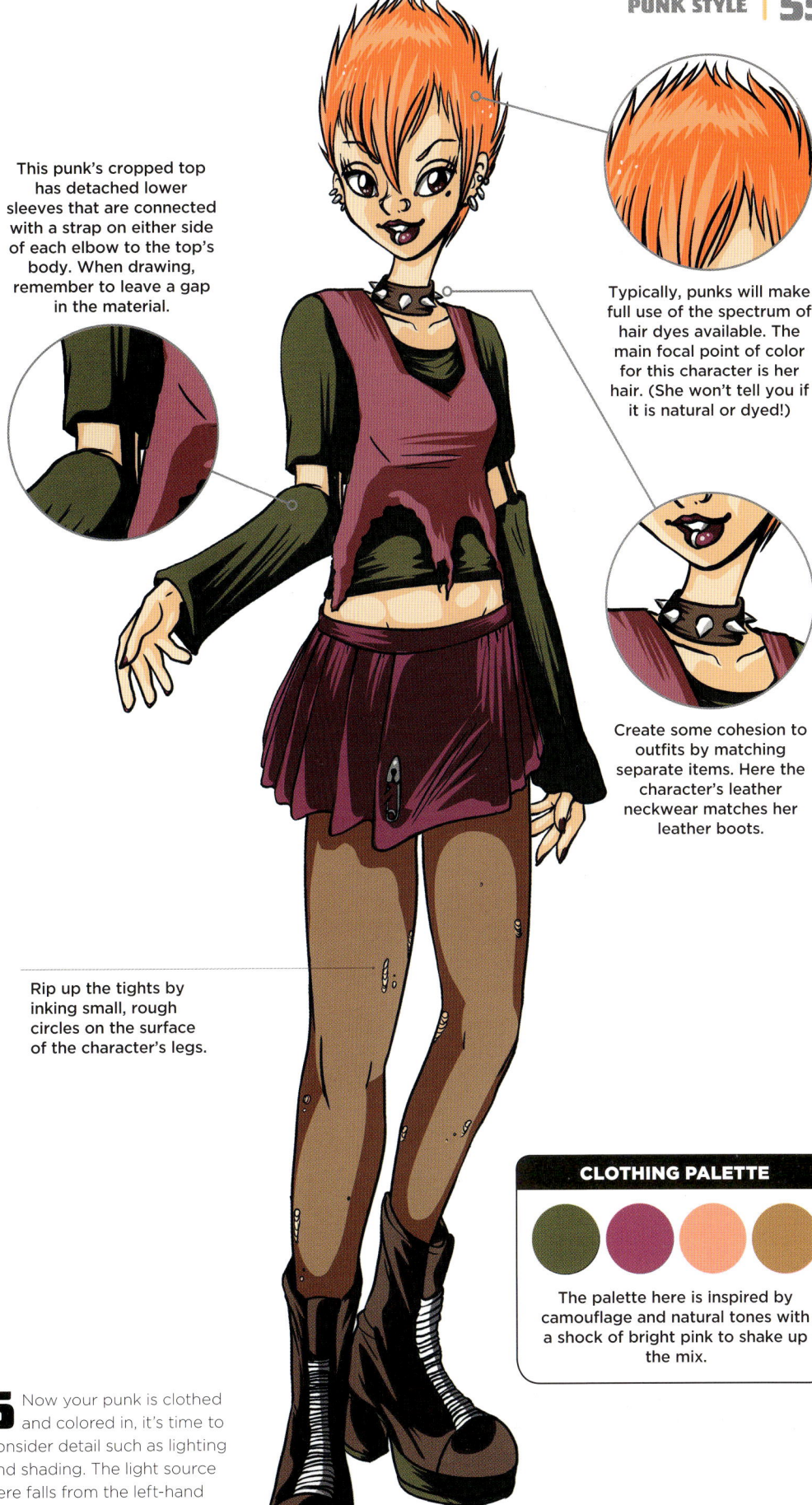

This punk's cropped top has detached lower sleeves that are connected with a strap on either side of each elbow to the top's body. When drawing, remember to leave a gap in the material.

Typically, punks will make full use of the spectrum of hair dyes available. The main focal point of color for this character is her hair. (She won't tell you if it is natural or dyed!)

Create some cohesion to outfits by matching separate items. Here the character's leather neckwear matches her leather boots.

Rip up the tights by inking small, rough circles on the surface of the character's legs.

CLOTHING PALETTE

The palette here is inspired by camouflage and natural tones with a shock of bright pink to shake up the mix.

5 Mix up your color schemes by using brights to accent duller colors such as black and gray. The scheme chosen here is bright and punchy, but with subdued tones for the top and bottom clothing. The safety pin and jewelry are a plain 50% gray.

6 Now your punk is clothed and colored in, it's time to consider detail such as lighting and shading. The light source here falls from the left-hand side. Color shadow using a darker tone to denote shade on the opposite side.

56 | THE COLLECTIONS

Punk has developed to adapt everyday objects (trash bags, safety pins, ripped clothing) for a striking visual effect. Punk music and fashion covers many subgenres, such as ska, glam, skate, hardcore, horror, and psychobilly. The look is a contradictory combination of dressing down while dressing up.

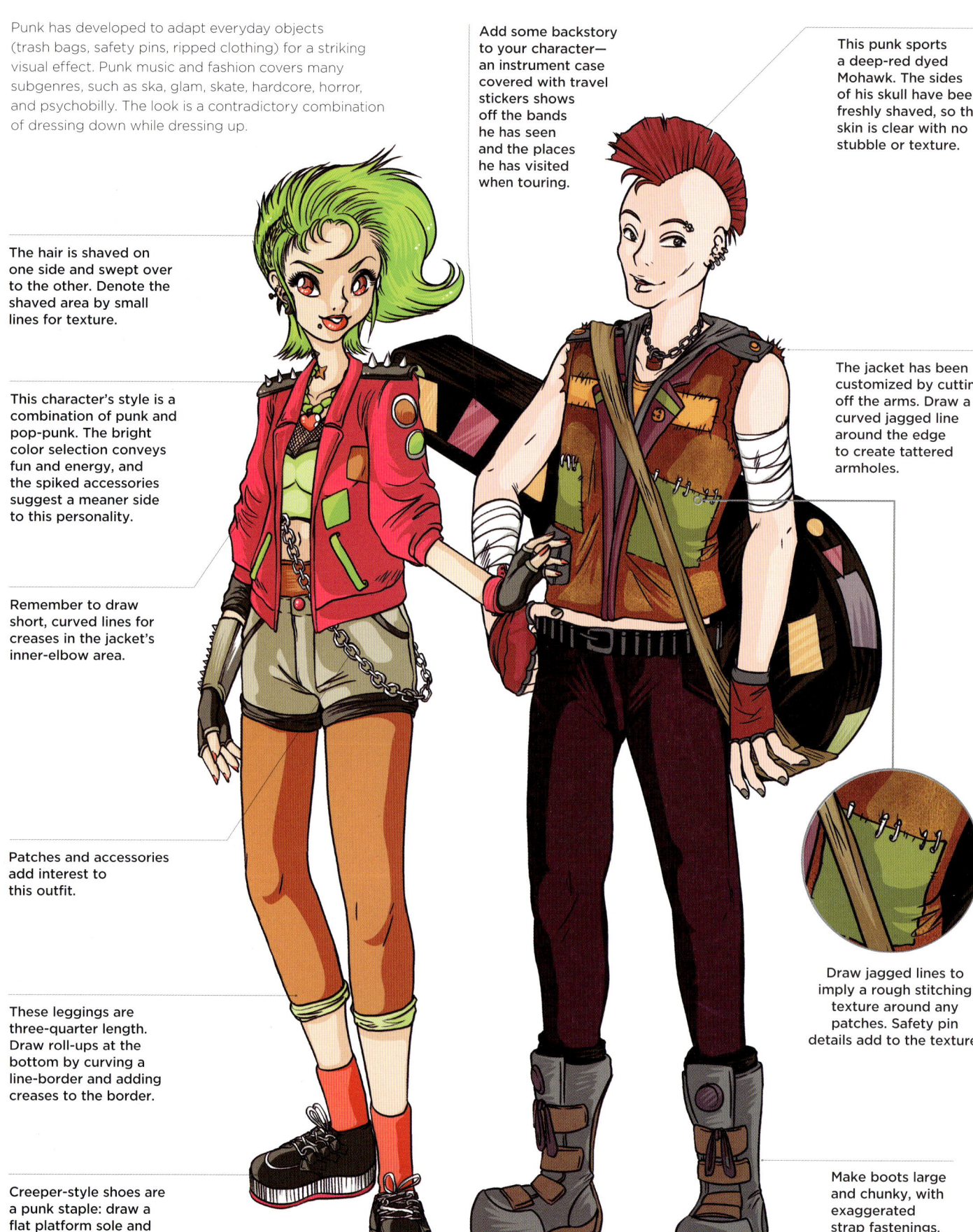

Add some backstory to your character—an instrument case covered with travel stickers shows off the bands he has seen and the places he has visited when touring.

This punk sports a deep-red dyed Mohawk. The sides of his skull have been freshly shaved, so the skin is clear with no stubble or texture.

The hair is shaved on one side and swept over to the other. Denote the shaved area by small lines for texture.

This character's style is a combination of punk and pop-punk. The bright color selection conveys fun and energy, and the spiked accessories suggest a meaner side to this personality.

The jacket has been customized by cutting off the arms. Draw a curved jagged line around the edge to create tattered armholes.

Remember to draw short, curved lines for creases in the jacket's inner-elbow area.

Patches and accessories add interest to this outfit.

These leggings are three-quarter length. Draw roll-ups at the bottom by curving a line-border and adding creases to the border.

Draw jagged lines to imply a rough stitching texture around any patches. Safety pin details add to the texture.

Creeper-style shoes are a punk staple: draw a flat platform sole and add short vertical lines to the sole's base.

Make boots large and chunky, with exaggerated strap fastenings.

PUNK STYLE | 57

ACCESSORIES AND CLOTHING

This split-Mohawk hairstyle will appeal to goth punks in particular. Use softer, curved lines for the bottom of the hair to contrast with the straight, spiked lines at the top.

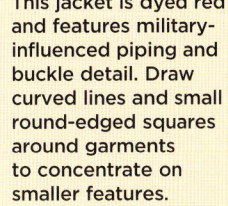

This jacket is dyed red and features military-influenced piping and buckle detail. Draw curved lines and small round-edged squares around garments to concentrate on smaller features.

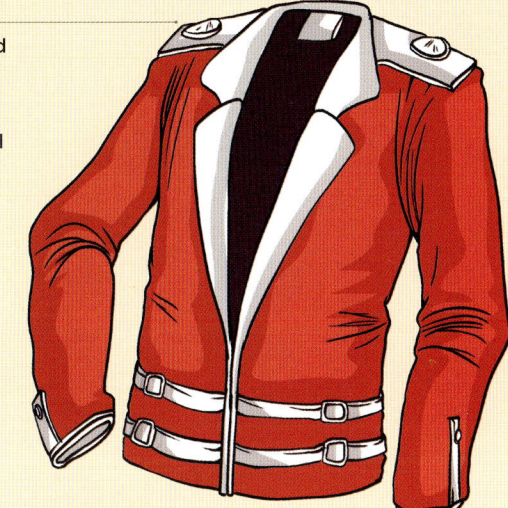

Messenger-style bags are big enough to hold vinyl records as well as art materials. Draw squares and long lines for the body of the bag, and parallel arches for the straps.

Accessories are inspired by tribal designs, ear stretchers, rough beads, and DIY jewelry. A chain of safety pins on a wire necklace would have been made by the character wearing it—there's no finesse here.

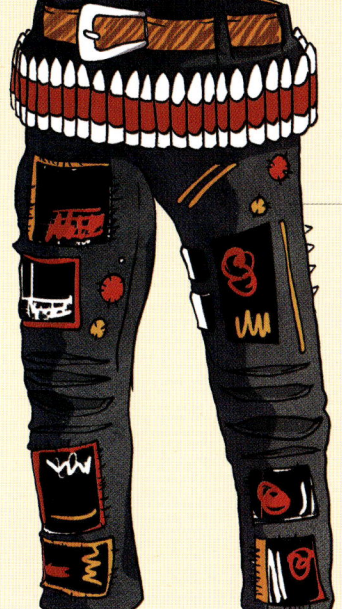

Jeans are often ripped and can feature a loose, chunky bullet belt. Add patches, small badges, and accessories such as DIY spikes and safety pins around the front of the legs, pockets, and seams.

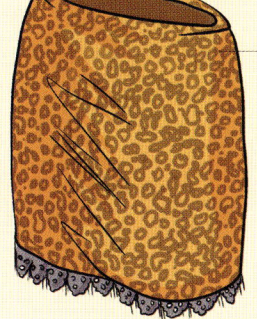

A leopard-print pattern added to this knee-length wriggle skirt creates a rockabilly-punk aesthetic. To re-create the look of lace, draw a combination of bubbly-edged triangles and small circles. Small threads drop down for the tattered look.

A strapless top is created with stretchy fabric and is designed to be worn on top of something more modest. Draw lines around your character's torso and join them up using round corners and small lines to denote stretch.

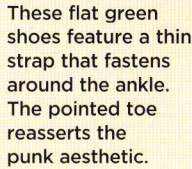

These flat green shoes feature a thin strap that fastens around the ankle. The pointed toe reasserts the punk aesthetic.

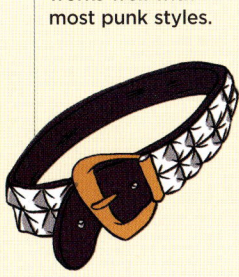

The studded belt is a staple for any alternative-music-centric wardrobe, and the purple color scheme works well with most punk styles.

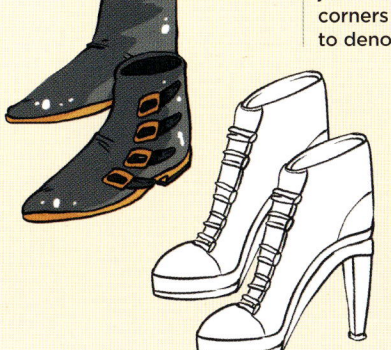

Exaggerated features—whether it's tall heels, thick soles, multiple buckles on winklepickers, or spiked strapping—will go a long way in punking up your footwear collection.

HOLLYWOOD GLAM

WE'RE ALL FAMILIAR WITH THE **GLAMOROUS DRESSES SHOWCASED ON HOLLYWOOD'S RED CARPETS**, BUT HAVE YOU EVER WANTED TO DESIGN SOME OF YOUR VERY OWN? WHETHER INSPIRED BY THE **GOLDEN AGE STARLETS OF THE 1930S** OR CREATED FROM ENTIRELY MORE **MODERN INFLUENCES**, THERE ARE HUNDREDS OF **BEAUTIFUL DRESSES** OUT THERE TO INSPIRE YOU TO KICK-START YOUR VERY OWN RED CARPET **GLAM** LABEL.

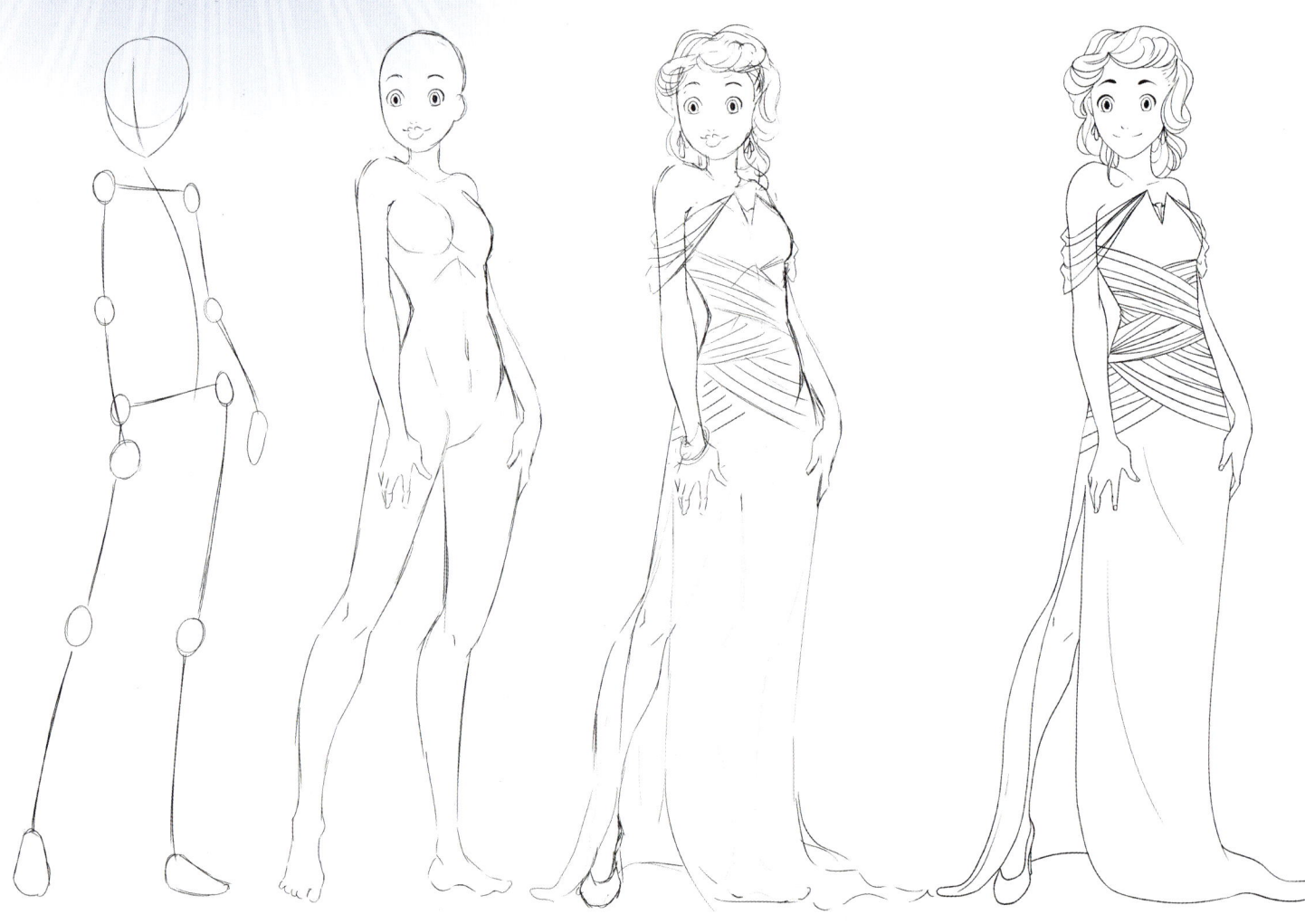

1 If your model is going to be rocking the red carpet, she's got to look confident! Standing with her feet slightly apart and her spine curved will give her a bolder and more upbeat posture.

2 Draw the rest of the model's body around the Step 1 skeleton. A lot of red carpet dresses are very form-fitting, so make sure that you have the model's anatomy right before you move on to the next step, or your dresses won't look right.

3 Now it's time for the fun part—designing your look. Try looking at recent red carpet events for inspiration, since they're a great display of what's currently in style; you may start to notice that certain elements, such as curled, up-styled hair and wrap-style bodices, are classic looks from vintage Hollywood, and are always a safe and stylish choice.

4 When adding the final lines to your sketch, make sure to add enough details to help describe the fabrics being used. For example, the sleeves here are semi-opaque, so you can see the model's arms beneath them, and the silk of the dress itself pools attractively on the floor.

HOLLYWOOD GLAM | **59**

CLOTHING PALETTE

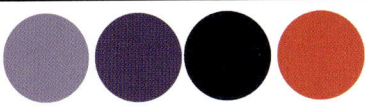

Just the word "Hollywood" is evocative of many things, but, above all else, it conjures images of luxury, wealth, and glamour. Rich jewel colors are always prominent on the red carpet, as are gold, silver, and classic black. This outfit is purple, a color often associated with royalty or nobility.

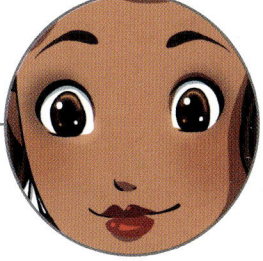

Since the Hollywood look is all about the clothes, you don't have to go too over the top when it comes to your model's makeup and hair. Go for something simple but classic—look at how the starlets of the 1930s presented themselves. A simple blush, some lipstick, and neatly shaped eyebrows should be more than enough.

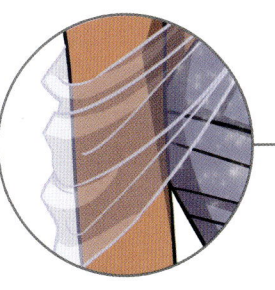

It's the finishing details of a dress that will really make it stand out, so try using multiple fabric types to add those extra little areas of interest. Sheer fabrics such as lace, gossamer, and silk make for delicate sleeves or overskirts.

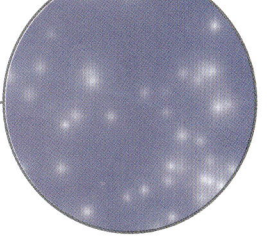

A lot of detail isn't always necessary to create some really striking effects. Adding sparkles can make a garment really come to life—and make it stand out from the crowd, which is what the red carpet is all about.

5 Using the choices from your palette, start to block in the colors of your outfit. To break up the single color of the dress, give your model a darker shade of purple for her shoes and add some splashes of alternate color in her makeup. Nails, lips, and cheeks are good places to add some complementary hues.

6 A red carpet isn't complete without a suitable amount of dazzle. Covering your model's dress with sparkles makes it look as though it is covered in rhinestones or sequins; or perhaps it's the material itself that's catching the light from so many cameras. Highlights in the sleeves and the model's hair help brighten the look and make it look suitably eye-catching.

If you're going to use geometric designs in your dresses, how about varying it up with different fabrics? Use panels of sheer fabric to show the model's skin beneath, or different shades of the same color to add interest.

Designing formal dresses really is an excuse to go wild when it comes to exercising your imagination. There are so many inspirations to draw from—Grecian, Slavic, and other historical influences are hugely popular, as well as more modern movements such as Art Deco. Anything goes, so here's your chance to really stun with your collection.

Don't forget to think about the backs of your dresses: a dress has to look impressive from all angles, so if you can flatter your model with a dipped back or unusual jewelry, she'll be sure to make an impression.

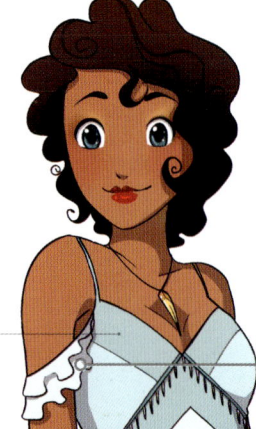
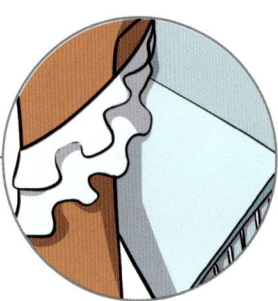
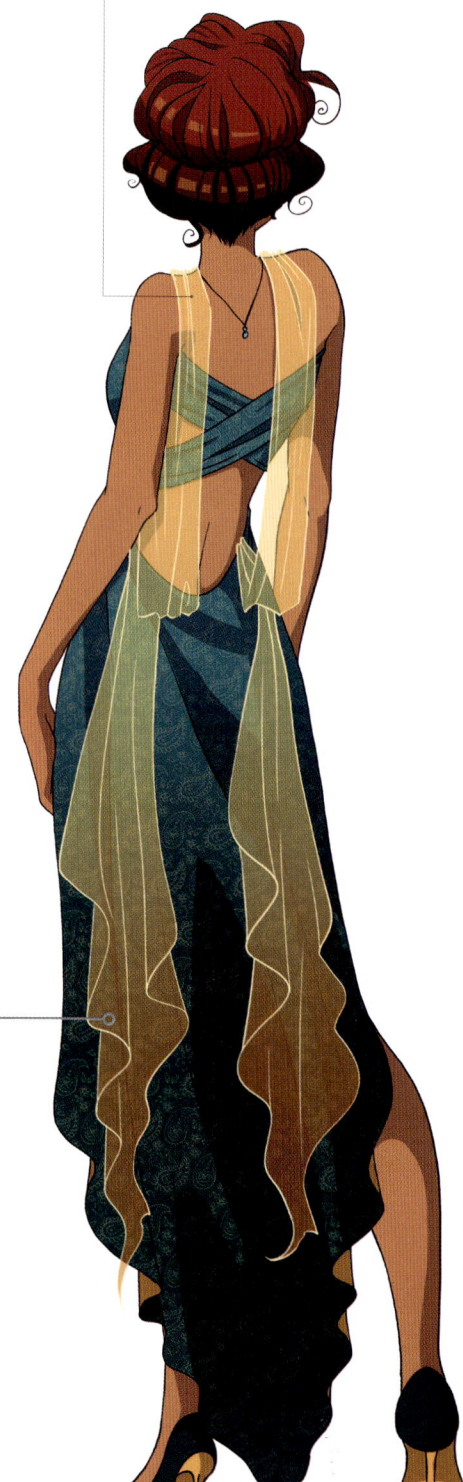

Detailing such as bead trims and ruffled sleeves can help draw attention to certain parts of an outfit. Be wary about using too much, as you don't want your dresses to look overdone, but small areas of trim to exaggerate the shapes of areas such as the bust or the waist can make a big difference.

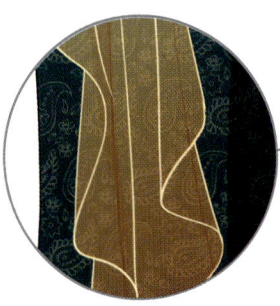

If your outfit has a lot of solid, block colors, try adding an ombré dye to parts of the design. This dress fades into a darker blue at the bottom, and the same happens for the gold scarves as they fade into a deep orange.

HOLLYWOOD GLAM | 61

DRESSES AND ACCESSORIES

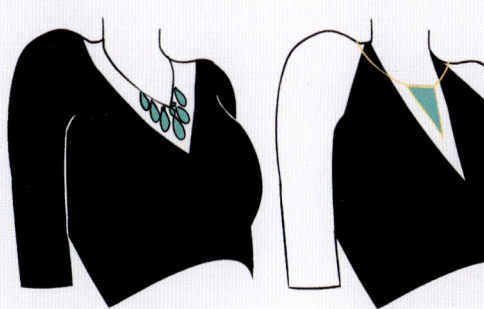
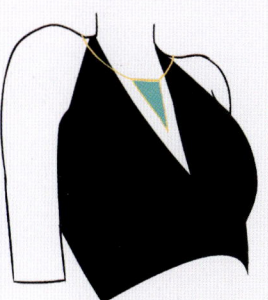
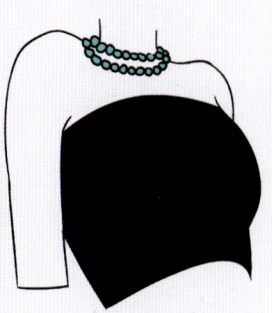
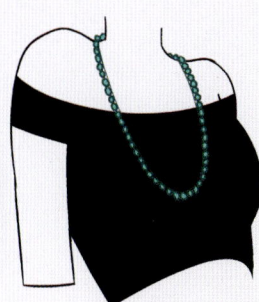

V-neck/statement   Halterneck/long   Sleeveless/feature choker   Boatneck/long

Match the necklace to the neckline
The dress might be the first thing that people look at, but don't forget the right kind of jewelry to complement it. Every style of neckline should have the right shape of necklace that serves to balance and complement the outfit and its wearer.

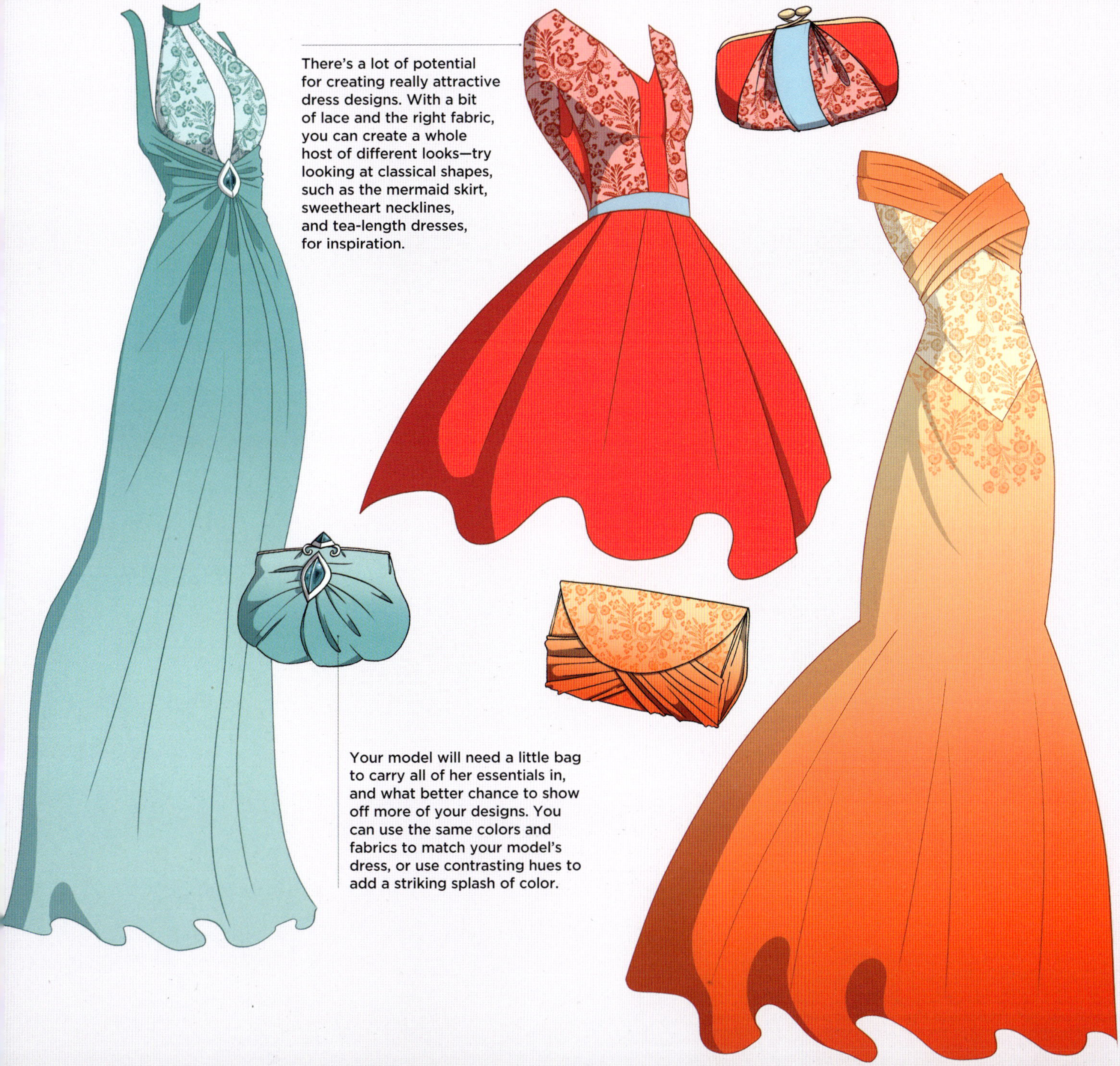

There's a lot of potential for creating really attractive dress designs. With a bit of lace and the right fabric, you can create a whole host of different looks—try looking at classical shapes, such as the mermaid skirt, sweetheart necklines, and tea-length dresses, for inspiration.

Your model will need a little bag to carry all of her essentials in, and what better chance to show off more of your designs. You can use the same colors and fabrics to match your model's dress, or use contrasting hues to add a striking splash of color.

ROCK ROYALTY

62 | THE COLLECTIONS

ROCK STARS ARE AMONG THE LEADING FIGURES IN FASHION, BRINGING BACK STYLES THAT ARE CONSIDERED OUT OF DATE AND CREATING NEW LOOKS THAT RAPIDLY **TAKE THE FASHION WORLD BY STORM**. ROCK MUSIC AND FASHION HAVE GONE HAND IN HAND SINCE THE 1960S, BRINGING **PUNK, MOD, AND GRUNGE** STYLES INTO THE MAINSTREAM AND KEEPING THEM THERE FOR LONGER THAN MOST FASHION TRENDS REMAIN.

CLOTHING PALETTE

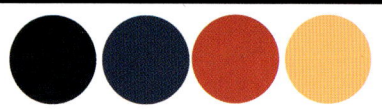

Dark, muted colors almost always form the base of any rock star's look. However, splashes of rich, bright colors—such as red or purple—ensure the look is not too dark. This palette in particular uses dark blues, with shades of red and gold for contrast.

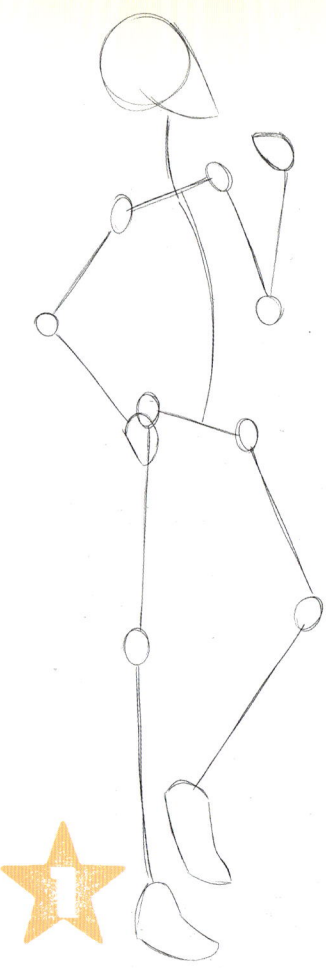

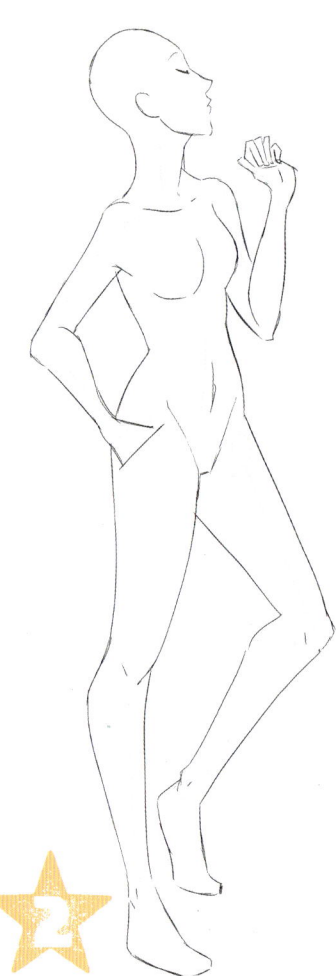

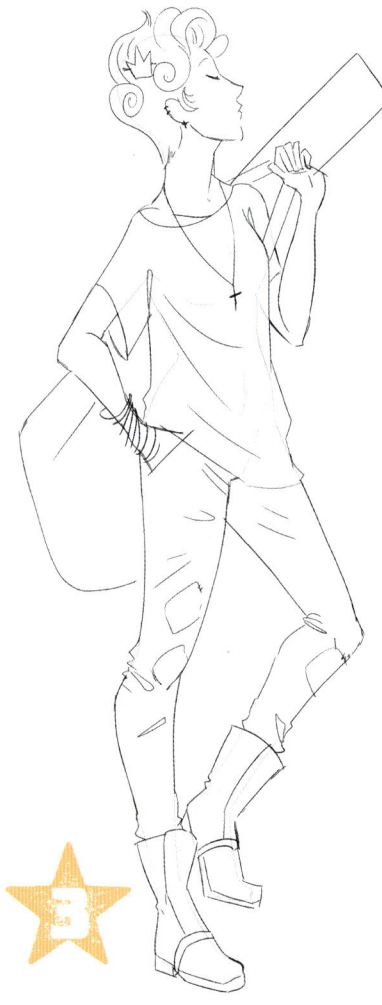

1 Start your sketch by drawing in a rough, simple skeleton; this will help you get the anatomy and pose right before you get weighed down with details. If there's one thing every rock star needs—beyond a rocking outfit—it's confidence! An outward-curving spine and uptilted face gives her an air of self-assurance, perfect for showing off your collection.

2 Once you're happy with the skeleton, sketch in the rest of the model around it. You can see here how drawing in the basic bones has created a dynamic pose, instead of one that looks static; the model has plenty of personality that shines right through.

3 The essence of rock fashion is to throw conventions to the wind, and a lot of female rock stars will wear their hair short and sport androgynous clothes. In this look, a neatly styled hair and men's T-shirt provide the main components of the look, but close-fitting jeans and delicate accessories keep the outfit feminine.

ROCK ROYALTY | **63**

4 When adding more detail to a sketch, remember to keep the fall and folds of the fabric in mind. When a model is wearing a baggy garment, such as the T-shirt in this outfit, the fabric will bunch at the base as gravity pulls it down. However, with tight denim, it gathers only where it bunches at the groin and knee. Any other creases are created by the fabric stretching across the model's legs, such as at the thigh and shin.

5 After adding in the darker base colors, you'll be able to pick out areas where you need to add accent colors—in this case red and gold. Adding diamonds and areas of gold helps to break up the larger, darker areas of color—achieved here by the chains on the boots, the necklace, and the rhinestones on the jeans and boots.

6 It's the little touches of luxury that upgrade this outfit from "rock" to Rock Royalty—and one of them is that extra sparkle! More rhinestones on the hair tie, bracelets, and necklace give an extra dash of glam, and bold makeup adds plenty of attitude.

To further break up areas of dark color, why not add in a few rock-star-style designs? A logo, illustration, or graphic adds detail to large areas such as T-shirt fronts and this model's guitar case.

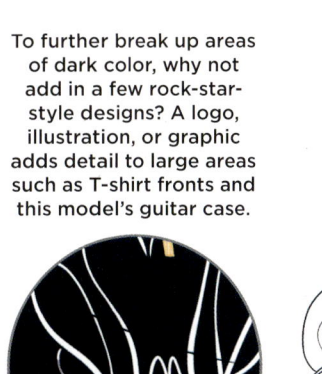

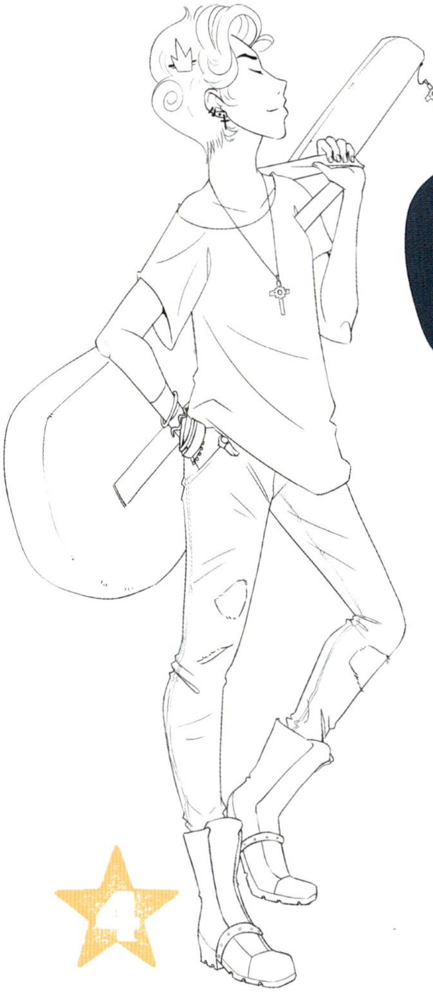

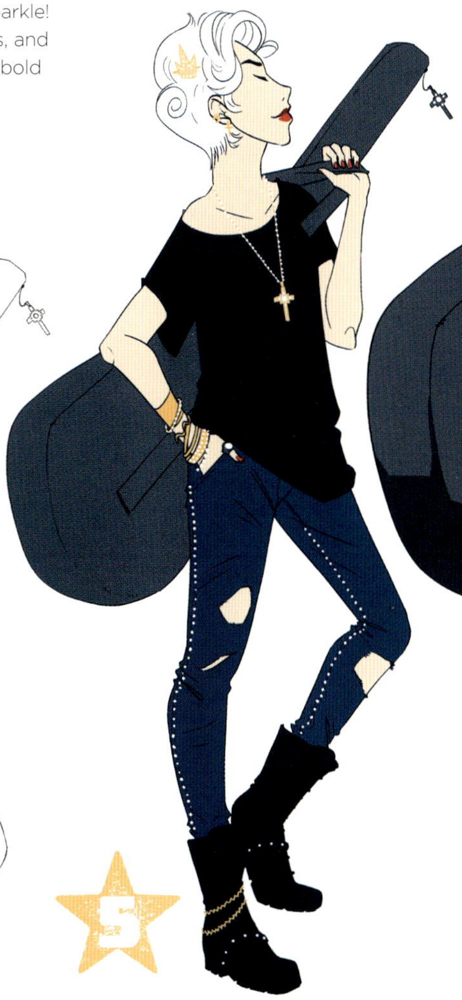

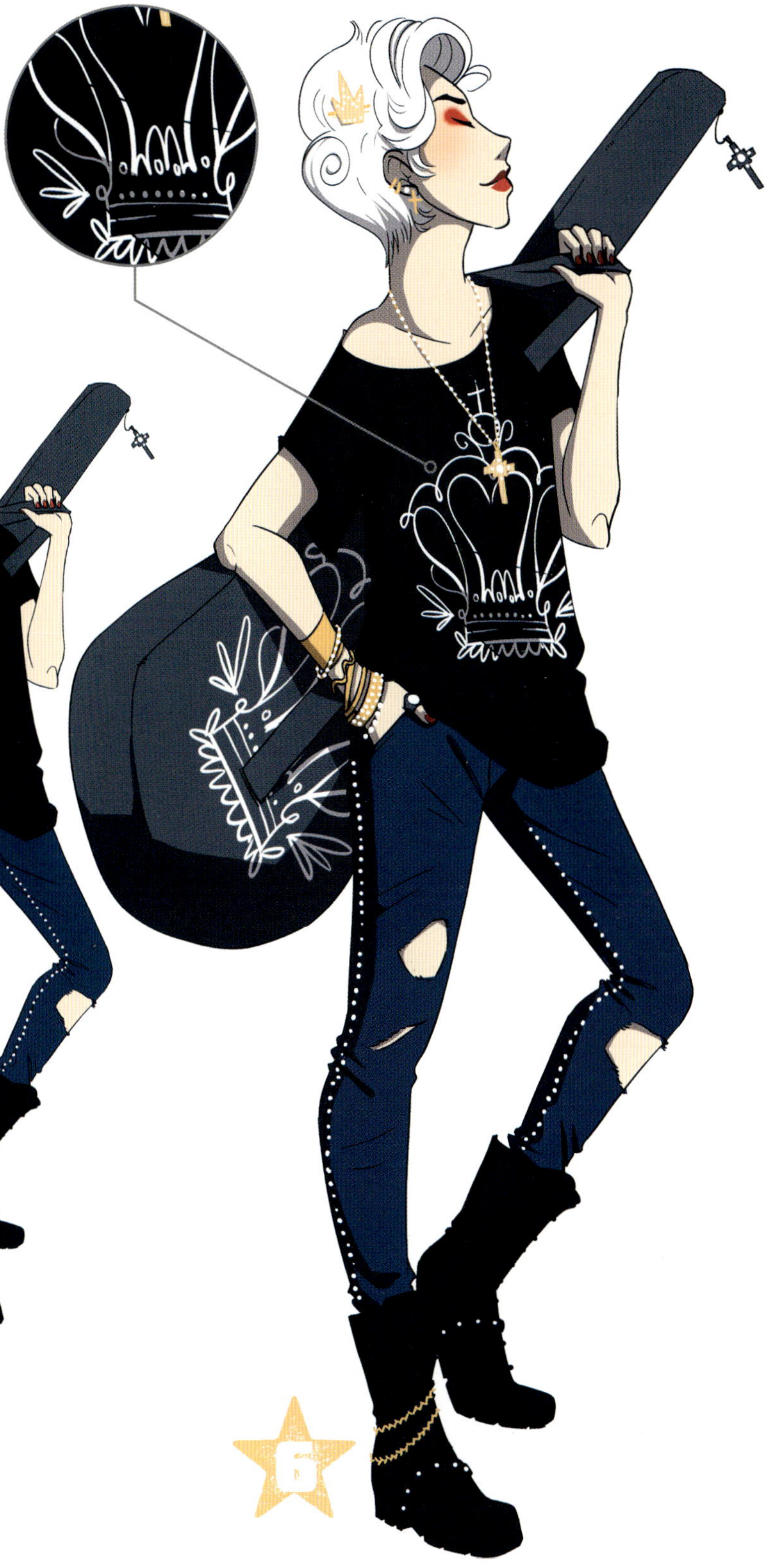

64 | THE COLLECTIONS

A true rock queen needs to look at home no matter where she is—whether that's on stage, on the red carpet, or just going to buy groceries. Unlikely combinations add that quirky, devil-may-care style—such as fancy dresses paired with casual jackets, or vests and full skirts together.

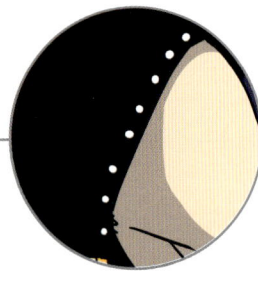

Just because rock fashion is grungy doesn't mean it can't be girly. Soft pinks, warm blushes, and natural lip colors contrast with the rougher, grittier outfits of the collection.

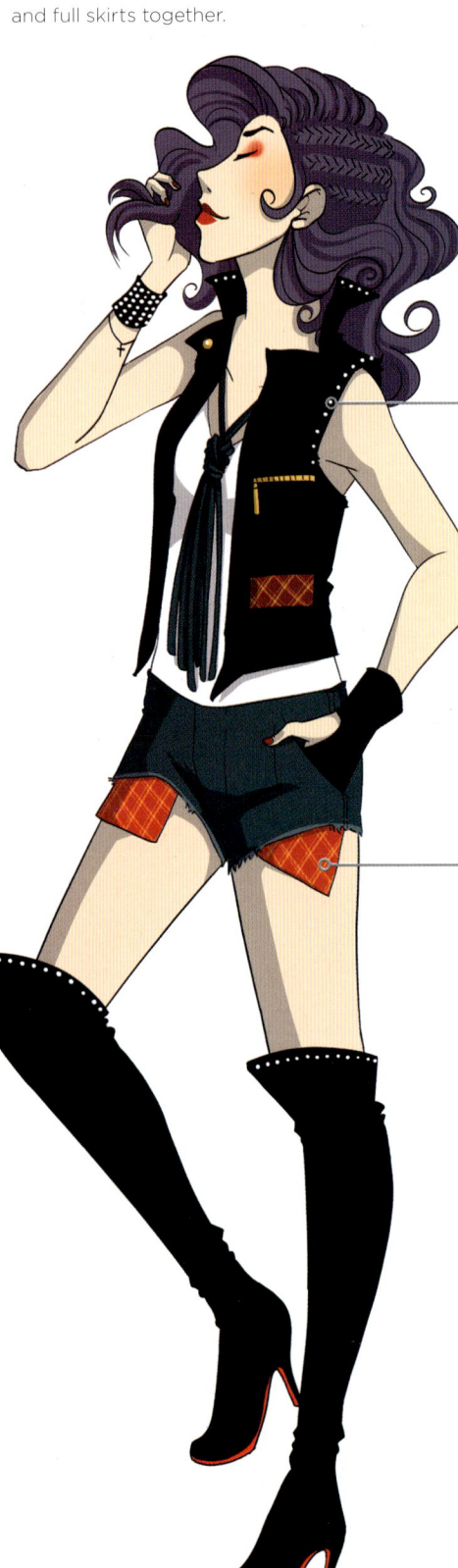

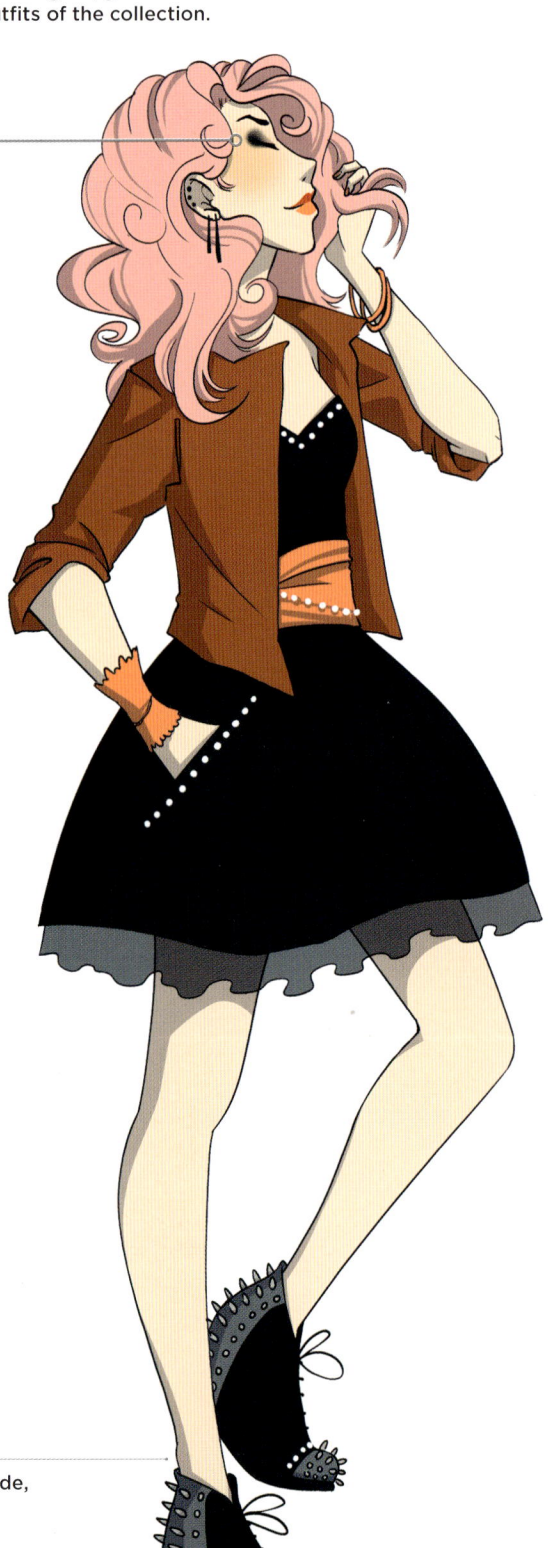

Rhinestones give an extra dazzle to even the darkest of outfits. Pop up a shirt's collar and line the edges with diamonds for even more sparkle.

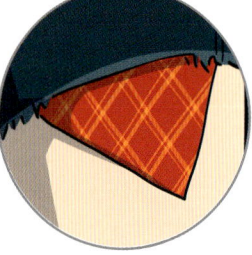

True to its punk roots in the 1980s, tartan still crops up frequently in rock couture. Too much can be overwhelming, but small sections—perhaps in sewn-on patches or pocket linings—add a glimpse of detail and color.

Every rock queen needs attitude, and what better way to look tough than with a pair of big boots? Pair heavy spikes with sparkling diamonds to create the perfect, tough, femme fatale.

CLOTHES AND SHOES

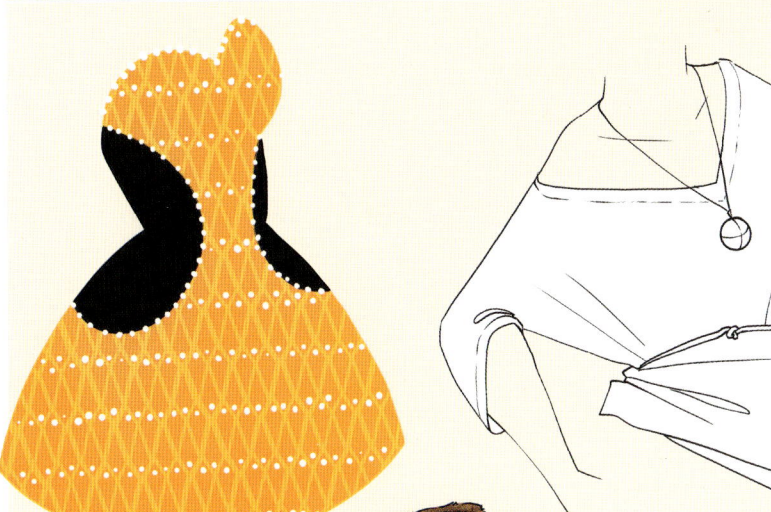

A true rock star knows how to take any outfit and make it work. With the right accessories, jewelry, and attitude, the entire wardrobe is at your disposal to inspire your designs.

Any rock chick will know her A–Z of kings and queens, so be prepared to pay homage to famous musicians and bands—such as David Bowie and KISS—in your choice of makeup, hair, and accessories.

Heavy heels, bulky straps, and bold stripes are designed to catch the light on stage and make a really stomping impact.

TEE DESIGNS

A good design can make a plain band tee interesting to look at. And if you've already got a logo for your fashion designs, it's a great place to advertise just who you are! Common themes for band logos and tees include royal crowns, edgy skulls, and romantic hearts.

Royal crown

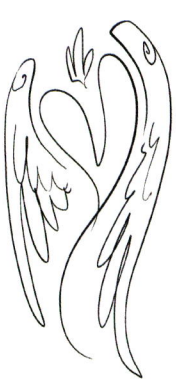

Romantic hearts

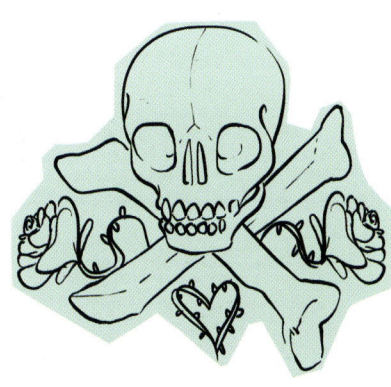

Edgy skull

GOTHIC FASHION
BY EMMA VIECELI

GOTHIC FASHION SHOULD NOT BE CONFUSED WITH GOTHIC LOLITA (SEE PAGES 74–75). WHILE THE LOLITA STYLE TAKES A LOT OF CUES FROM GOTHIC FASHION, GOTHIC IS VERY MUCH ITS OWN BRAND—AND YOU'LL RARELY SEE FRILLS OR PETTICOATS HERE. INSTEAD, IT'S ABOUT **FIGURE-HUGGING SHAPES, CURVES**, AND, OF COURSE, A LITTLE **DARKNESS**.

1 For this look, don't opt for too flamboyant a stance. Consider how the clothing might limit your model's pose—in this case we'll be drawing a skirt that gathers at the knee.

2 This figure is a little different in that we're warping natural shape a little by adding a corset—a common feature of Gothic Fashion. Include this cinched waist in your form sketch.

3 Remember: no frills in sight, but do consider ways to contrast the figure-hugging shape with sheer, loose sleeves and a small overskirt.

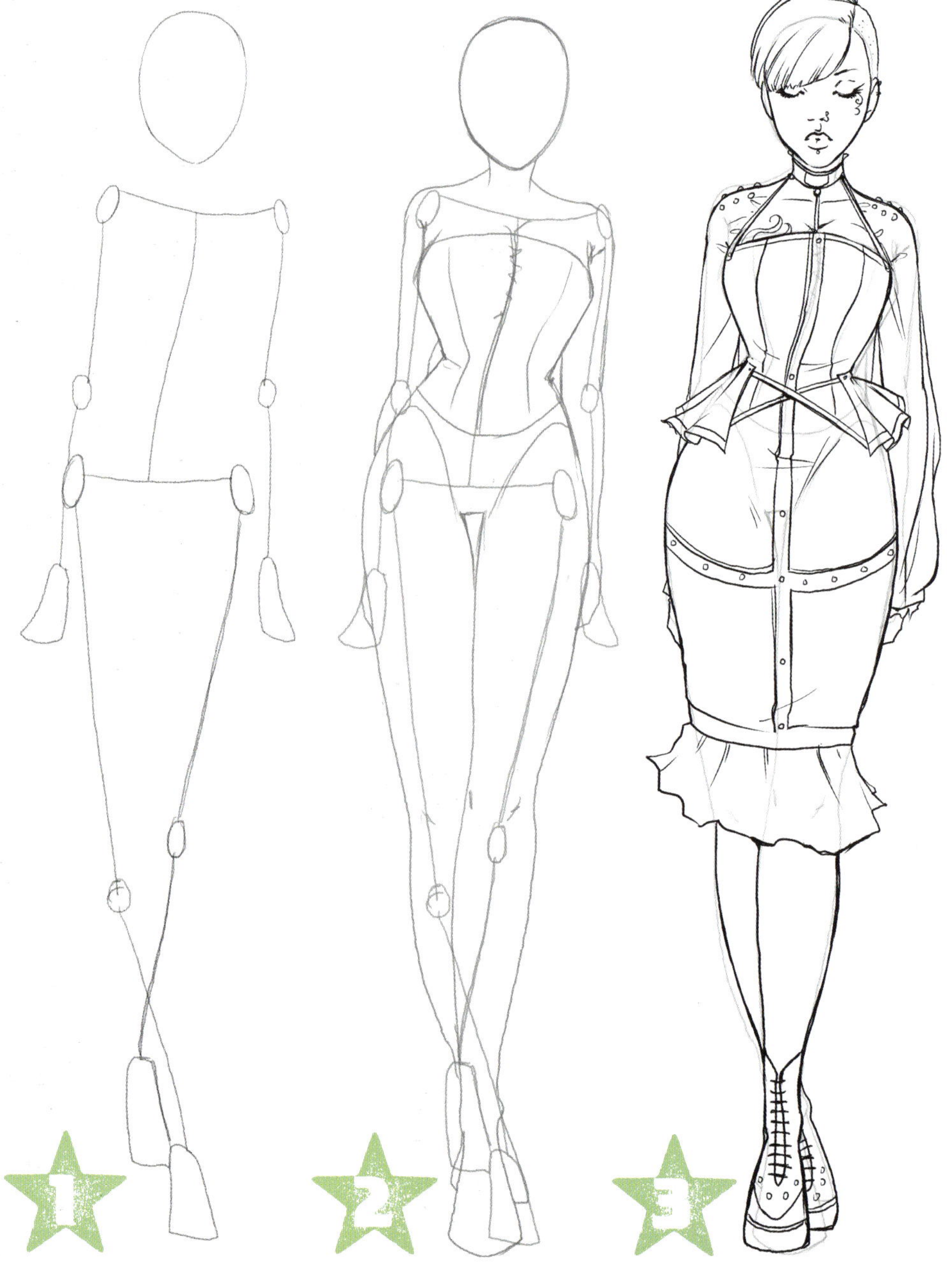

CLOTHING PALETTE

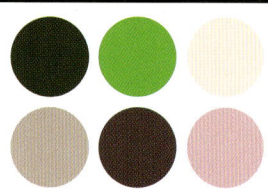

Gothic Fashion is often about black, black, and more black. But using accent colors can really bring out the design. And there is not only one shade of black. Be sure to use different textures, patterns, and shades of gray to show up areas of your design.

GOTHIC FASHION | **67**

4 Gothic Fashion really has some fun when it comes to hairstyles. Dye it, shave it, shave patterns into it—research some gothic hairstyles and try to emulate them.

5 Consider small details that add to the overall design, such as lipstick to match an outrageous hair color, or the tip of a tattoo showing underneath clothing.

6 Highlights such as those on the hair and lips help bring the model to life. Try using a white gel pen or correction fluid to add highlights over existing colors. Your model might have pale skin, but using a shade of red or pink for shadows gives warmth and life.

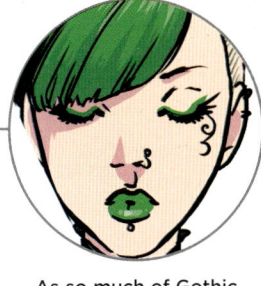

These sheer sleeves were created digitally, but, as an alternative effect on paper, try using colored pencil over marker.

As so much of Gothic Fashion is made up of grays and blacks, you can jazz up a style by using an accent color. The green of the hair is reflected in the model's makeup.

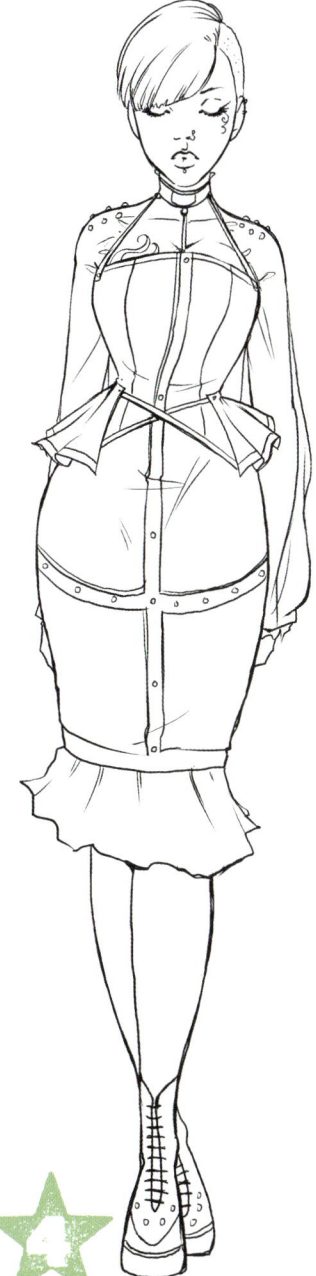

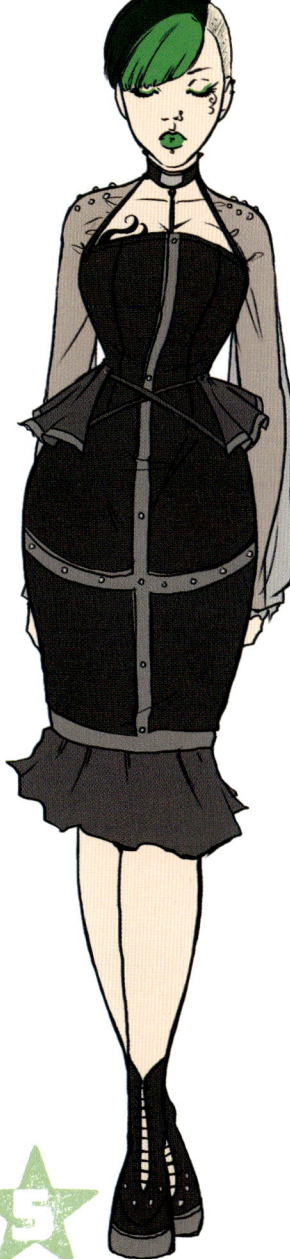

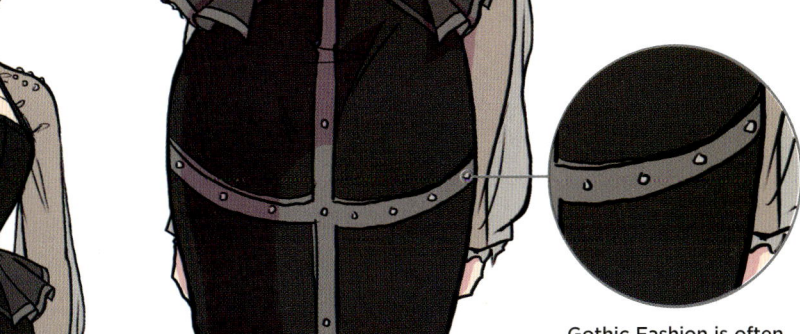

Gothic Fashion is often about contrasts and subverting the expected. Metal studs here contrast against the dress that they're attached to.

Try to avoid ever using solid black in a design because you'll lose your line art. Instead, try shades of dark gray.

THE COLLECTIONS

Modern Gothic Fashion challenges existing popular ideas and enjoys subverting standard fashion choices. If it's seen as feminine to have long, flowing locks, then a gothic model may set out to prove that a shaved head can be equally feminine. Likewise, piercings and tattoos can be used effectively. The "Morticia Addams" approach is an older but still effective look: elegance, grooming, and swathes of dark colors—true gothic style.

Gothic Fashion is expressed in makeup as much as in clothing. For this character, one eye is highlighted with exaggerated liner, and blue lipstick has been added to give an otherworldly look.

Pinstripes are mostly associated with a dapper and smart style, and Gothic Fashion is all about subverting, so take pinstripes and mix them with something less dapper.

Fairytale- or historical-styled dresses can also form part of a gothic wardrobe, as long as they stay dark. Flowing and pretty styles are fine, but always in dark shades.

Though you may be limited in palette with the goth style, you can play with layers and variations on texture and opacities. Here, a sheer top is layered with a solid corset.

To draw chunky boots, consider where the bottom of the foot would fall and then add a new layer of sole beneath that. Make sure the boot will cover the character's foot.

Rips and tears are easily drawn. Make sure they reflect the contours beneath them and bend where the material would be stretched.

Drawing lacing like this can be time-consuming, but worth it. Before you start, think about how lacing works and consider how the ribbon criss-crosses between eyelets.

GOTHIC FASHION | 69

ACCESSORIES AND CLOTHING

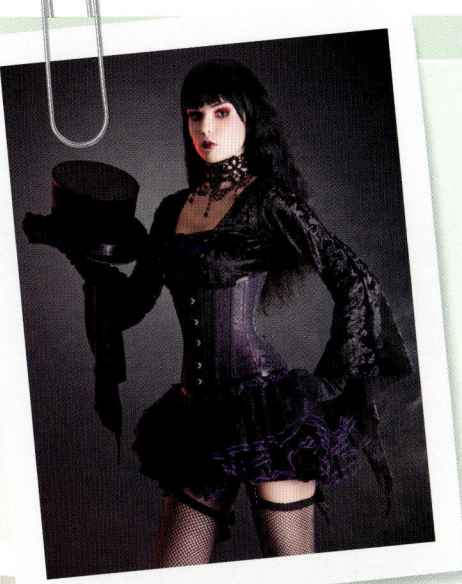

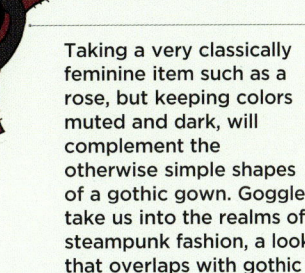

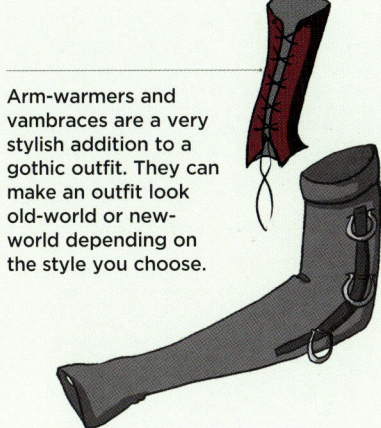

Taking a very classically feminine item such as a rose, but keeping colors muted and dark, will complement the otherwise simple shapes of a gothic gown. Goggles take us into the realms of steampunk fashion, a look that overlaps with gothic in a very stylish way.

Arm-warmers and vambraces are a very stylish addition to a gothic outfit. They can make an outfit look old-world or new-world depending on the style you choose.

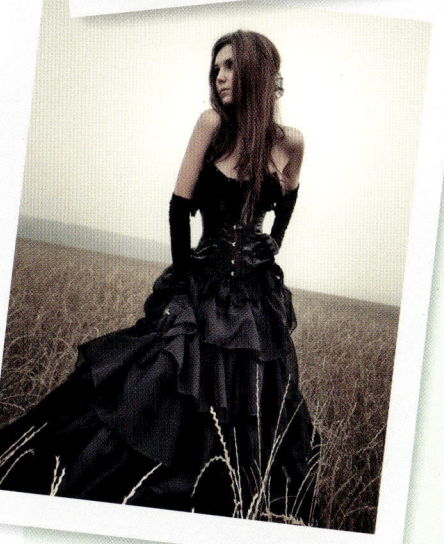

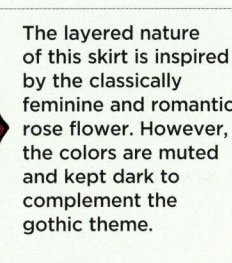

The layered nature of this skirt is inspired by the classically feminine and romantic rose flower. However, the colors are muted and kept dark to complement the gothic theme.

From glam to classic, tailor the gothic look to suit your character's personality and/or a special event she may be attending.

These high boots are close-fitting, so make sure you follow the contours of the leg for the shape.

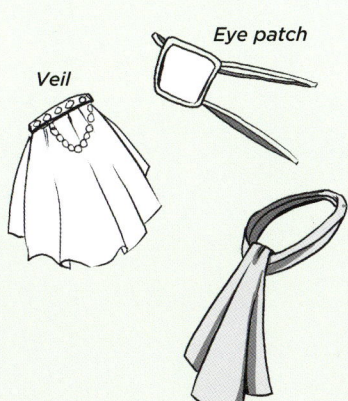

Veil

Eye patch

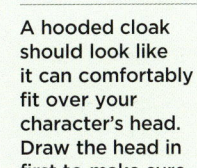

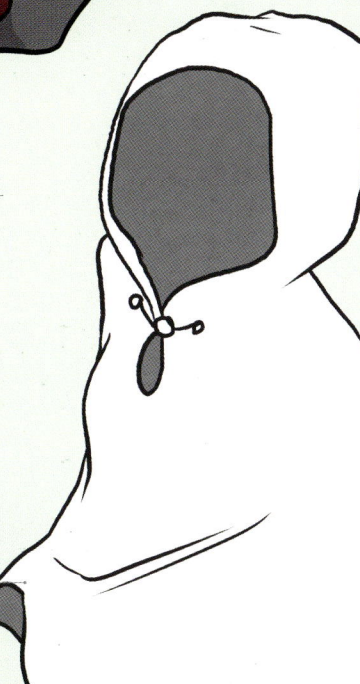

When drawing neckties or frills, consider how the material will fold, scrunch, or flair out from a fastening.

A hooded cloak should look like it can comfortably fit over your character's head. Draw the head in first to make sure.

CLASSIC LOLITA

AN **ELEGANT** STYLE OF DRESS THAT IS HIGHLY POPULAR IN JAPAN, CLASSIC LOLITA IS INFLUENCED BY **HISTORICAL** PERIODS SUCH AS ELIZABETHAN, ROCOCO, EDWARDIAN, AND THE RENAISSANCE. PROMINENT FEATURES OF THE STYLE ARE **LAYERED DRESSES**, COMBINATIONS OF **LACE AND RUFFLES, FULL SKIRTS**, AND **SOFT, FLORAL PATTERNS**. ACCESSORIES—PEARLS, BOWS, AND BROOCHES AS WELL AS LACE GLOVES AND HAIR ORNAMENTS—MATCH THESE HISTORICAL INFLUENCES.

1 Use basic shapes and simple lines to sketch out your figure. Drawing the spine as a slightly curved line gives movement to figures—don't worry about messy sketching at the moment, as the most important thing right now is making sure that everything is in proportion.

2 Lolita style is all about big skirts, big bows, and even bigger hair; try looking at existing Lolita dresses and fashionistas for inspiration. Use loose, curved lines while sketching to keep your designs looking lively.

3 Block in colors in your scheme of choice. Classic Lolitas dress in a lot of light and pastel colors—this model is wearing predominantly pale gold and cream, so by adding areas of purple (the complementary color to yellow), the outfit won't look bland.

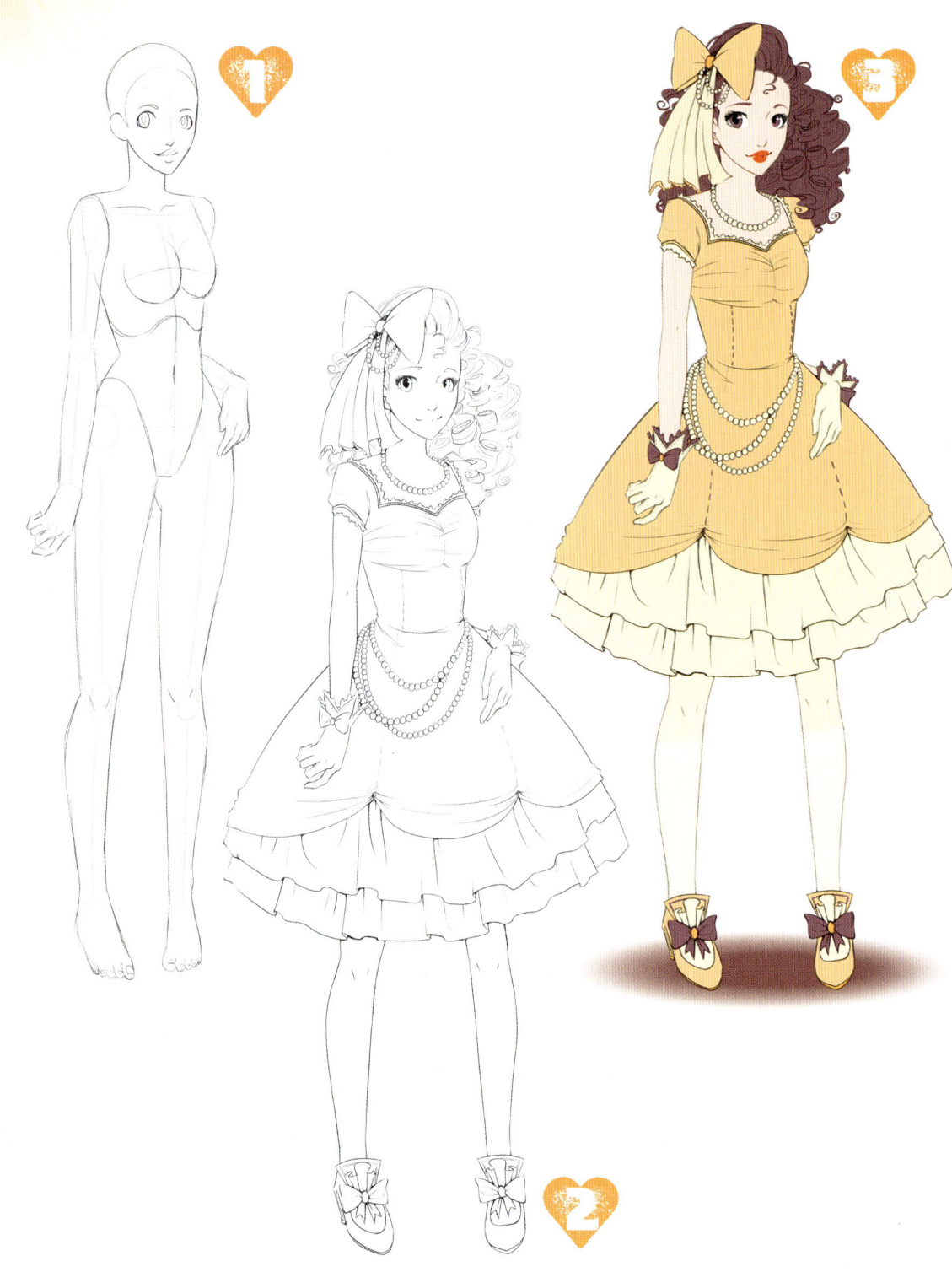

CLASSIC LOLITA | **71**

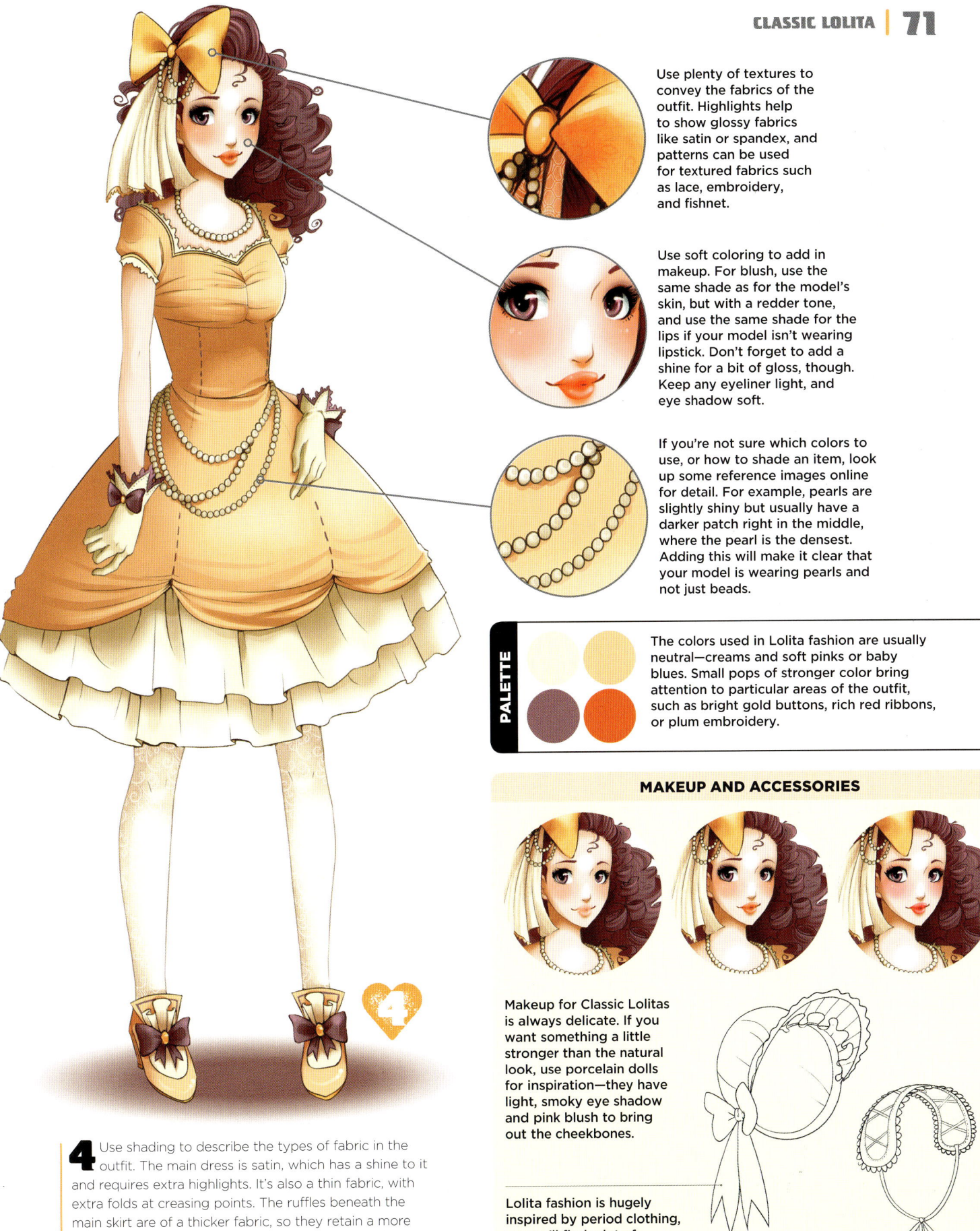

Use plenty of textures to convey the fabrics of the outfit. Highlights help to show glossy fabrics like satin or spandex, and patterns can be used for textured fabrics such as lace, embroidery, and fishnet.

Use soft coloring to add in makeup. For blush, use the same shade as for the model's skin, but with a redder tone, and use the same shade for the lips if your model isn't wearing lipstick. Don't forget to add a shine for a bit of gloss, though. Keep any eyeliner light, and eye shadow soft.

If you're not sure which colors to use, or how to shade an item, look up some reference images online for detail. For example, pearls are slightly shiny but usually have a darker patch right in the middle, where the pearl is the densest. Adding this will make it clear that your model is wearing pearls and not just beads.

PALETTE

The colors used in Lolita fashion are usually neutral—creams and soft pinks or baby blues. Small pops of stronger color bring attention to particular areas of the outfit, such as bright gold buttons, rich red ribbons, or plum embroidery.

MAKEUP AND ACCESSORIES

Makeup for Classic Lolitas is always delicate. If you want something a little stronger than the natural look, use porcelain dolls for inspiration—they have light, smoky eye shadow and pink blush to bring out the cheekbones.

Lolita fashion is hugely inspired by period clothing, so you'll find a lot of bonnets and headbands on models.

4 Use shading to describe the types of fabric in the outfit. The main dress is satin, which has a shine to it and requires extra highlights. It's also a thin fabric, with extra folds at creasing points. The ruffles beneath the main skirt are of a thicker fabric, so they retain a more solid shape. Don't forget finishing touches like makeup, and lace patterns on her tights and veil.

SWEET LOLITA

72 | THE COLLECTIONS

THIS TYPE OF LOLITA FOCUSES LARGELY ON CHILDLIKE THEMES, CANDYLIKE COLORS, AND A FANTASTICAL **"ALICE IN WONDERLAND"** TENDENCY TOWARD **OVERSIZED ACCESSORIES**. BASED ON STRONG, **JUVENILE COLORS** AND **SOFT TEXTURES**, SWEET LOLITAS USUALLY CHOOSE A CENTRAL THEME FOR THEIR OUTFITS—SUCH AS PLUSH TOYS, CUTE ANIMALS, FLOWERS, OR CAKES AND CANDY. THE WHOLE LOOK HAS TO SCREAM **"CUTE."** KEY FEATURES OF THE STYLE ARE BIG, CURLED HAIR, A FULL SKIRT, AND LARGE DECORATIONS.

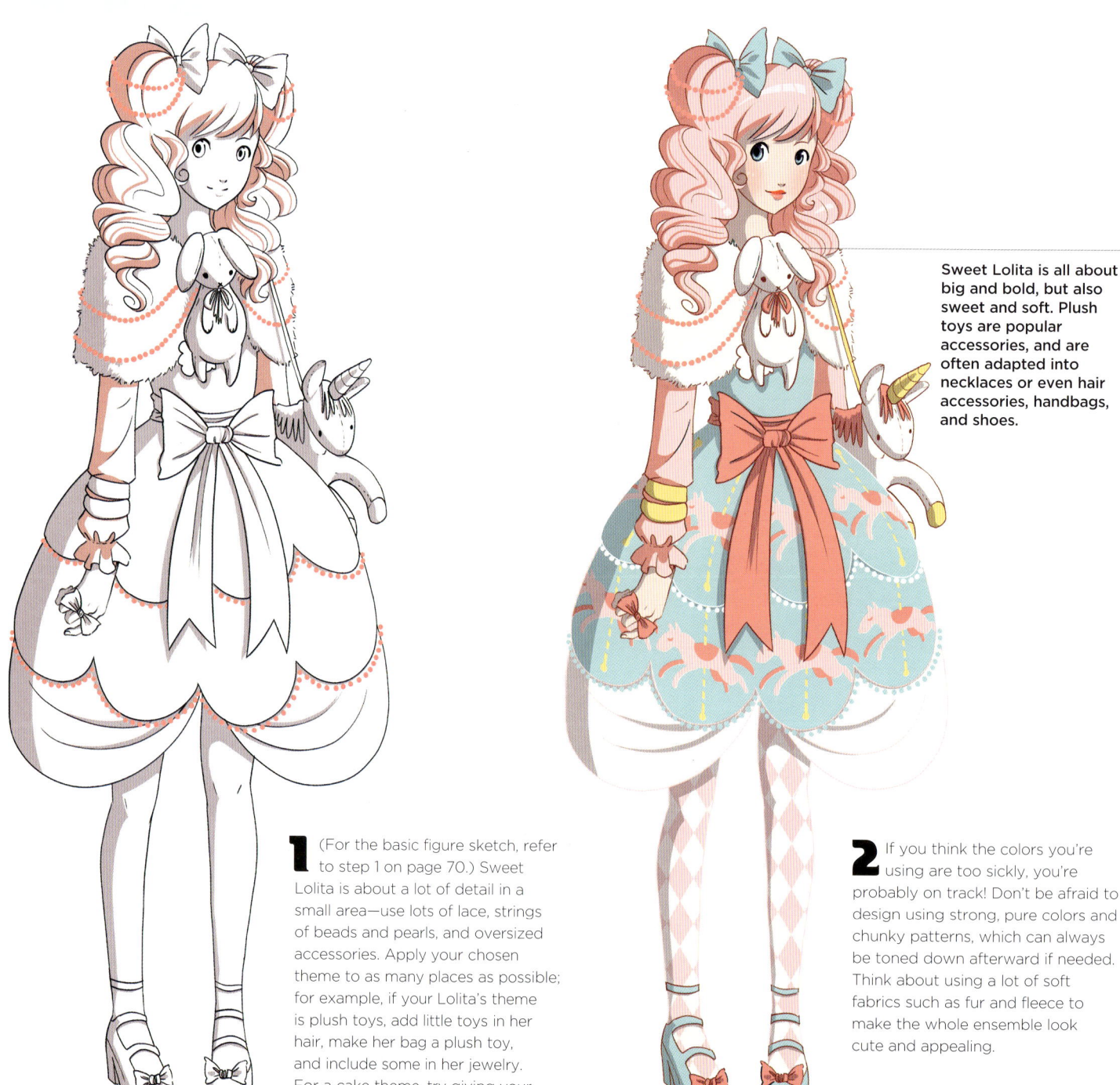

Sweet Lolita is all about big and bold, but also sweet and soft. Plush toys are popular accessories, and are often adapted into necklaces or even hair accessories, handbags, and shoes.

1 (For the basic figure sketch, refer to step 1 on page 70.) Sweet Lolita is about a lot of detail in a small area—use lots of lace, strings of beads and pearls, and oversized accessories. Apply your chosen theme to as many places as possible; for example, if your Lolita's theme is plush toys, add little toys in her hair, make her bag a plush toy, and include some in her jewelry. For a cake theme, try giving your model cake-topped shoes or a cake-shaped hat.

2 If you think the colors you're using are too sickly, you're probably on track! Don't be afraid to design using strong, pure colors and chunky patterns, which can always be toned down afterward if needed. Think about using a lot of soft fabrics such as fur and fleece to make the whole ensemble look cute and appealing.

SWEET LOLITA | 73

ACCESSORIES AND HAIR

PALETTE

As with Classic Lolita, Sweet Lolita palettes are very delicate. However, rather than being faded and pastel-colored, they are very much about baby colors—blues, pinks, and yellows—as well as large amounts of white and cream to balance out the palette.

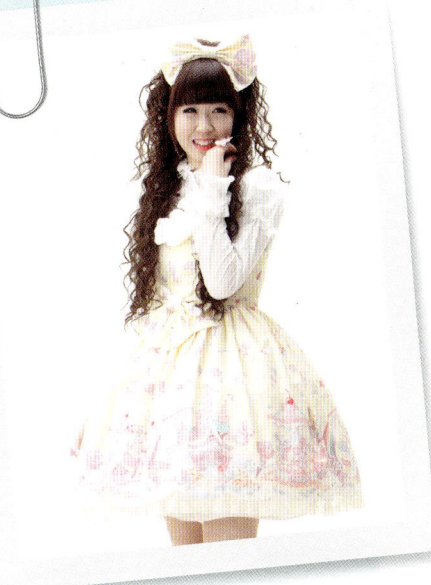

Every Sweet Lolita outfit should be full of big shapes and soft curves. Ruffled collars and cuffs soften the lines of the shirt under this model's dress, as does her curled hair and the rounded designs on her skirt.

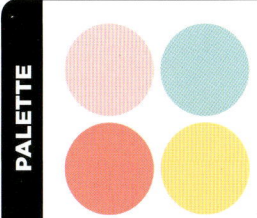
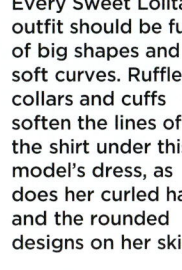

Once you have a theme for your outfit, designing the accessories is the fun part! Try drawing cake hats, or topping bows with fruit, wrapped candies, or little plush toys.

Don't neglect your Lolita's shoes! Look at Georgian and other historical periods for inspiration, and throw in plenty of lace, low heels, and cute accessories.

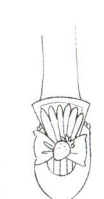

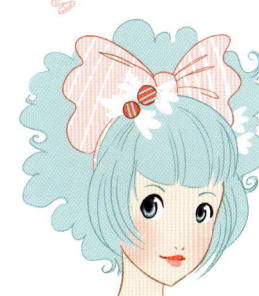

Big, curled hair is one of the most distinctive signs of a Sweet Lolita. Whether done up in an Afro or curled into long, low ringlets, the bigger the better. Try accessorizing with plenty of bows, barrettes, clips, and pins. The hair can be a great showcase for your chosen theme.

MAKEUP

As Sweet Lolita is a fantasy-based look, it's probably the most outlandish of the Lolita styles when it comes to makeup.

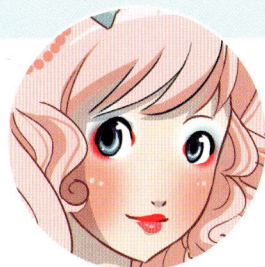

Using the standard Lolita blush and eye-shadow style as a base (see page 71), add bright, striking colors that contrast with the pastels.

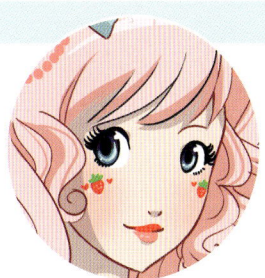

Try experimenting with cute designs—such as fruit, stars, or hearts—drawn on the cheeks.

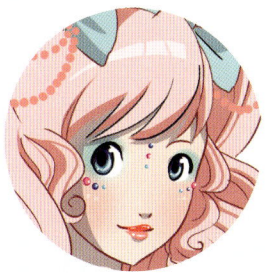

Sparkling gems are a popular accessory with Lolitas, since they're both colorful and eye-catching. They're commonly used to create designs on the cheeks and under the eyes.

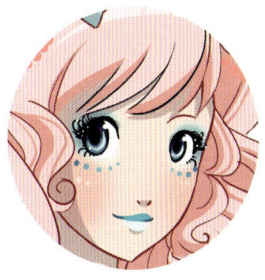

Long, oversized eyelashes add to the cute factor.

GOTHIC LOLITA

ONE OF THE MOST POPULAR AND RECOGNIZABLE FORMS OF THE "LOLI" MOVEMENT, GOTHIC LOLITA IS ALSO INSPIRED BY **PORCELAIN DOLLS AND HISTORICAL CLOTHING**, BUT IS CHARACTERIZED BY **DARK COLORS, HEAVY LAYERS, AND THICK MAKEUP**. THERE IS A FOCUS ON POPULAR GOTHIC ICONS, SUCH AS **CROWNS, CROSSES, AND ROSES**. ELEGANT GOTHIC LOLITA (FOR WOMEN) AND ELEGANT GOTHIC ARISTOCRAT (FOR MEN) ARE EVEN MORE EXAGGERATED AND VERY MUCH INSPIRED BY **ARISTOCRATIC FASHION AND "STEAMPUNK."**

1 For the basic figure sketch, refer to step 1 on page 70.) Since the dark colors of Goth Loli clothing can make it difficult to see details, make sure that you're happy with your sketch before you start adding colors. This is also a good time to think about lighting, since adding shadows will make the image even darker. When designing your outfits, include areas where you know you'll be able to add in flashes of lighter colors—for example, ribbons, bows, jewelry, and hair accessories.

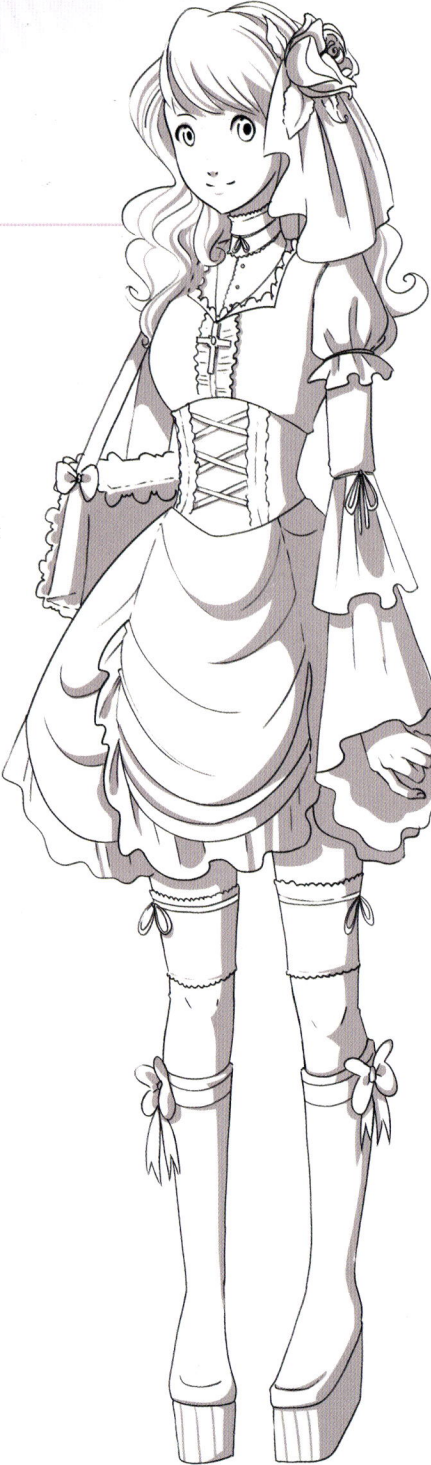

2 It's very easy to go too dark too quickly, so start with light colors and work your way darker. Try using a midtone for the majority of your clothing, such as a warm gray, and then add areas of darker gray and lighter colors to balance it out. Makeup is another opportunity to add a splash of color, and don't forget that pale skin—characteristic of the Lolita movement—will help to lighten your images as well as define your model's look.

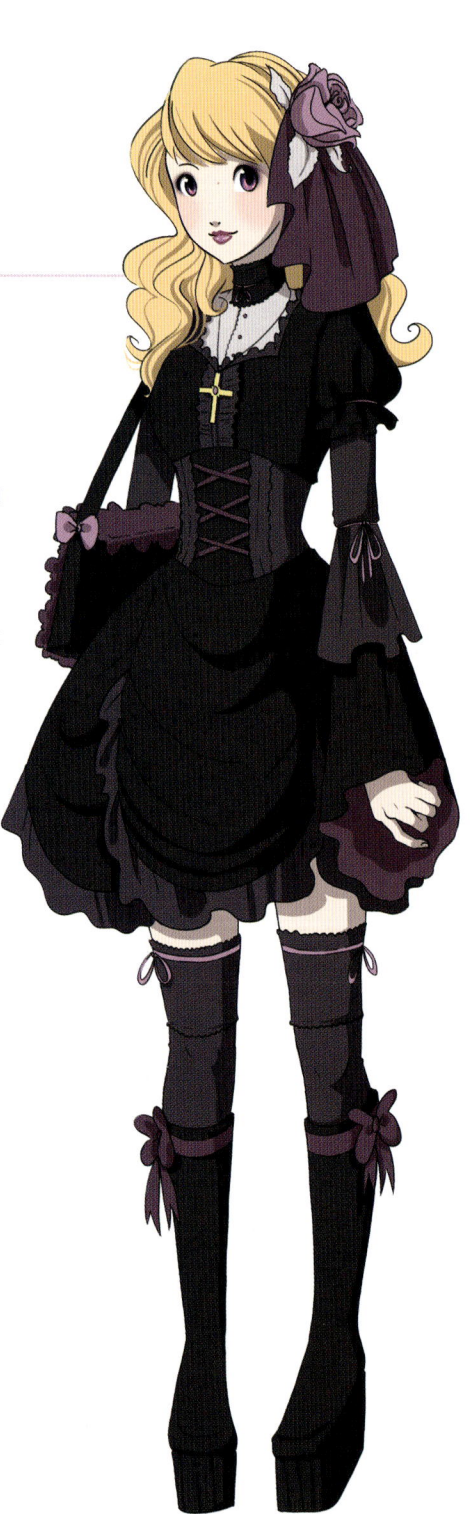

GOTHIC LOLITA | 75

ACCESSORIES AND CLOTHING

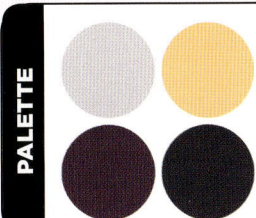

PALETTE

In contrast to the light, pastel colors of Classic Lolita, Gothic Lolita is very dark and often quite unremarkable. However, by using pops of rich colors such as purple, gold, and red, you can easily make your designs stand out.

There are plenty of ideas to draw on for your Goth Loli fashion collection. For example, you'll find that popular headwear often consists of crowns, miniature top hats, and veils. Don't forget to deck them out with plenty of decadent trimmings, such as lace, feathers, pearls, or velvet.

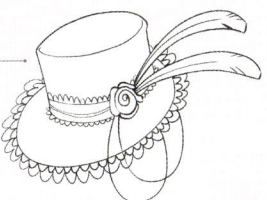
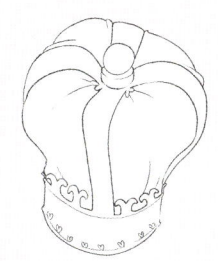
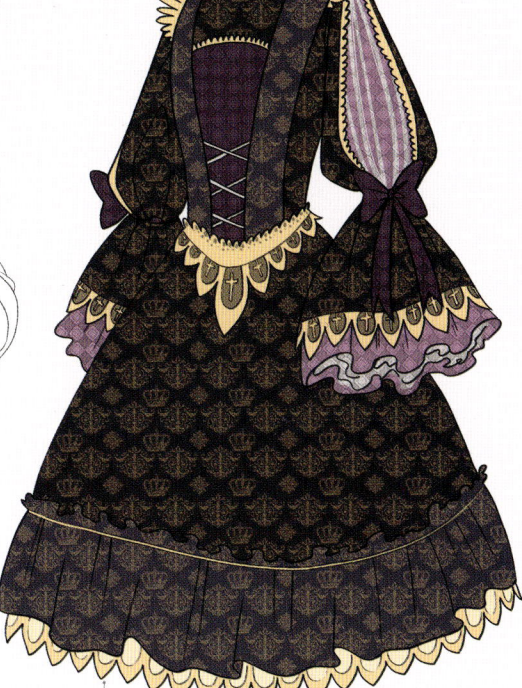

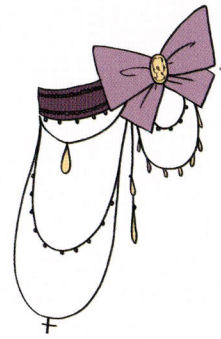

Gothic Lolita is inspired by the high-necked dresses and shirts popular in the Edwardian and Victorian eras, and necklaces are designed to replicate this look. Thick lace or velvet chokers, often covered in beads, Victorian cameos, and filigree embellishments are very popular.

Elegant Gothic Lolita is even more extravagant than the standard gothic style and features heavy, embroidered fabrics, plentiful layers, and historically accurate clothing. Try looking at historical costumes for inspiration.

MAKEUP

The Gothic Lolita look is similar to the Classic Lolita look, but there are plenty of variations to play with.

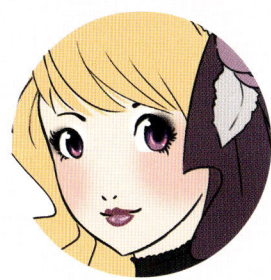

Smoky eye shadow, natural blush, and exaggerated lashes are carried through from the Classic Lolita look.

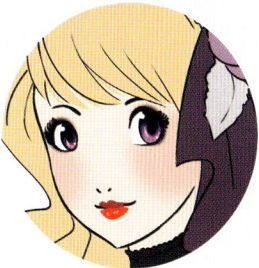

Dark eyeliner, fake lashes on the eyelids, and bright red lipstick outline the features and add contrast.

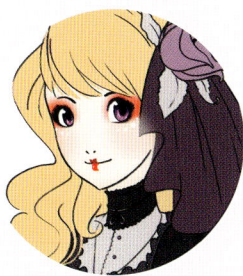

The bold, striking makeup of geisha is a suitable inspiration to draw on for your Lolita look. Pay homage to these amazing women with stylized red lips and red eye shadow.

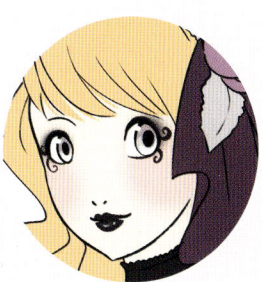

Toning down the blush and adding spookily colored or tinted contact lenses make your model more vampiric.

GANGURO

IF LOLITAS ARE THE DRESS-UP DOLLS OF JAPAN, THEN GANGURO ARE DEFINITELY THE **PARTY GIRLS!** A TREND THAT **STARTED IN THE MID-1990S**, GANGURO IS DISTINGUISHED BY **DARK TANS, WHITE MAKEUP, PLATFORM BOOTS, AND NEON CLOTHING**. WHAT **STARTED AS A REBELLION** AGAINST THE TRADITIONAL JAPANESE CONCEPT OF PALE-SKINNED BEAUTY HAS BECOME A **LONG-LASTING FASHION TREND**, ESPECIALLY IN THE NIGHTLIFE DISTRICTS OF TOKYO SUCH AS SHIBUYA AND IKEBUKURO.

CLOTHING PALETTE

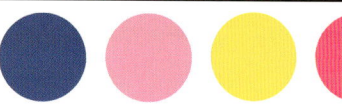

In ganguro fashion, brighter really is better. Ganguro girls are known for their love of bright, neon colors and clashing clothing; this outfit features neon pinks and yellows, which are always guaranteed to be popular in this particular style.

1 To start off your drawing, sketch your figure's pose by using simple lines to mark in the skeleton. Though ganguro girls are definitely not shy, this model is showing off her playful personality by playing coy—to show this, her toes and hands are pointing inward. This affects the whole pose, including her knees and elbows.

2 Using the skeleton as a base, draw in the rest of the figure. You can see here how thinking ahead about the pose has helped—the turned-in feet have turned the knees inward slightly as well, and the model's fingers are also loosely interlaced. If you find drawing hands difficult, try using your own as reference.

3 The majority of a ganguro's personality comes from her hair and makeup, not her clothes—but that doesn't mean that you can't have fun with them too! A lot of ganguro girls love flower motifs and chunky jewelry; this model is wearing a lei (a Hawaiian flower garland), and has continued this theme by wearing flowers in her hair and around her ankles.

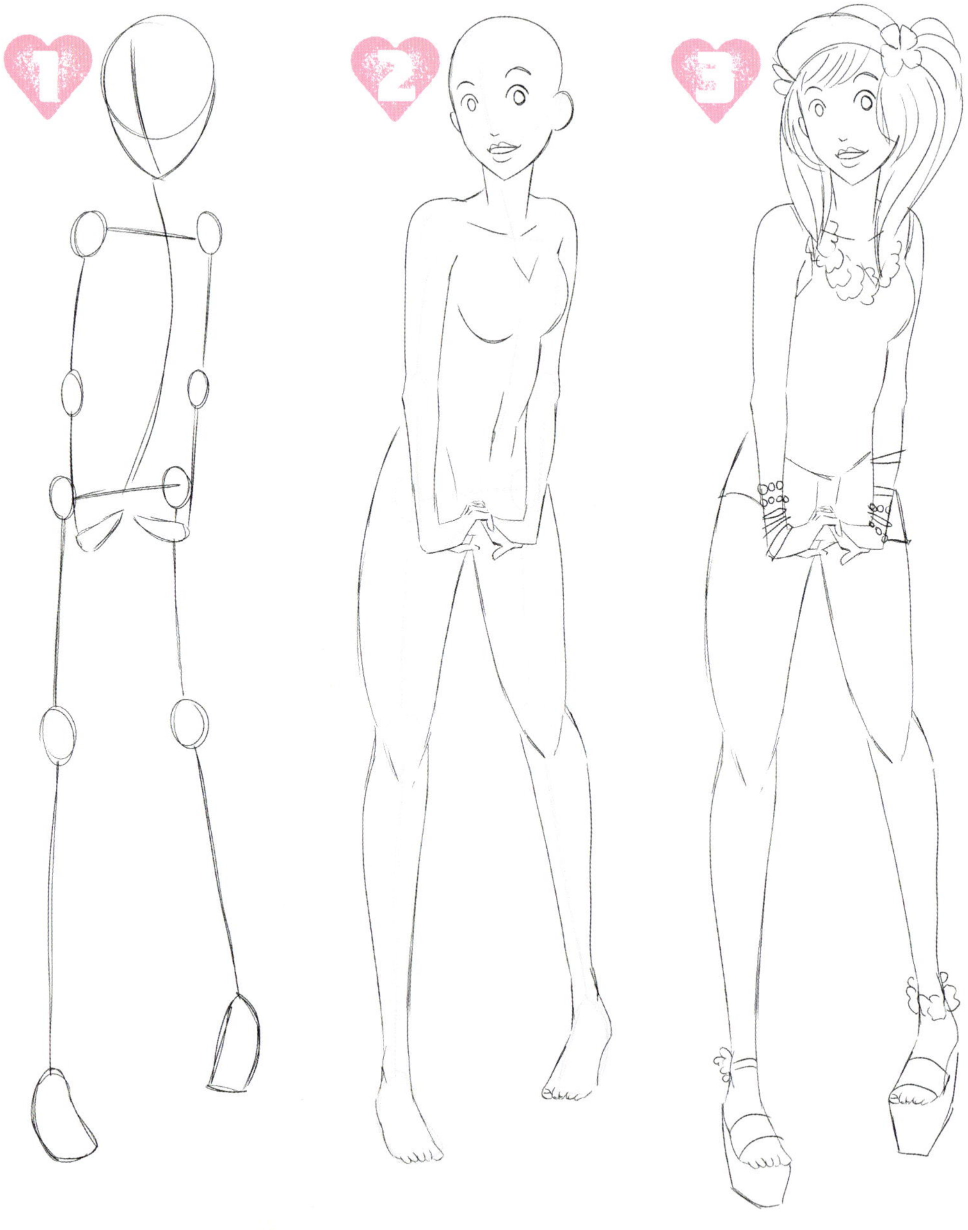

GANGURO | 77

4 You'll be able to draw in more details when you begin to clean up your sketch in this step—now you can really see all of the fun accessories. Stacks of bracelets create a playful, bright feature, and the flowers on her shoes make sure she's just as ready for the beach as she is for the club.

5 Bright colors will really begin to give the outfit personality. Most ganguro bleach their hair, and some even dye it bright colors again afterward; this model has pink hair to reflect the colors of the rest of her outfit. And don't forget the fake tan—a staple of the ganguro look.

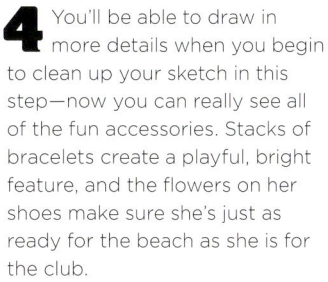

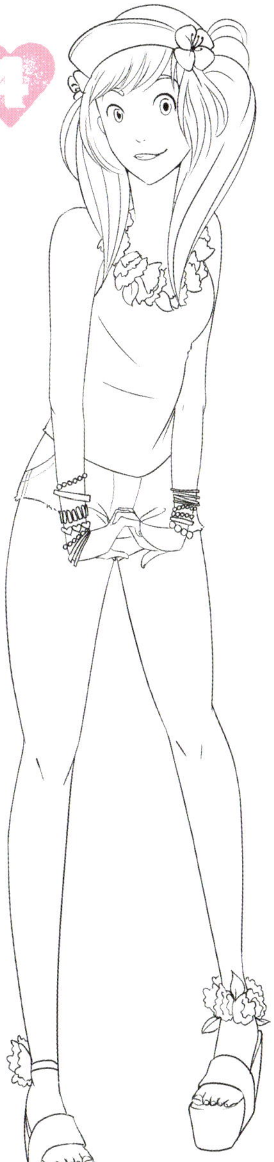

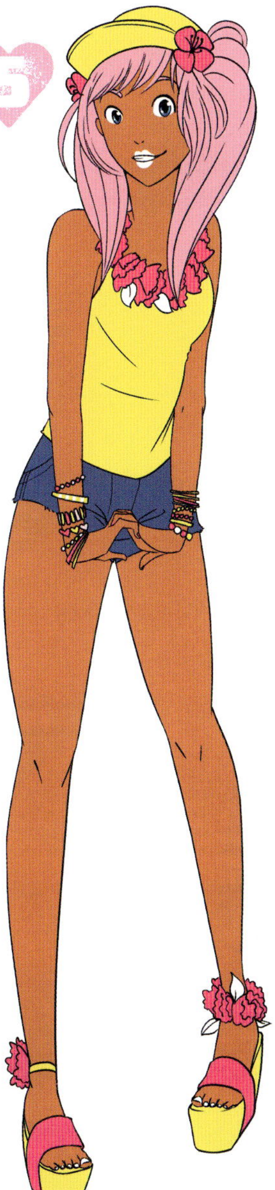

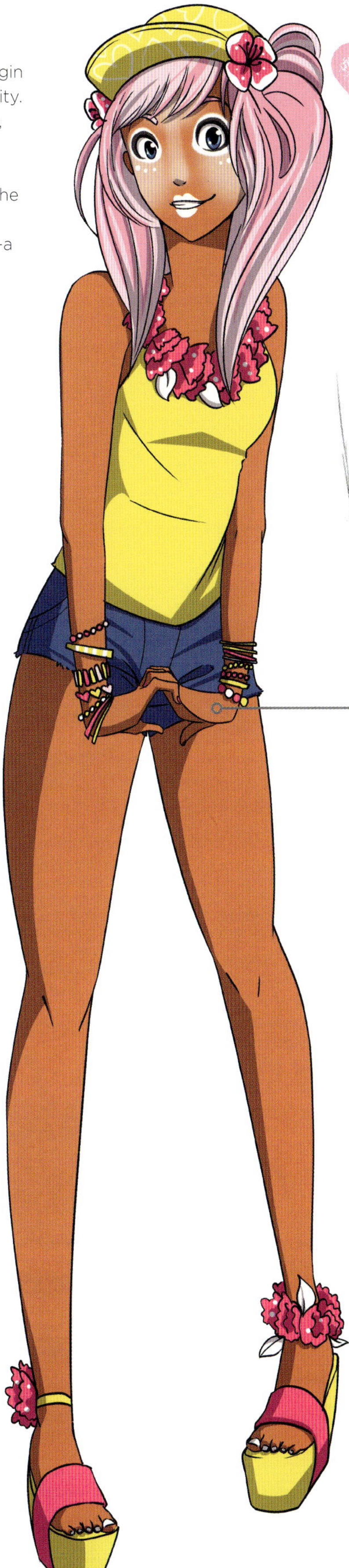

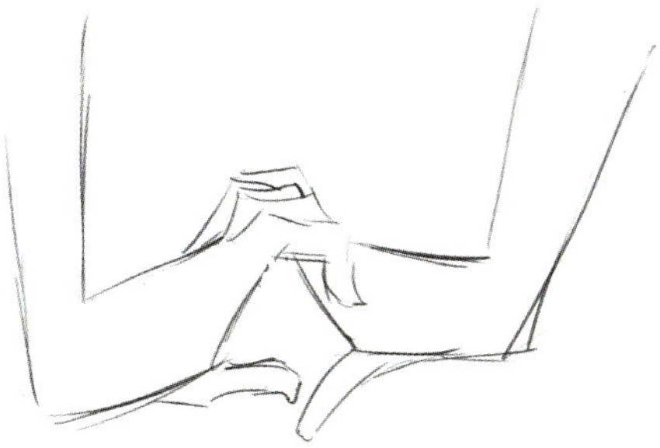

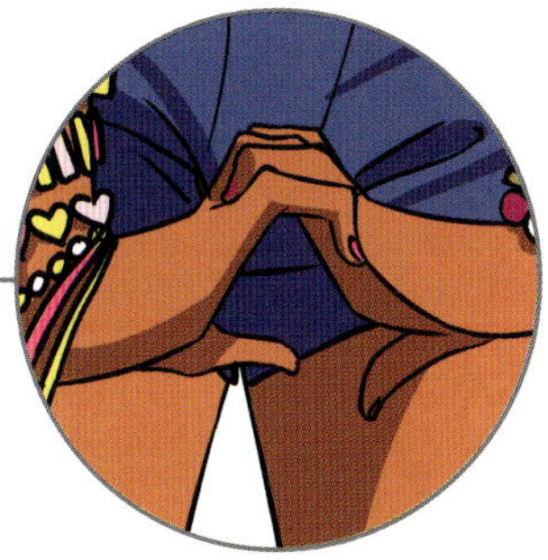

Hands can prove difficult for even the most experienced artist to get right. Luckily, you have two of your own to use as immediate reference—try using a mirror or taking photographs to see how different poses look. Making separate, more detailed sketches on a different piece of paper before you start can prove useful, as well as this being good practice in general.

6 It's important to focus on the white makeup of a ganguro, as this is the main feature of the style. Using white on the cheeks and the bridge of the nose adds shape to the model's face, while the bolder white lips and eye shadow really make the look pop.

It may seem at first that ganguro is quite a limited style, but that couldn't be farther from the truth. The style is surprisingly diverse, from the extreme, over-tanned look of the manba to the more subtle, relaxed style of the gyaru. In fact, there are more than 30 recognized subgenres of ganguro—looking them up online will give you plenty of inspiration for your own collection.

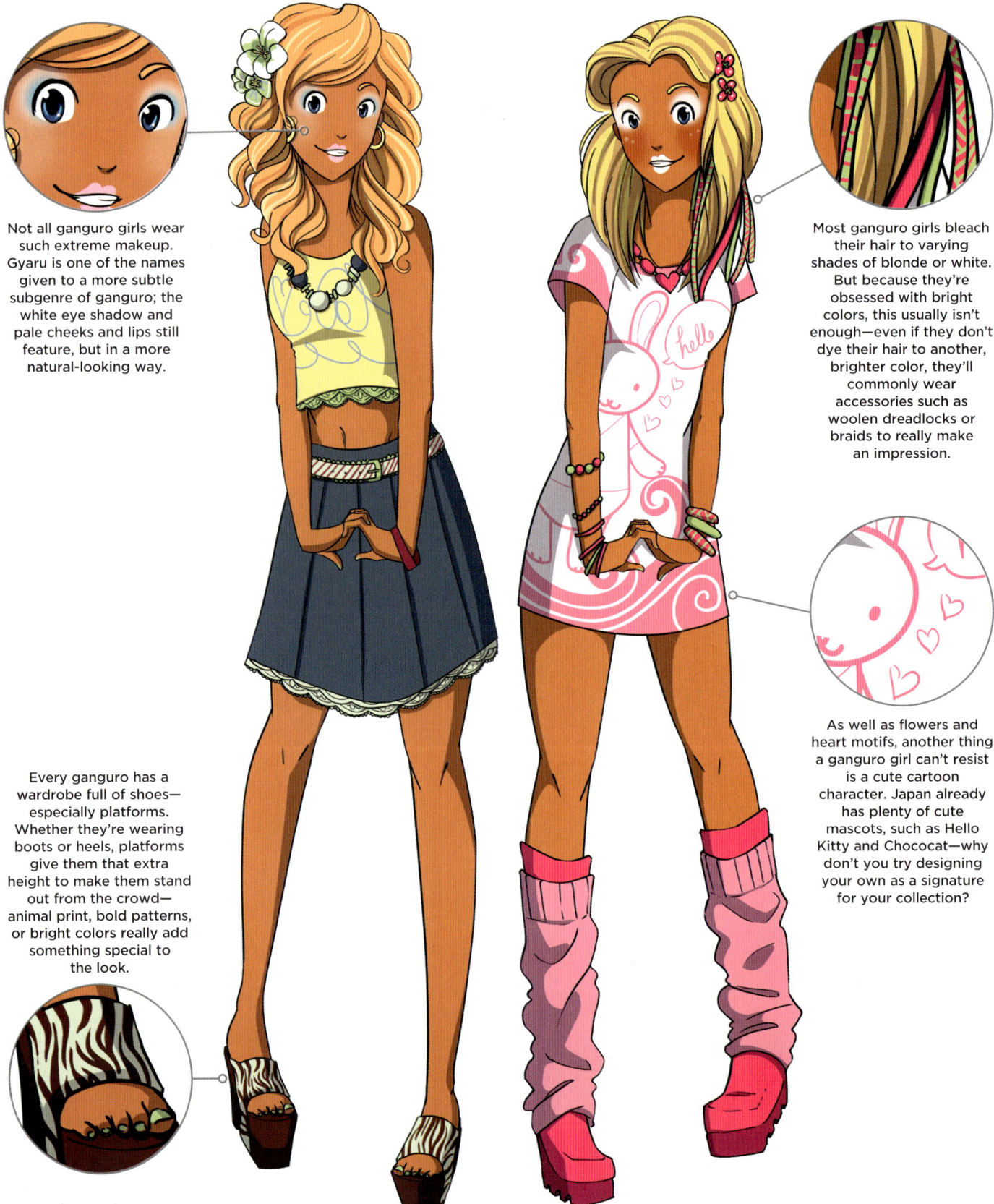

Not all ganguro girls wear such extreme makeup. Gyaru is one of the names given to a more subtle subgenre of ganguro; the white eye shadow and pale cheeks and lips still feature, but in a more natural-looking way.

Every ganguro has a wardrobe full of shoes—especially platforms. Whether they're wearing boots or heels, platforms give them that extra height to make them stand out from the crowd—animal print, bold patterns, or bright colors really add something special to the look.

Most ganguro girls bleach their hair to varying shades of blonde or white. But because they're obsessed with bright colors, this usually isn't enough—even if they don't dye their hair to another, brighter color, they'll commonly wear accessories such as woolen dreadlocks or braids to really make an impression.

As well as flowers and heart motifs, another thing a ganguro girl can't resist is a cute cartoon character. Japan already has plenty of cute mascots, such as Hello Kitty and Chococat—why don't you try designing your own as a signature for your collection?

GANGURO | 79

ACCESSORIES AND CLOTHING

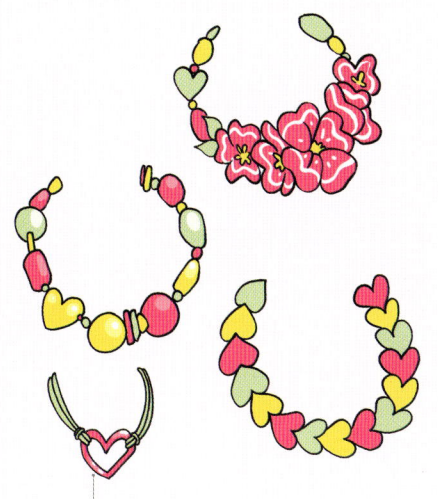

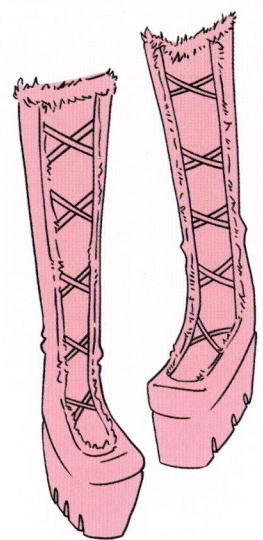

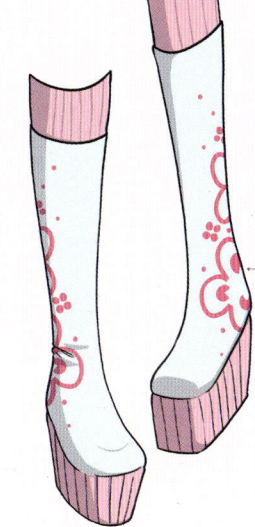

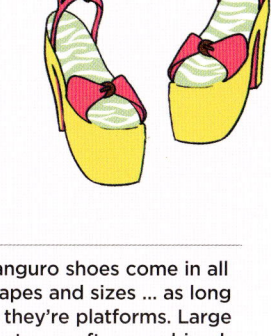

The ganguro girl loves her chunky jewelry, and anything brightly colored is bound to attract her attention. Large plastic beads are a common feature in necklaces, bracelets, and rings, especially if they're in cute shapes like hearts or stars; flowers make an appearance, too, in the trademark neon colors.

Ganguro shoes come in all shapes and sizes ... as long as they're platforms. Large boots are often combined with high-topped socks or fur trim; shoes are often in bright colors, and look as though they'd be just as fashionable on vacation as they would be shopping or clubbing. Adding patterns to the insoles injects a style detail that other designers often overlook.

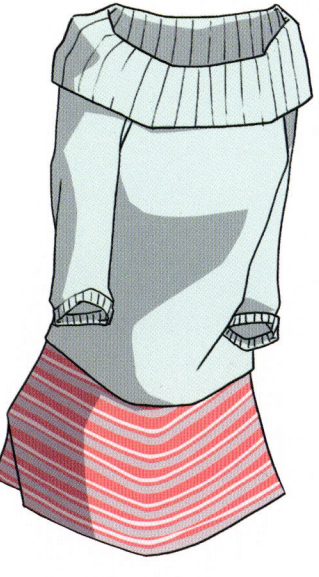

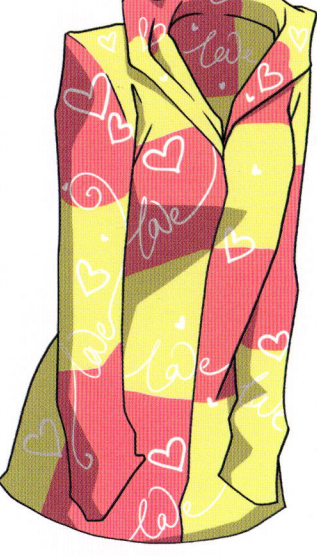

If it's not bright, bold, and outrageously over the top, it's not ganguro! Blue, pink, and yellow are staple colors for any ganguro girl—throw these colors together in mismatched stripes, checkers, harlequins, and other chunky patterns. Top with big, bright words or designs, or pair with another brightly colored garment for the ultimate ganguro look.

MAKEUP

Here are examples of the various styles of ganguro makeup. As you can see, it can look good whether it's subtle or very extreme. The most hardcore ganguro commonly use glitter, cute stickers, or colored gems on their cheeks while out partying, as well as colored contacts for added dazzle.

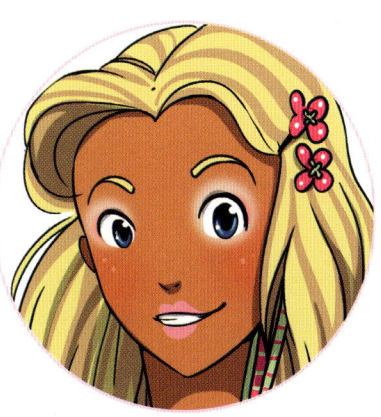

Sweet pastels

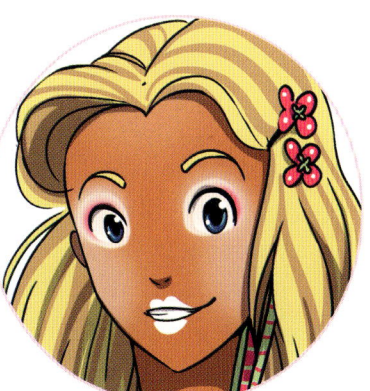

Exaggerated highlights

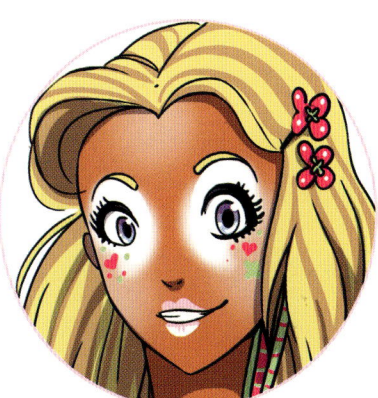

Extreme ganguro!

HIPSTER

THE TERM "HIPSTER" HAS BEEN AROUND SINCE THE 1990S, BUT ROSE TO POPULARITY MOST RECENTLY AROUND 2010. IT REFERS TO A WAY OF LIVING THAT **EMBRACES OLD-FASHIONED AND NON-MAINSTREAM IDEALS**, AS WELL AS BEING **CONSCIOUS OF ENVIRONMENTAL ISSUES**; AS A RESULT, THE MAIN CONCEPT OF HIPSTER CLOTHING IS TO **REPURPOSE OLD FASHIONS** THAT ARE SEEN AS OUT OF DATE, SO AS TO AVOID SUPPORTING MODERN DEPARTMENT STORES. MOST OUTFITS ARE FOUND IN **THRIFT STORES** AND FASHIONED INTO SOMETHING MORE MODERN.

CLOTHING PALETTE

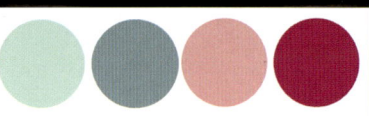

Because hipsters build their outfits from "found" clothes, there's no particular color palette that the look adheres to. However, natural colors and pastels commonly make an appearance—this particular outfit focuses on pastel blues, greens, and berry purples.

1 Sketch out a basic skeleton for your model to work out the anatomy and pose. Even at this early stage, you can add in some character—a spine curving inward gives your model a bit of a slouch, for added attitude.

2 Using the skeleton as a base, start to sketch in the bulk of the model's body. It doesn't matter if your lines are rough. If there are elements of the outfit that you already know you're going to include that will change the way your model is standing—for example, this model will be wearing heels—take these into consideration now so you can adjust the position of feet and legs accordingly.

3 Now it's time to start designing! Knitted hats and Daisy Duke shorts are staples of female hipster fashion, so this model is showcasing these—a rough sketch also shows where she'll have a tattoo to add an extra splash of detail and color to the outfit.

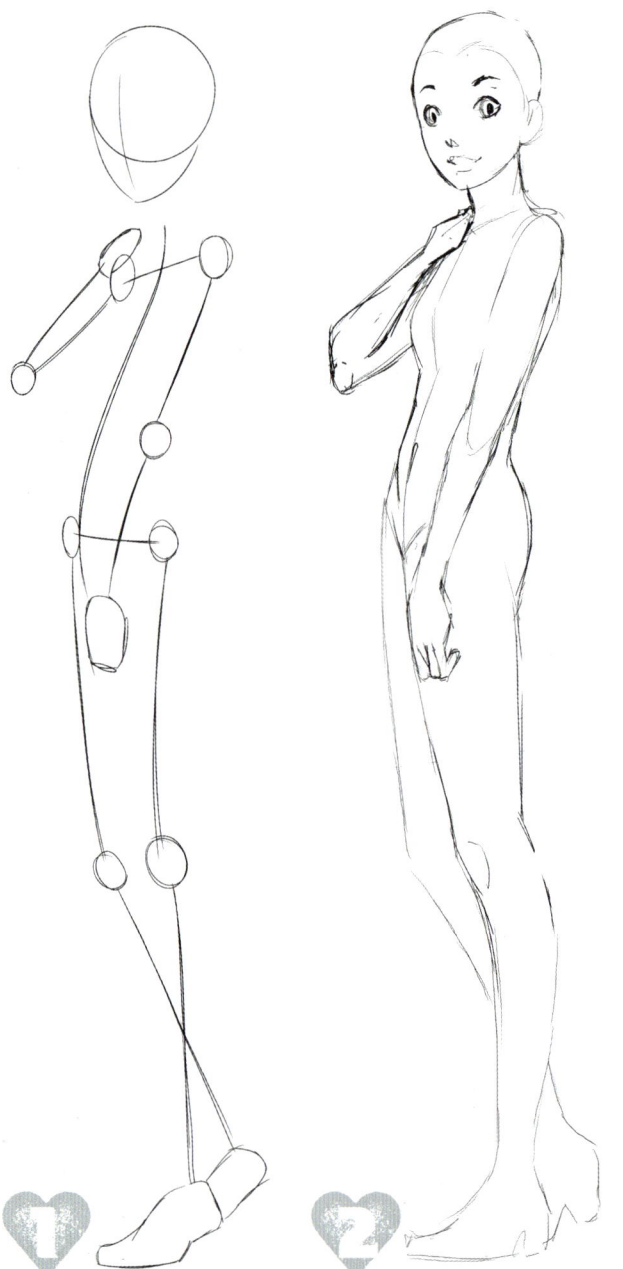
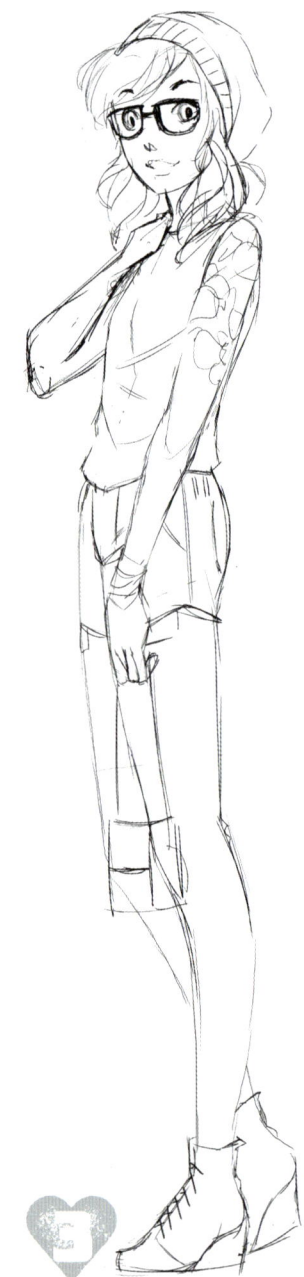

HIPSTER | **81**

4 Now that you've got a chance to clean up your sketch, don't forget to add areas of detail. Start describing what fabrics your model is wearing—thin lines around the ankle of the boot and the band of the hat suggest a soft, ribbed fabric, and flat-felled seams on the shorts show they're made of denim.

5 Adding color will give extra definition to different areas of the outfit. The hipster look is all about mixing and matching fabrics, textures, and patterns; it's quite common to see hipsters wearing leggings or patterned tights with shorts or skirts, as well as odd combinations of fabrics—such as suede and knitted wool in the boots—to add further character to their wardrobe.

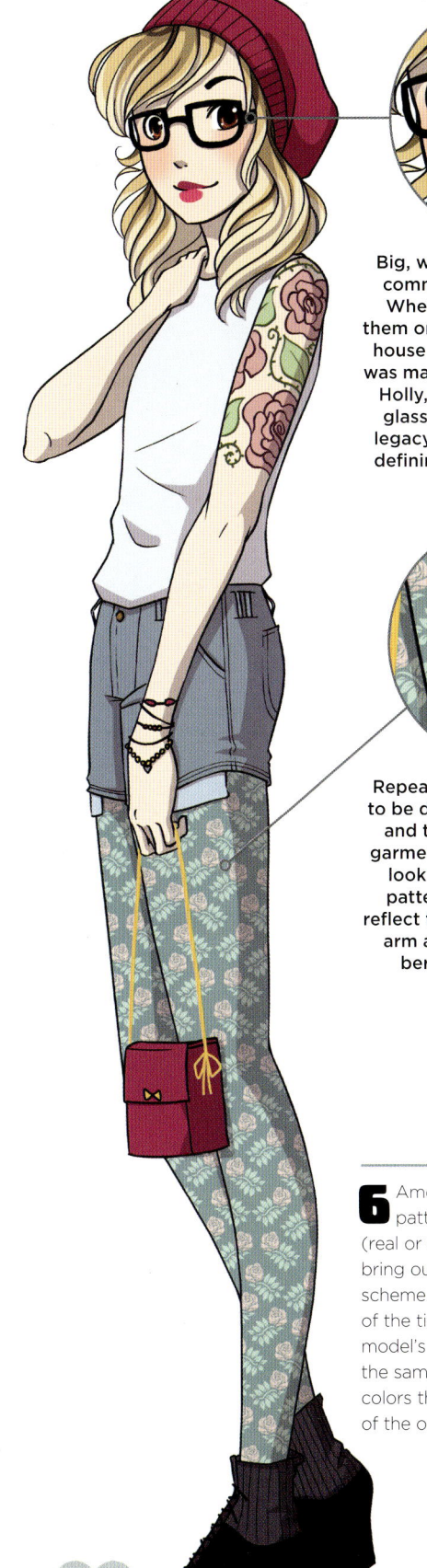

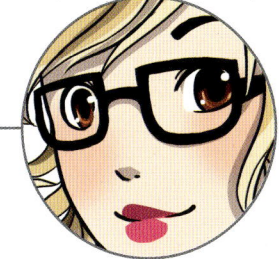

Big, wide-rimmed glasses are common in the hipster look. Whether your model needs them or not, they can't leave the house without them! The style was made fashionable by Buddy Holly, who wore Faosa brand glasses—and the company's legacy has become one of the defining traits of hipster style.

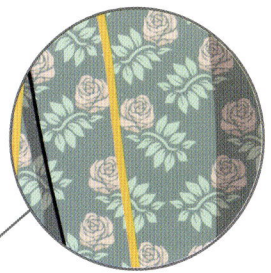

Repeating patterns don't have to be detailed to look effective, and they can add texture to garments that might otherwise look too plain. Here, a rose pattern has been chosen to reflect the tattoo on the model's arm and to complement the berry colors throughout the outfit.

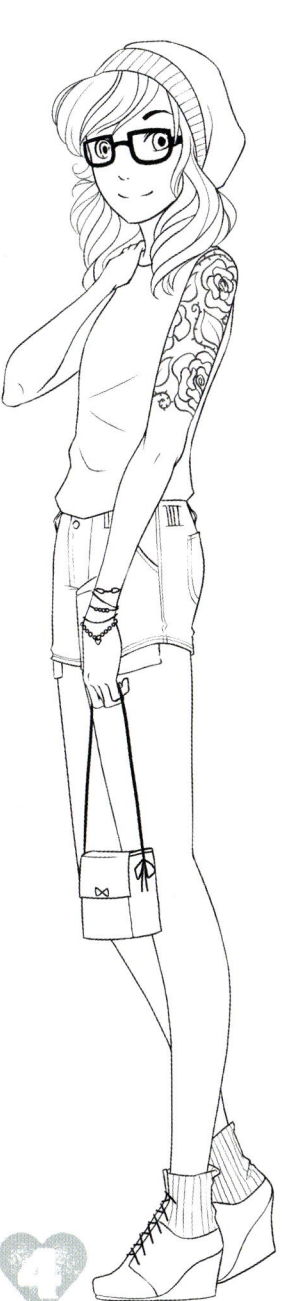

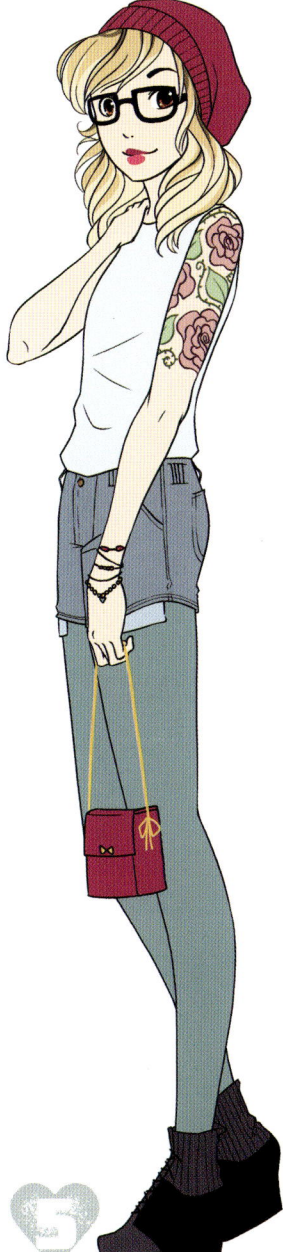

6 Among other things, patterned fabrics and tattoos (real or fake) are a great way to bring out new elements of a color scheme. In this outfit, the roses of the tights are reflected in the model's tattoo—both bring out the same berry and blue/green colors that are sampled in the rest of the outfit.

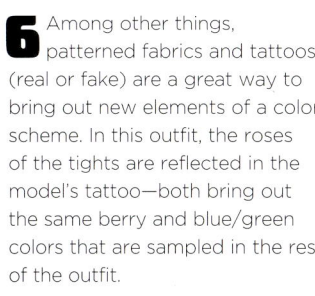

82 | THE COLLECTIONS

Considering that hipster fashion is intended to be out of style and old-fashioned, it may seem a daunting challenge to create flattering outfits. High, close-styled necklines and baggy tops are popular, along with muted colors, but by layering other, brighter-colored clothes over the top, there are a lot of potential looks to work with.

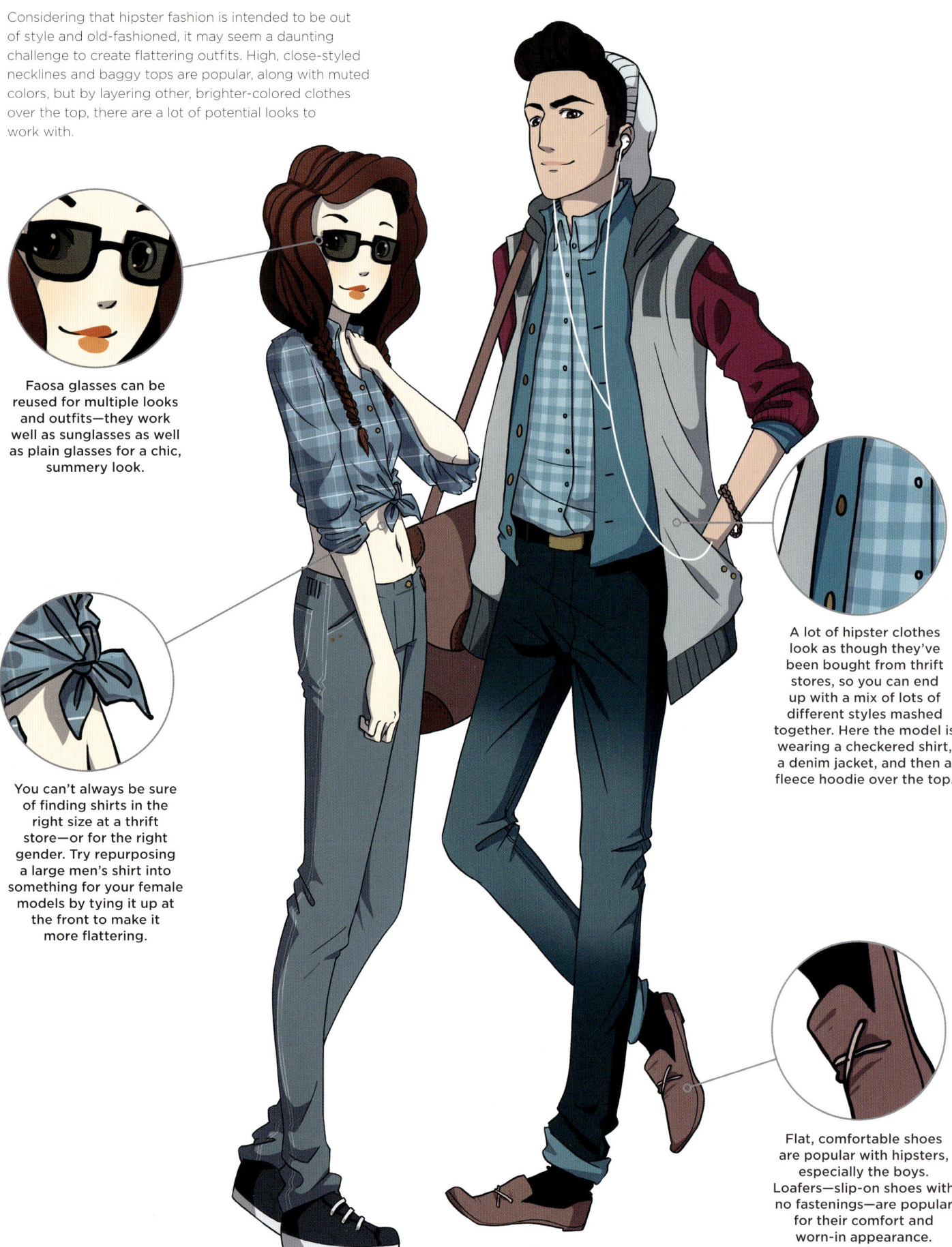

Faosa glasses can be reused for multiple looks and outfits—they work well as sunglasses as well as plain glasses for a chic, summery look.

You can't always be sure of finding shirts in the right size at a thrift store—or for the right gender. Try repurposing a large men's shirt into something for your female models by tying it up at the front to make it more flattering.

A lot of hipster clothes look as though they've been bought from thrift stores, so you can end up with a mix of lots of different styles mashed together. Here the model is wearing a checkered shirt, a denim jacket, and then a fleece hoodie over the top.

Flat, comfortable shoes are popular with hipsters, especially the boys. Loafers—slip-on shoes with no fastenings—are popular for their comfort and worn-in appearance.

HIPSTER | 83

CLOTHING AND BAGS

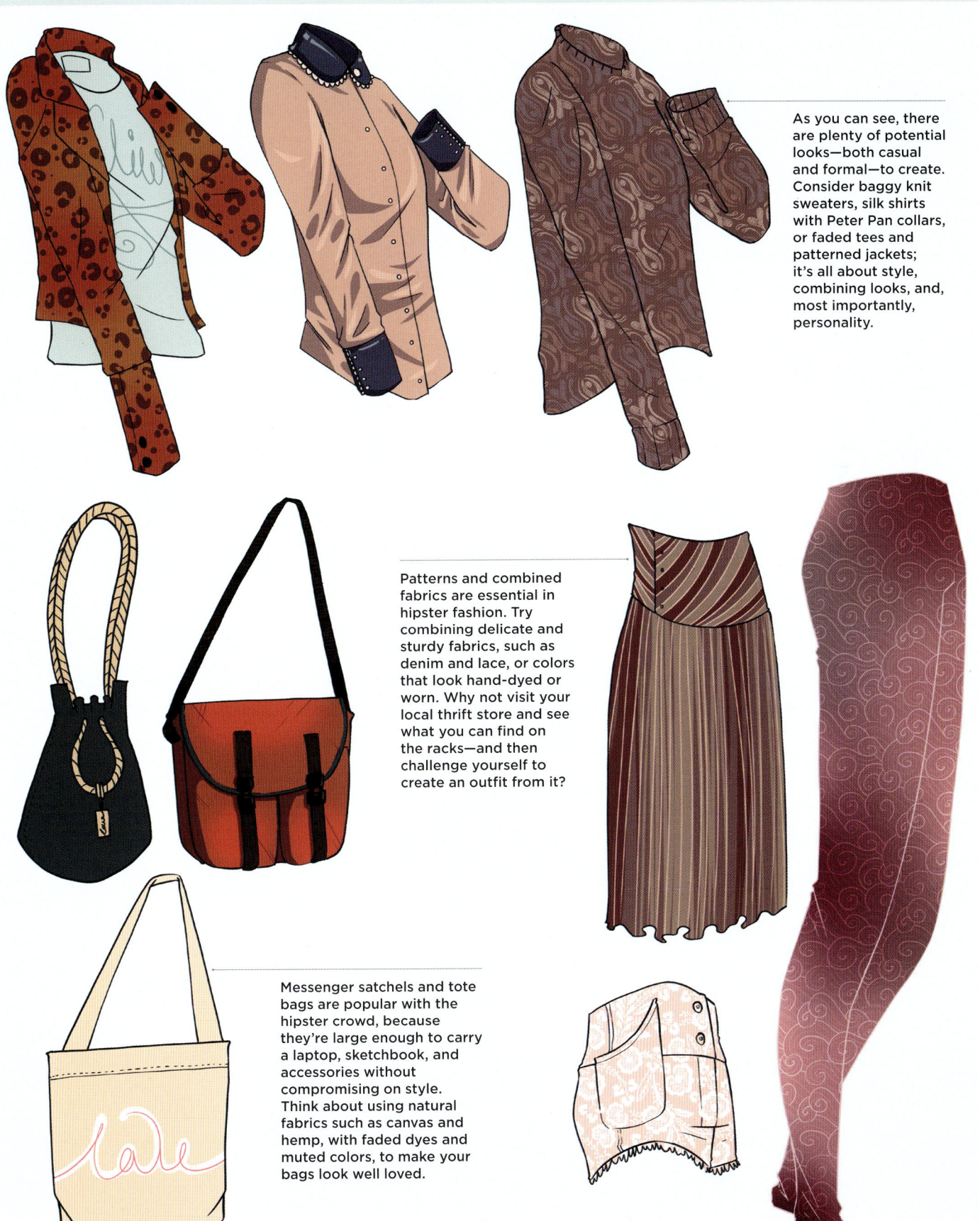

As you can see, there are plenty of potential looks—both casual and formal—to create. Consider baggy knit sweaters, silk shirts with Peter Pan collars, or faded tees and patterned jackets; it's all about style, combining looks, and, most importantly, personality.

Patterns and combined fabrics are essential in hipster fashion. Try combining delicate and sturdy fabrics, such as denim and lace, or colors that look hand-dyed or worn. Why not visit your local thrift store and see what you can find on the racks—and then challenge yourself to create an outfit from it?

Messenger satchels and tote bags are popular with the hipster crowd, because they're large enough to carry a laptop, sketchbook, and accessories without compromising on style. Think about using natural fabrics such as canvas and hemp, with faded dyes and muted colors, to make your bags look well loved.

84 | THE COLLECTIONS

EMO AND SCENE
BY LAURA WATTON-DAVIES

THERE IS BOTH CROSSOVER AND SEPARATION BETWEEN EMO AND SCENE STYLES. EMO HAS ORIGINS IN HARDCORE PUNK, MELODIC MUSICIANSHIP, AND EXPRESSIVE LYRICS. IT IS ASSOCIATED WITH BEING **EMOTIONAL AND SENSITIVE**, WITH **SUBDUED—EVEN MONOCHROMATIC—COLORS**, AND **FEW TEXTURE/PATTERN COMBINATIONS**. IN RESPONSE TO EMO FASHION, SOME TEENAGERS BEGAN WEARING **BRIGHT COLORS AND CARTOON PRINTS**, WHICH DEVELOPED INTO A **PARTY-FOCUSED SCENE FASHION**.

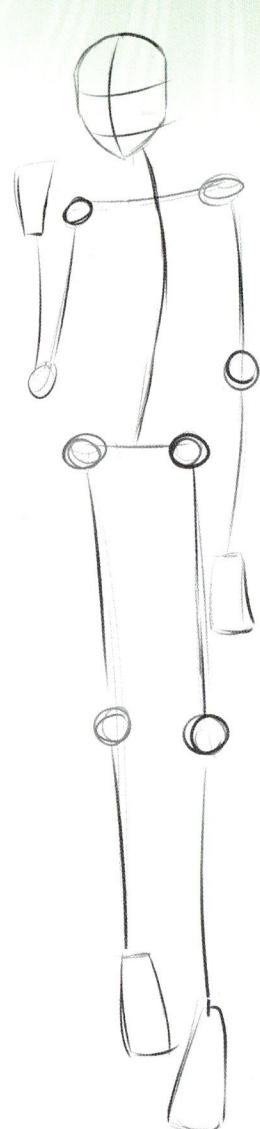
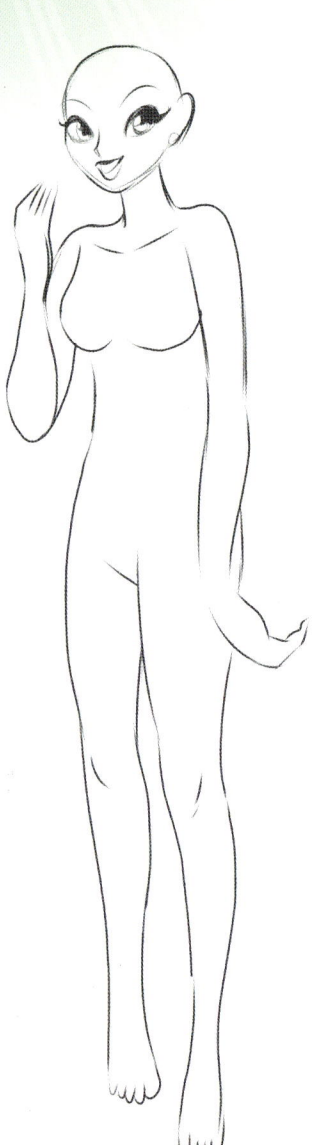
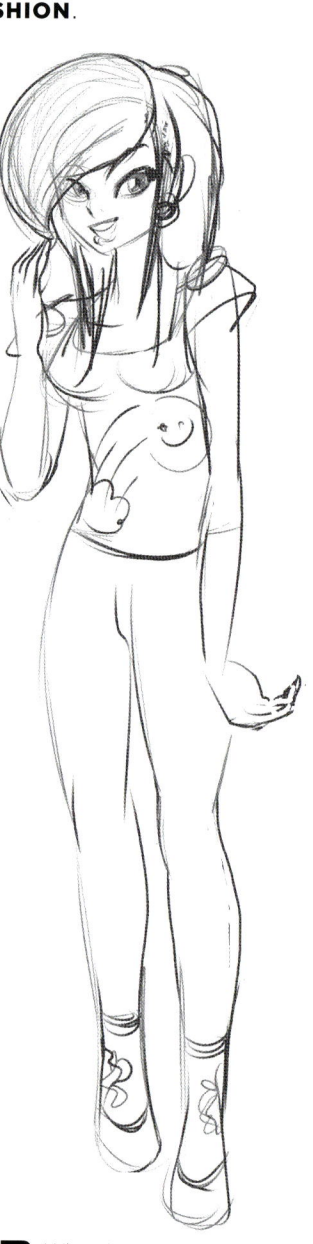
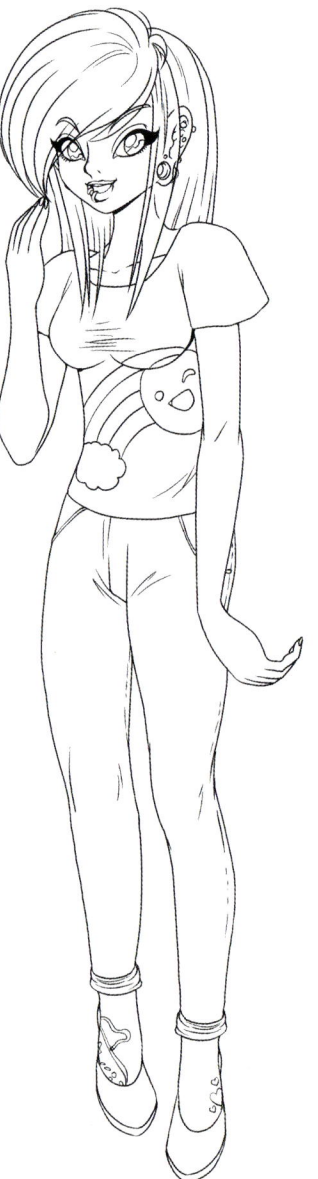

1 Using light pencil lines, draw body joints and lines to physically show the inner emotion that your character is to have.

2 Draw your character's body type over the skeletal sketch. Flesh out limbs and solidify the body.

3 When it comes to Scene hair, it's a case of the bigger, the better! Draw the hair protruding out from the scalp of your character. Sketch clothing and shoes over the body sketch and closely to the body shape, using curved lines and details.

4 Choose one solid line to ink over your pencil work. Small strokes imply creases and texture bumps over knees as well as strands of hair.

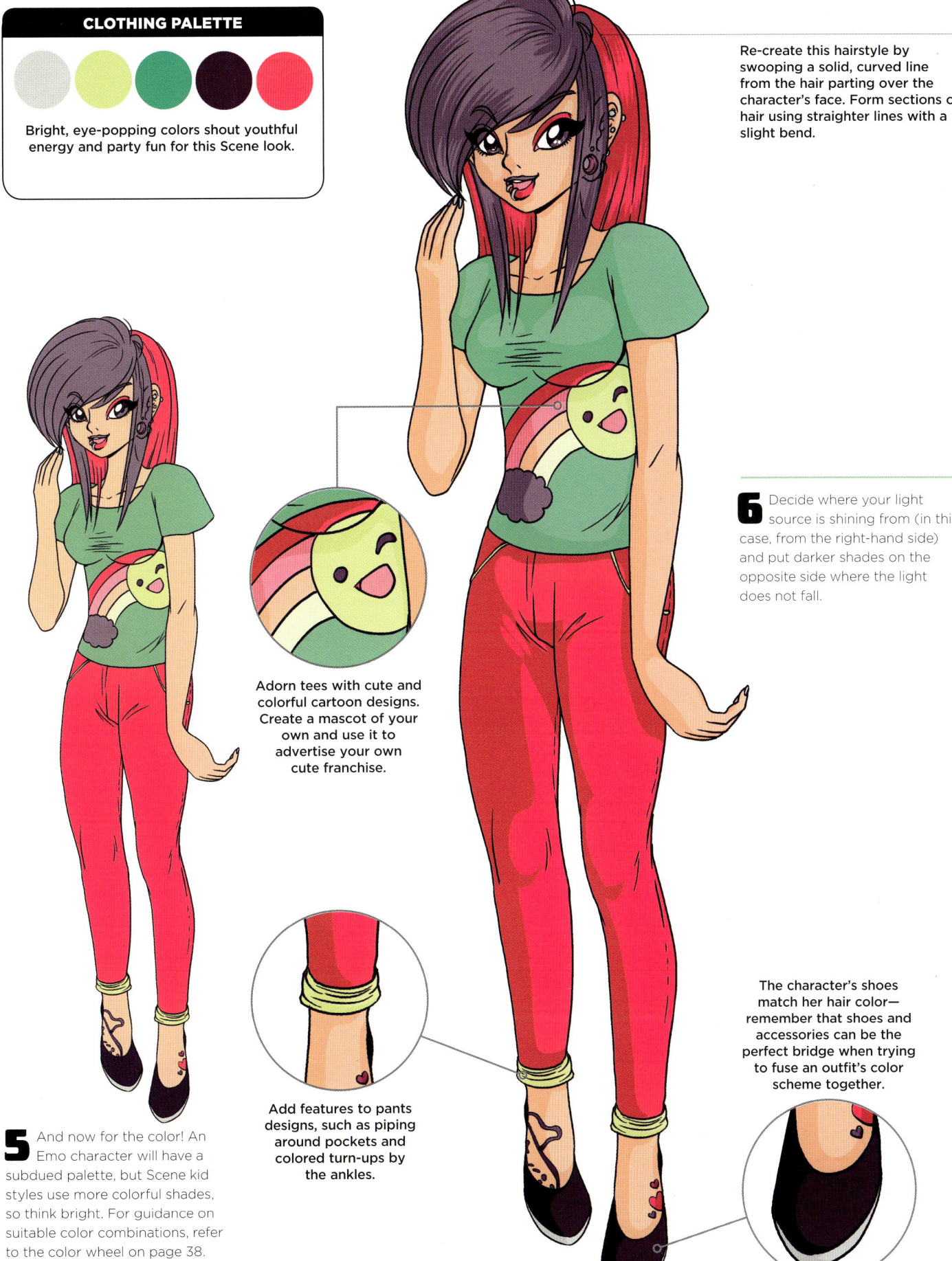

EMO AND SCENE | 85

CLOTHING PALETTE

Bright, eye-popping colors shout youthful energy and party fun for this Scene look.

Re-create this hairstyle by swooping a solid, curved line from the hair parting over the character's face. Form sections of hair using straighter lines with a slight bend.

6 Decide where your light source is shining from (in this case, from the right-hand side) and put darker shades on the opposite side where the light does not fall.

Adorn tees with cute and colorful cartoon designs. Create a mascot of your own and use it to advertise your own cute franchise.

Add features to pants designs, such as piping around pockets and colored turn-ups by the ankles.

The character's shoes match her hair color—remember that shoes and accessories can be the perfect bridge when trying to fuse an outfit's color scheme together.

5 And now for the color! An Emo character will have a subdued palette, but Scene kid styles use more colorful shades, so think bright. For guidance on suitable color combinations, refer to the color wheel on page 38.

86 | THE COLLECTIONS

The Emo and Scene movements share similar silhouettes—slim and skinny fit. None are intended for a particular gender and cross over quite frequently. Skinny layers and flat colors are the focal points. Use color schemes and your character's expressions to convey emotions and whether he or she is part of the Emo (see the figure to the right) or Scene (see the figure near-left) style.

Such big, swooping bangs provide volume and a pompadour silhouette, and cry out for on-theme hair accessories.

Nose, lips, and ears are common piercing areas for Emos; Scene styles lean toward snakebites, septum, gauges, and even cheek piercings.

To draw the skirt, start with the waistband and draw long lines that curve outward slightly to imply volume. The bottom of the skirt is layered with tulle—draw a number of wobbly lines to convey this.

Jewelry is layered and brightly colored. Add a white dot or two for a shiny surface.

Take inspiration from animal print for an outfit's main focus, with an emphasis on an RGB color scheme. The tiger stripe pattern is drawn over the bright leggings with a darker color, layered to create texture.

This Scenester's shoes are ballet-flat pump style and made of leather. The texture is streaked and shiny.

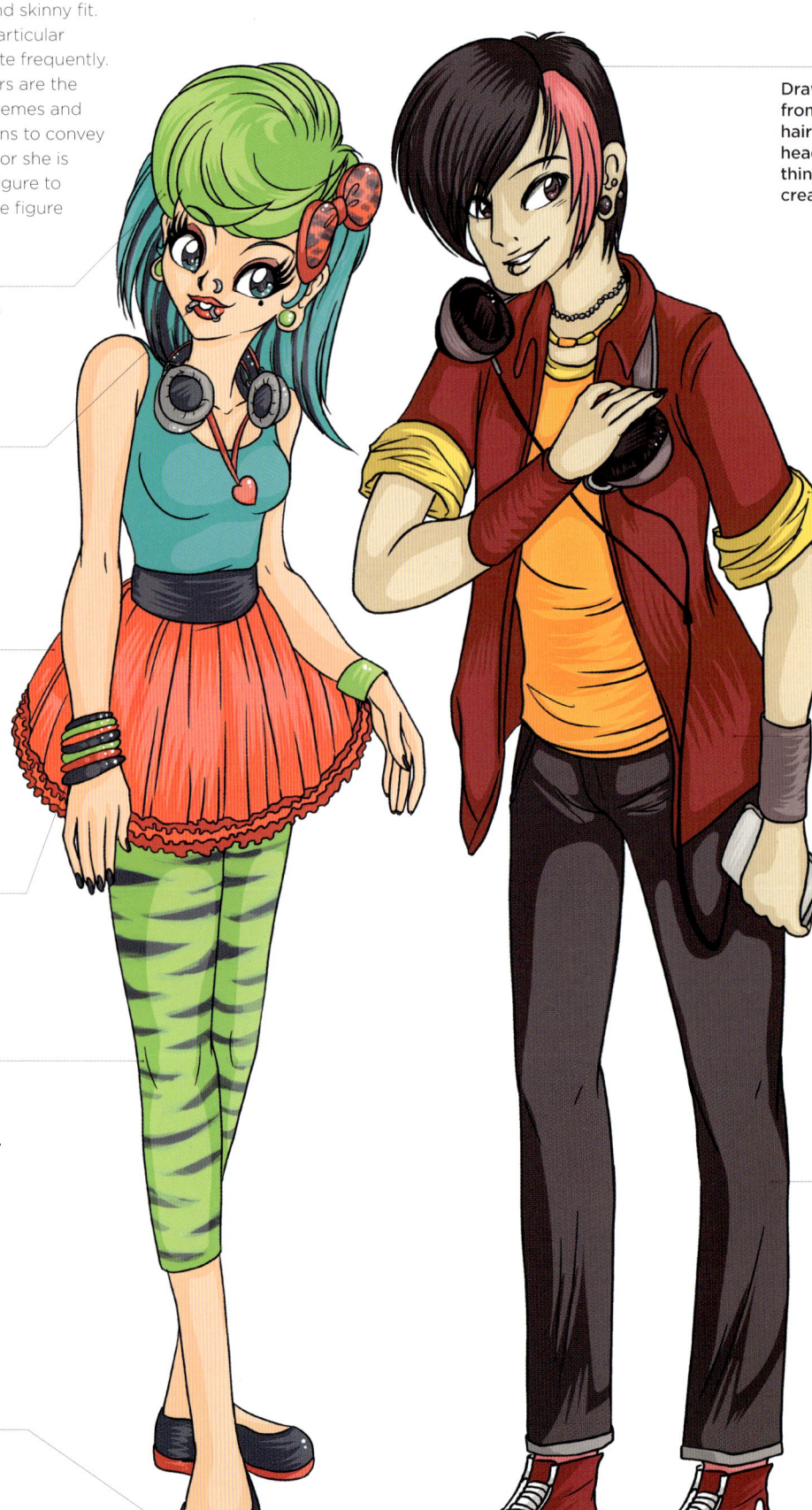

Draw curved, long lines from where the character's hair parts at the top of his head and put down long, thin, curved zigzags to create long bangs.

For casual, rolled-up sleeves, draw lines to make creases.

The textures are generally cotton-like, so you can add a bit of shade using zigzags or plain lines to give some volume.

The jeans are a regular denim gray, which make the overshirt and tee colors pop. This character also wears jewelry subtly, which matches the subdued color scheme.

EMO AND SCENE | 87

ACCESSORIES AND CLOTHING

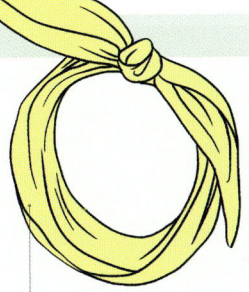

A 1950s-style headband loops around the character's head and knots into a bow at the top. Popular with punk subcultures, this is a classic band. Loose circles denote volume and creased material.

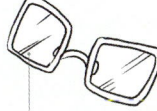

Sunglasses are the ideal accessory for a sensitive soul to use when he or she does not want to talk to anyone. Draw ovals or squares over the eyes, shade, and bridge with a small arch in between the lens frames.

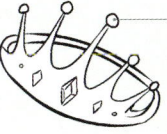

A homage to the late '90s Riot Girl movement, grungy princess fashions have experienced a resurgence with Scene style. Tiaras are easy to draw using curved arches with circular dots on each tip.

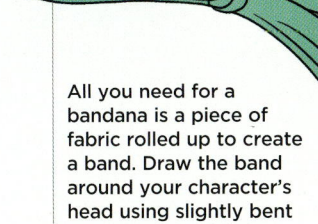

All you need for a bandana is a piece of fabric rolled up to create a band. Draw the band around your character's head using slightly bent lines and extra strokes for creases, leaving enough space for some hair to protrude from it.

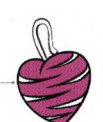 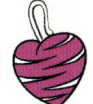

Colorful earrings are playful and punky—geometric shapes like round-cornered stars or hearts are popular.

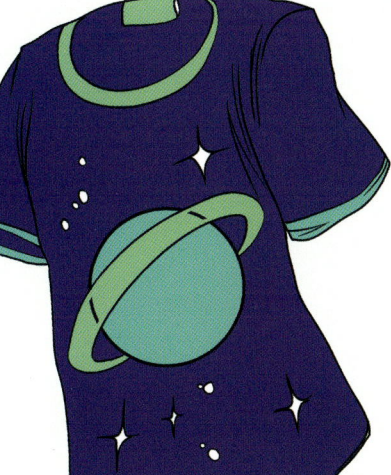

Bright, colorful tees are a staple for any Scenester's wardrobe; cartoon graphics with funny slogans feature frequently.

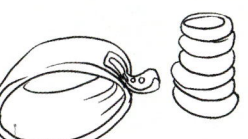

A beanie hat is useful for keeping warm when lining up to get into a gig. This should be loose fitting to be able to fit the hair underneath.

Made of leather or plastic, bangles are a staple part of punk-influenced Emo and Scene fashion. Draw circles around your character's wrists, and layer up to create a mass.

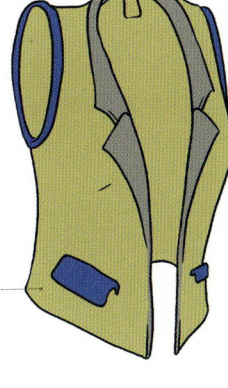

A vest is a stylish addition to a youthful fashion style. Streamlined curves with triangular lapels make this item simple to draw.

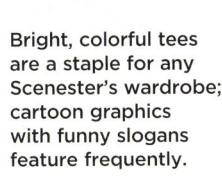

When it comes to skinny jeans, the more rips the better. Draw in the rips using pointed-edged ovals.

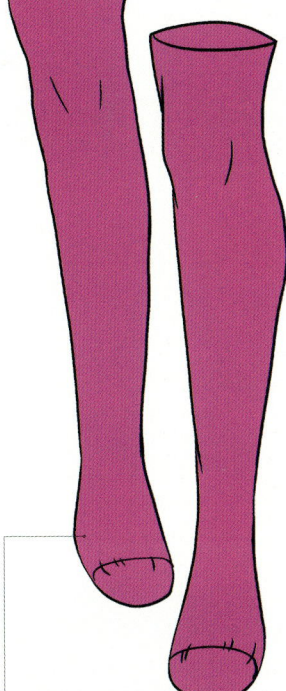

Thigh-high socks worn with skirts or shorts are a very simple shape. If your character is not wearing shoes, don't forget to draw in the sock toe tips and heels, using small lines to show the stitched construction.

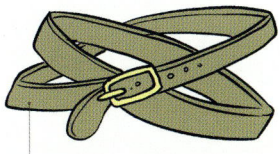

For an extra-long double-wrap belt, draw overlapping ovals, and a rectangle frame for the belt buckle, with a small oval to imply the buckle pin poking through the belt.

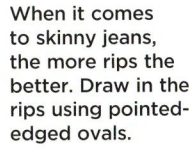
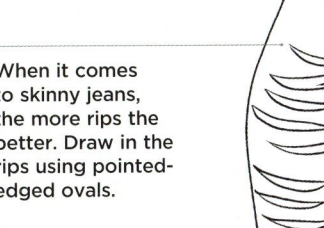

MIAMI BEACH

THE COLLECTIONS

WHAT BETTER WAY TO **WELCOME IN SUMMER** THAN WITH A COLLECTION OF BEACH FASHIONS. THE EPITOME OF THE SUMMER SEASON, BEACHWEAR HAS RAPIDLY EXPANDED FROM BEING JUST ABOUT SWIMSUITS TO ENCOMPASSING DRESSES, SKIRTS, AND EVERYTHING THAT YOU MAY NEED FOR YOUR **ULTIMATE VACATION WARDROBE** SO THAT YOU CAN **HIT THE STREETS STRAIGHT AFTER CHILLING ON THE BEACH**, AND STILL LOOK STYLISH.

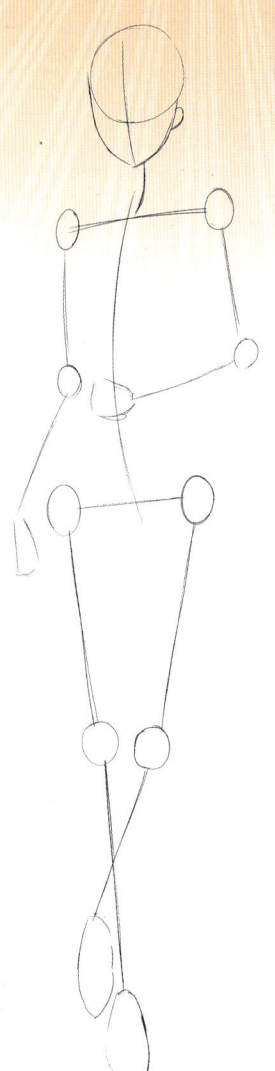 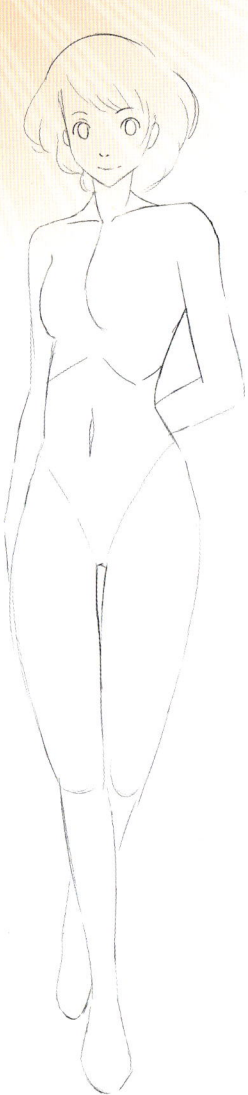 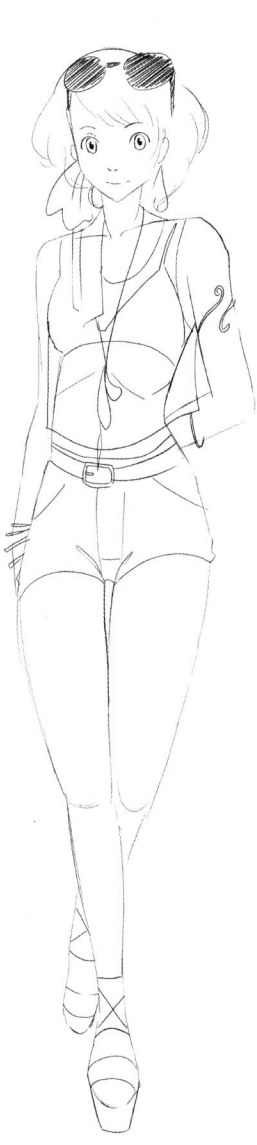 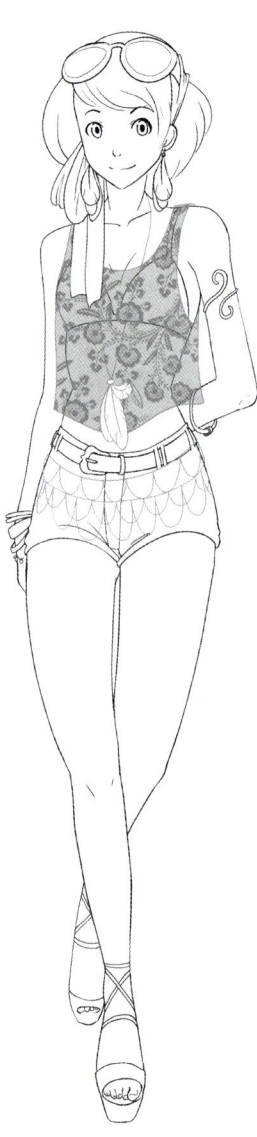

1 Your model should be showing off as much of her outfit as possible, so draw her from front-on. Add some movement with bent joints and a slight curve in her back. In this pose one hand will be hidden behind her back, but sketch this in anyway so that you can make sure everything's in proportion.

2 Block in the rest of your model's body as well as giving her a face and hair. Because she's walking, her hips and shoulders are twisted in different directions. Unlike other collections, where most of the body will be hidden by clothes, you'll be seeing more of your model when she's in beachwear—so spend some extra time making certain that her proportions are right.

3 The most predominant feature of beachwear is loose, usually opaque, shirts or dresses over swimwear. Baggy clothes can be unflattering, so either make them cropped short, so that they still show off the waist and hips, or draw them with a belt or tailored waistline. Don't worry about sketching loosely while you're trying out different ideas; you'll clean it up in the next step.

4 In this step, clean up your sketch and start adding in some clean lines for coloring. This outfit is bohemian, so the model has feathered jewelry and a tribal coin belt, as well as lots of bangles and a headscarf. Don't be too hesitant to combine different styles and looks.

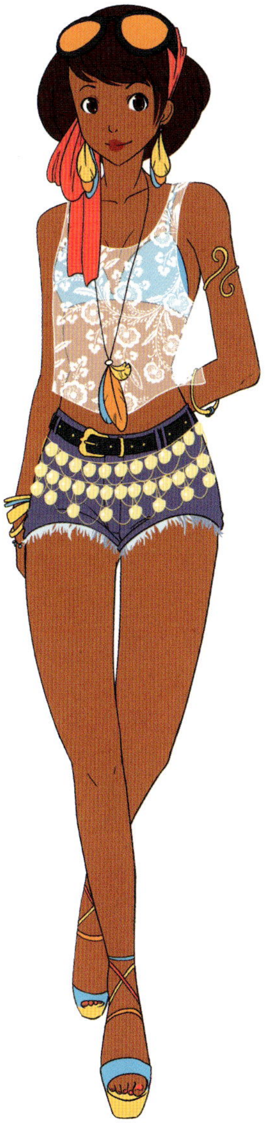

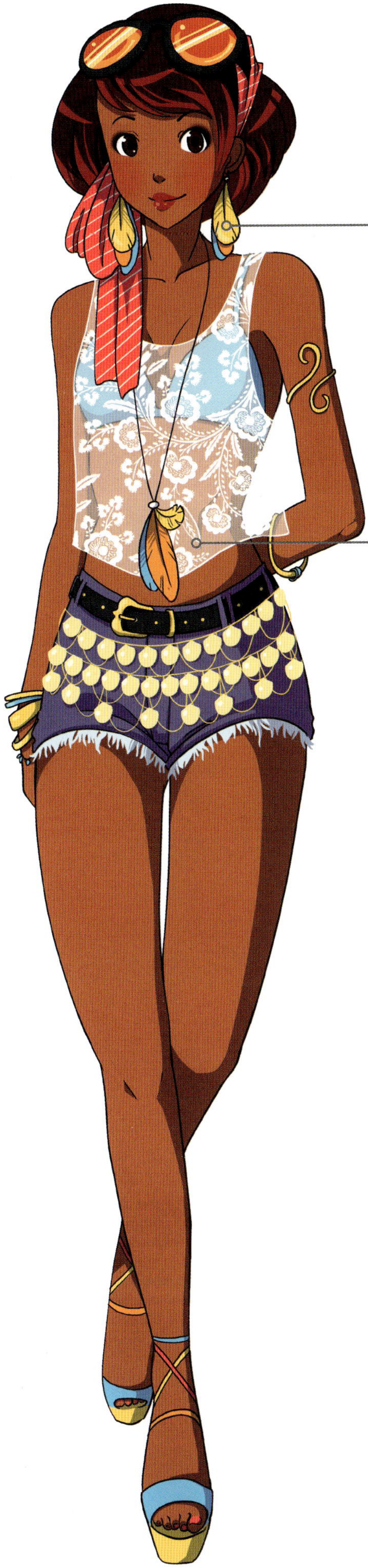

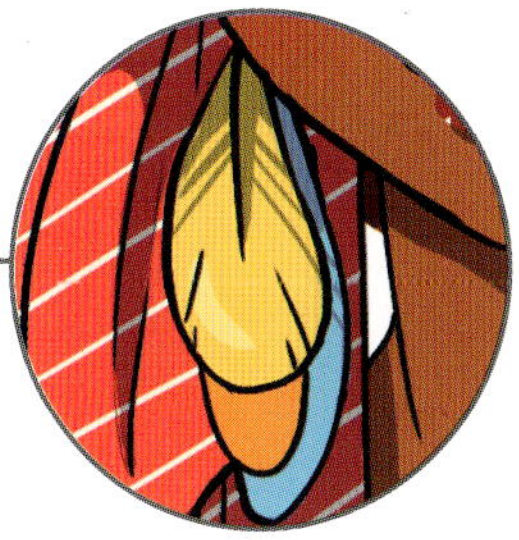

MIAMI BEACH | **89**

Don't be afraid to use lots of bright, bold colors to make your designs extra summery. This design uses three analogous colors (next to each other on the color wheel)—red, orange, and yellow. Adding blue, which complements all three of these colors, helps to balance the design.

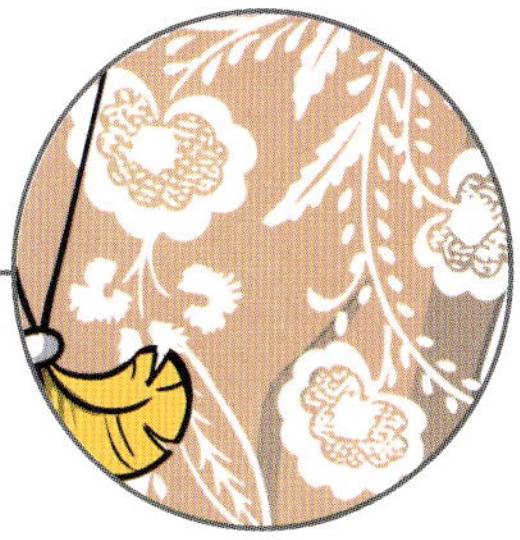

One of the main appeals of the beach is the sun, so make sure that outfits are light and airy enough to keep your models cool. Lace garments preserve modesty while still being attractive, and the pattern of the lace gives a delicate, feminine touch.

6 Using shading and bold patterns, add in any final details that will really make the outfit stand out on the catwalk. Give your model a healthy glow in her cheeks, and don't forget to add light reflections in any metal or glass, such as her sunglasses and belts.

5 Using the color scheme that you decided on earlier, block in colors to make your model bright and summery. Blue and gold are a great combo since not only are they complementary colors, but they're also inspired by the sea, which is exactly where your model will be showing off her outfit.

CLOTHING PALETTE

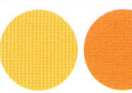

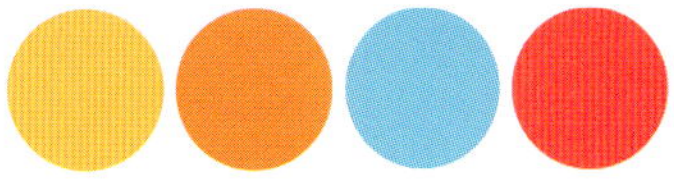

Since beachwear is all about summer, the sun, and the sea, it's got to be colorful! Jewel colors and gold are popular choices—take inspiration from tropical birds, the beach, and mocktails. This outfit uses lots of nice hot colors: vibrant yellows, oranges, and reds. Little pops of blue make the whole ensemble more balanced.

THE COLLECTIONS

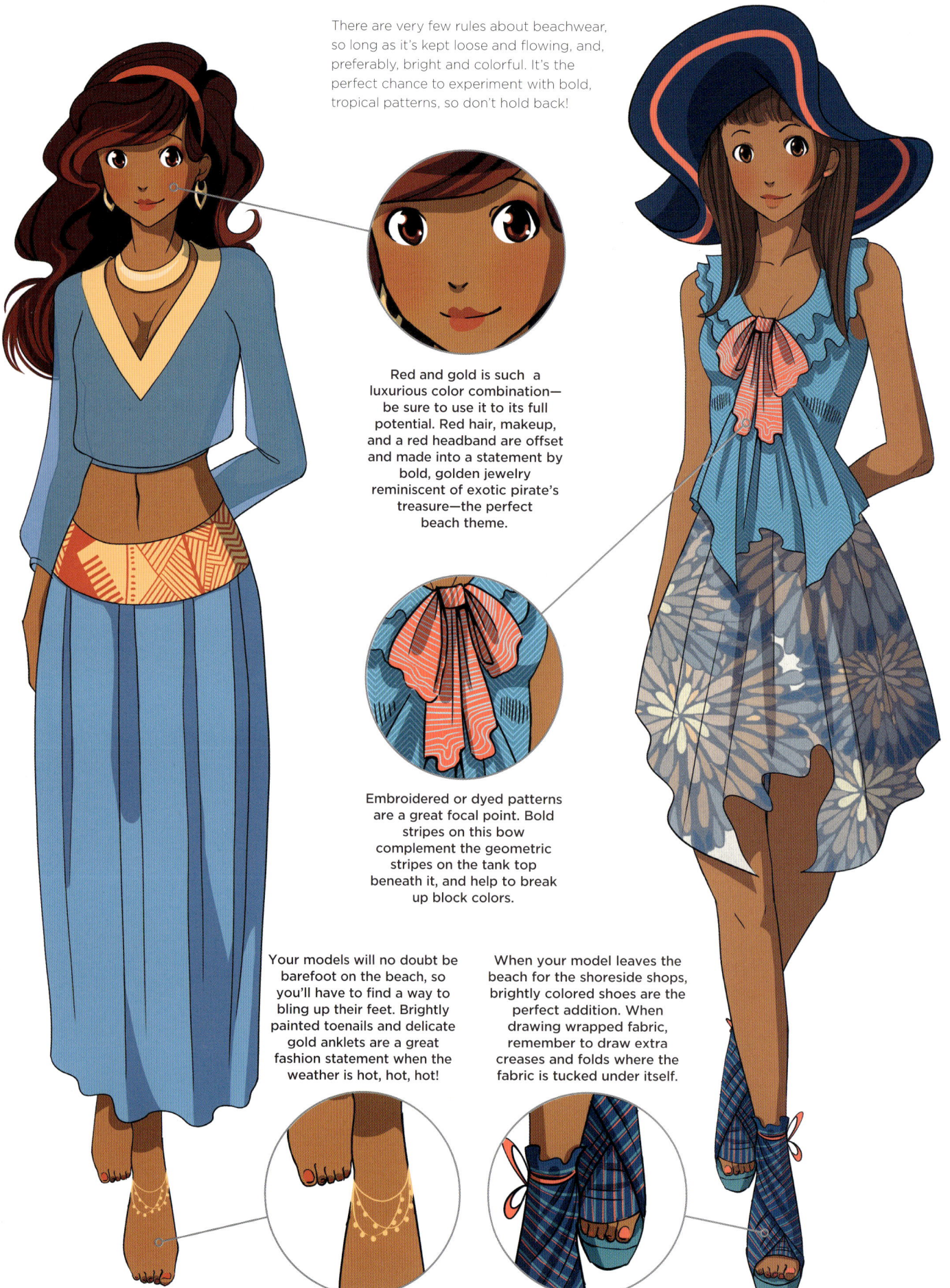

There are very few rules about beachwear, so long as it's kept loose and flowing, and, preferably, bright and colorful. It's the perfect chance to experiment with bold, tropical patterns, so don't hold back!

Red and gold is such a luxurious color combination—be sure to use it to its full potential. Red hair, makeup, and a red headband are offset and made into a statement by bold, golden jewelry reminiscent of exotic pirate's treasure—the perfect beach theme.

Embroidered or dyed patterns are a great focal point. Bold stripes on this bow complement the geometric stripes on the tank top beneath it, and help to break up block colors.

Your models will no doubt be barefoot on the beach, so you'll have to find a way to bling up their feet. Brightly painted toenails and delicate gold anklets are a great fashion statement when the weather is hot, hot, hot!

When your model leaves the beach for the shoreside shops, brightly colored shoes are the perfect addition. When drawing wrapped fabric, remember to draw extra creases and folds where the fabric is tucked under itself.

MIAMI BEACH | **91**

ACCESSORIES AND CLOTHING

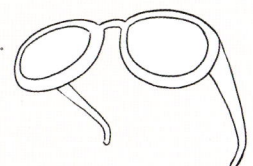

Since your model will be spending her time on the beach, you'll need to know how to add some sunny reflections in her glasses.

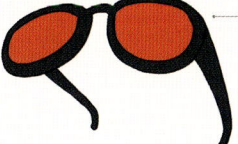

1 Block in your colors first—some tinted lenses will really make her stand out.

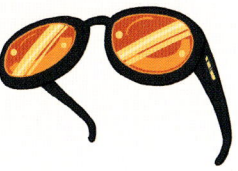

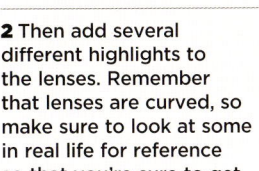

2 Then add several different highlights to the lenses. Remember that lenses are curved, so make sure to look at some in real life for reference so that you're sure to get it right.

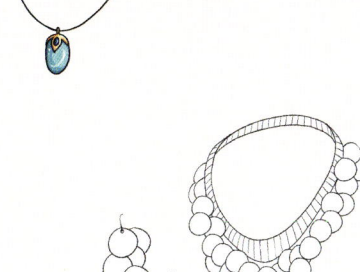

Beachwear is usually inspired by one of two influences: a boho look, inspired by natural materials such as feathers, shells, and wood, and a pirate-inspired look, which features lots of beaten gold or brass and heavy metallic jewelry. Both are perfect for the beach. Decide which one you'd like to focus on and design your whole outfit around it.

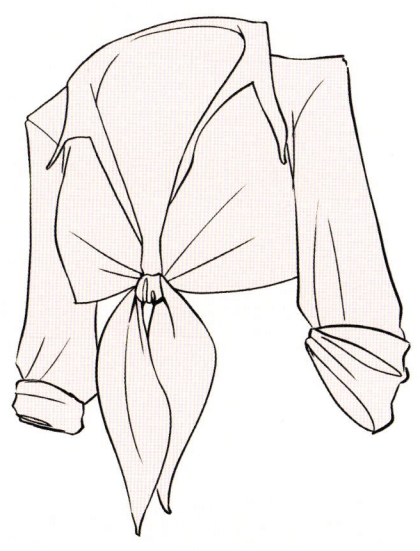
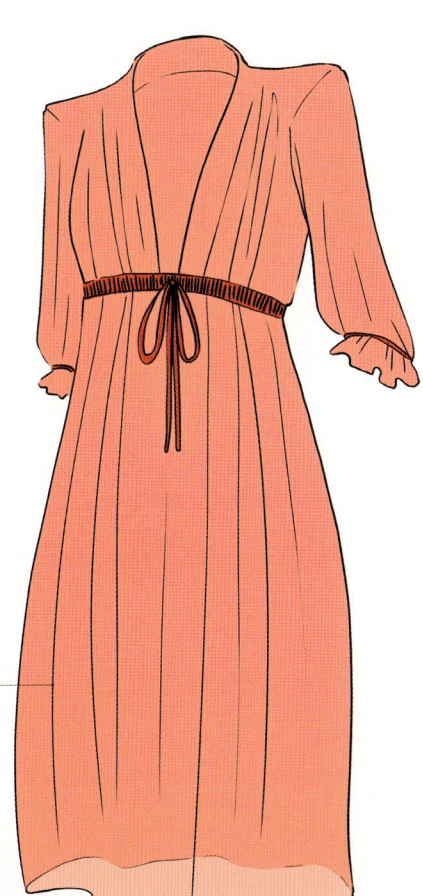
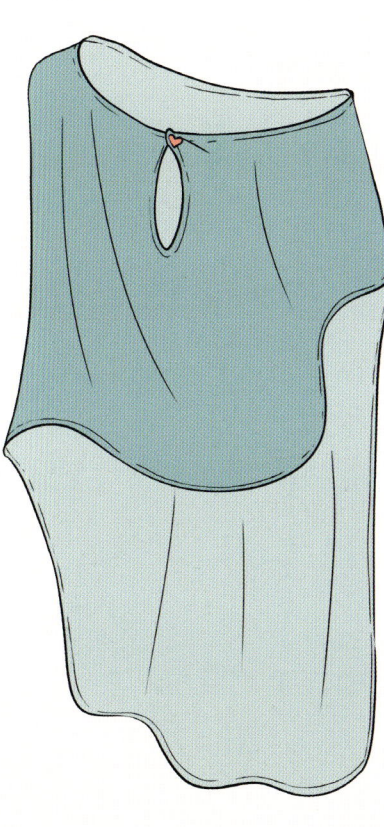

Just because your model is covering up doesn't mean that she can't look stylish at the same time. Cover her swimwear with a semi-opaque shrug, or with a dress that's cut low enough to show off the design of her swimsuit. Alternately, try dressing her in a man's shirt that's tied up at the front to make it more flattering. There are lots of options!

VINTAGE COLLECTION

THE MOST POPULAR FORM OF VINTAGE FASHION IS LATE '40S AND '50S, OR THE **POST-WAR ERA**: IT'S NOT UNCOMMON TO HEAR THE TERM VINTAGE AS REFERRING TO THIS ERA SPECIFICALLY. DURING THIS TIME THE WORLD WAS RECOVERING FROM WARTIME RATIONING ON CLOTHING, SO YOUNG PEOPLE WHO HAD ONLY KNOWN RATIONED FABRICS AND DRAB WARTIME FASHIONS WERE ALLOWED TO SPLASH OUT IN **BRIGHT COLORS, EXTRAVAGANT DRESSES, AND ELABORATE OUTFITS**. WITH THE INVENTION OF **ROCK AND ROLL**, FASHION BECAME ALL ABOUT **CLOTHES THAT COULD BE DANCED IN**—SWING DRESSES, CROP PANTS, AND SIMPLE SWEATERS AND TEES BECAME POPULAR.

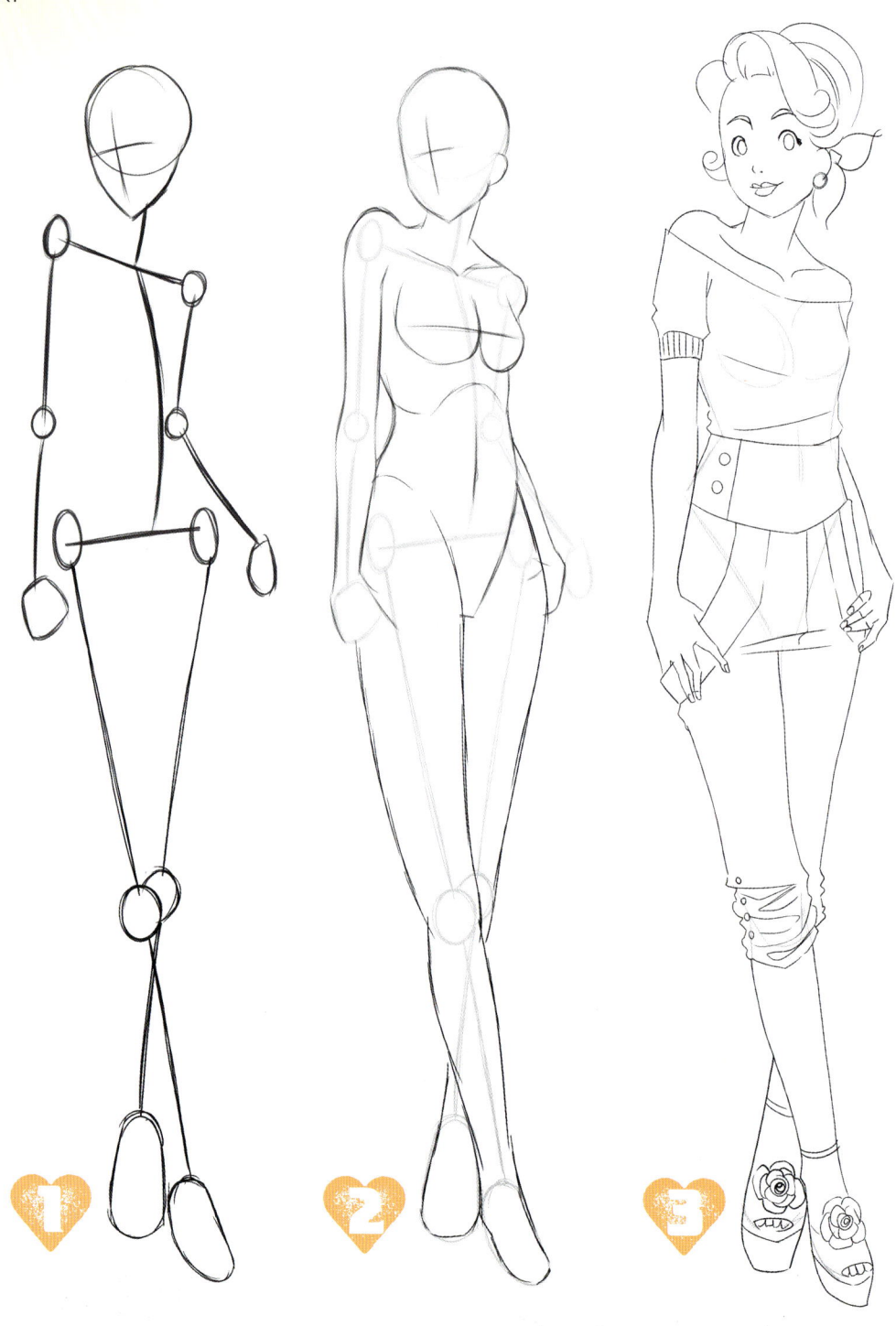

1 Begin sketching out your figure by using a very basic skeleton to work out your model's pose. Curving the spine will add a sense of movement, as will bending the knees and elbows. Remember to keep it looking natural.

2 Flesh out your figure over the skeleton that you've drawn. Think of your sketch as your model's bones—you don't have to get too anatomical, but knowing where the body's muscles are will help you get your figure looking right and ready to dress.

3 Swing dresses are the most famous piece of vintage fashion, but try thinking creatively about your collection. Typically, male fashion, such as pants and sweaters, became popular for ladies around this time. Do some research to help yourself come up with ideas. It's a perfect excuse to watch some old movies.

VINTAGE COLLECTION | 93

4 All of your sketches up until this point should have been rough and loose, so now's your chance to neaten up your drawing. Using your sketch as a base, neaten up the line work and add in important details, such as creases, ruffles, and elasticized hems, and elaborate on previous details, such as hairstyle and any decorations on the shoes.

5 With your figure drawn up neatly, add in some colors. Using plain blocks of color, work out what sort of scheme you want to use. This outfit is very summery, so we'll be going with light blues and strong yellows. Red lipstick was a makeup staple in this era, and you can use the same color for the model's finger- and toenails.

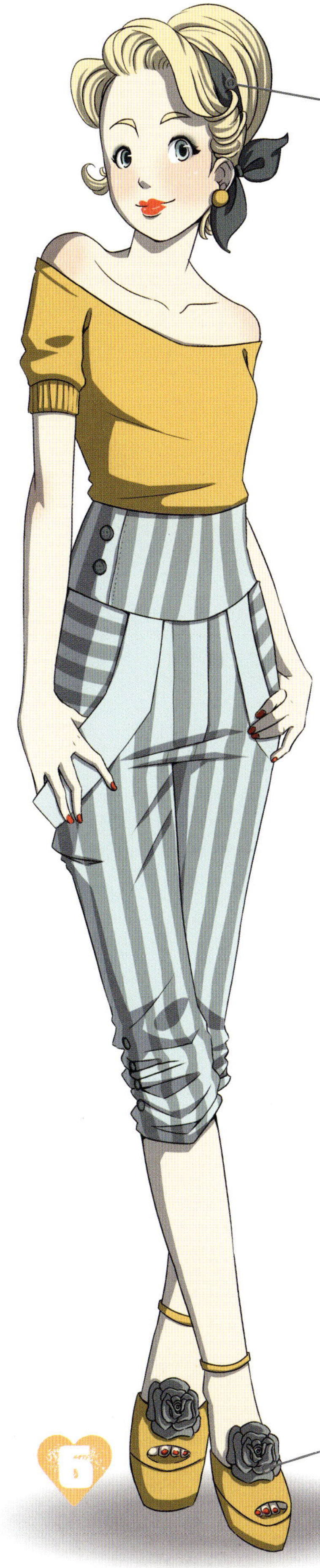

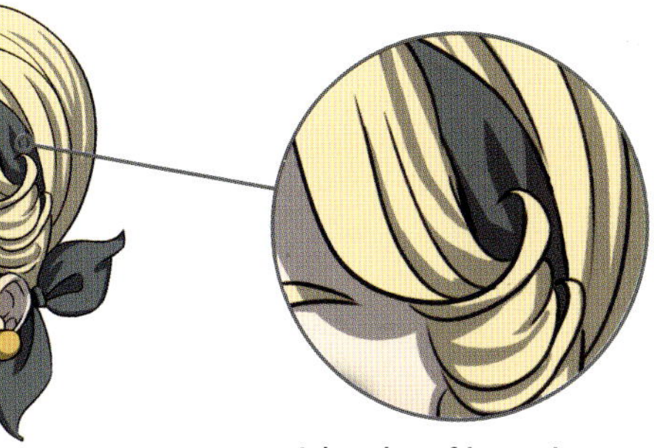

A headscarf is not just a practical way of keeping hair out of the face, but it is a key fashion statement too. A dusky blue complements the model's blonde hair and her yellow earrings.

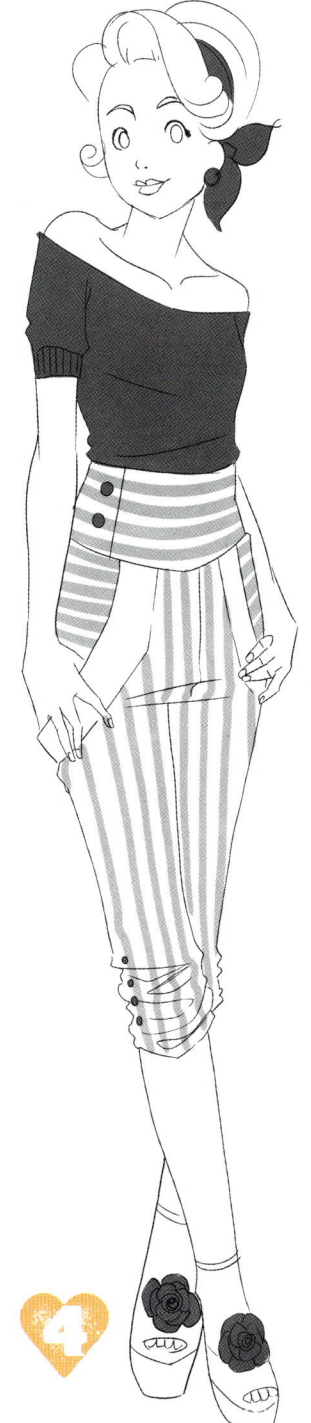

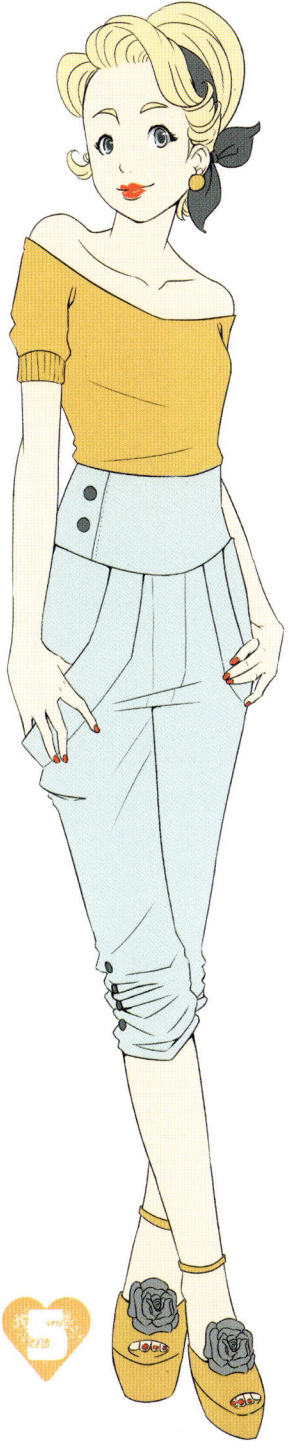

6 To finish off your model, add in last-minute patterns, such as the stripes on the pants, and extra details, such as makeup and a light source. Don't use too much shading, or your image will look dark and clothing details may be lost. A light source should help make your designs look more realistic and your artwork more interesting.

Original vintage shoes can sometimes be quite chunky and plain, so adding an area of extra detail, such as the roses on the front of this pair of heels, can help to break up these areas.

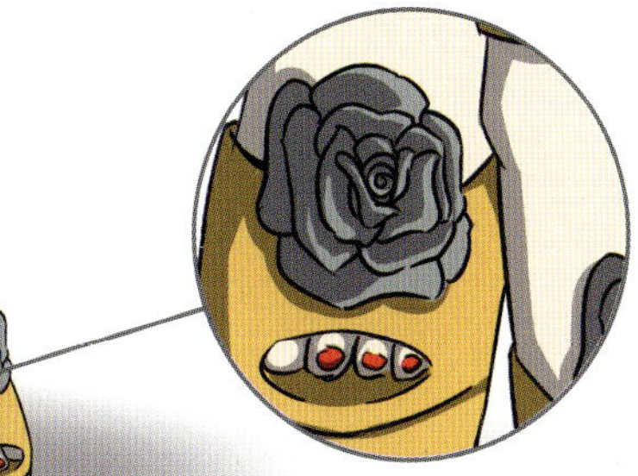

94 | THE COLLECTIONS

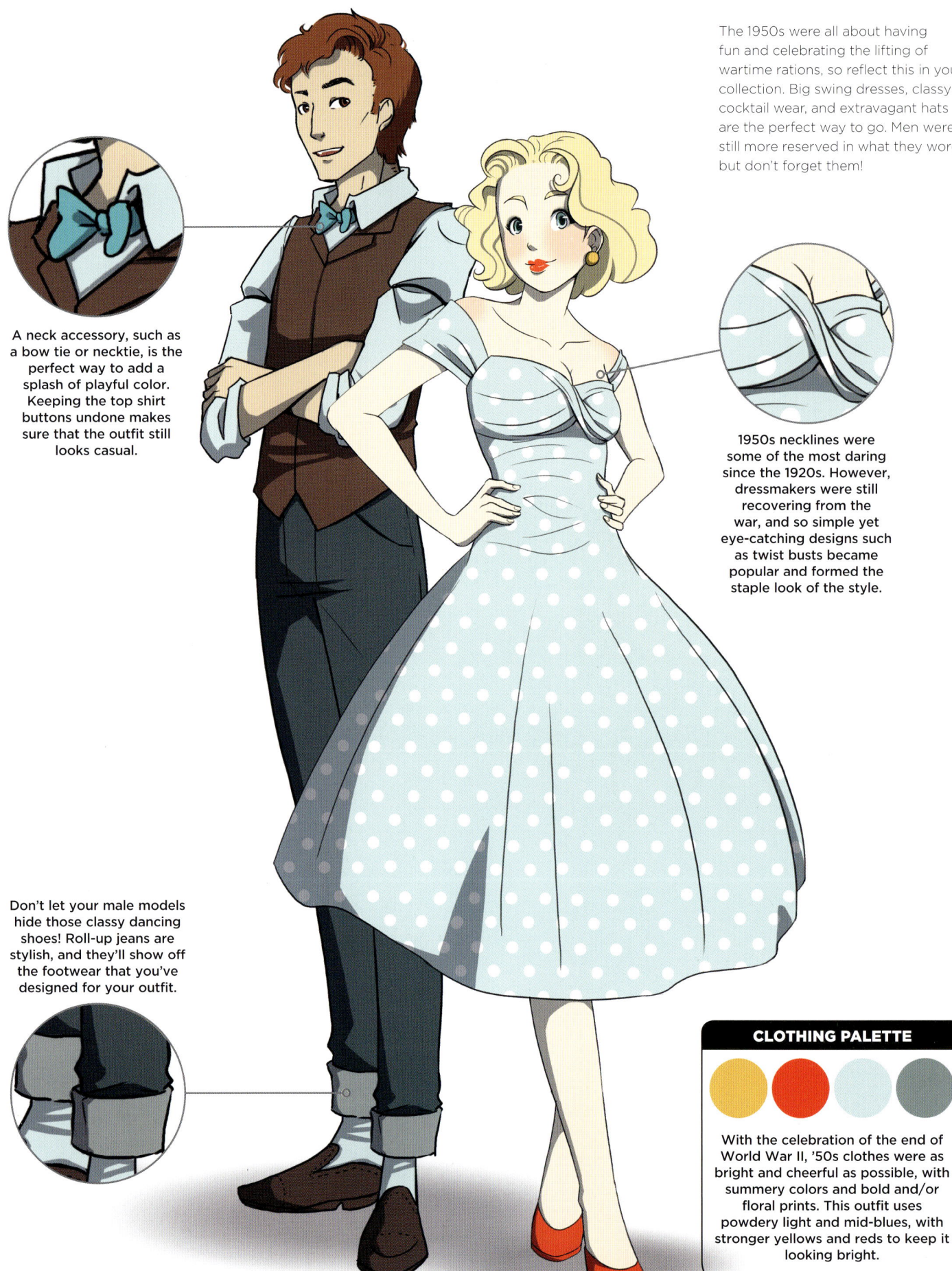

A neck accessory, such as a bow tie or necktie, is the perfect way to add a splash of playful color. Keeping the top shirt buttons undone makes sure that the outfit still looks casual.

Don't let your male models hide those classy dancing shoes! Roll-up jeans are stylish, and they'll show off the footwear that you've designed for your outfit.

The 1950s were all about having fun and celebrating the lifting of wartime rations, so reflect this in your collection. Big swing dresses, classy cocktail wear, and extravagant hats are the perfect way to go. Men were still more reserved in what they wore, but don't forget them!

1950s necklines were some of the most daring since the 1920s. However, dressmakers were still recovering from the war, and so simple yet eye-catching designs such as twist busts became popular and formed the staple look of the style.

CLOTHING PALETTE

With the celebration of the end of World War II, '50s clothes were as bright and cheerful as possible, with summery colors and bold and/or floral prints. This outfit uses powdery light and mid-blues, with stronger yellows and reds to keep it looking bright.

VINTAGE COLLECTION | 95

ACCESSORIES AND CLOTHING

The '50s really were the era of self-expression, especially for women, and there was a huge boom in terms of clothing available. Women could look chic and fashionable even in the office, and especially when going out in the evening. For inspiration, look at the kind of dresses that starlets and celebrities of that era were wearing.

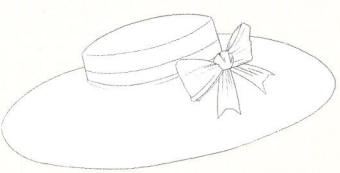
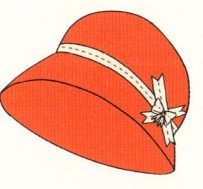
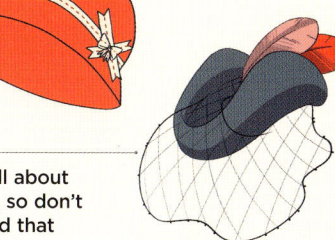

Fashion in this era was all about looking glam and stylish, so don't forget a stylish hat to add that bit of extra wow factor. Use bows, feathers, and veils to make your designs unique—they also provide an opportunity to add an extra pop of color to the outfit.

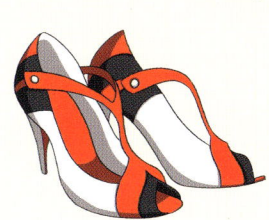
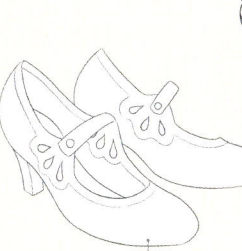

The key to being a dapper '50s gent was to look smart at all times, so don't neglect your model's shoes. Try looking at brogues or Oxford shoes for ideas, as these were smart, popular pieces of footwear for both the office and dancing alike.

As with everything else, everyday shoes received a makeover in the late '40s and '50s. Most still had quite low and thick, practical heels, but evening shoes were much more elegant—play around with styles and patterns to accentuate the rest of your outfit.

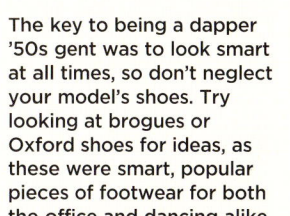
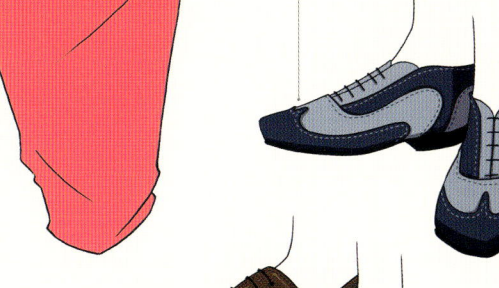
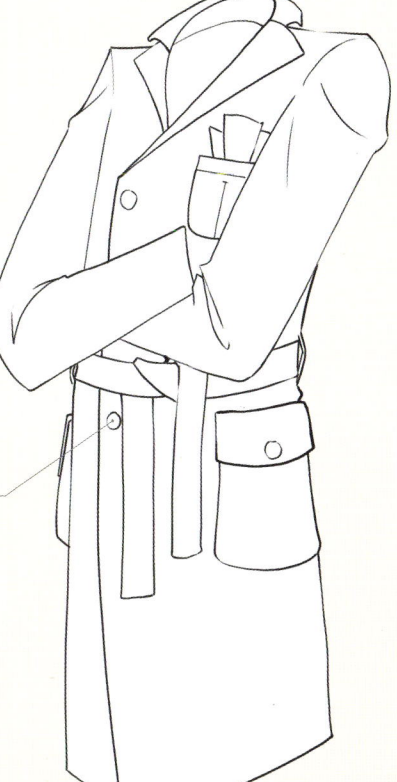

Men's hats were a little more conservative than the ladies', but still a key element of their outfits. Whether the flat, ivy cap (more commonly called a "Ben Hogan" after the golfer who made it fashionable) or the porkpie hat made popular by zoot suiters and bankers, hats can easily be customized and made more colorful to match the wearer's clothes that day.

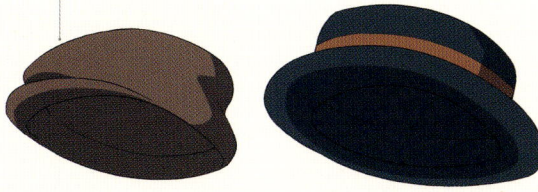

Women certainly benefitted from the freedom of the '50s, but that didn't mean that men couldn't look stylish too. It wasn't uncommon for them to wear the heavy, thick coats from the war era, but to jazz them up with colored, patterned handkerchiefs and/or bright, shiny buttons.

DOLLY KEI

A JAPANESE FASHION MOVEMENT HEAVILY INFLUENCED BY **EUROPEAN FAIRYTALES**, DOLLY KEI IS ALSO HEAVILY STYLED ON **SLAVIC FOLKLORE, ROMANY GYPSY FASHION, AND GOTHIC INFLUENCES**. IT IS A TYPICAL CASE OF "MORE IS MORE"—IT'S ALL ABOUT **DARK, RICH COLORS, HEAVILY PATTERNED FABRICS, AND MIXED TEXTURES**. IT IS NOT UNCOMMON TO SEE **HEAVY FABRICS** SUCH AS FUR AND VELVET MIXED WITH LACE AND **DELICATE EMBROIDERY**, AND THE LOOK IS USUALLY ACCESSORIZED WITH **DOLL PARTS, RELIGIOUS SYMBOLS, OR EVEN BONES**.

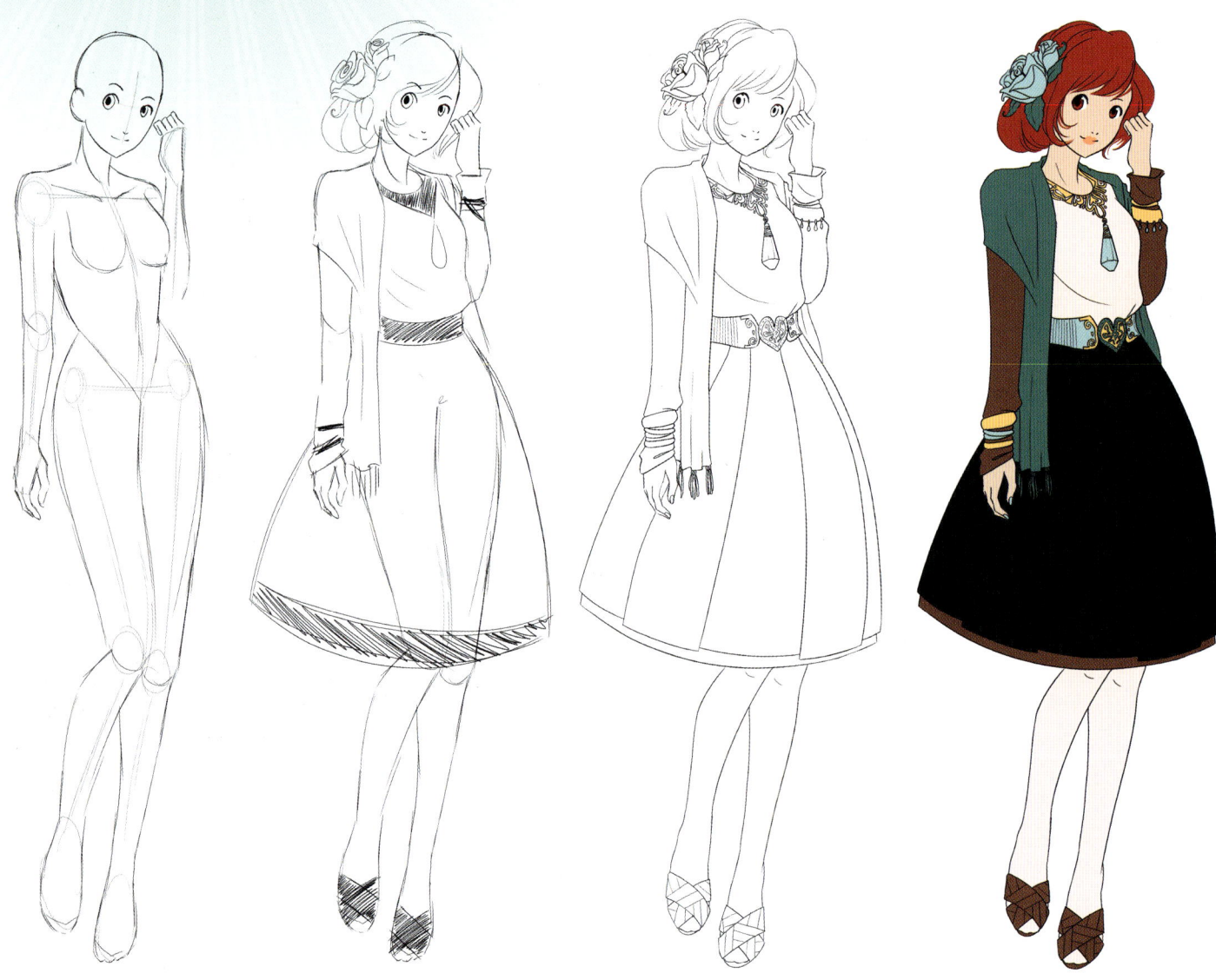

1 As always, sketch out your figure before you start to think of clothes. It's important to get the proportions right now, so that you don't have to change things later on.

2 Over your rough sketch, draw in the basic shapes of your outfit. Think of where the clothes puff out and where they're pulled in close to the figure—baggy clothes will look flattering so long as they tuck in at key points, such as the waist and wrists. Think about your model's hair and how to style it to match the fashion.

3 Now that you've got everything sketched in, neaten up your lines and begin to add details. Dolly Kei is all about small details and intricate accessories. This model has an ornate belt and necklace, as well as tassels on her scarf and roses in her hair, to add texture and detail.

4 Before you start worrying about clothing textures, think about which colors to use first. This outfit could come out looking very dark if you're not careful, but by adding a pale pink shirt and tights, as well as small areas of intense brights to the belt and other accessories, the outfit is lightened while retaining that Dolly Kei look.

DOLLY KEI | 97

ACCESSORIES AND CLOTHING

5 Now we get to the fun part! Go wild with adding some textures—most Dolly Kei fashion is based on Eastern European styles, so try looking at Slavic embroidery, gypsy clothing, and Russian artwork for inspiration.

A versatile accessory like a scarf is a perfect addition to a layered outfit. Not only can it be knotted at the neck or worn as a shawl, but it can also double as a belt, or be tied around a bag strap as a feature piece.

Most Dolly Kei clothing looks as though it was picked up in an antiques store, so try looking at some vintage bags for inspiration. Bags and other accessories are a great place to add fresh colors and textures, while creating a focus point on a model.

Since Dolly Kei is based on European folklore, try looking at traditional folk patterns to inspire your extra details. You don't have to copy designs exactly, but using their main elements will add an authentic element to your designs.

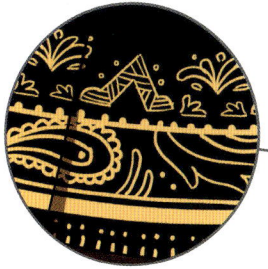

CLOTHING PALETTE

So far as color palettes are concerned, there are two styles of Dolly Kei: one focuses on light, airy creams and pastels; the other uses deep, jewel-like colors and dark blues, browns, or blacks. For this outfit, rich blues and browns form the base of the design, with little sections of turquoise and gold to make it stand out.

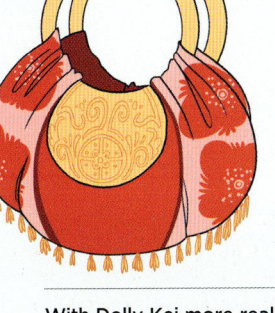

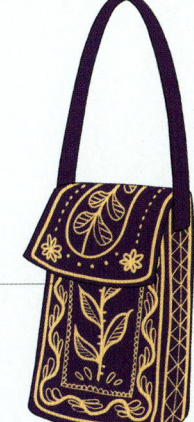

With Dolly Kei more really is better, so don't hold back with textures, colors, and layers. Throw together three or more different colors, look at balancing out rich, jewel colors with browns and plums, and go wild with mixing fabrics such as lace trims and velvet waistbands.

KIMONO STREET STYLE

THE KIMONO IS A **TRADITIONAL JAPANESE ROBE** THAT IS STILL WORN BY WOMEN DURING **FORMAL EVENTS** OR **CEREMONIES**. THOUGH TRADITIONALLY MADE OF HEAVY SILK AND WORN IN A VERY SPECIFIC WAY, MORE RECENTLY ITS STYLE HAS BEEN UPDATED AND REDESIGNED INTO GARMENTS SUITABLE FOR **EVERYDAY WEAR**, BOTH IN JAPAN AND IN THE WEST.

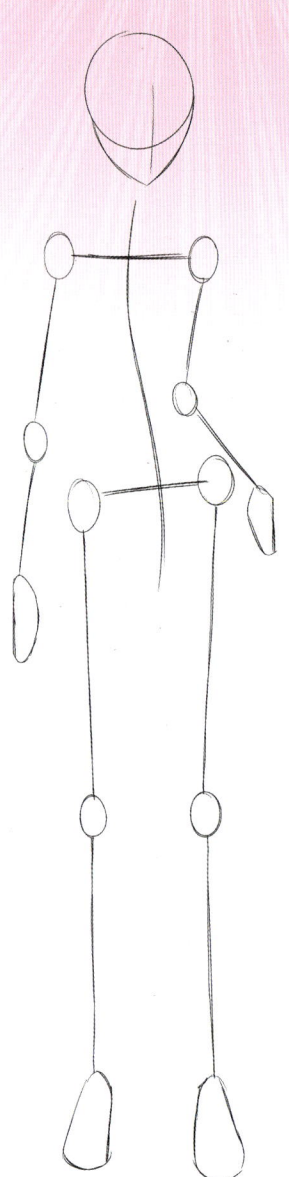 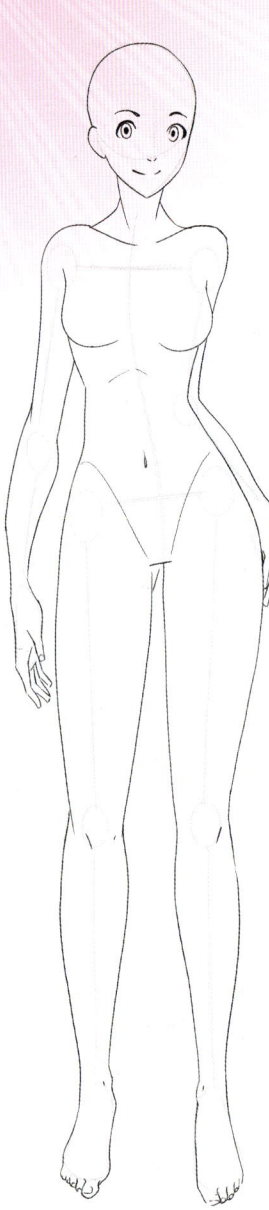 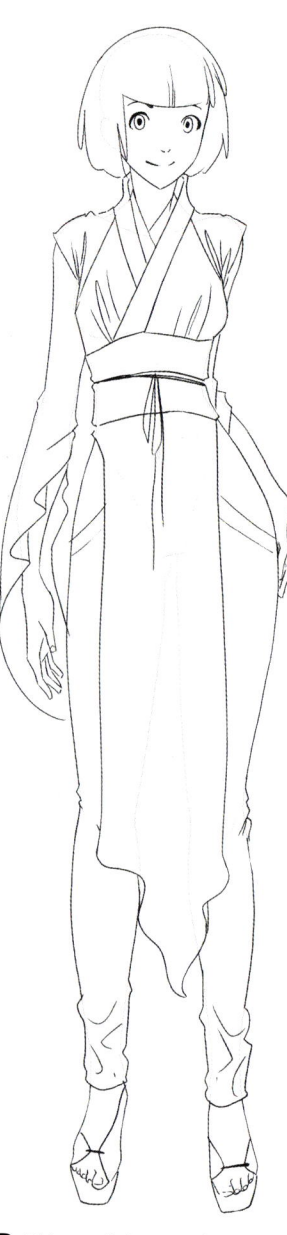 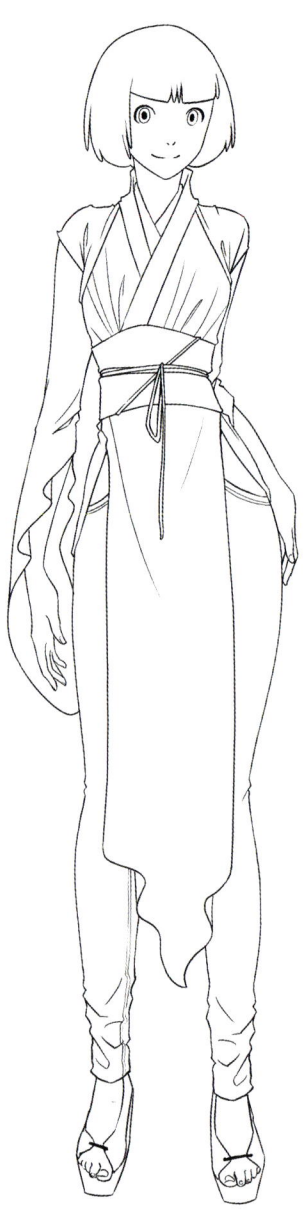

1 Start your sketch with a basic skeleton. This will help you work out how your model is standing—by having the shoulders and hips slightly tilted toward each other, your model will appear more natural and comfortable.

2 Here you can see how drawing the skeleton first has helped make the second sketch look more natural. Even though the majority of the model's figure will be covered by her outfit, drawing it in will make sure that the clothes sit properly on her.

3 This outfit is a modern interpretation of the kimono, so it combines the traditional kimono robe with fashionable jeans and a pair of heels. Substituting a lighter fabric for the heavy silk means the base of the robe and the sleeves have a loose, airy ruffle. The model's hair reflects a traditional style worn by Japanese women.

4 Cleaning up the sketch helps to make subtle details more obvious, such as the ruffles in the sleeves and the detailing in the jeans. Extra creases and folds in the kimono top help to show it as a thinner fabric, and thicker creases around the ankles show that this fabric is denim.

KIMONO STREET STYLE | 99

There are many intricate and detailed traditional Japanese hairstyles that can be used to enhance your collections. However, this model's outfit already stands out easily on its own, so a simpler hairstyle complements, rather than competes with, the look.

CLOTHING PALETTE

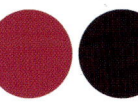 

Kimonos are traditionally made from heavy hand-dyed and embroidered silks, and though a lot of modern replicas are made of lighter fabrics, the rich colors of the originals are often replicated to keep the traditional look. This outfit uses deep, jewel purples, with gold as a complementary hue.

Traditionally, the obi is the sash worn over a kimono. Women's obis are traditionally thicker than men's, and, in a fashion design, they're the perfect place for a flash of color or pattern.

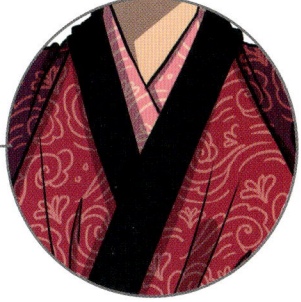

The layered neckline of a kimono is one of its most recognizable details. Usually, two or three garments are worn underneath it to create extra layers—and these are a great place to add complementary colors or patterned fabrics.

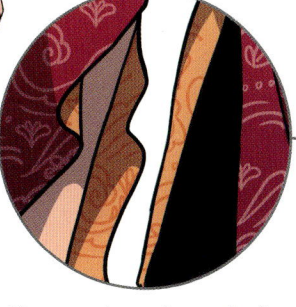

The complementary color to purple is yellow, or in this case gold. By placing areas of gold in the garment—for example, the inner lining or on the obi—you'll be bringing out the colors of the purple and making your clothes really memorable.

Adding a darker gradient to the front of the robe helps make the garment more eye-catching.

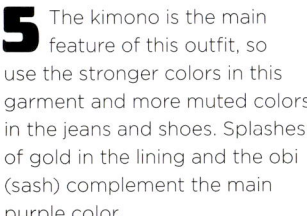

5 The kimono is the main feature of this outfit, so use the stronger colors in this garment and more muted colors in the jeans and shoes. Splashes of gold in the lining and the obi (sash) complement the main purple color.

6 Adding patterns to the kimono and the obi—in this case, stripes and cloud designs—not only makes the whole outfit stand out, but it is also a nod toward the traditional way that kimonos were dyed or embroidered with elaborate patterns.

Denim skinny jeans aren't exactly a traditional part of Japanese fashion, but in a modern reimagining, they look right at home! Don't forget to add creases and folds where the denim gathers at the ankles and knees.

THE COLLECTIONS

Your collection will be kimono-inspired, but you don't have to use the full garment in your outfits to retain that Japanese look. Try thinking about what makes the kimono so distinctive in the first place—for example, the obi sash, the wrapped neckline, or the painted silk—and incorporate these elements into your designs.

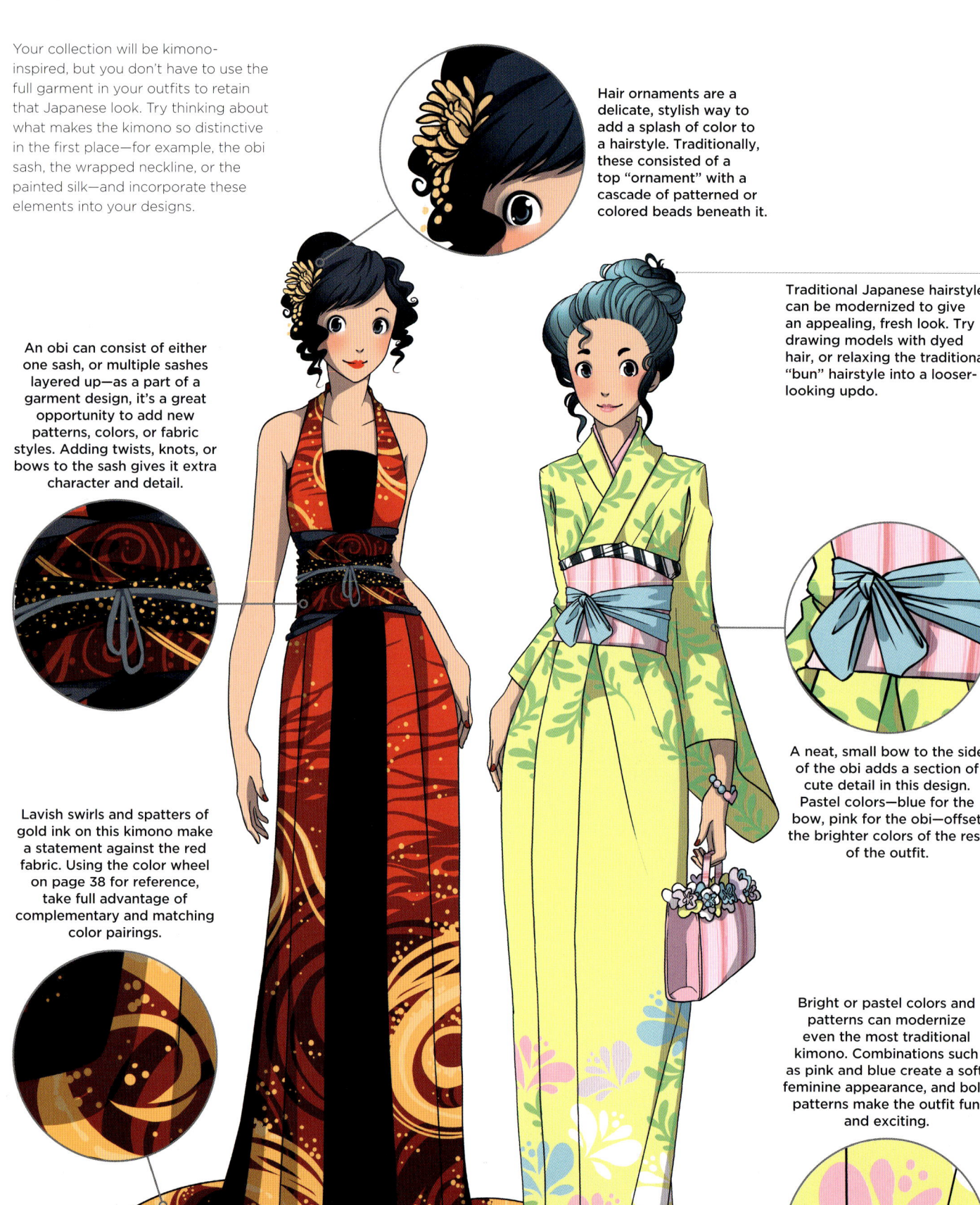

Hair ornaments are a delicate, stylish way to add a splash of color to a hairstyle. Traditionally, these consisted of a top "ornament" with a cascade of patterned or colored beads beneath it.

Traditional Japanese hairstyles can be modernized to give an appealing, fresh look. Try drawing models with dyed hair, or relaxing the traditional "bun" hairstyle into a looser-looking updo.

An obi can consist of either one sash, or multiple sashes layered up—as a part of a garment design, it's a great opportunity to add new patterns, colors, or fabric styles. Adding twists, knots, or bows to the sash gives it extra character and detail.

A neat, small bow to the side of the obi adds a section of cute detail in this design. Pastel colors—blue for the bow, pink for the obi—offset the brighter colors of the rest of the outfit.

Lavish swirls and spatters of gold ink on this kimono make a statement against the red fabric. Using the color wheel on page 38 for reference, take full advantage of complementary and matching color pairings.

Bright or pastel colors and patterns can modernize even the most traditional kimono. Combinations such as pink and blue create a soft, feminine appearance, and bold patterns make the outfit fun and exciting.

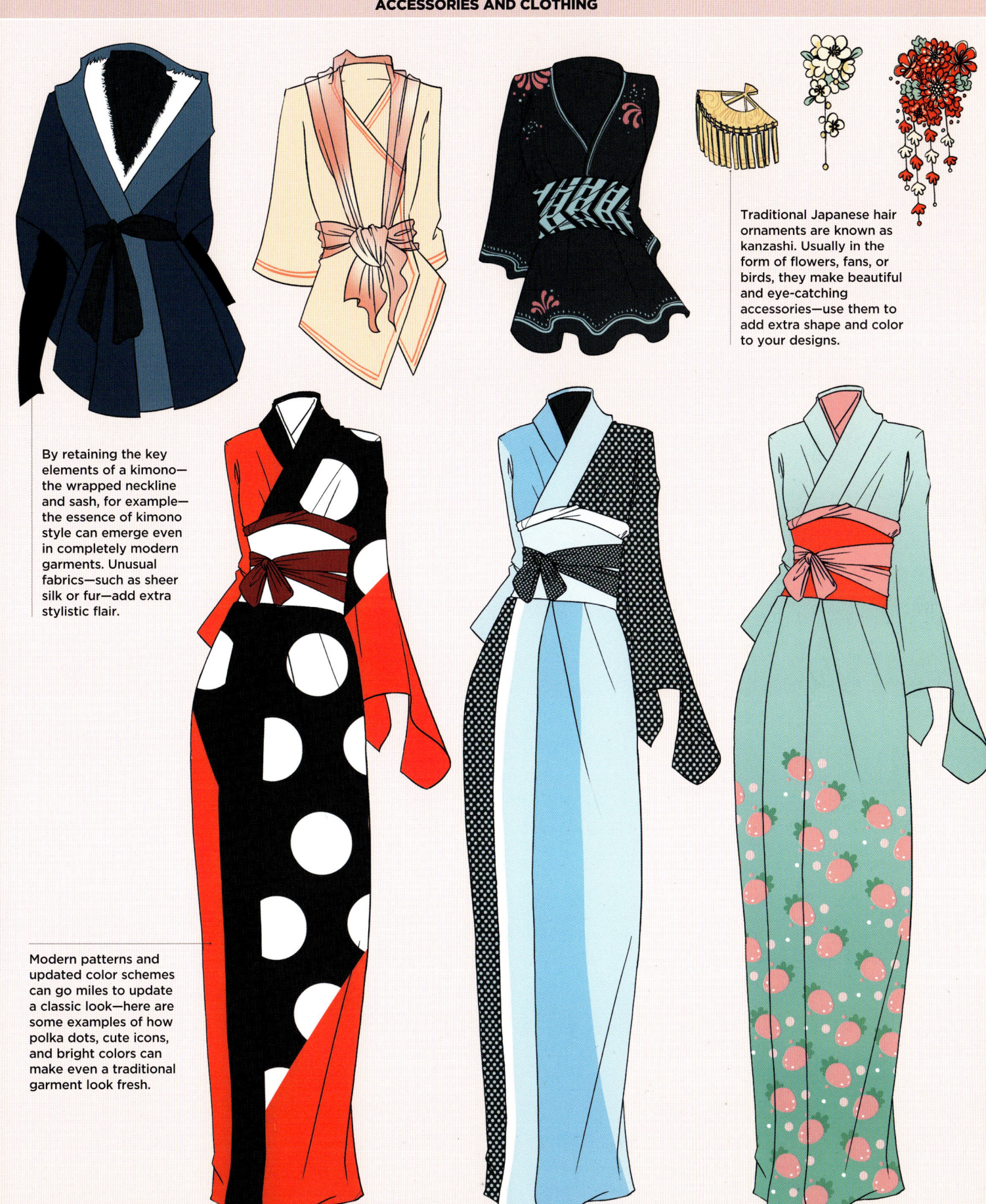

ACCESSORIES AND CLOTHING

Traditional Japanese hair ornaments are known as kanzashi. Usually in the form of flowers, fans, or birds, they make beautiful and eye-catching accessories—use them to add extra shape and color to your designs.

By retaining the key elements of a kimono—the wrapped neckline and sash, for example—the essence of kimono style can emerge even in completely modern garments. Unusual fabrics—such as sheer silk or fur—add extra stylistic flair.

Modern patterns and updated color schemes can go miles to update a classic look—here are some examples of how polka dots, cute icons, and bright colors can make even a traditional garment look fresh.

CYBERPUNK
BY LAURA WATTON-DAVIES

THE EARLY ROOTS OF CYBERPUNK WERE IN 1980S NOVELS SET IN A **FUTURISTIC JAPAN**. AS TIME WENT ON, THESE THEMES WERE INCORPORATED INTO THE NATION'S ARCHITECTURE, ALONGSIDE THE ENVIRONMENTS FEATURED IN FILMS AND COMICS—**SCI-FI/TECHNOLOGICAL IMAGERY** INTERTWINED WITH **CYBERNETIC HACKERS**, WORKING AGAINST OR ALONGSIDE HUGE (EVIL) CORPORATIONS. CHARACTERS FIND THEMSELVES IN A **DARK DYSTOPIA**, ARMED WITH **POCKETFULS OF GADGETS** AND I.T. KNOWLEDGE, IN STORIES THAT ALSO FEATURE ELEMENTS OF DETECTIVE FICTION.

1 Lightly draw out your character in the pose you like. Light lines make it easy to erase mistakes, or change your mind about the stance. This character has a proud pose with a prominent torso.

2 Drawing shapes around the joint circles and pose lines, create the body outline of your character. Remember—if the character is wearing heels, draw them as if they are standing on their toes.

3 The silhouette of a cyberpunk-themed fashion outfit relies on thin piping, padded panels, and streamlined contours. Draw smooth parallel lines, and push them around your character's shape.

4 Details such as motherboard circuitry patterns are made using parallel lines and small circles. You can use this over a large area. Other details can be replicated elsewhere on the outfit, or on jewelry. Draw a border using thin lines to create a piped effect.

5 Fill in areas with one area of color. Use a white pen and ink or digital colors to dot circuit imagery on top of base colors such as forest green.

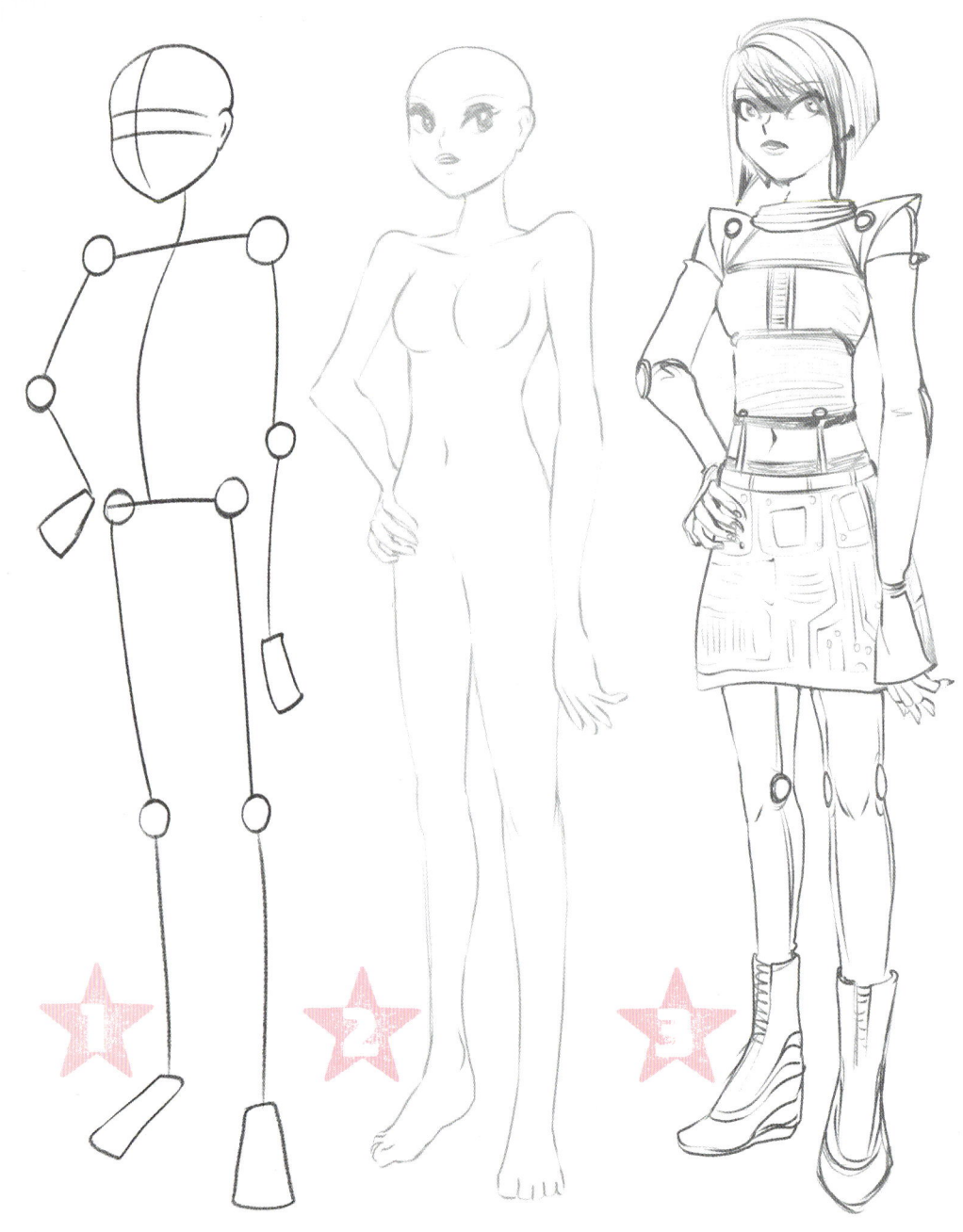

CYPERPUNK | 103

CLOTHING PALETTE

Neon colors contrasted with darker tones are crucial to the cyberpunk look.

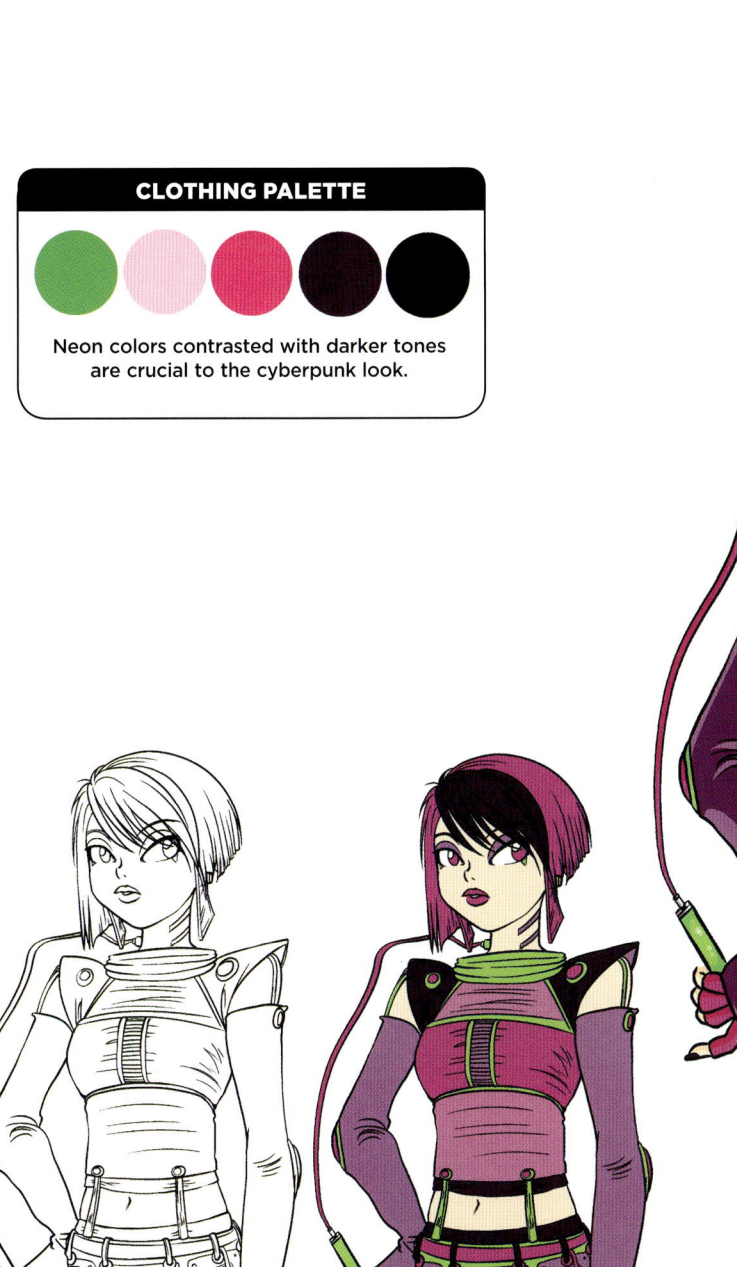

Note how the horizontal crease lines convey the tight fit of the top—see pages 24–25 for more information on folds and creases.

Look at underlighting for dramatic shading effects. Select where your light source is, and shade around the opposite surfaces.

6 Minimalist color schemes work well for cyberpunk fashion; flat dark shades or saturated colors make good combinations. Very bright, almost neon colors will make the character stand out in a dark environment.

THE COLLECTIONS

Cyberpunk fashion has developed in waves, which have included digital cowboy chic and gumshoe design, and an advancement of '80s neon fashion. The third wave picked up on '90s industrial subculture and real-life cyberpunk scenes. Now, the fashion is represented with increasing frequency in futuristic films and animation. Are you ready for the digital future, no matter what it brings?

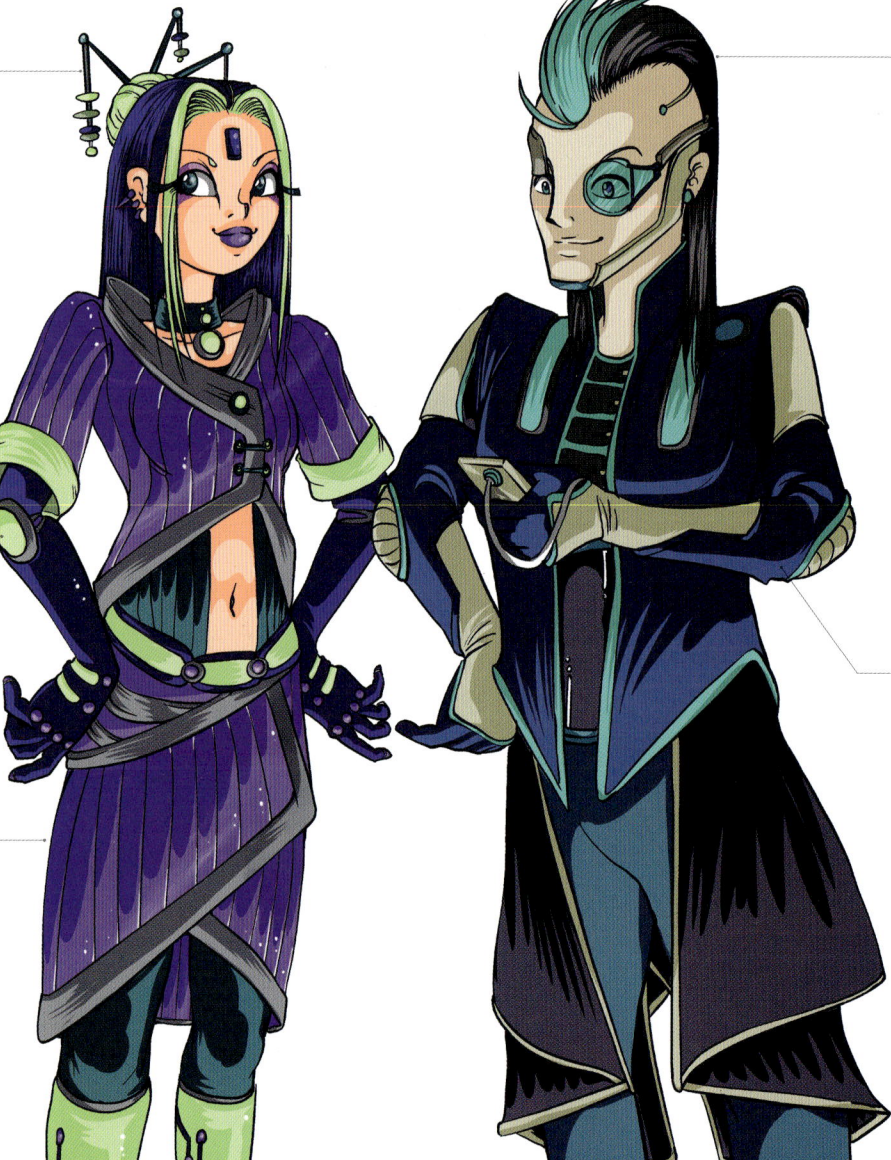

Hair accessories stick out, with small details hanging down. Remember that if the model is moving, details will trail to show the direction she is headed.

Small elbow guards and boot-style shin guards add stylish protection. Add detail using pipes and circles.

The coat and wrap skirt have thick padding in strips to create smooth contours. Draw these strips in the same direction, curving over contours of the body.

This character's style amalgamates traditional geisha inspirations with modern fashions such as tights and platform shoes. Draw clothing as close to the body form as possible, and allow little bumps for wrinkles to show where the material folds around the joints.

The model's head is shaved from one point around his head (called an undercut), with long strands left on top to create a long Mohawk. He is wearing technological accessories made with round lenses and pipes, which sit on his jawline. Draw a small shield that contours around his jaw and add small circles to show where the circuitry is attached (if your character has undergone some cybernetic surgery and wants to connect to the digital world biomechanically).

The sleeves are like gauntlets, layered over each other. The shapes that make up the lower half of the jacket hang from the hips and fold in and out, creating an angular form; these are created using slightly curved long strokes and piped around the edges using thin lines.

Though his jacket is modern, his pants and boots are of an older style. Traditional (but pocketless) combat pants are tucked into leather military boots, with straighter lines and curved areas near the tops of the boots to show the volume of the pants being folded into the top of the boot.

CYPERPUNK | 105

ACCESSORIES AND CLOTHING

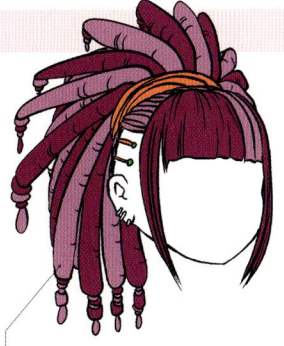

This hairstyle is a combination of dreadlocks, beading, and an undercut. Two strips of cybertechnical inputs are fastened at the side of the head. Draw deadlocks using long, thin balloon shapes, and adding texture using small lines dotted along the edges.

Mirrored aviator shades are a fashion constant; draw them using parallel oval shapes and straight lines.

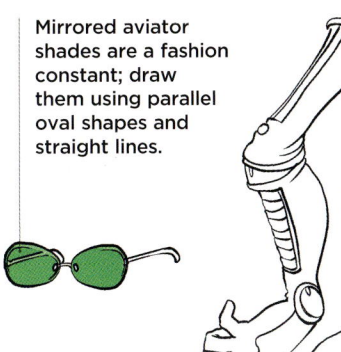

These long gloves have spheres, padded strips, and piping details. Create them using long strips for the piped edging, short curved lines for the padded strips, and circles for the crystal spheres embedded over the wrists.

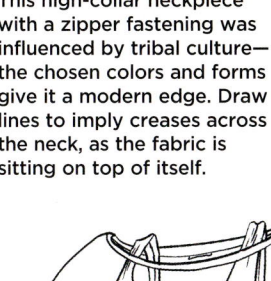

This high-collar neckpiece with a zipper fastening was influenced by tribal culture—the chosen colors and forms give it a modern edge. Draw lines to imply creases across the neck, as the fabric is sitting on top of itself.

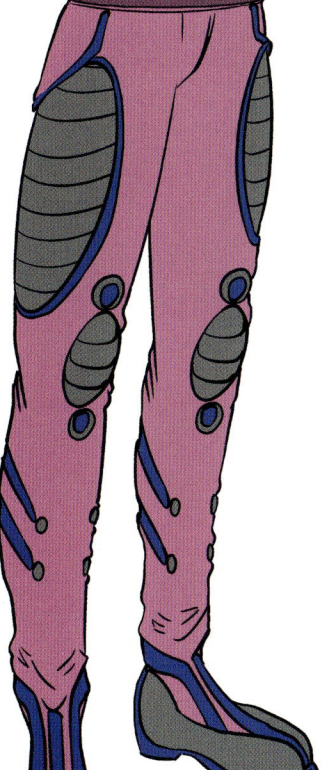

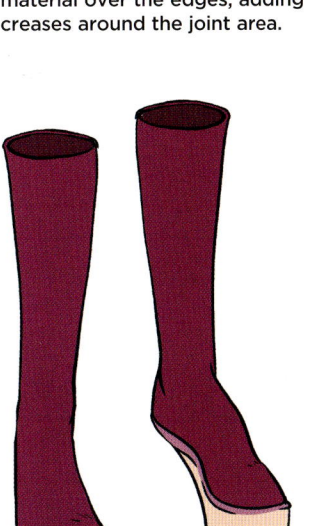

Hotpants are fun, and the wearer can move about freely if they are engaged in action scenes. Draw hoops around the waist and the tops of the thighs, and draw material over the edges, adding creases around the joint area.

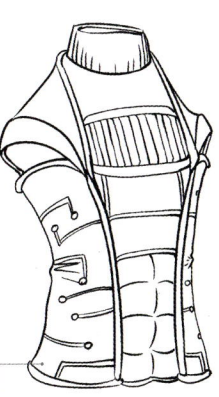

This top combines the function of a corset and the form of a tank top. The piece is paneled using small curved lines to denote abdomen protection and ribbed fabric over the neck and upper chest to show warmth.

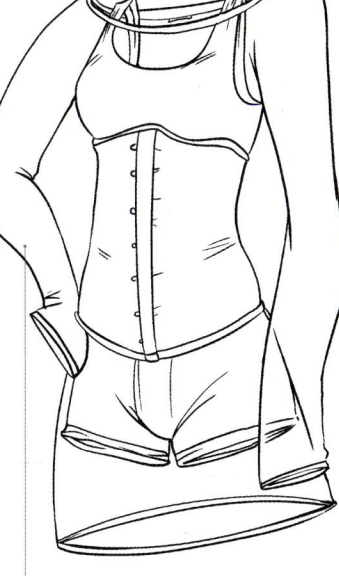

This top and dress fits the character on page 103 and would be perfect for clubbing. The dress is made of crochet fabric, and the top, corset, and shorts are synthetic fabrics with smooth textures. Color the undergarments first, and draw with circular motions over the top to create the crochet texture by hand.

These pants are slim-fitting, and contain durable panels for action or adventure. Draw ovals around the areas you want to protect, and add curved lines around the body to give an impression of depth.

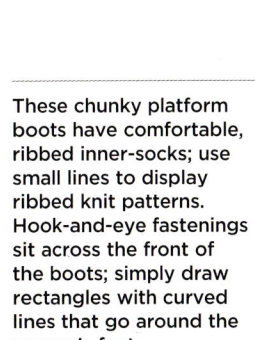

These long, plain boots have no heel; the wearer's body weight is concentrated into the front of the foot, and held up by a strengthened platform sole.

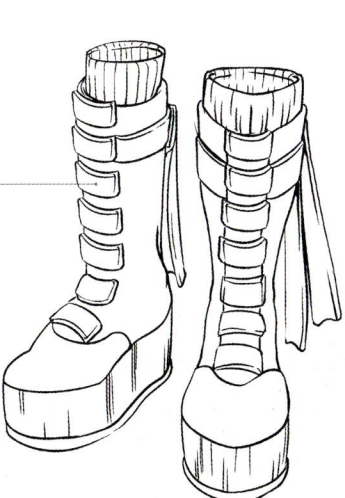

These chunky platform boots have comfortable, ribbed inner-socks; use small lines to display ribbed knit patterns. Hook-and-eye fastenings sit across the front of the boots; simply draw rectangles with curved lines that go around the wearer's feet.

SUNDAY LOUNGEWEAR

BY EMMA VIECELI

WHETHER PUTTING ON AN OUTRAGEOUSLY CUTE KIGURUMI (ANIMAL-THEMED ONESIE), GRABBING A SET OF LOOSE SWEATS, OR SIMPLY PULLING A BATHROBE OVER A PAJAMA SET, **LOUNGEWEAR IS ABOUT COMFORT** ABOVE ALL ELSE. THIS TYPE OF CLOTHING IS OFTEN SOMETHING PERSONAL, RARELY SEEN BY OTHERS, BUT MORE RECENTLY, IT'S BECOME FASHIONABLE TO MAKE IT **STYLISH AS WELL AS COMFORTABLE**.

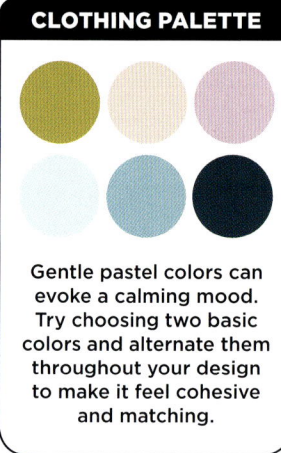

CLOTHING PALETTE

Gentle pastel colors can evoke a calming mood. Try choosing two basic colors and alternate them throughout your design to make it feel cohesive and matching.

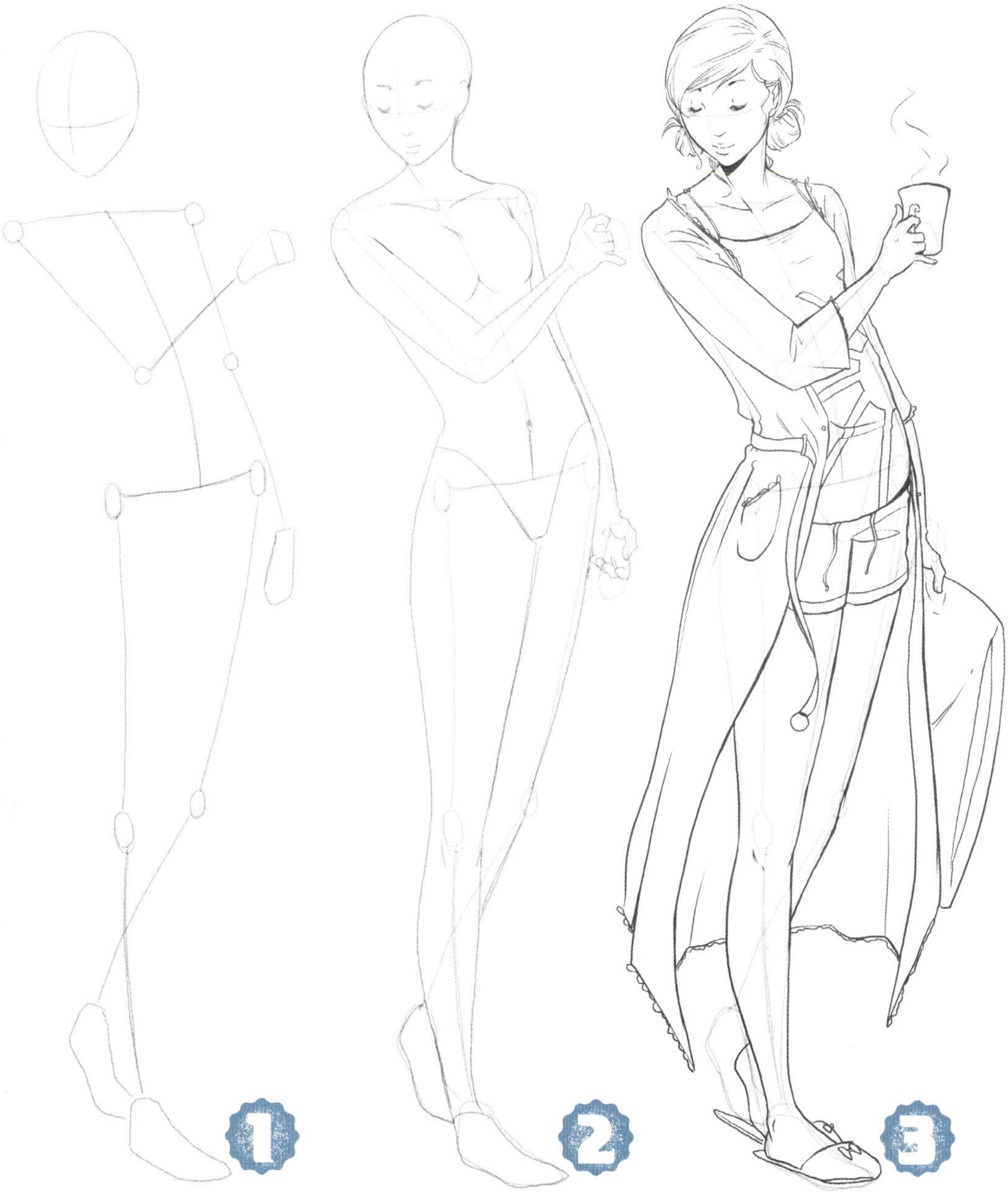

1 The lines here already suggest a casual and relaxed feel. Drop a hip and have the shoulders loose and hanging low. Arch the back and push the hips forward, giving a sense of confidence.

2 At this stage you can start to consider details and props. Prepare the hands for where they may be holding props, such as the Sunday-essential hot drink, in this case.

3 It can be easy to lose the shape that the initial construct lines provide as you're finalizing line work, so be mindful not to lose your initial pose. Trust your own planning.

4 Hands can be tricky to draw—why not take a photo of a friend holding a mug to be sure how it would look? In this example, the thumb is used to steady the mug and the little finger supports the base, while the index finger is hooked through the handle.

SUNDAY LOUNGEWEAR | **107**

5 Loungewear is all about comfort and relaxation. Avoid bright or oversaturated colors in favor of soft, calming tones. Try to keep a sense of cohesion to your palette—here, pastels reflect the lazy mood of the outfit, and the sunburst design ties in the tank top with the shorts.

6 There's little in the way of highlight or reflective surface in this image. Shading is simple and in a pinkish hue. Reds, oranges, and pinks make for gentle, warm, and relaxing shade choices.

When lazing around the house, the priority for hair is something easy and non-fussy. Try some half-up, half-down styles, or hair roughly pulled into bunches or ponytails.

The thickness of a gown's material will affect the shape. In this image, the gown is made of thin cotton, so it drapes downward and bunches only slightly out from the gathering at the waist.

There's something vintage in the design of this gown, with its lace trim, that contrasts with the modern sun design on the tank top beneath. Experiment with combining vintage and modern design inspirations.

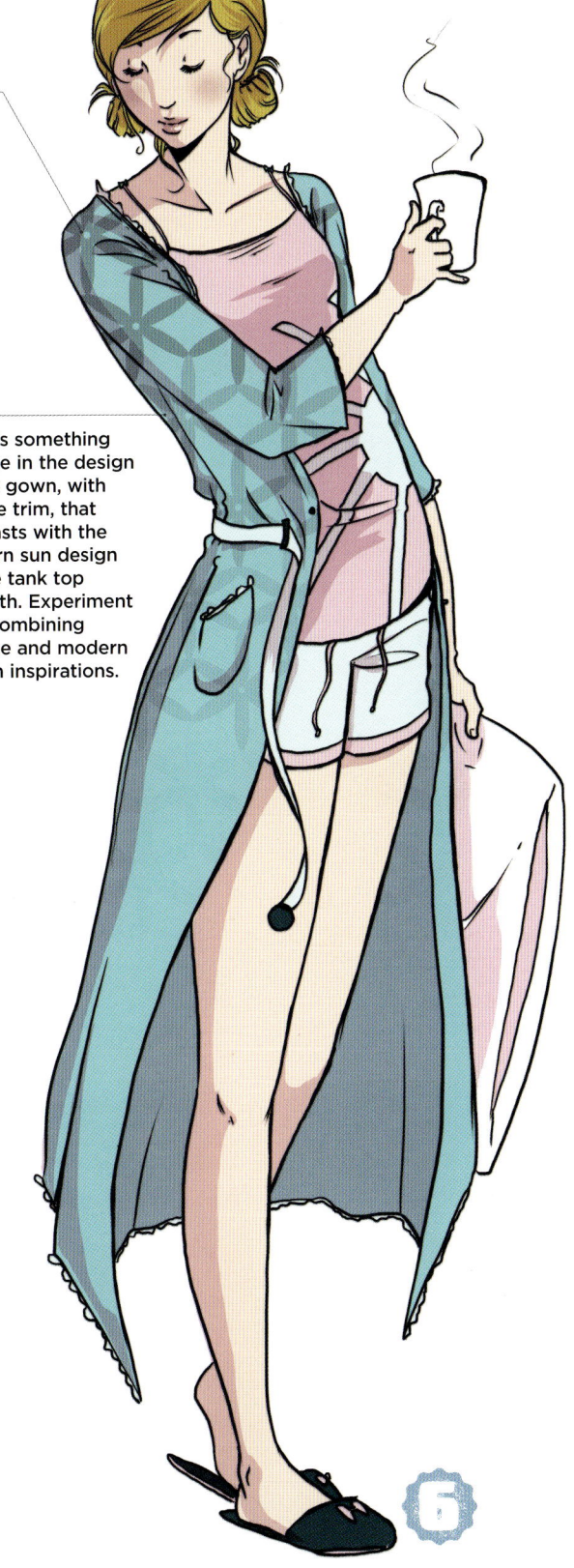

108 | THE COLLECTIONS

Loungewear is a comprehensive term that can simply refer to the clothes your models wear when winding down at home. These are not garments designed for leaving the house: footwear doesn't need heavy soles, and materials can be all about comfort and coziness, or elegant breeziness.

Onesies follow the same rules as hoods or hats in that you'll need to draw in or imagine the full figure beneath to make sure the onesie is sitting on the character as clothing rather than becoming the figure itself. These garments are rarely close-fitting. Imagine a small gap between skin and the material, and make sure your hood easily covers the character's head.

When drawing something soft being hugged, like a pillow, make sure the folds and creases where the object is depressed originate out from what's holding it. Here we can see the creases spreading out and away from the character's arms.

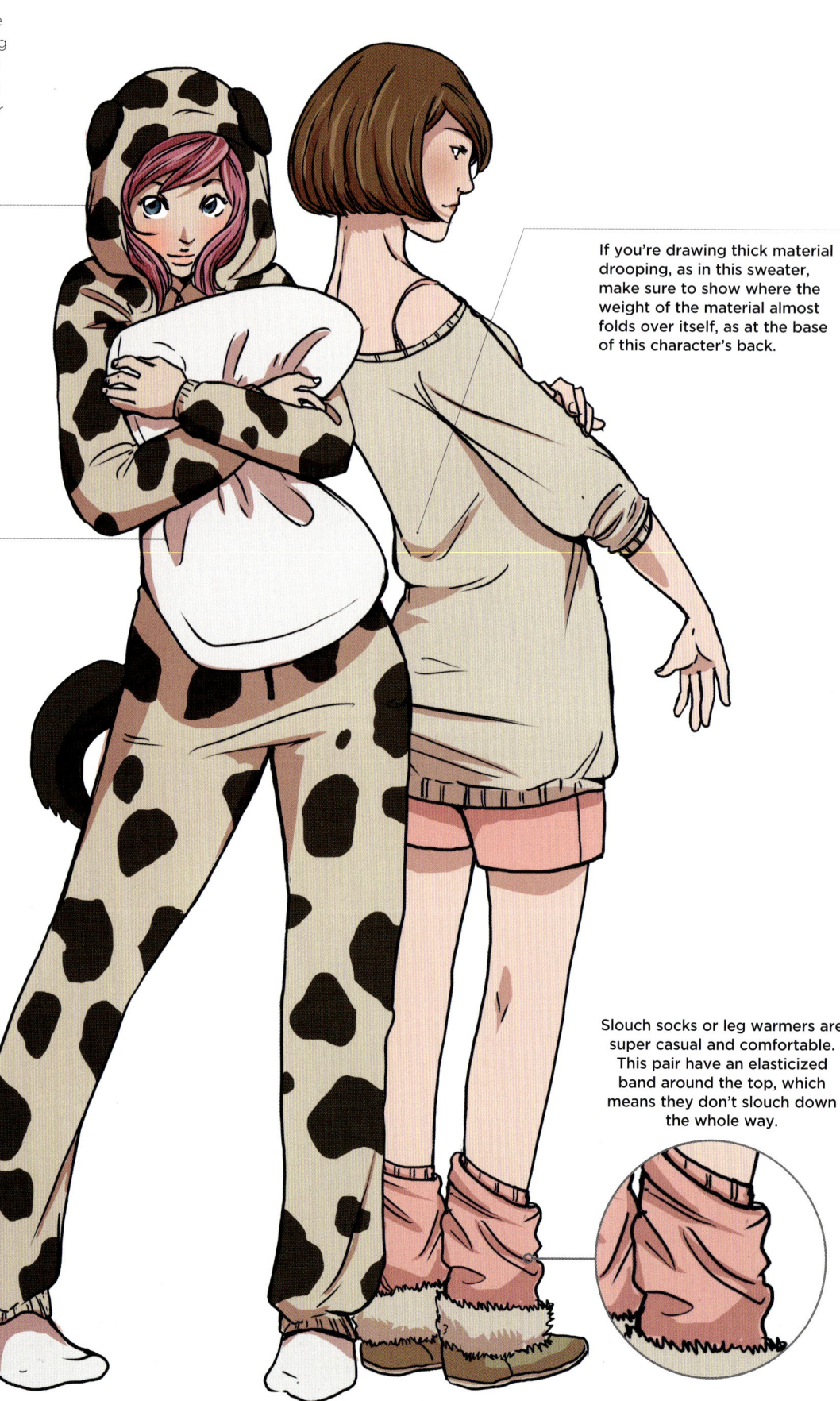

If you're drawing thick material drooping, as in this sweater, make sure to show where the weight of the material almost folds over itself, as at the base of this character's back.

Slouch socks or leg warmers are super casual and comfortable. This pair have an elasticized band around the top, which means they don't slouch down the whole way.

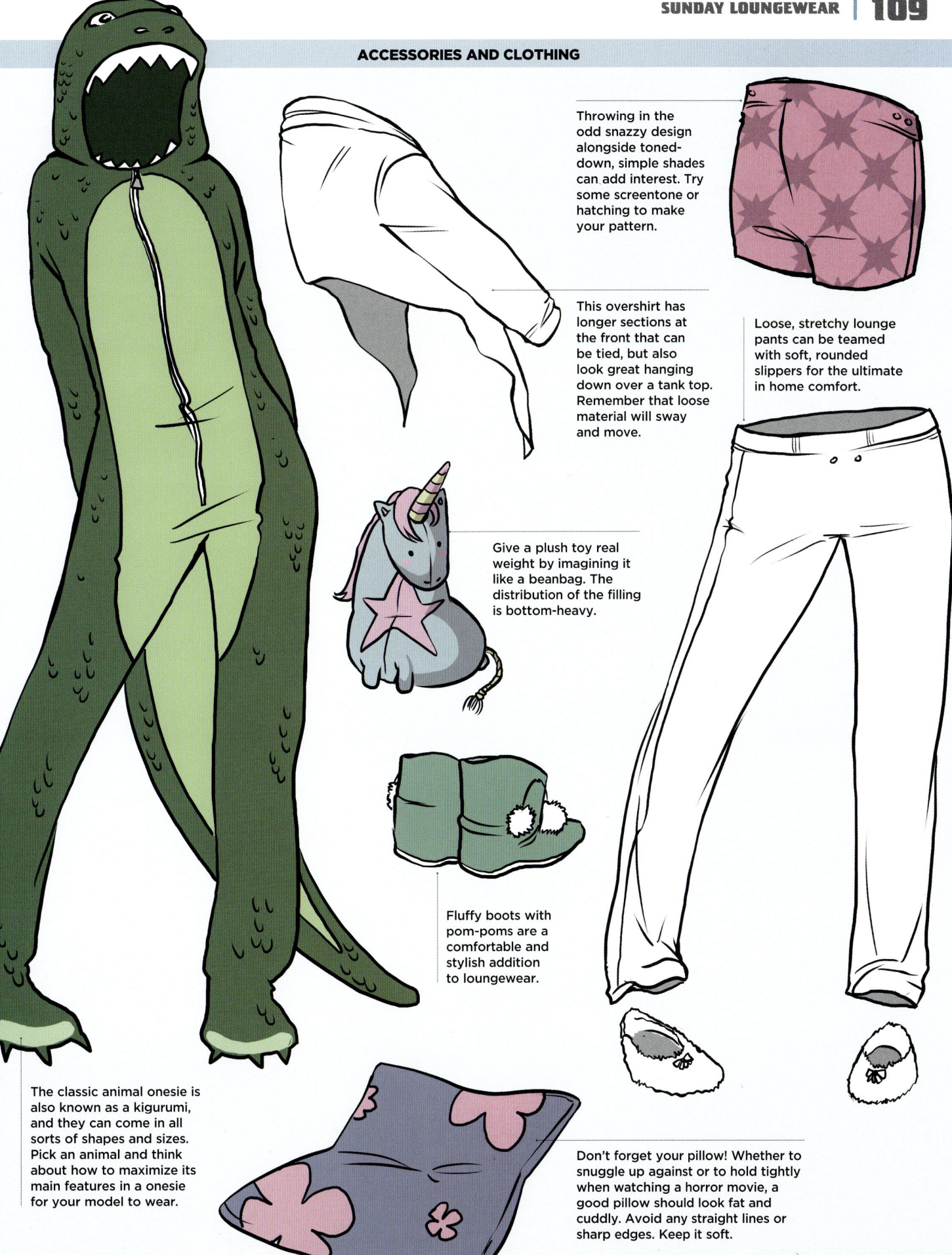

110 | THE COLLECTIONS

WILDERNESS CHIC

IN A WORLD OF TECHNOLOGY, DEADLINES, AND TRAFFIC, A DISTINCTIVE **"BACK TO NATURE"** TREND HAS BEGUN TO CROP UP IN THE FASHION INDUSTRY. ONE OF THE MOST PREDOMINANT OF THESE LOOKS IS THE **LUMBERJACK LOOK** FOR MEN—A UTILIZATION OF **PLAID SHIRTS, OUTDOOR BOOTS, AND FLANNEL**. HARKING BACK TO THE EARLY DAYS OF **AMERICAN SETTLERS**, THE RUGGED OUTDOORS LOOK HAS QUICKLY TAKEN HOLD IN THE FASHION WORLD.

1 Begin by drawing in the basic skeleton of your model, so that you can be sure to get the proportions and pose right first. If you already know that his arms are going to be posed in a certain way—for example, holding something in his hands or with his hands in his pockets—pose the arms roughly for now and be prepared to adjust them later.

2 With your skeleton sketched out, block in the rest of your model's body. Remember that men are blockier and more angular than women—give your model broad shoulders, a deep chest, and a square jaw. The legs and arms are also more muscular.

3 The rustic look has to be practical as well as fashionable, so keep this in mind when designing your outfit. Think about warm layers, jeans tucked into boots, rolled-up cuffs, and a wild, messy hairstyle, of course.

4 In cleaning up your sketch, you'll have a chance to add in more details. A scruff of stubble makes your model look more rugged. Add lots of rumpled folds to his jeans to make them look worn and loved.

5 Block in your colors, keeping in mind the choices that you made at the beginning of your design. Don't worry if this process makes your model's clothes look too crisp and clean; they'll start looking more natural in the next step.

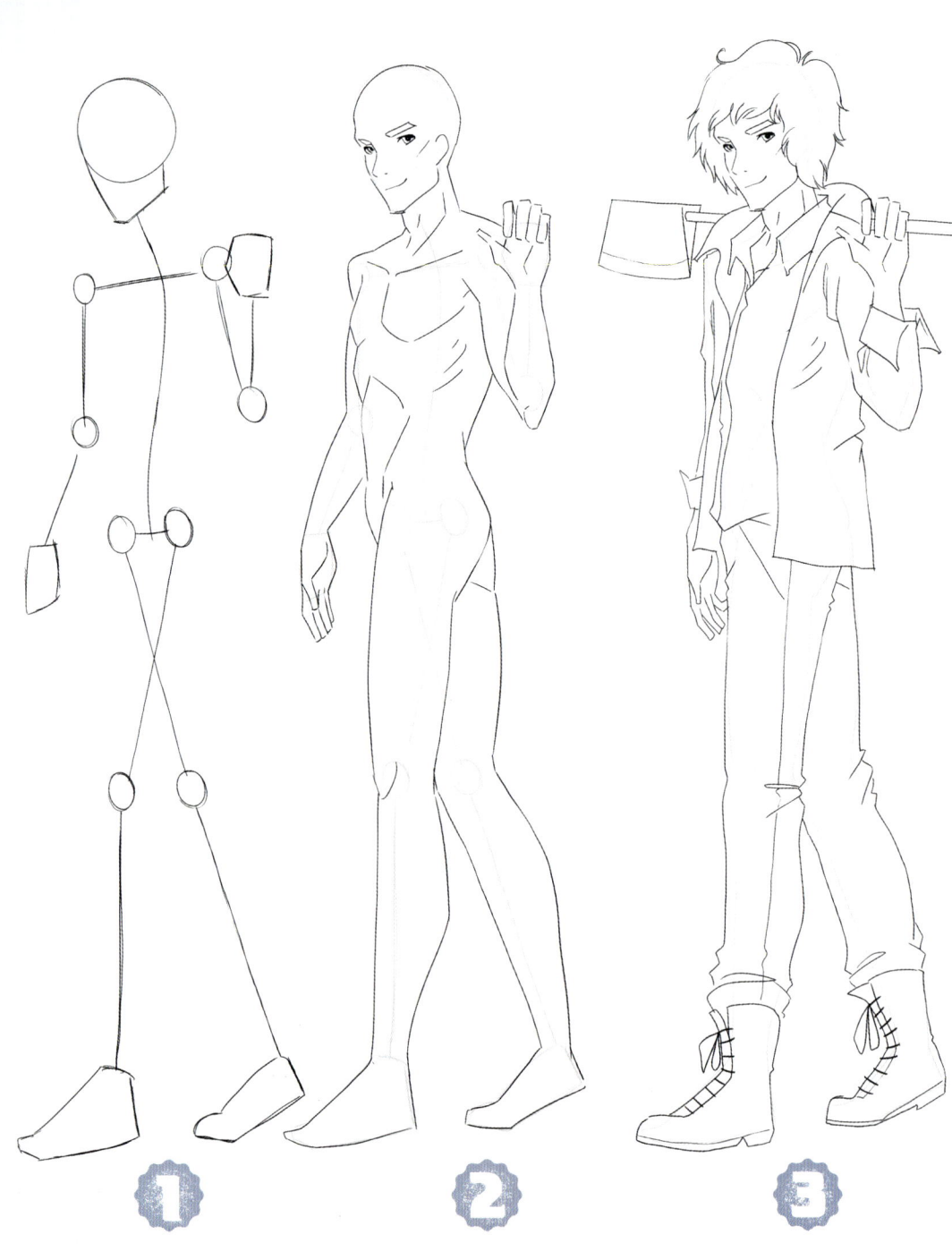

WILDERNESS CHIC | 111

6 Create a plaid effect by using several layers of light colors and blocking them over each other in a grid pattern. The traditional lumberjack plaid is red with black stripes, but you can use any combination of colors, or even add in extra colors for a tartan effect. Use a lighter blue at the front of the model's jeans to make them look faded.

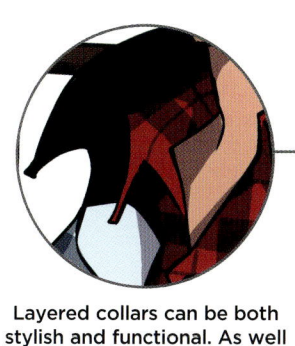

Layered collars can be both stylish and functional. As well as providing a warm outfit for all of your model's outdoor needs, it's a great way to introduce new colors, textures, and fabrics, such as offsetting a darker fleece on the inside of the jacket collar with the red plaid shirt underneath.

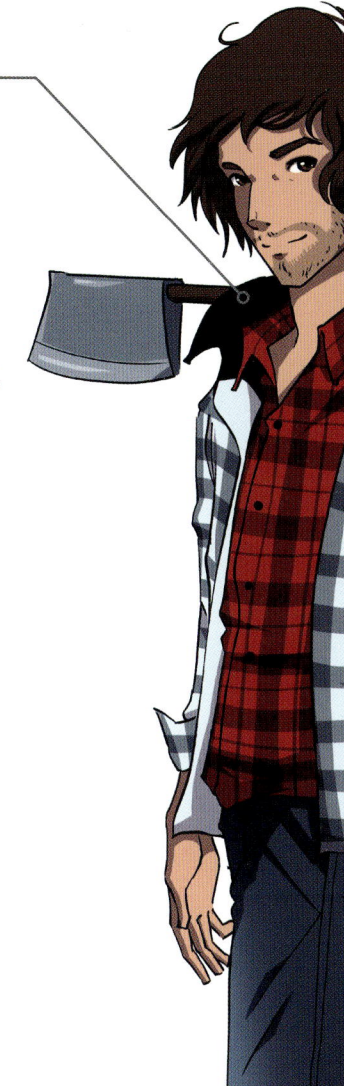

Denim naturally fades with wear, and this aged look has become popular in fashion. To create a stonewashed effect, find areas where the jeans would be naturally stretched (across the tops of the thighs and at the knees, for example) and use a lighter color to show the fading.

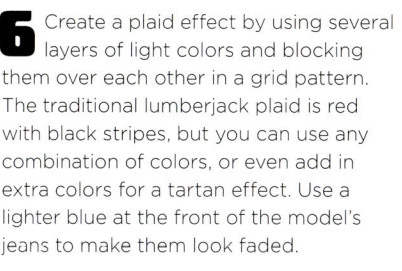

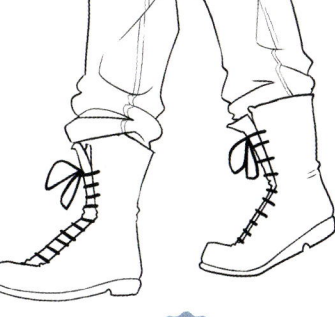

THE COLLECTIONS

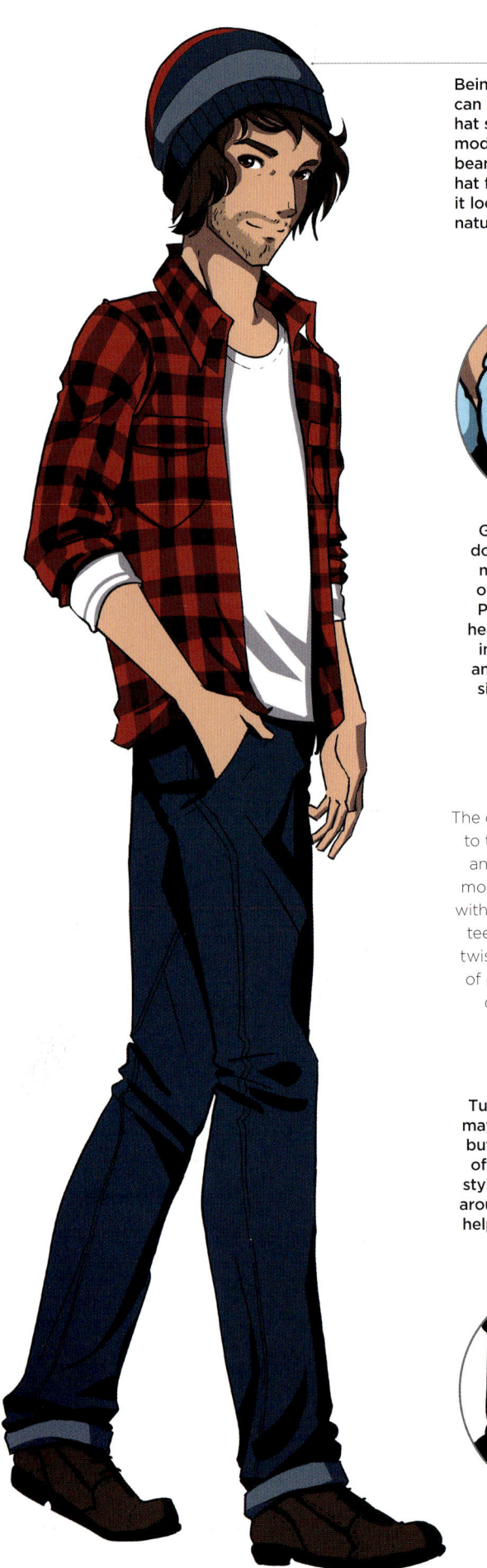

Being an outdoorsman can be cold work, so a hat should help keep your model warm. For a knitted beanie, draw the rim of the hat first to make sure that it looks like it's sitting naturally over the head.

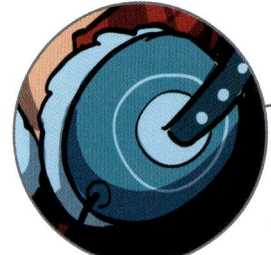

Going back to nature doesn't mean that your model has to give up on all home comforts. Place accessories like headphones by drawing in the headband first, and making sure that it sits naturally over the model's body.

The outdoors look harks back to the days of lumberjacks and woodsmen, but your models can be modernized with a leather jacket or white tee to give a metropolitan twist that wouldn't look out of place in the fashionable districts of New York.

Tucking jeans into socks may sound unfashionable, but it's a chance to show off a bit more color and style. Drawing the ribbing around the top of the sock helps suggest that they're made of a thick, comfortable wool.

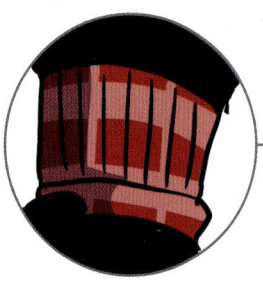

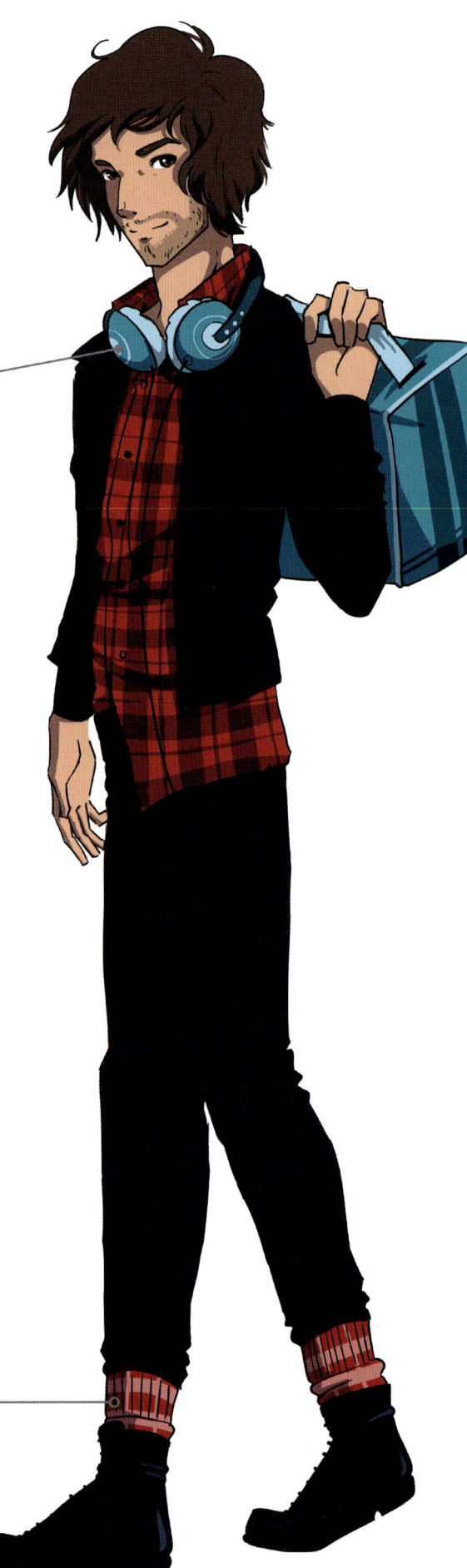

WILDERNESS CHIC | **113**

SHIRTS AND SHOES

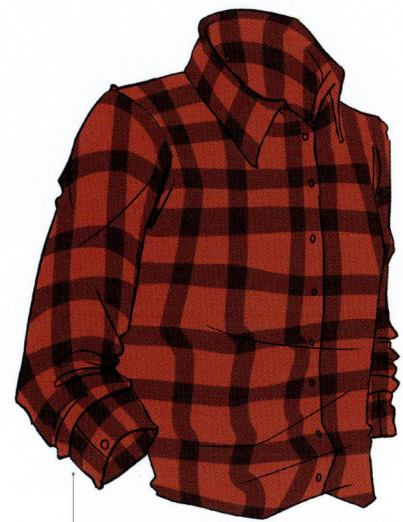
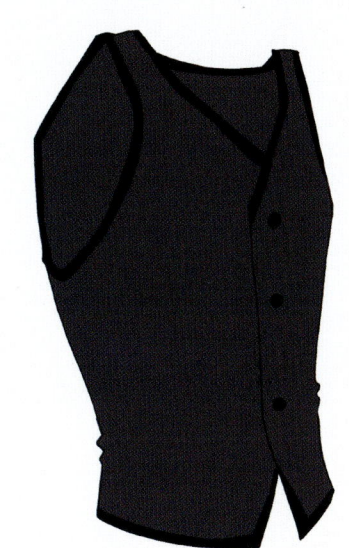
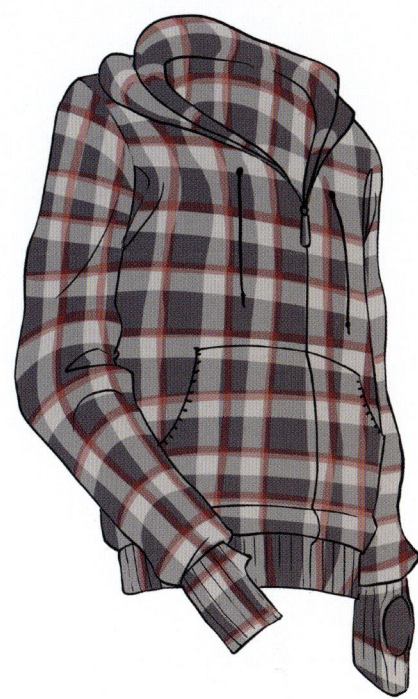

There is lots of potential for this fashion collection: try combining shirts and vests or adding the plaid motif to less likely garments, such as hoodies and socks. Remember to keep it casual.

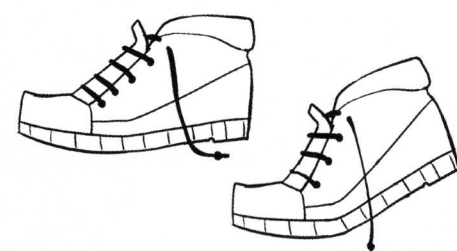

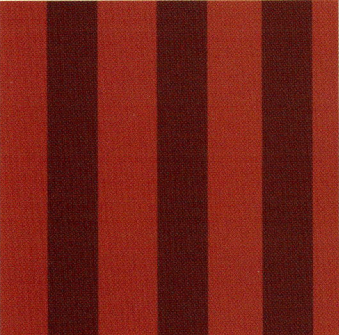

Every outdoorsman needs a dependable, solid pair of shoes, even in the fashion world. Look at walking or military boots and adapt them to match the rest of the outfit. Keeping the toes thick and the heels chunky will retain that heavy, hardwearing look.

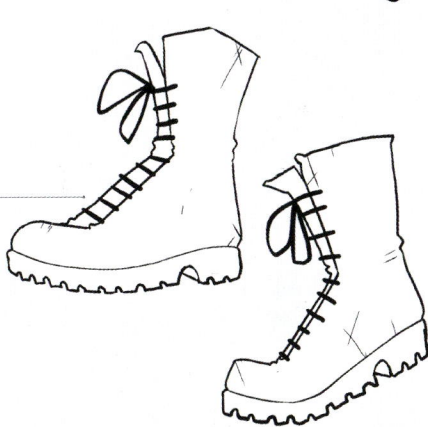

PLAID PATTERNS

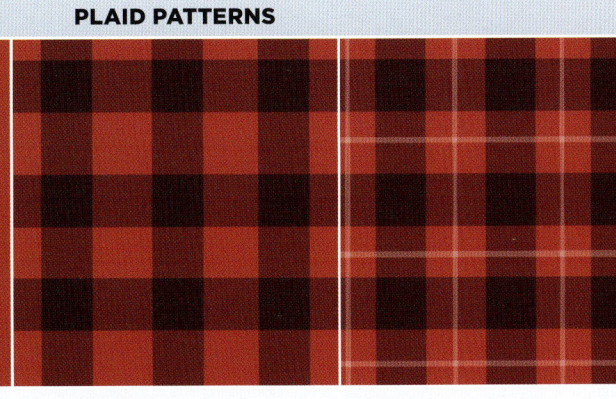

1 Creating a plaid effect isn't difficult at all. Begin by choosing two colors—either a light base color and a darker one for the stripes, or vice versa.

2 Keeping the stripes light so that you can see below to where they cross over, create a bold grid pattern.

3 Add more colors for more of a tartan look.

CLOTHING PALETTE

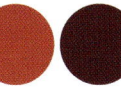

The woodsman look is immediately distinctive—a glimpse of red and blue and you're immediately certain what to expect. However, use muted and darker versions of these colors—because this is a natural, outdoors look, bright colors will only look garish and out of place.

MILITARY

MILITARY INFLUENCES ARE NEVER FAR FROM THE FASHION WORLD. OFTEN APPEARING IN THE FORM OF **EPAULETTES, NAUTICAL BRASS BUTTONS, AND STRIPED CUFF DETAILING**, ELEMENTS FROM MILITARY **UNIFORMS ACROSS THE WORLD** HAVE ALWAYS PLAYED A PART IN OUR FASHIONS. WHETHER AS FORMAL, HISTORICALLY INFLUENCED COATS AND JACKETS OR AS MORE CASUAL, MODERN ARMY ATTIRE, THE MILITARY LOOK IS A **PROUD AND SMART STATEMENT** TO MAKE ON THE STREET.

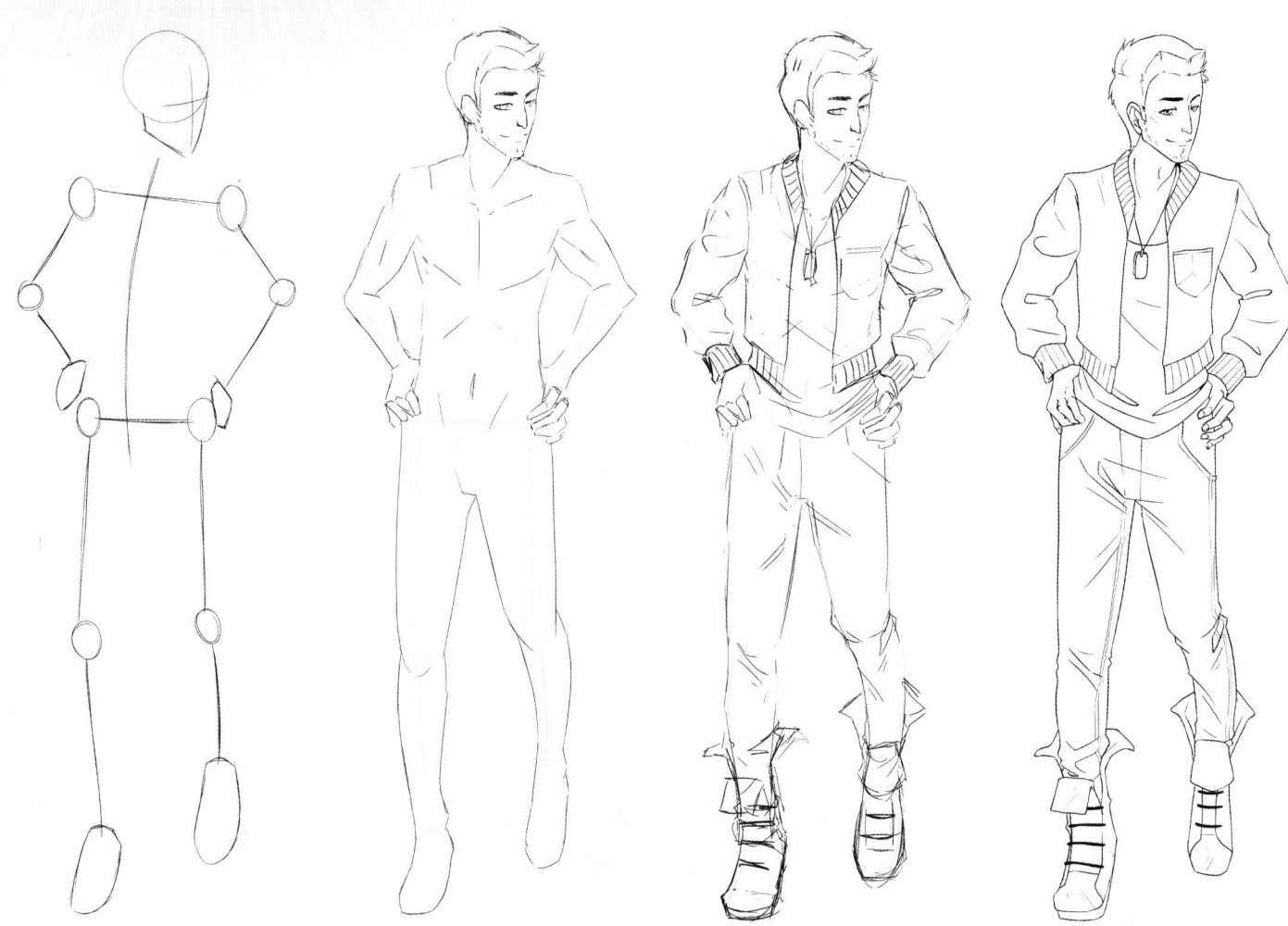

1 Use a very basic skeleton to decide on your model's pose. Before you get wrapped up in adding any details, use the first sketch to work out how he will be standing, the basic proportions of his face, and to check that your anatomy is correct.

2 With the skeleton in place, start to block the shape of the body over it. Even though your model will be clothed, be sure to think about muscle structure—this will help you to add in the drape and cut of your outfits correctly.

3 Military style doesn't always mean that you are restricted to formal wear. Try combining a pair of military boots, a bomber jacket, and dog tags with a more casual tank top and jeans. Don't worry about messy sketching at this point.

4 Now that you're cleaning up your sketch, you'll have a chance to add in details that will help identify which fabrics your collection consists of. Draw in seams and wide, linear folds to show the stiff denim of the jeans, and broad, rounded creases to make the jacket look like it's made of a thick, lined material.

MILITARY | 115

Every new recruit into the military is given a standardized haircut. Buzzcuts don't have to be unflattering, though—a combed top and pushed-up bangs create a neat, casual look that's both attractive and fashionable.

The dog tag is one of the ultimate military accessories, which has been adopted by the fashion world both for men and for women. Engrave them with the logos of fashion labels or simply leave them blank.

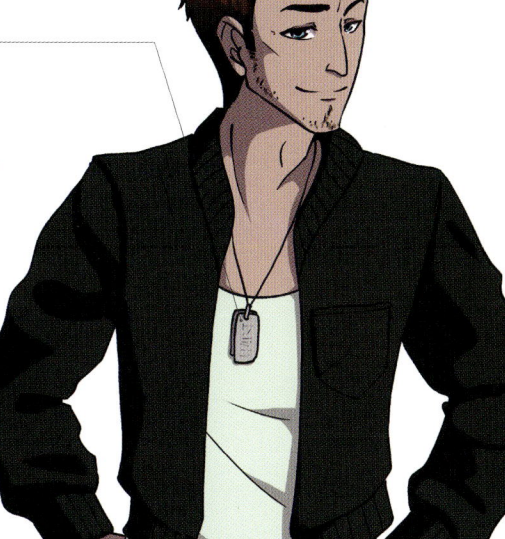

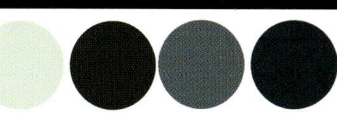

CLOTHING PALETTE

The color of military uniforms varies depending on their country of origin, but the most distinctive and classical look is usually comprised of khaki or other dusky, mid-tone shades. The most common base color for infantry, khaki can be paired with other desaturated colors, such as blue or red, as well as acting as a suitable background for small areas of bright brass or other bright hues. Since this model is wearing one of the more classic military street looks, we'll be sticking to these traditional colors.

6 Using soft areas of color, you can brighten up dark areas again without losing the effect of a darker fabric. For example, this outfit is all about looking sharp yet comfortable—fading the dye at the front of the jeans makes it look as though they have been worn frequently, and adding a patch of brighter color to the model's hair makes it look glossy and clean.

Every soldier has a clean pair of boots polished and ready for inspection, but in the fashion world, it's acceptable—encouraged, even—to lean toward the scruffier look instead. Think about ways to turn an ordinary pair of army boots into a style statement—how about lacing them up halfway and flipping the top sides down like a cuff?

5 Try using reference images of modern army camouflage to inspire your color choices. Your colors might look too dark at first, but use areas of lighter colors, such as the lighter tank top, to balance out the image again. You can always use additional effects, such as the ones mentioned in the next step, to lighten things up further while still keeping the intended look.

Bear in mind that when jeans are pushed into the tops of boots, they tend to bunch upward. Denim is quite a stiff fabric, so draw folds and bunches with sharp lines and contours. The flat-felled seam helps to give jeans their distinctive look, so don't forget to add that in as well.

116 | THE COLLECTIONS

It may seem like there isn't much that you can do with army khakis, but the military look has a surprisingly large potential. Historically inspired jackets can add a certain amount of romantic chic to any formal occasion, and felted wool military coats are perfect for cold weather. Try looking at both modern and antique military dress for inspiration.

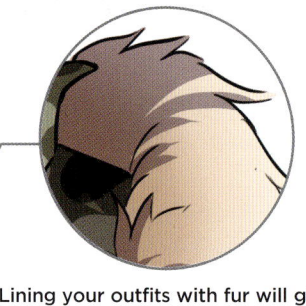

Lining your outfits with fur will give them an appearance of both luxury and practicality, especially in coat hoods or around the cuffs. Using natural, undyed fur in this look helps it to fit in with the rest of the outfit, though for a formal outfit, you could use white or even gold-dyed fur for effect.

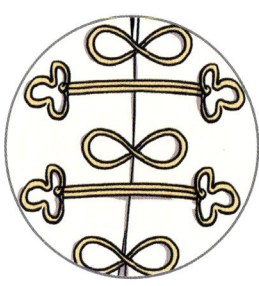

This coat features "frogs," which is the name for an oriental braided closure. Frogging became popular on military uniforms during the 17th–19th centuries, and has returned in modern years as a fashionable nod to historical uniform jackets.

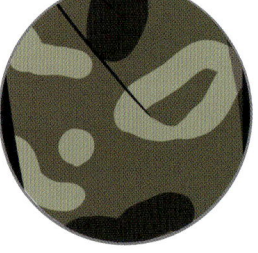

Basic camouflage is created from three colors: a mid-tone, such as khaki, beige, or blue; and a lighter and a darker color, to create the mottled effect. On the opposite page you can see examples of the three most common camouflage patterns.

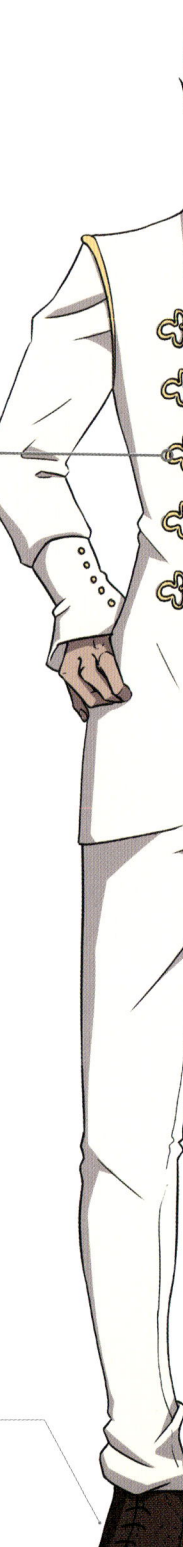

When wearing formal wear, your models don't have to be restricted to the heavy army boots most often found in military fashion collections. Consider classy but practical footwear, such as brogues or Oxfords.

MILITARY | **117**

CLOTHING AND ACCESSORIES

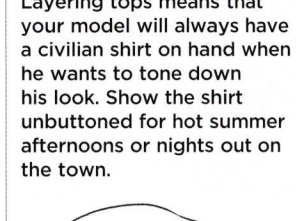

Layering tops means that your model will always have a civilian shirt on hand when he wants to tone down his look. Show the shirt unbuttoned for hot summer afternoons or nights out on the town.

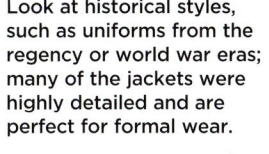

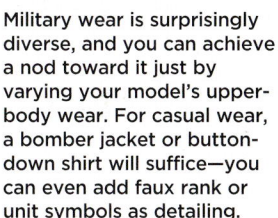

Look at historical styles, such as uniforms from the regency or world war eras; many of the jackets were highly detailed and are perfect for formal wear.

Military wear is surprisingly diverse, and you can achieve a nod toward it just by varying your model's upper-body wear. For casual wear, a bomber jacket or button-down shirt will suffice—you can even add faux rank or unit symbols as detailing.

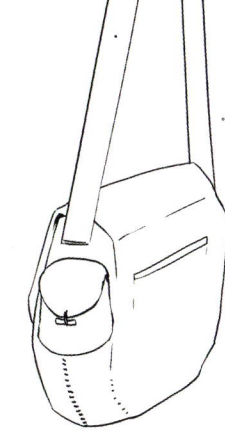

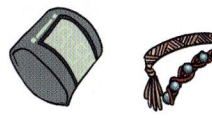

Soldiers need to be able to pack up and move on at short notice, so a practical bag is a must. Duffel and messenger bags are a stylish statement; either in black and gray or matching camouflage, they can be accessorized with military patches and patriotic colors.

Add extra detail to your looks by adding accessories such as watches, wristbands, and bracelets. The military look is versatile enough that you can add high-tech watches, woven hemp bracelets, or classical cufflinks, and they'll fit right in with your outfits.

CAMOUFLAGE PATTERNS

Camouflage material doesn't always have to be green. Although khaki is the color that we associate most with the military, there are actually 12 main patterns that are used for different terrain, and to the right are the three most common—woodland, desert, and snow.

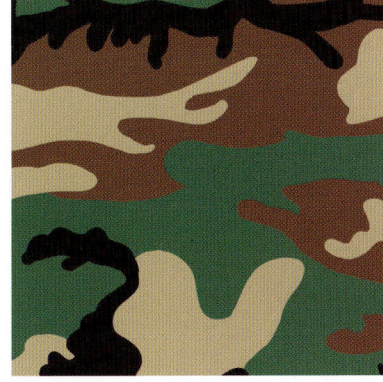
Woodland

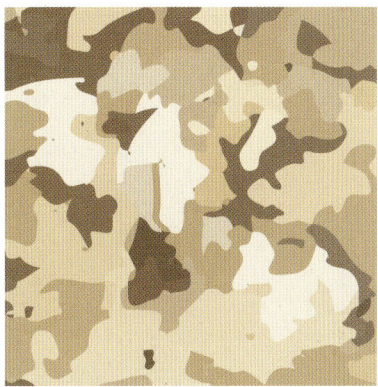
Desert

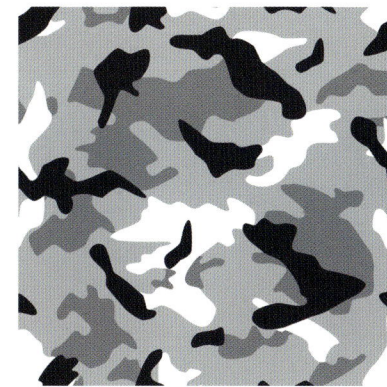
Snow

WINTER KNITWEAR

KNITTED CLOTHING HAS BEEN PRODUCED FOR THOUSANDS OF YEARS, BUT IT WASN'T UNTIL **COCO CHANEL** BEGAN USING IT IN HER COLLECTIONS IN THE 1910S THAT IT BECAME A **POPULAR FASHION STAPLE**. WHETHER FOR USE IN **SKIWEAR, NIGHTWEAR, OR WINTER WEAR**, IT'S A **VERSATILE FABRIC** THAT HAS BECOME A WELL-KNOWN STYLE ALL OF ITS OWN IN RECENT DECADES.

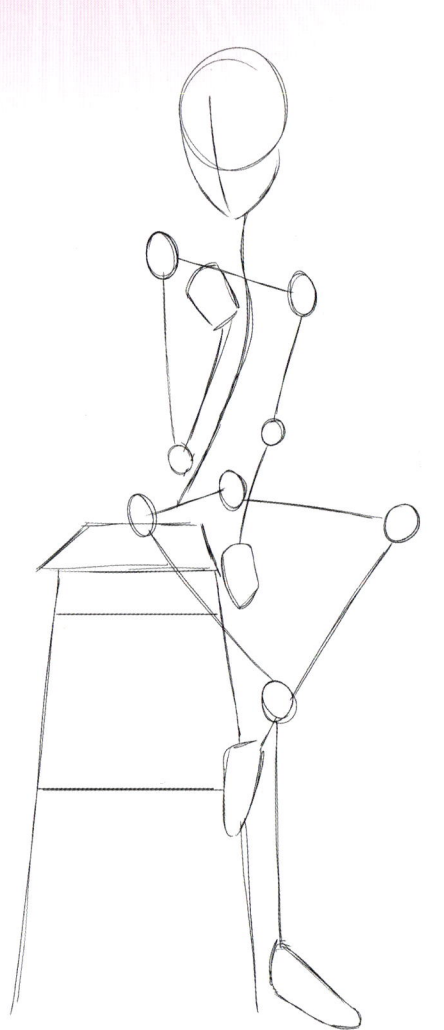
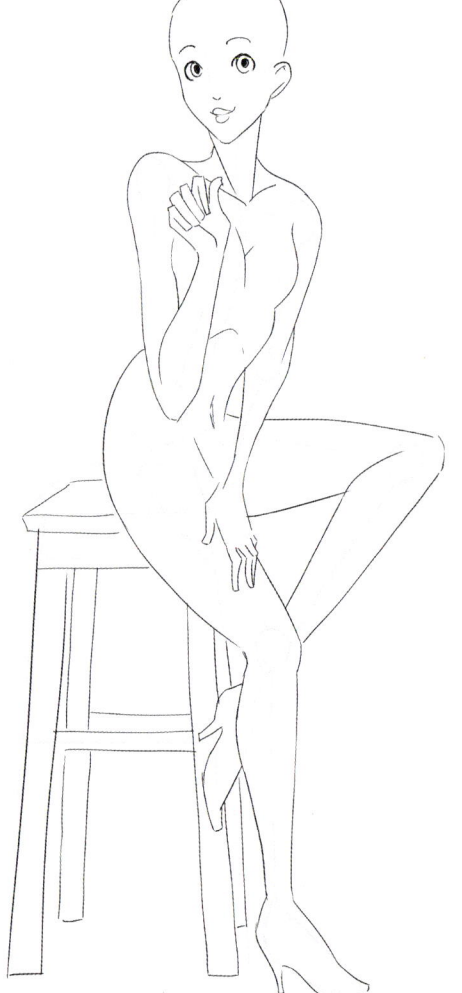
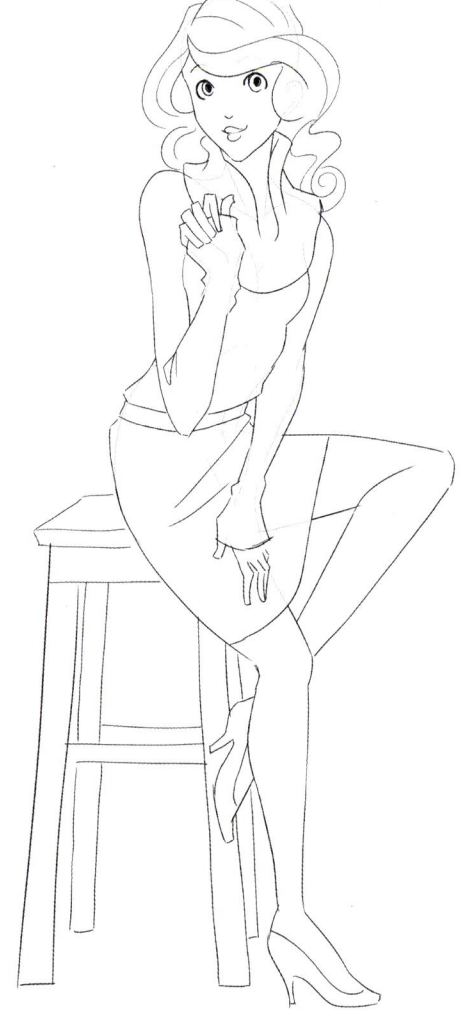

1 To add a bit of variation, our model will be sitting down in this sketch. Sketch in the stool first, so that you can be sure to check that her pose is looking natural before you've added in too much detail.

2 Draw the shapes of your model's body over your skeleton. Propping one foot up against the stool gives her a feminine appeal—you don't want just your clothes to look good, but your model as well.

3 Thinking about the sort of outfit you want to give your model, begin to sketch in the shapes of the clothes. Knitted clothing can be quite baggy and loose, so cinch it in at the waist with a belt to keep it flattering. Don't forget to give your model some hair—soft and natural suits the clothing.

WINTER KNITWEAR | 119

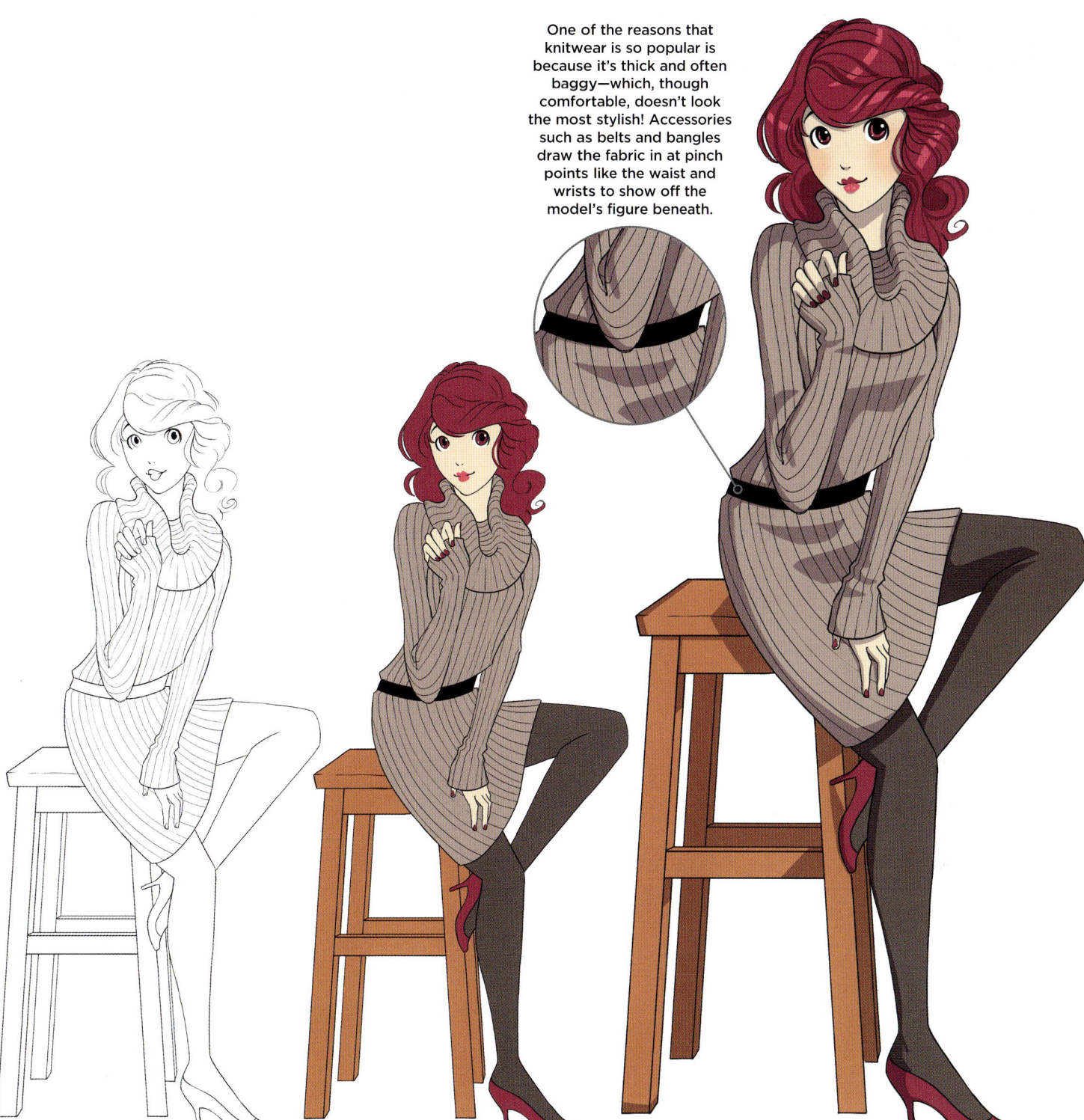

One of the reasons that knitwear is so popular is because it's thick and often baggy—which, though comfortable, doesn't look the most stylish! Accessories such as belts and bangles draw the fabric in at pinch points like the waist and wrists to show off the model's figure beneath.

4 When cleaning up your sketch, add in some details to help describe your fabrics. Woolen fabric is often ribbed, so draw in thin, delicate lines to show this. It also doesn't crease or fold in the same way that thinner fabrics do, so keep your creases large and soft. In some areas you can get away with not drawing the creases at all, as they usually do not show.

5 Gray is a popular color for knitwear, especially as it's a common winter style—however, you don't want it to look too boring. By adding in dark pinks and reds, you can make it stand out without losing that winter look. When coming up with color schemes, try to stick to warm hues to blow away those winter blues.

6 Keeping in mind the thicker nature of knit, use soft shadows to describe the folds that you left out in the earlier steps. Adding highlights to the model's hair will make it look extra shiny—a nice contrast to the soft look of the dress.

120 | THE COLLECTIONS

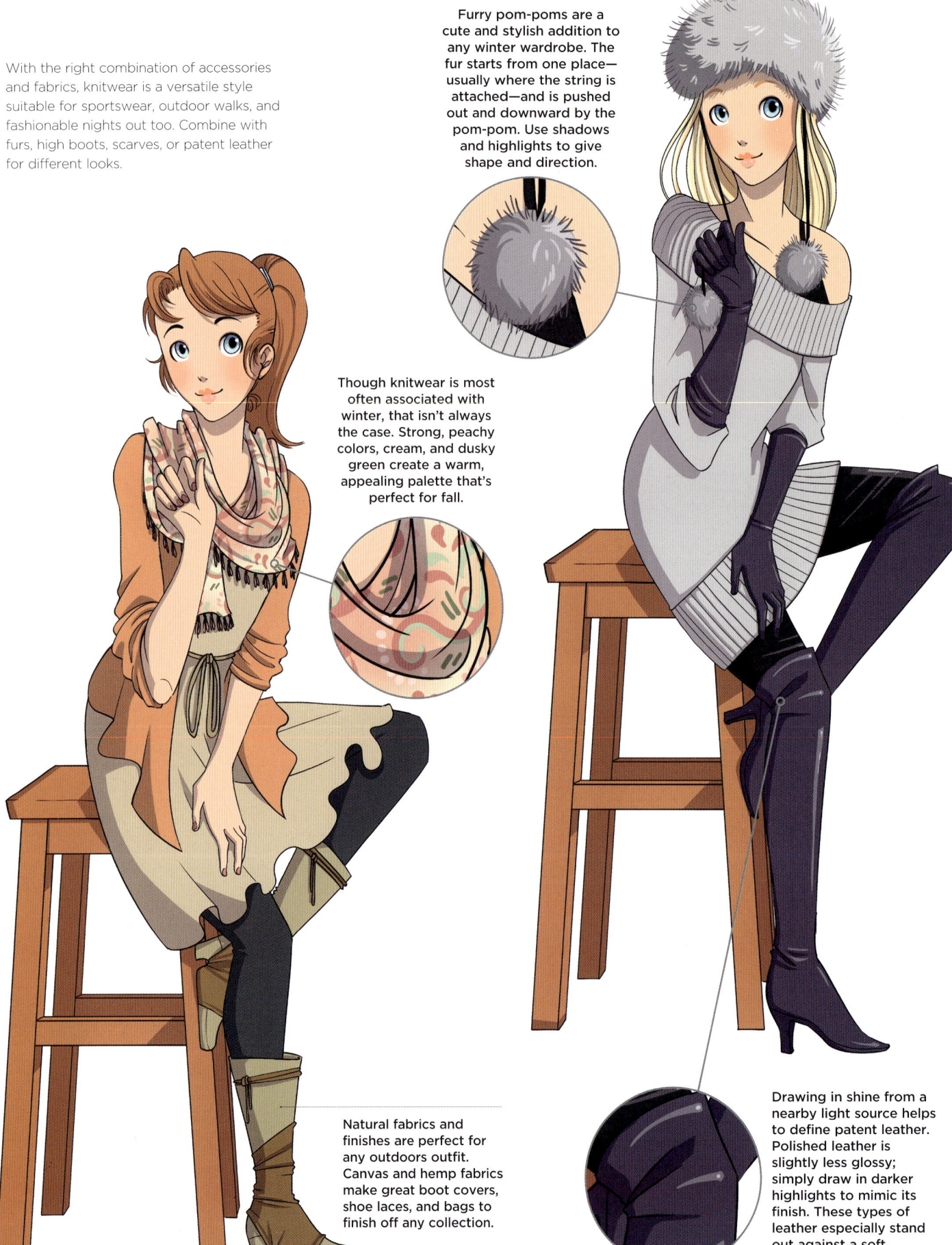

With the right combination of accessories and fabrics, knitwear is a versatile style suitable for sportswear, outdoor walks, and fashionable nights out too. Combine with furs, high boots, scarves, or patent leather for different looks.

Furry pom-poms are a cute and stylish addition to any winter wardrobe. The fur starts from one place—usually where the string is attached—and is pushed out and downward by the pom-pom. Use shadows and highlights to give shape and direction.

Though knitwear is most often associated with winter, that isn't always the case. Strong, peachy colors, cream, and dusky green create a warm, appealing palette that's perfect for fall.

Natural fabrics and finishes are perfect for any outdoors outfit. Canvas and hemp fabrics make great boot covers, shoe laces, and bags to finish off any collection.

Drawing in shine from a nearby light source helps to define patent leather. Polished leather is slightly less glossy; simply draw in darker highlights to mimic its finish. These types of leather especially stand out against a soft, matte wool.

WINTER KNITWEAR | 121

ACCESSORIES AND CLOTHING

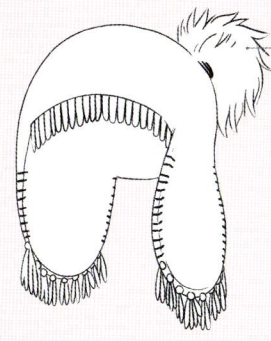

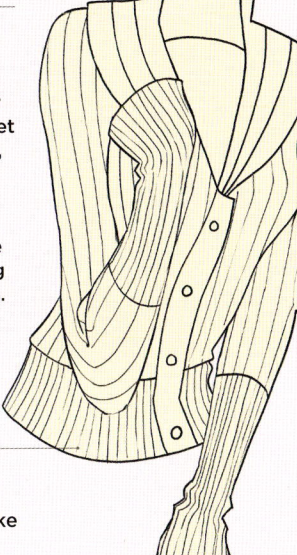

We all think of a winter hat when we think of knitted headwear, but there are plenty of other options out there. A beret is a smart, stylish option, or by using different knitting styles—a cable knit or a lace stitch, perhaps—you can create some interesting-looking items for your collection.

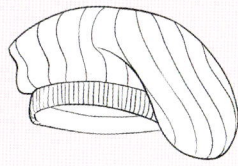

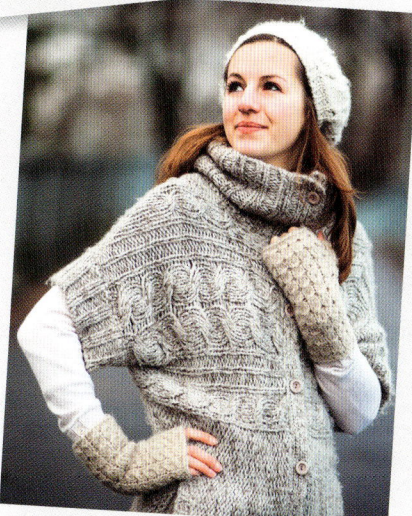

Knitwear can be quite loose and easily end up looking unflattering. Make sure that it is pulled in at the waist and the neckline, by a belt or a fitted hem, to give it shape and prevent it from swamping your model.

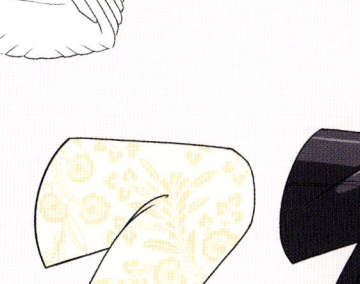

Any talented knitter could tell you all about the many different patterns that can be knitted into woolen garments. As you can see in these photos, wool has the potential for some lovely, unique textures and designs—you could even have your fashion label's logo knitted in!

Knitwear looks great when mixed and matched with other fabrics. Try combining it with patent leather, so that the shininess serves as a contrast to the look of the wool, or try combining lacy tights or other patterned fabrics for different looks.

CLOTHING PALETTE

 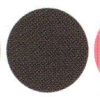

One of the appeals of knitwear is its natural look and feel. As a result, try to keep its charm by using nature-inspired grays and raspberry pinks.

ANDROGYNOUS
BY EMMA VIECELI

IT'S KEY TO REMEMBER THAT AN ANDROGYNOUS LOOK DOESN'T MEAN THAT THE MODEL SHOULD LOOK LIKE A BOY: ANDROGYNY IS ABOUT **WALKING A LINE** THAT SHUNS **GENDER BIAS**, AND SOMETIMES FLIPS IT INTENTIONALLY ON ITS HEAD. THIS IS ABOUT **DRESSING NEITHER LIKE A BOY NOR A GIRL** ... AND WHATEVER THOSE TERMS ARE SUPPOSED TO DICTATE.

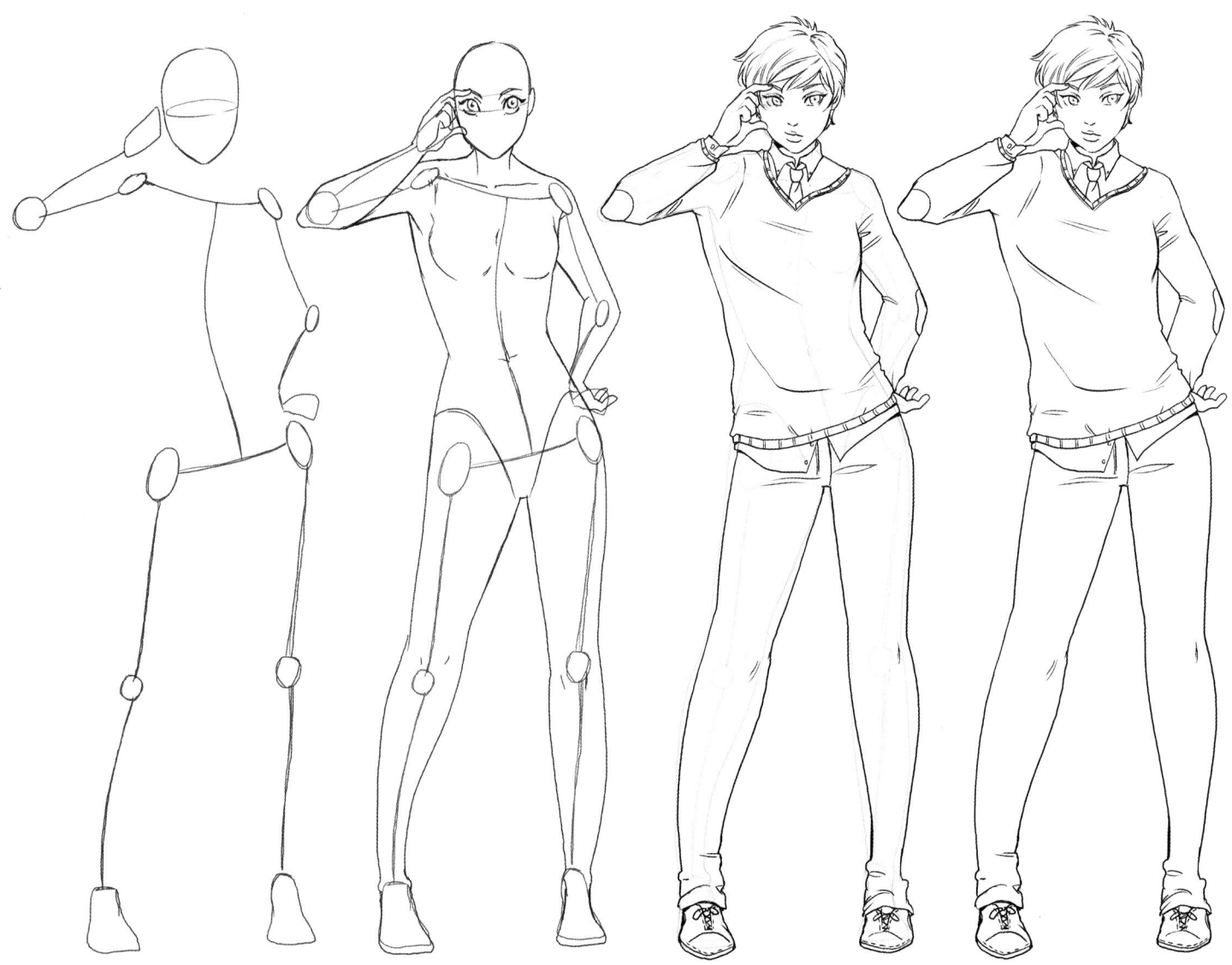

1 Create a confident, bold pose, but keep something distinctly feminine in the slant of the hips.

2 Be careful to avoid the pitfalls of drawing an androgynous female with a male figure. Remember to keep hips no narrower than the shoulders.

3 If you have a held accessory planned (glasses, in this case), make sure the hand is drawn in the correct position.

4 This is a casual, slightly messy look. Give the model tousled, boyish hair to match the outfit, remembering that the bone structure and body shape will contrast with this.

ANDROGYNOUS | 123

CLOTHING PALETTE

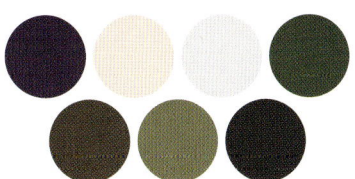

This outfit has a bit of a school uniform feel to it, though worn as something far more casual. It uses fall tones and browns and greens. Avoid anything too outlandish.

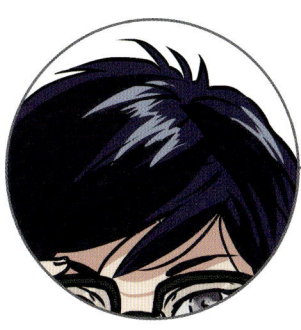

The model's hair is not in a classically feminine manga style—draw it to specifically convey your character's look. Try some variations!

Clothing in this design should not be form-fitting or cut according to women's fashion, as that would miss the point. The sweater here is slightly oversized and out of shape.

This outfit requires a lot of confidence and sass to pull off, not least of all in these rather old-fashioned shoes. No heels or straps here!

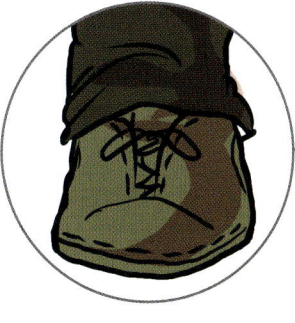

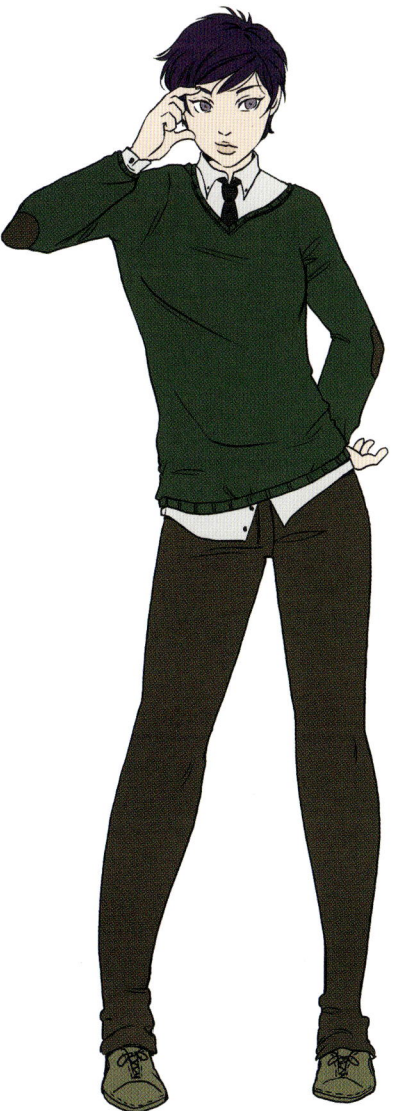

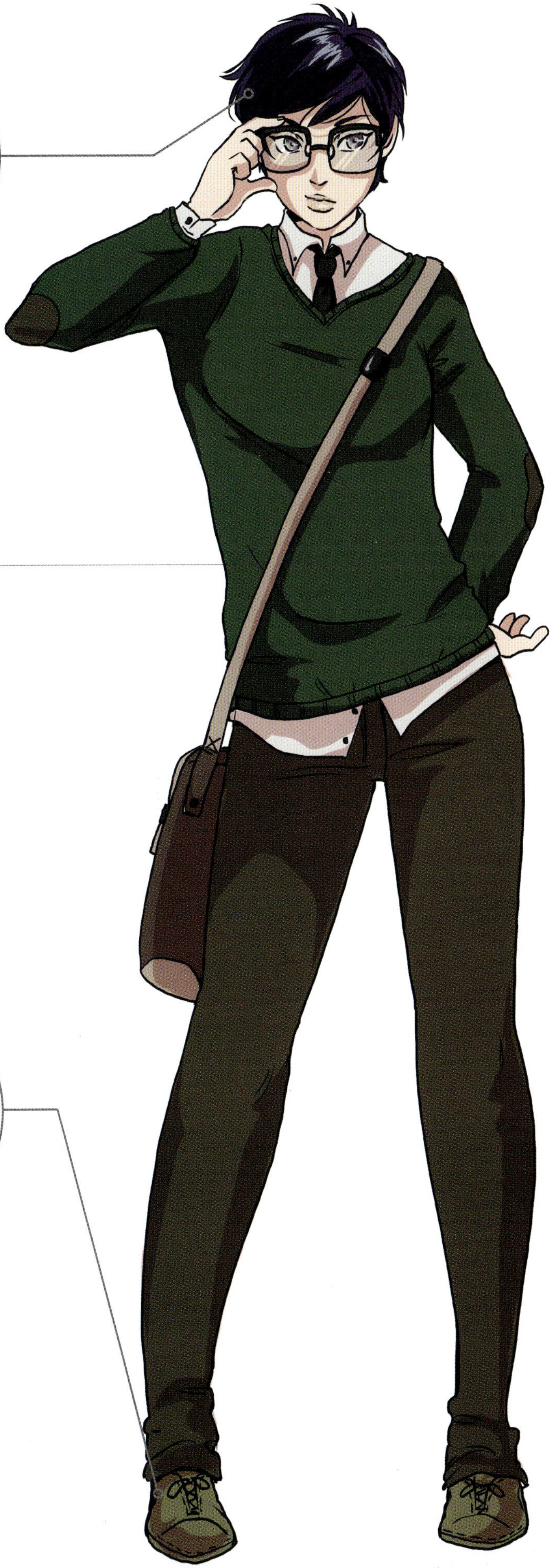

5 While you could decide to add some fantastic makeup for a brilliant bit of contrast, here we keep to a natural look, because this model is all about contrasting actual body form with boyish dressing.

6 A pair of oversized glasses and a satchel complete the look. If you're struggling to draw glasses, draw the full face first and then add the glasses over it, making sure that the character's eyes are set evenly behind the lenses.

124 | THE COLLECTIONS

There is no one androgynous look, of course. For as many ways as there are to dress in a way we would label "female" or "male," there are as many ways again to subvert those ideas. Research some male fashion outfits and try applying them to a female model. With a little additional tailoring, you should find that any outfit can fit feminine curves. Or, for that rumpled, cute look that we achieved on page 123, simply forget the tailoring!

Neckties look smart on male and female characters. If your character has a turned-down collar, you may only see the central part of the tie, but some collar styles, like this one, require you to think about the way the loop of the tie goes around the character's neck. This classy lady has a small pin holding the two loose pieces together.

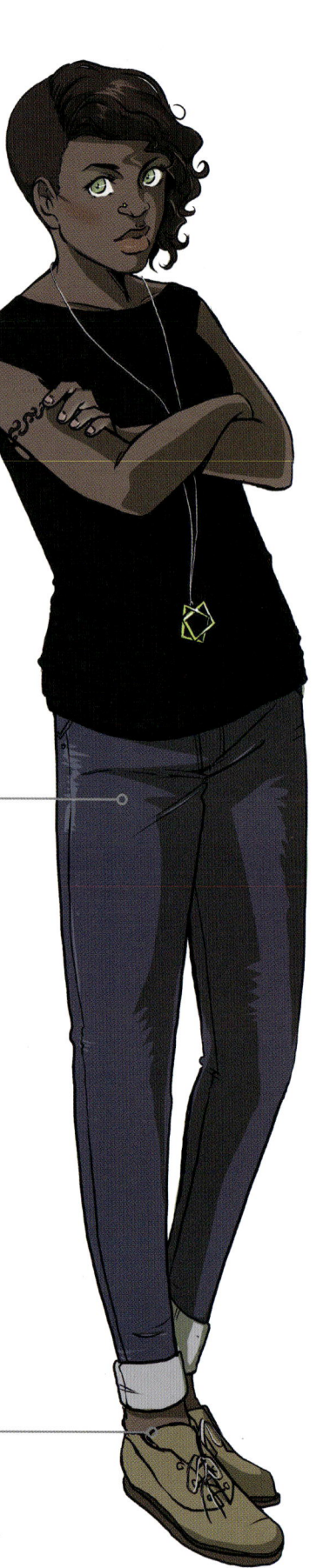

Tailoring of pants will greatly affect how creases will sit around the top of the legs. Avoid the temptation to always draw creases that follow the line of the groin; sometimes they'll flow diagonally downward or straight across.

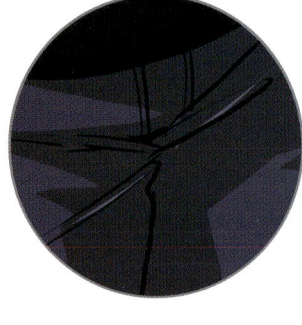

To imply tailored pants, think about seams and creases. A strong line down the front and back of the legs adds a flattering length and a certain sharpness.

In this design, the character wears long socks that show off her spat-style shoes, and her pants have a hem that sits over the socks, rather than having the socks holding the pants in place. If you're drawing full-length pants, consider and reference the way they fall on the top of shoes.

A good approach to drawing laced shoes and sneakers is to draw the tongue first and then draw the laces and panels that cover it to form the shoe.

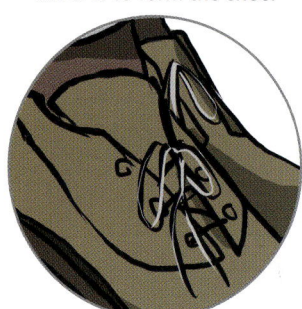

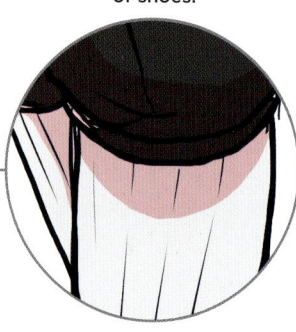

ANDROGYNOUS

CLOTHING AND ACCESSORIES

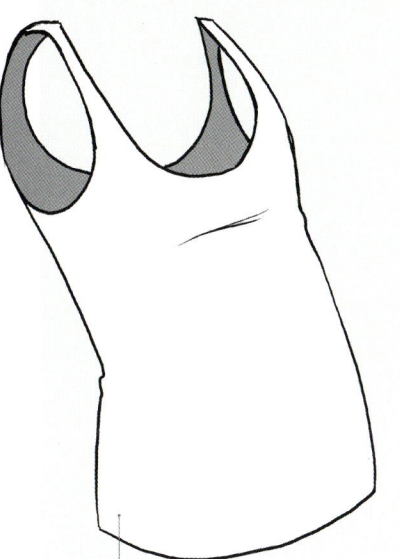

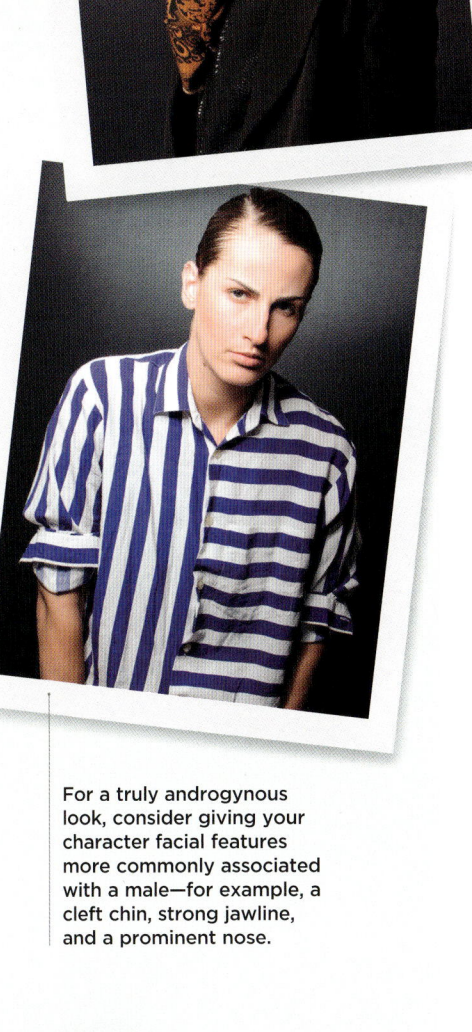

A layered look can work well for androgynous style. Start with a classic undershirt and build up from there.

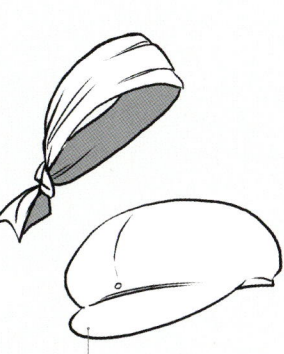

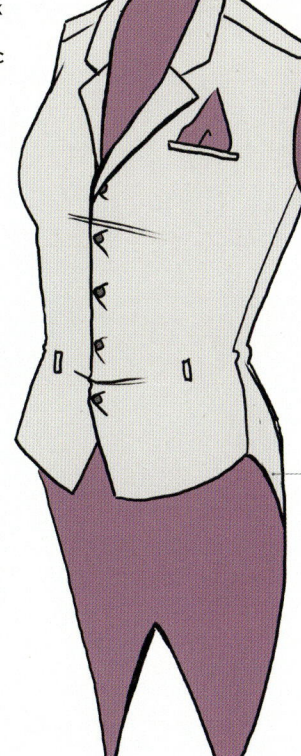

When it comes to suits and refined tailoring, why let men have all the fun? If you're drawing something tailored, make sure it fits your model correctly. Remember that women have a different body shape from men, so tailored suits will fit differently, especially around the waist. Embellish with a stylish cravat to complete the look.

Continuing the layering theme (see undershirt, above), consider dual headgear, such as a bandana underneath a cap.

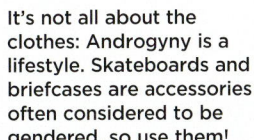

It's not all about the clothes: Androgyny is a lifestyle. Skateboards and briefcases are accessories often considered to be gendered, so use them!

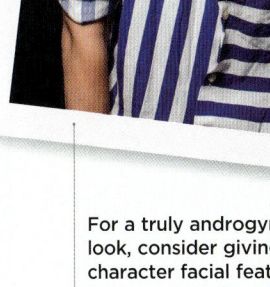

For a truly androgynous look, consider giving your character facial features more commonly associated with a male—for example, a cleft chin, strong jawline, and a prominent nose.

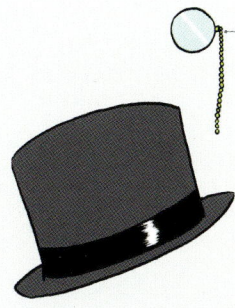

If you're trying out the dapper look, go the whole hog and add a monocle and top hat. Draw the model's full head before adding a hat, to make sure that the hat sits in a believable way.

HIP-HOP

ORIGINALLY CREATED BY **AFRICAN-AMERICAN YOUTHS** IN THE UNITED STATES DURING **THE 1970S**, HIP-HOP FASHION—ALSO KNOWN AS **URBAN FASHION**—HAS BARELY CHANGED SINCE ITS INCEPTION. A CELEBRATION OF **CULTURE AND DIVERSITY**, AND A LOVE OF **MUSIC AND DANCE**, IT IS A STYLE THAT IS PRACTICAL FOR **SPORTS AND DANCING**, YET CRAMMED FULL OF **ATTITUDE**.

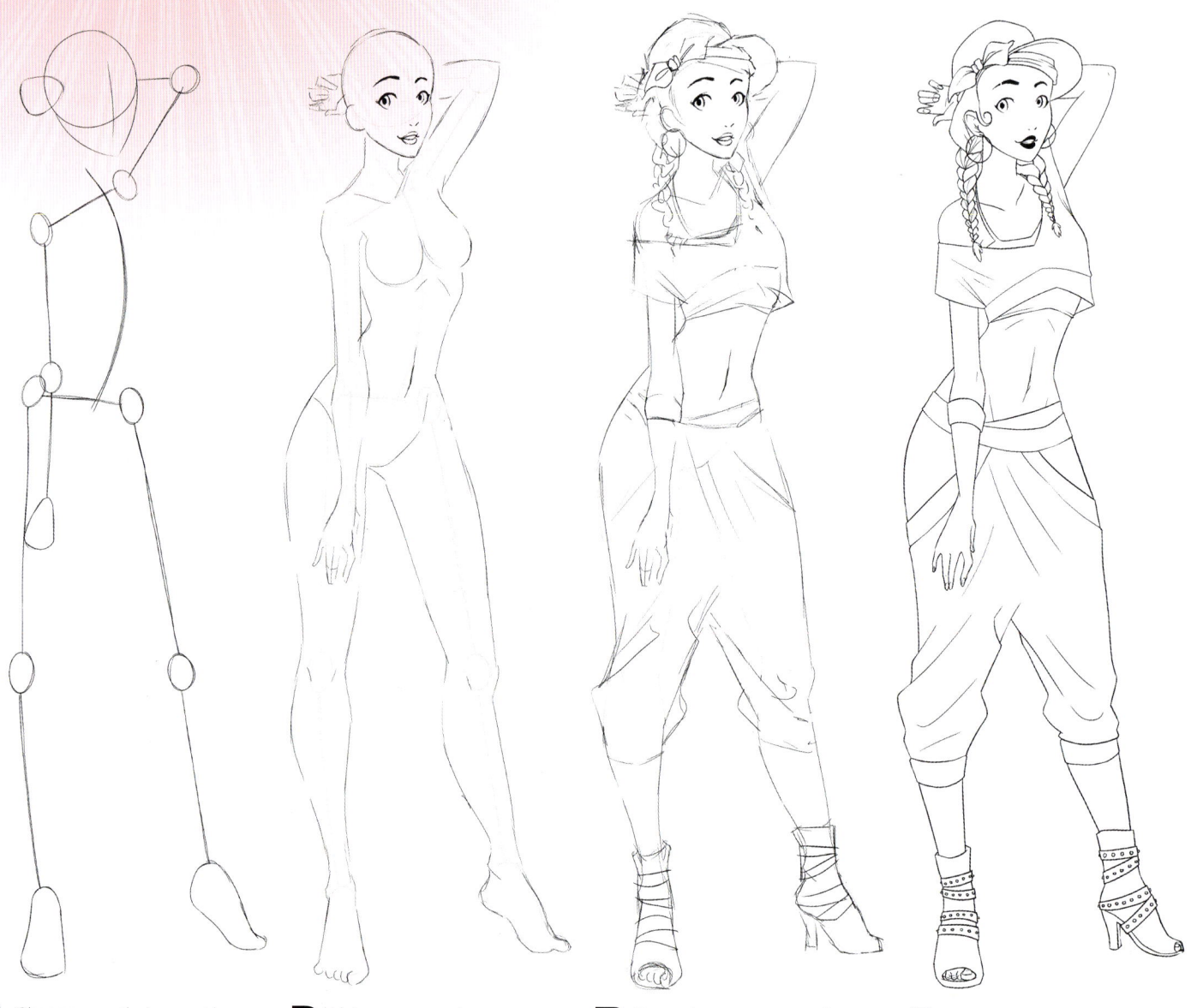

1 Chances are that any girl rocking the hip-hop look knows how to flaunt it—so make sure that your models do too! Standing with the feet apart, one arm back, and the back curved will give your model the right amount of attitude—help yourself work out the pose by drawing it as a simple skeleton. Make sure you're happy with it before you carry on to the next step.

2 Make sure you give your model the right amount of muscle for all the dancing she's going to do. Let the skeleton that you drew in the previous step help you with the pose—and if you have difficulties drawing the hands, use a mirror to study your own for reference.

3 Baggy harem pants and crop tops are popular as they leave the body free to move, and bandanas, hats, and braids keep the hair out of the face. Add some big jewelry, striking makeup, and a pair of sturdy heels, and you've got yourself a look.

4 Harem pants are designed to be baggy around the thighs and groin but tight around the shins. They should bunch around the waistband, but most of the folds will fall at the bottom of the legs, where gravity pulls the fabric downward. The same goes for a baggy top—it bunches at the armpit, but hangs loose everywhere else.

HIP-HOP | **127**

CLOTHING PALETTE

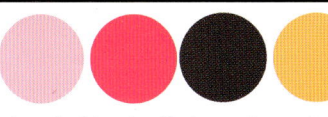

Hip-hop fashion is all about the attitude, so bright colors—and a lot of gold jewelry—will go a long way toward making it stand out. Female urbanites are all about rocking their gender—there's no shame in wearing a lot of pink. This outfit uses gray as a base color, with flashes of bright pink and gold for impact.

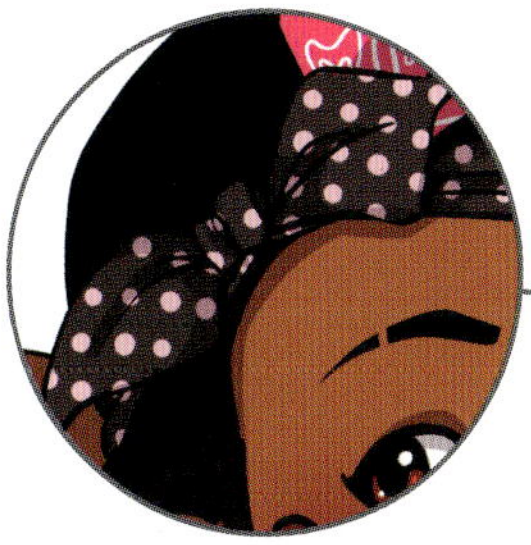

A bandana will help keep your model's hair out of her face when she goes out dancing, but just because it's practical doesn't mean it can't look good too. Polka dots are a cute, feminine pattern for any accessory, but using a gray and pink color palette keeps it looking edgy.

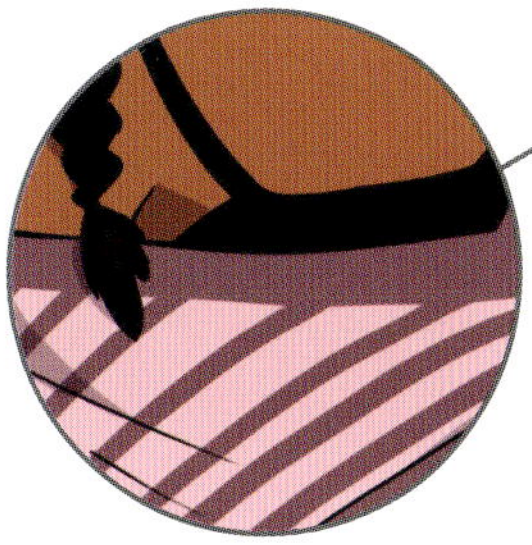

Practicality is the number-one criteria for hip-hop fashion, so it's important that clothes are designed to fit well, as well as look good. A sports tank helps to support this model's figure while she's dancing, and a looser top over it adds a splash of color and style.

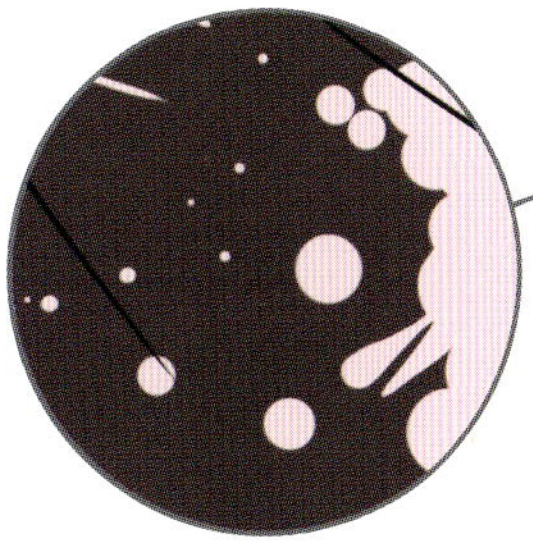

Patterns and designs on a garment will help break up large areas of flat color. Living's a busy job, so a splash of paint helps make these harem pants look well-loved—whether it was designed to look that way or not.

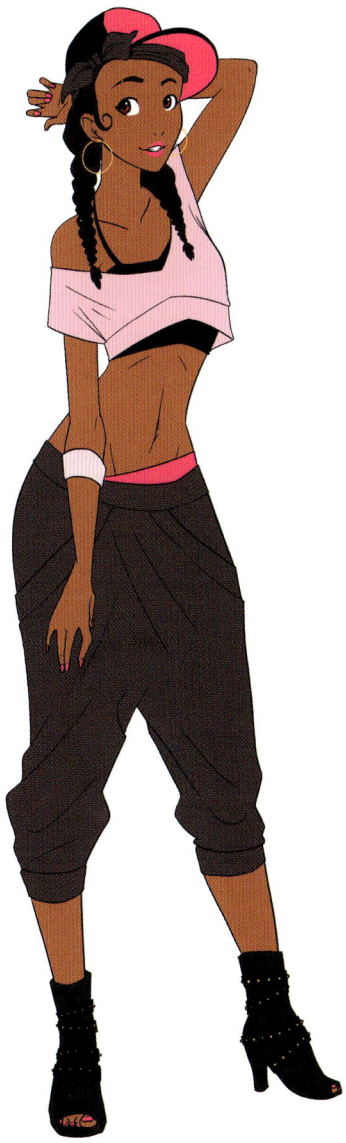

5 Using your chosen color palette, block in the main areas of the outfit. Bright sections of pink give it a cool, modern attitude, but too much wouldn't look right—use more neutral colors such as gray and a lighter pink in the larger garments to tone it back down again.

6 Hip-hop culture is all about having fun and making an impression, and bold patterns will complete this look. Make sure to take advantage of every area that you've got. A stripy top and patterned bandana add areas of detail, along with the design on the model's hat, paint textures on her pants, and chunky straps about her boots.

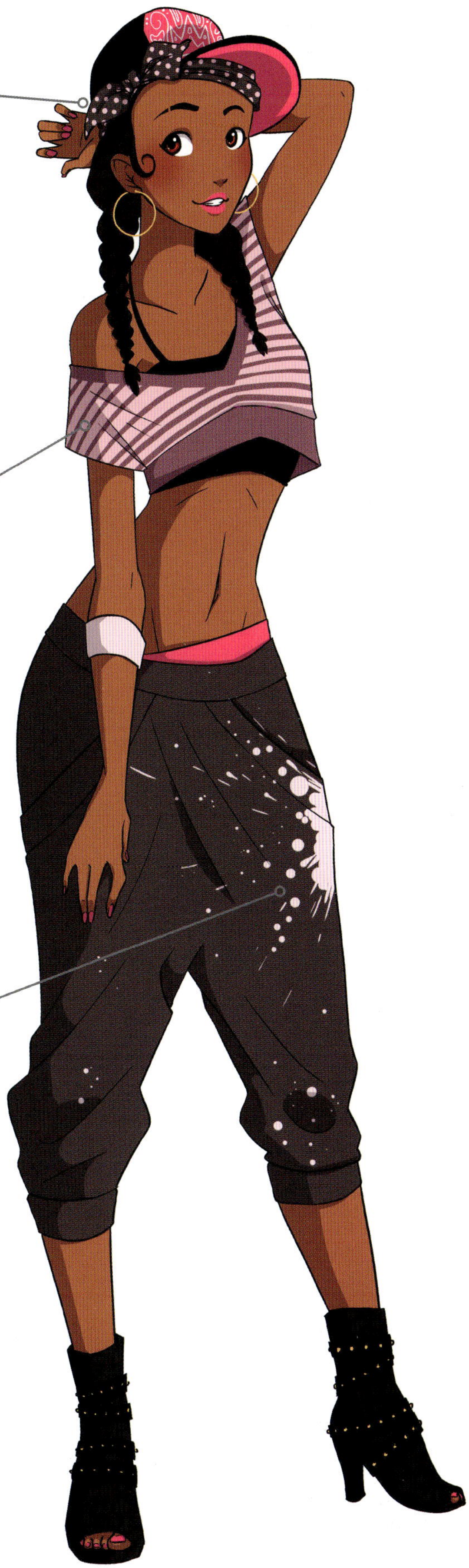

128 | THE COLLECTIONS

If you're going to go out dancing, there's a whole host of different looks out there for you. Whether you prefer comfortable, practical sportswear, or heels and short shorts, there are plenty of ways for you to show off your personality through urban fashion. Just remember to bling up your jewelry and throw on some bold lipstick, and you're set!

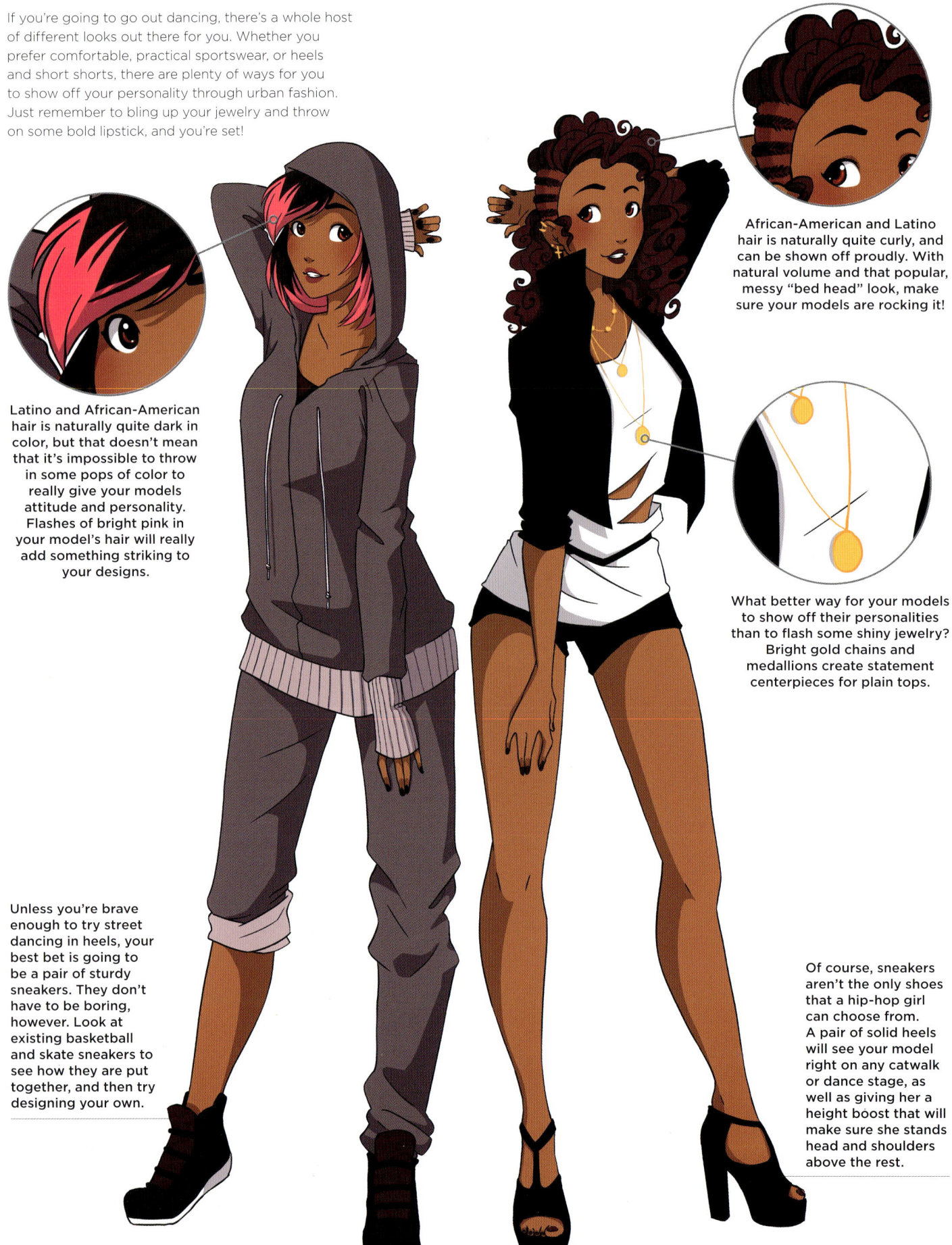

Latino and African-American hair is naturally quite dark in color, but that doesn't mean that it's impossible to throw in some pops of color to really give your models attitude and personality. Flashes of bright pink in your model's hair will really add something striking to your designs.

African-American and Latino hair is naturally quite curly, and can be shown off proudly. With natural volume and that popular, messy "bed head" look, make sure your models are rocking it!

What better way for your models to show off their personalities than to flash some shiny jewelry? Bright gold chains and medallions create statement centerpieces for plain tops.

Unless you're brave enough to try street dancing in heels, your best bet is going to be a pair of sturdy sneakers. They don't have to be boring, however. Look at existing basketball and skate sneakers to see how they are put together, and then try designing your own.

Of course, sneakers aren't the only shoes that a hip-hop girl can choose from. A pair of solid heels will see your model right on any catwalk or dance stage, as well as giving her a height boost that will make sure she stands head and shoulders above the rest.

HEADGEAR AND CLOTHING

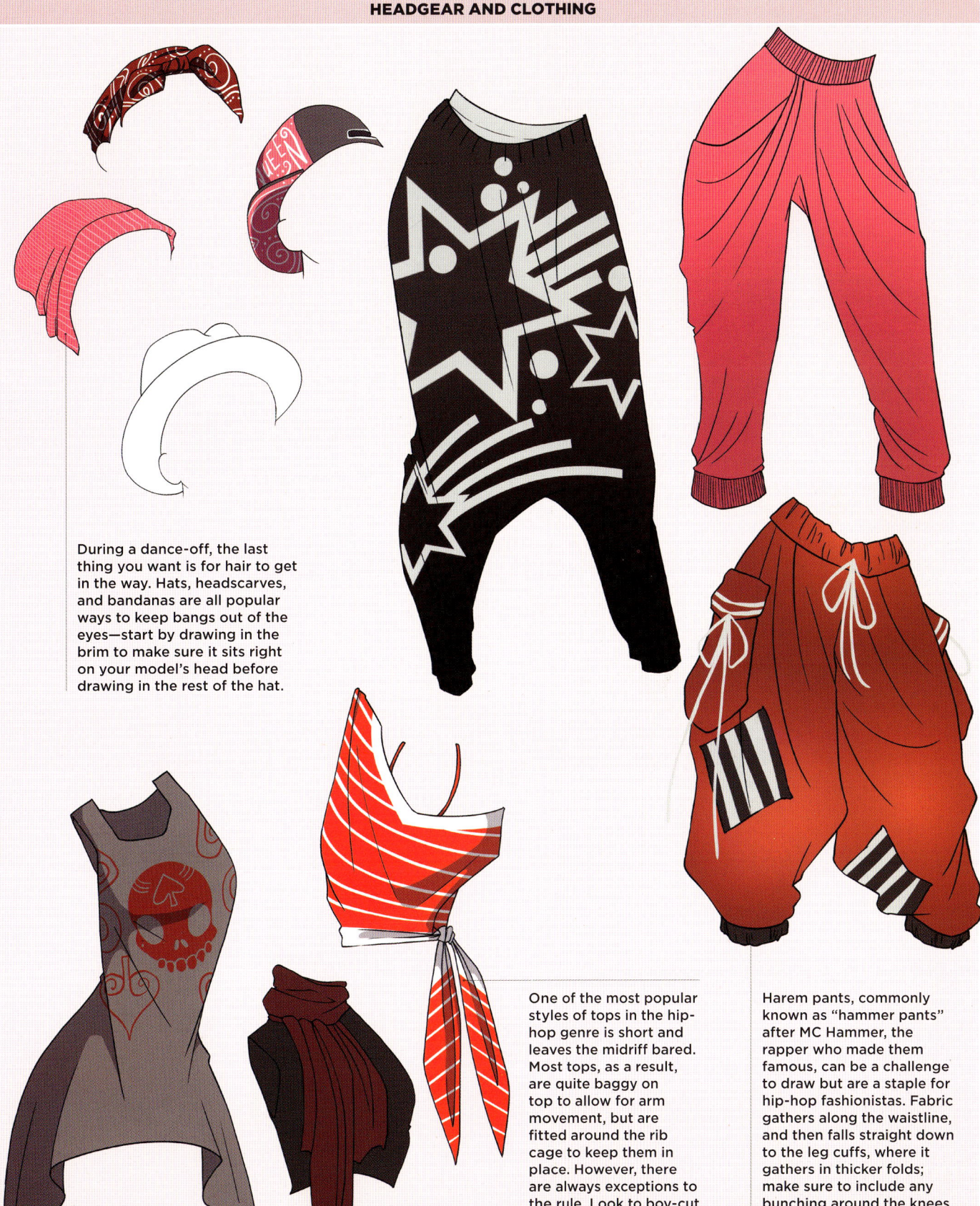

During a dance-off, the last thing you want is for hair to get in the way. Hats, headscarves, and bandanas are all popular ways to keep bangs out of the eyes—start by drawing in the brim to make sure it sits right on your model's head before drawing in the rest of the hat.

One of the most popular styles of tops in the hip-hop genre is short and leaves the midriff bared. Most tops, as a result, are quite baggy on top to allow for arm movement, but are fitted around the rib cage to keep them in place. However, there are always exceptions to the rule. Look to boy-cut T-shirts, baggy tanks, and oversized hoodies to vary your designs.

Harem pants, commonly known as "hammer pants" after MC Hammer, the rapper who made them famous, can be a challenge to draw but are a staple for hip-hop fashionistas. Fabric gathers along the waistline, and then falls straight down to the leg cuffs, where it gathers in thicker folds; make sure to include any bunching around the knees and groin area also.

APOCALYPSE STYLE
BY LAURA WATTON-DAVIES

IN A FUTURISTIC WORLD, IT IS **SURVIVAL OF THE FITTEST**—AND SAVVIEST. CLOTHING IS SCAVENGED FROM THAT LEFT BEHIND; **UTILITY RULES**. SHOWCASED IN POPULAR SCI-FI FILMS LIKE *THE TERMINATOR* AND *MAD MAX*, APOCALYPSE STYLE HAS BEEN INCREDIBLY POPULAR SINCE THE '90S. TODAY'S INTERPRETATION OF THIS LOOK IS EVEN MORE **UTILITARIAN** AND **FUTURISTIC**—THIS LOOK IS BACK, AND **AIMS TO KILL**.

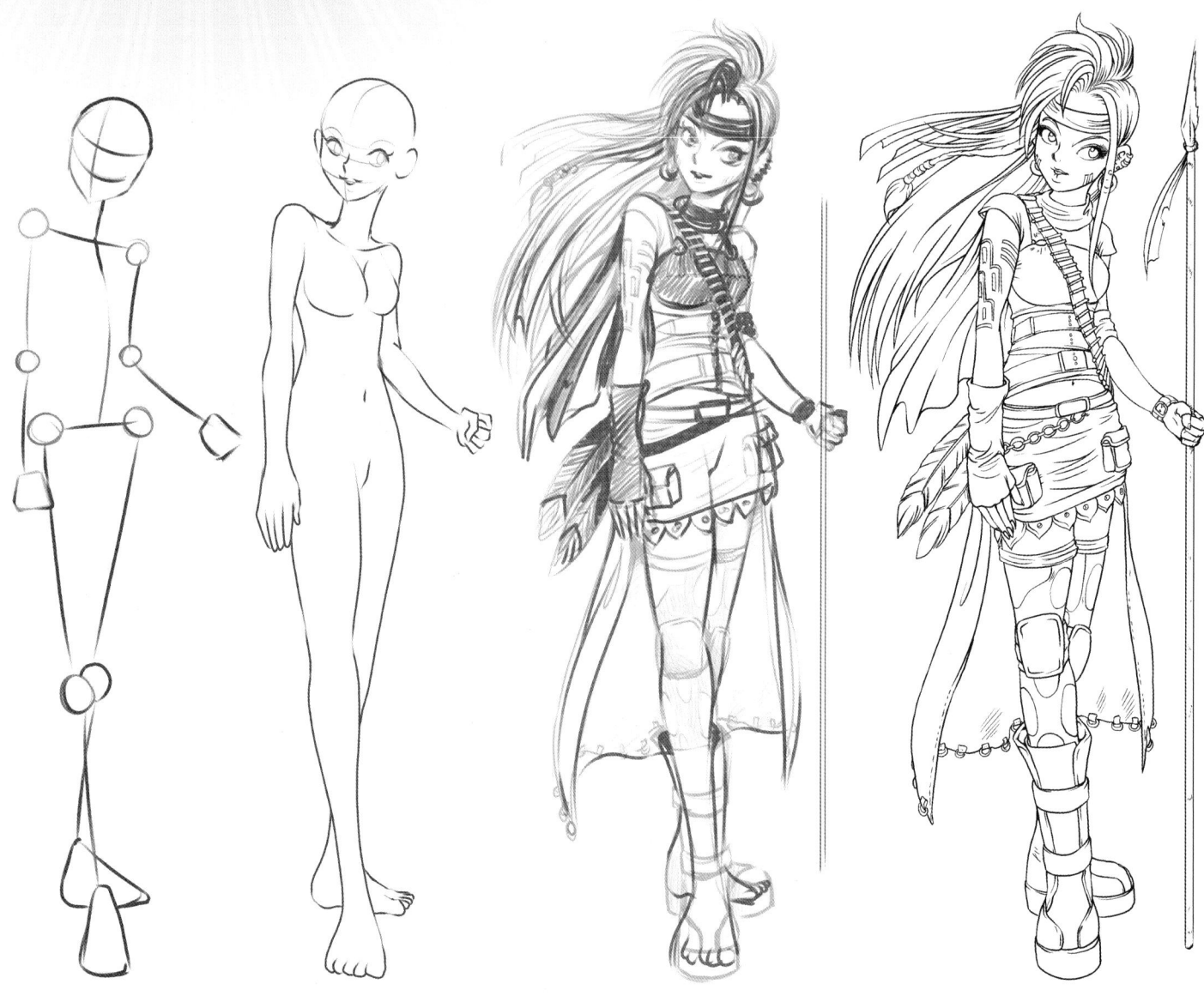

1 Rough out your character pose by first imagining the mood of your character, and reflect it using curved bends in your straight lines. For joints, use small circles. Facial features can be laid out using rough guidelines on the skull.

2 Rounded pencil lines and body contours help shape the weight, body language, and expression of your character. Draw around your rough character pose and create a stance using contoured, light lines.

3 Add as much detail as you want at this stage (refine it in Step 4). Block out clothing ideas using rough strips and rounded shapes. There may be a "breeze" in your scene, which means loose fabrics should flow in the same direction; use long strokes to imply this.

4 Select which rough line you feel is best with a quality stroke—be confident! Add extra creases by making short lines that swipe backward and forward for texture. Add smaller details like hoop earrings by drawing small curves around the ears.

APOCALYPSE STYLE | **131**

CLOTHING PALETTE

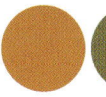  

An urban palette with khaki themes blends the wearer into their background. The stronger and brighter colors pop and contrast with the moodier selections.

Flowing ribbons, straps, and light feathers contrast with the character's harsher but practical clothing choices; they signify potential team leadership and rebelliousness.

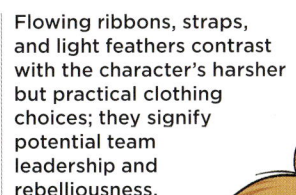

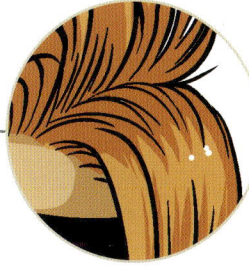

Use white spots to highlight areas that shine (for example, lips, eyes, hair). Facial makeup marks imply tribal belonging. These can be applied using a small paintbrush tip, tiny brushes, or sharpened pencil points.

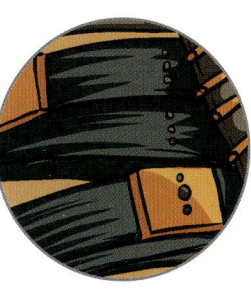

You can create texture that's useful for strappy, stretched materials by applying dark strokes over light areas.

Nonmatching gloves are a fashion point. Other accessories (spears, etc.) can be good to use for urban photoshoots or cosplay.

Smoother patterns can be applied by concentrating on light and heavy strokes of the same color, or by choosing different but darker shades.

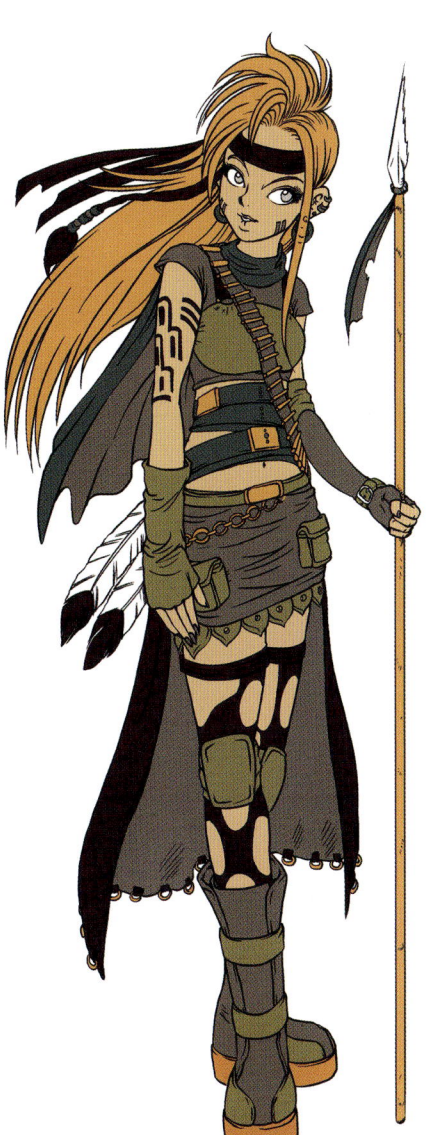

5 Fill in areas with flat, block color. Break up more mundane, desaturated areas with stronger colors.

Boots made from panels of leather or other durable materials are practical and suitable for this style. Draw round-edged shapes around the foot and ankle and fill with a matte color.

6 Select slightly darker colors to shade in areas using your palette choices. Think of the direction from which your light source falls (in this illustration, from top-right) and think where shadows would lie (for example, behind this character's spear). If you layer up your colors (via either digital or hand-applied color), you can create darker shades.

132 | THE COLLECTIONS

Wasteland chic mixes and matches aesthetics—it doesn't matter what silhouette the wearer has, because layering, taping, and strapping items together from found objects is at the core of this look. Use muted and saturated colors so that your characters blend in with their environment, and remember that practicality is key to survival.

The headscarf can be adapted into a shawl. Shade in between the creases to create depth. The area behind the character's head can be darkened to give more depth. Long, curved strokes convey flowing fabric.

Thin dreadlocks brushed back and styled into a faux-Mohawk bouffant shape are created using long, thin, string-shaped pipe forms.

Goggles are a style point. This item doubles as a headband. Small strokes of lighter color on the lenses imply a flat, shiny surface.

Use a large ponytail holder to constrain the huge dreadlocks hanging down the model's back; thick, round sausage shapes are useful for this hairstyle.

Knee-guards can be punched into cropped-leg combat pants. Draw rectangles for the patches with small dots as fabric bolts in each corner. Color in using highlights if made of a shiny material; color in the same way as the pants if the texture is the same.

A ribbed panel top is a practical piece as well as a fashion item. The extra strips of reinforced fabric help protect against knocks with their strength.

Rubberized Japanese jika-tabi boots provide comfort and flexibility. Draw around the big toe as one part of the toe cap, and draw another shape around the rest of the toes for the rest of the toe cap.

Steel-toe-capped boots protect the feet in harsh environments. Draw a big, round toe cap area over the sketch of your character's feet.

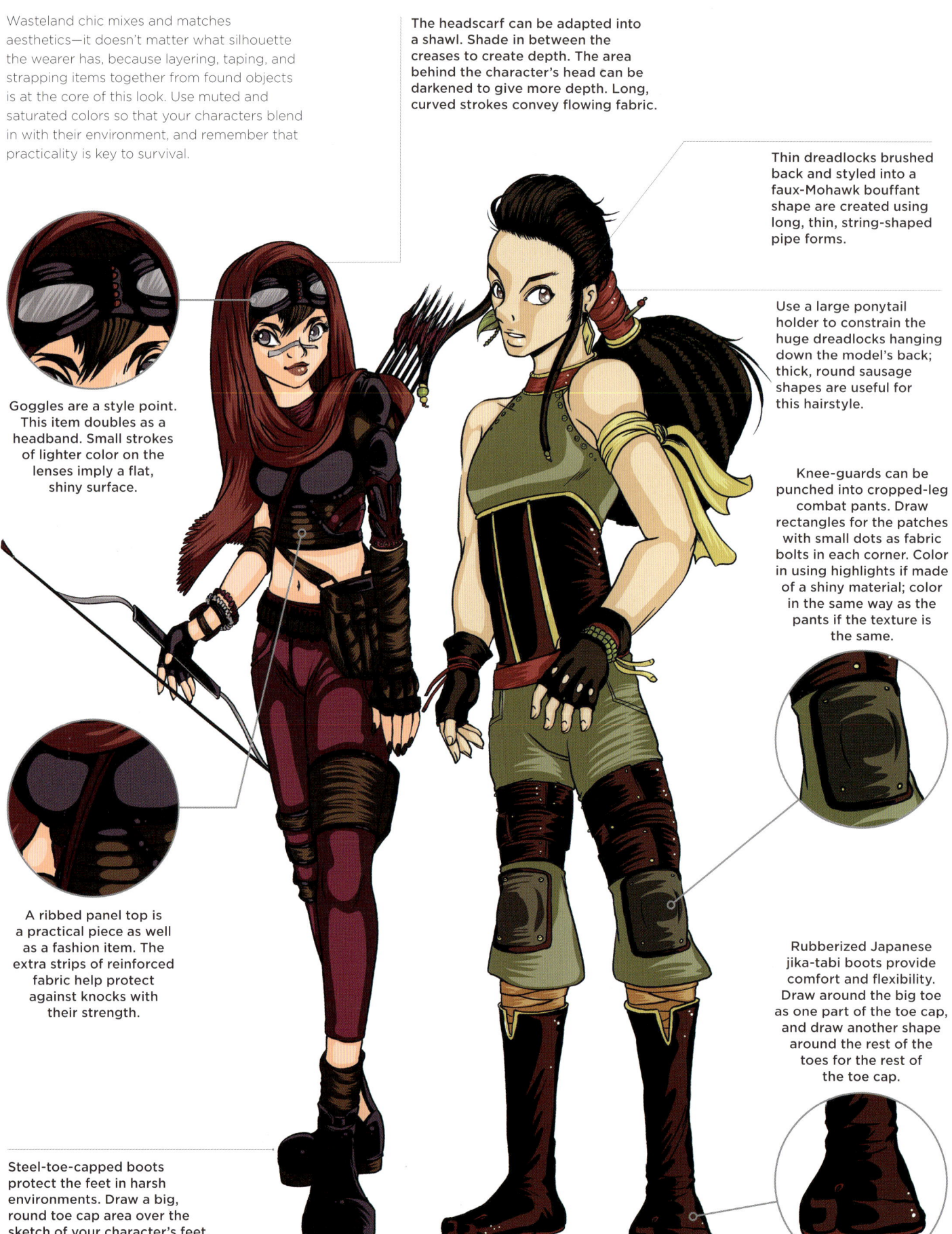

APOCALYPSE STYLE | 133

ACCESSORIES AND CLOTHING

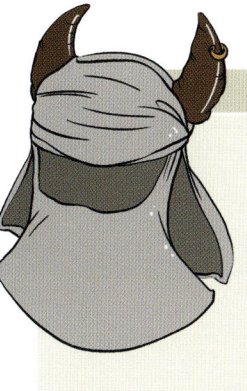

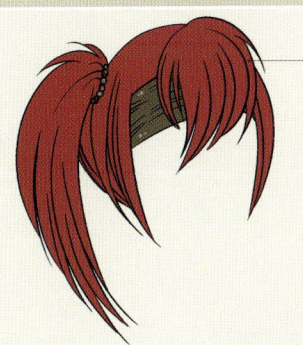

A balaclava will cover the face completely and create an unusual silhouette, especially with added horns! A bandana or headband will work under or over hair as an accessory or for practicality. Draw lines under the bangs or over the forehead, curving the strip around the forehead shape.

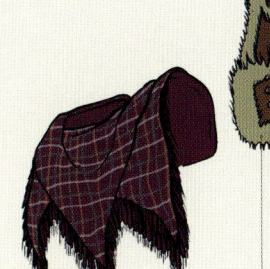

A scarf can be used as a neck decoration, for practical warmth, or to adapt into a head covering. Draw loose triangle shapes from the neck and shoulder area, and draw small tassels across the edges that hang straight down. This green/brown furry neck wrap works as a stand-up collar—small brushstrokes drawn in a thin "U" shape sit closely together, mimicking a furry texture.

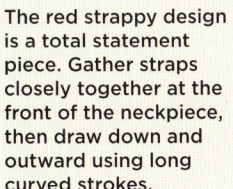

The red strappy design is a total statement piece. Gather straps closely together at the front of the neckpiece, then draw down and outward using long curved strokes.

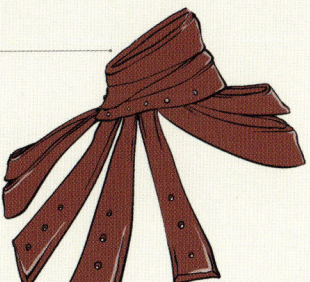

A utility belt should be easy to reach, and can hold money and documents. Draw a flat hoop with cubes to form pockets on the outside. This brown sidebag has a multi-sectioned purse that can keep items flat and safe. The pouch can be unhooked and a different-sized bag reattached.

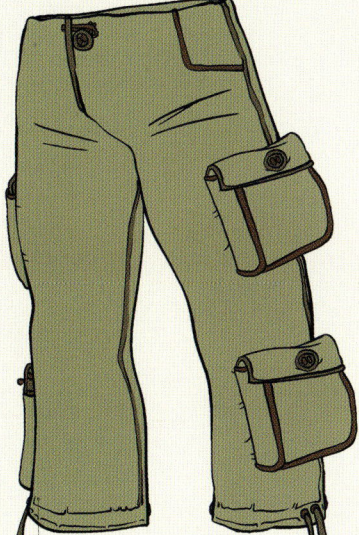

A document pouch can be used for larger items. It's simply one large rectangle with a utilitarian zipper design on the front. Draw using two thin strips and a zigzag pattern in between each strip. This gray bag will allow your character easy access to smaller or more valuable items. Shape using a rectangle base and a flat strap shape attached to each top corner.

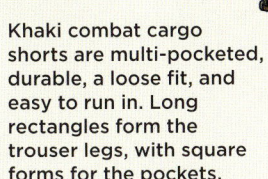

Khaki combat cargo shorts are multi-pocketed, durable, a loose fit, and easy to run in. Long rectangles form the trouser legs, with square forms for the pockets.

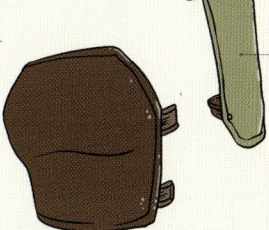

Chest and upper armpieces made of leatherette are not too heavy, and help shape the upper body. Curve the lines around the limbs or torso where required.

These leg warmers will keep ankles warm and adapt shoes into a boot-look style. Draw over the shins of your character and draw thin, curved lines from the outside lines to imply a wooly weight.

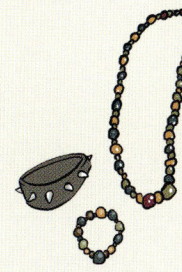

Small circles bunched together form tribal beaded strings. To create a spiked collar, place a flat leather strap around the character's neck using small spike shapes facing outward, drawn along a radius from a center point.

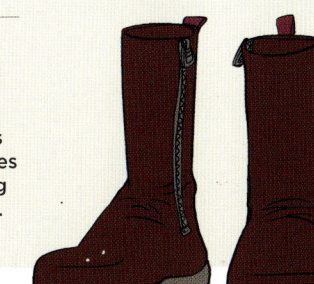

Draw around the foot and bulk outward, depending on how chunky you want your military boots to look and feel.

SPORTSWEAR
BY EMMA VIECELI

WHETHER IN A GYM, ON A TRACK, OR BY THE SEA, **FITNESS AND ATHLETICS** CAN TAKE MANY FORMS—AND THERE ARE MANY WAYS TO DRESS FOR THE OCCASION. FOR THE MOST PART, **PRACTICALITY** IS THE MOST IMPORTANT FACTOR WHEN DRAWING SPORTSWEAR. CLOTHING SHOULD **FACILITATE**, AND NOT INTERFERE WITH, THE ACTIVITY. BUT THERE'S PLENTY OF OPPORTUNITY FOR MAKING THINGS **FUN** TOO.

CLOTHING PALETTE

Anything goes, especially with beach sportswear. But this model has chosen some relaxing and soft colors to complement simple grays.

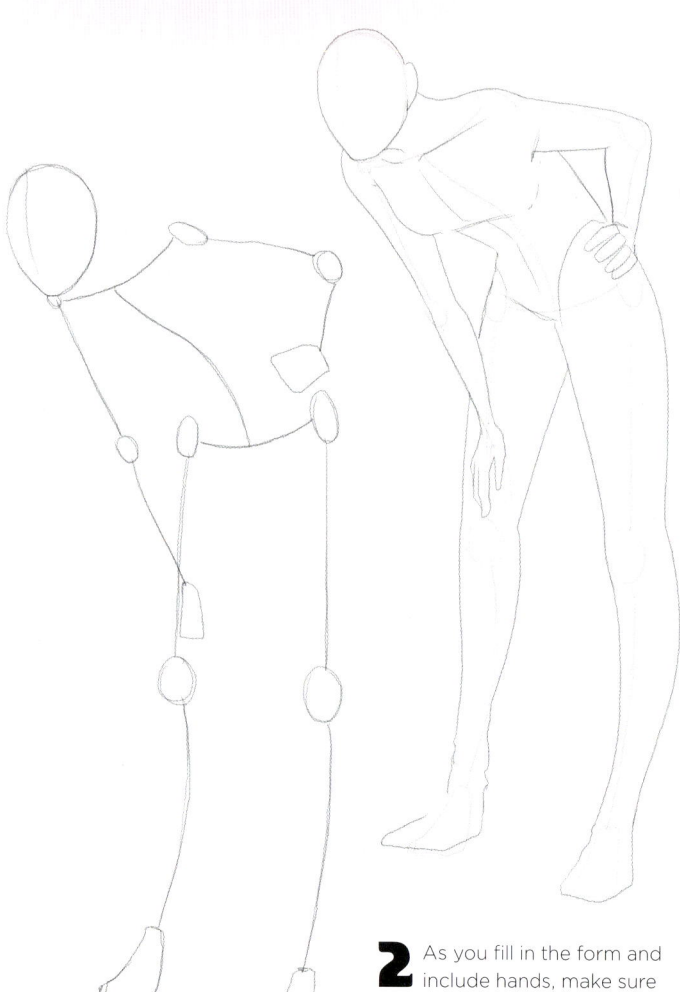

1 When drawing a leaning figure, make sure the proportions aren't warped—arm length is one to watch in particular.

2 As you fill in the form and include hands, make sure that, if the model is standing, the elbows will still sit at waist level, the wrists at the hips.

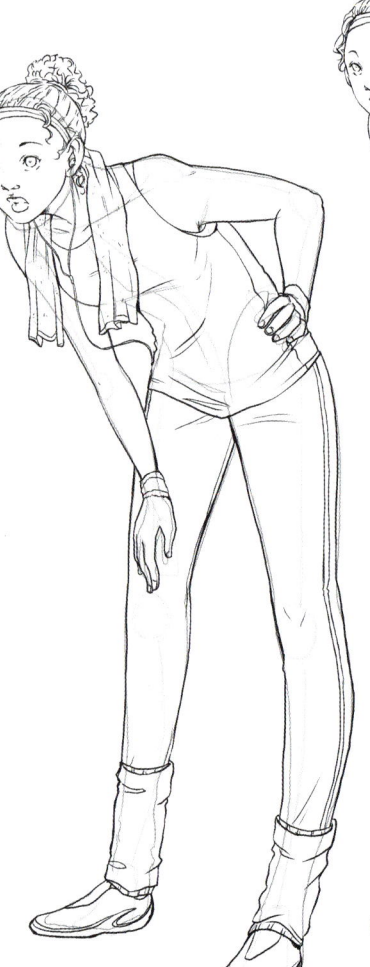

3 As always, consider rules like gravity. This model is leaning, so the towel around her neck will fall downward. Don't be tempted to have it follow her body shape.

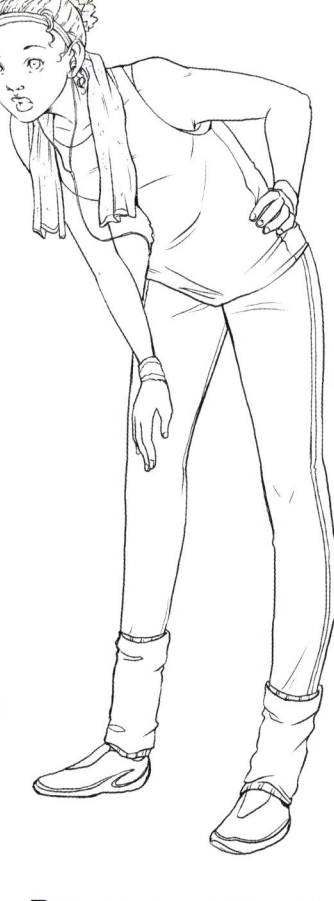

4 Consider how clothing will fall or cling. In this case, the model's top is figure-hugging, so it follows the body's shape as it bends.

SPORTSWEAR | 135

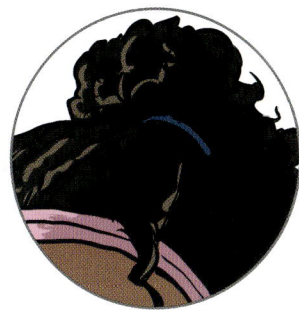

Thick, curly hair will reflect light in a different way from sleek and smooth hair. Always consider the surface you're highlighting and don't rely on the same tricks for all types.

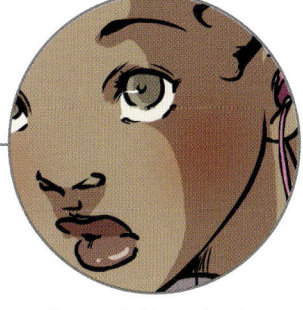

The model has glowing red cheeks here. Remember that exercise will get the blood flowing!

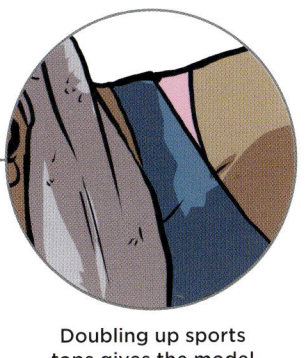

Doubling up sports tops gives the model an opportunity to lose a layer if she's hot, but also creates some cute color combination opportunities.

These sporty leg warmers are practical and streamlined, but they still have some looseness that you can show with a few well-placed creases.

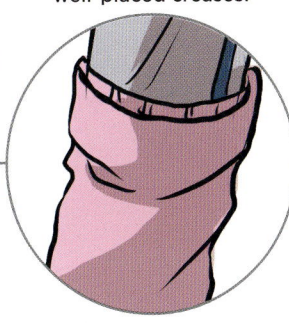

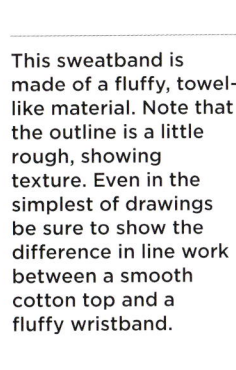

This sweatband is made of a fluffy, towel-like material. Note that the outline is a little rough, showing texture. Even in the simplest of drawings be sure to show the difference in line work between a smooth cotton top and a fluffy wristband.

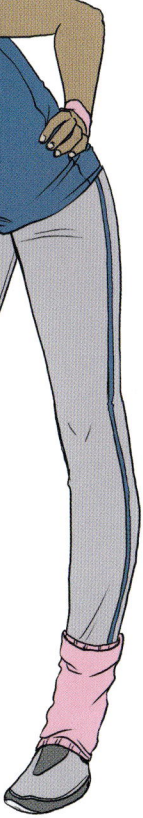

5 There's no limit to color in casual sportswear. Does your model want to stand out in a crowded gym or cheer herself up mid-activity with some bright shades? Keep things coordinated within the design, but have fun.

6 To create a cohesive outfit, be sure to use some repeating color themes. Here, the model's leg warmers and sweatbands match the undershirt she's wearing.

136 | THE COLLECTIONS

Sportswear is a broad topic that covers team sports, gym wear, and extreme sports. Remember that for some sporty looks, you can put your own creative stamp on a team uniform.

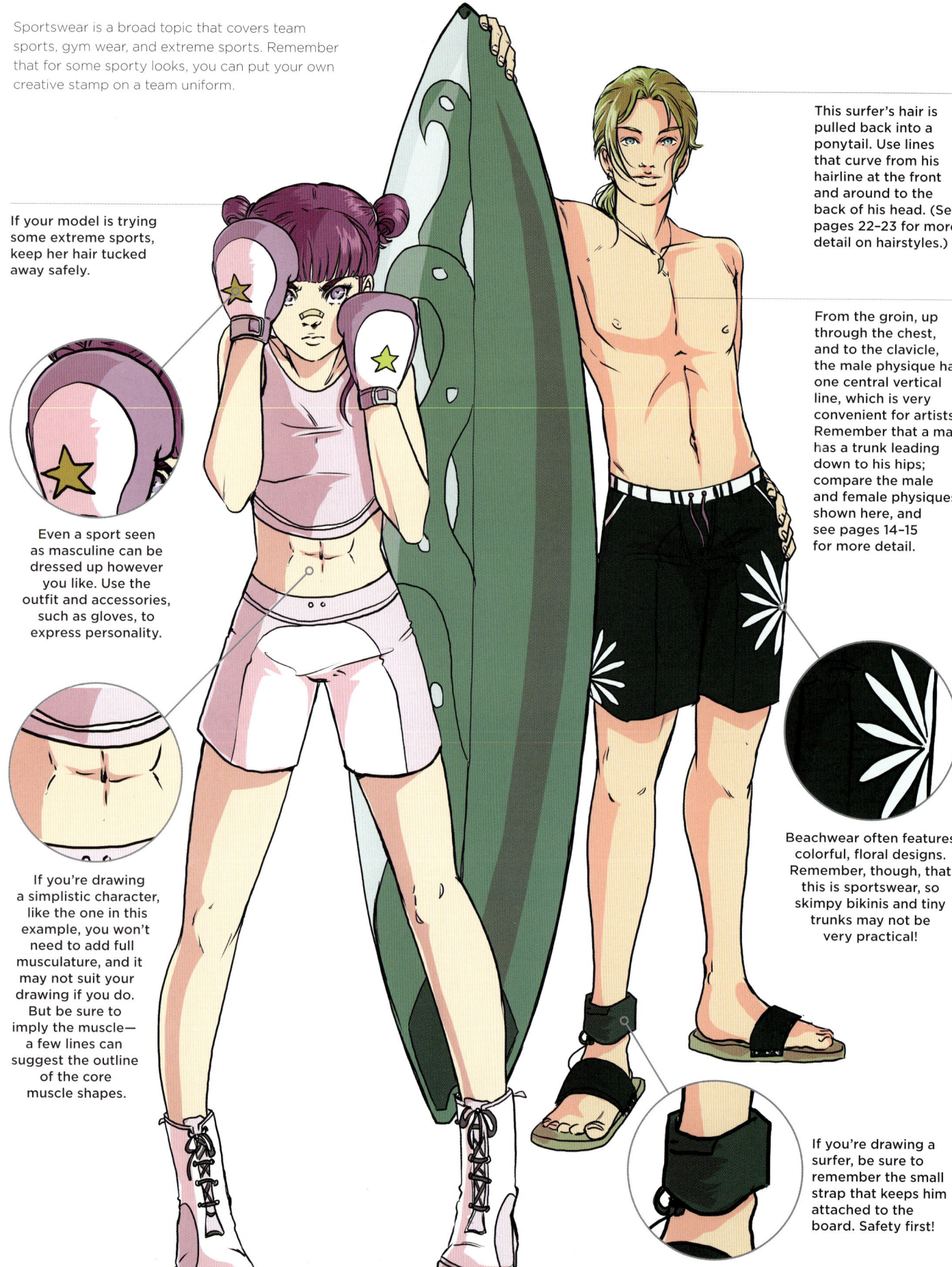

If your model is trying some extreme sports, keep her hair tucked away safely.

Even a sport seen as masculine can be dressed up however you like. Use the outfit and accessories, such as gloves, to express personality.

If you're drawing a simplistic character, like the one in this example, you won't need to add full musculature, and it may not suit your drawing if you do. But be sure to imply the muscle—a few lines can suggest the outline of the core muscle shapes.

This surfer's hair is pulled back into a ponytail. Use lines that curve from his hairline at the front and around to the back of his head. (See pages 22–23 for more detail on hairstyles.)

From the groin, up through the chest, and to the clavicle, the male physique has one central vertical line, which is very convenient for artists. Remember that a male has a trunk leading down to his hips; compare the male and female physiques shown here, and see pages 14–15 for more detail.

Beachwear often features colorful, floral designs. Remember, though, that this is sportswear, so skimpy bikinis and tiny trunks may not be very practical!

If you're drawing a surfer, be sure to remember the small strap that keeps him attached to the board. Safety first!

CLOTHING AND ACCESSORIES

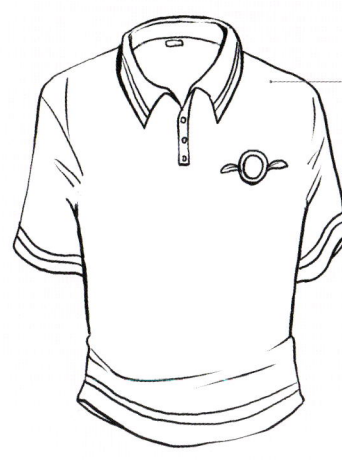

Here, the turned-down collar of this polo shirt is held in place by the buttons. If the buttons are left undone, the collar will flare out a little more.

Look up athletic figures online to study muscle usage and shape.

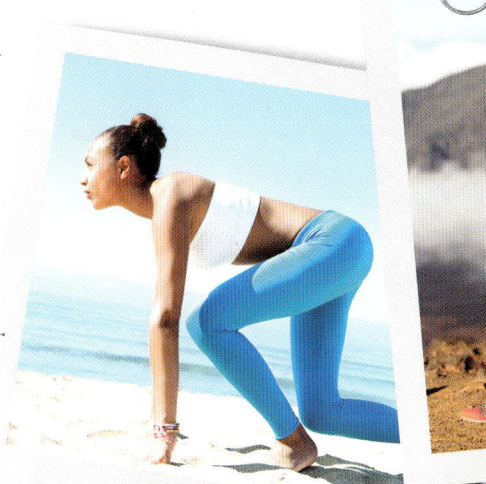

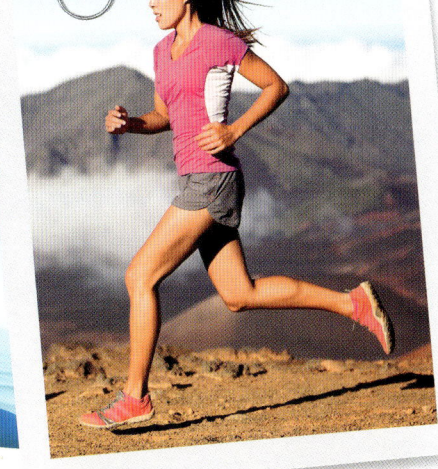

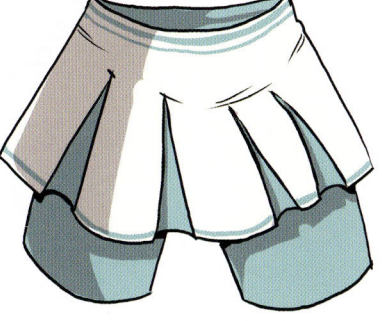

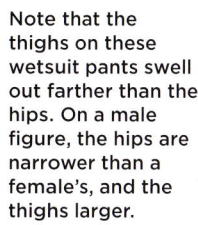

This tank top is designed for the male, opposite. The single-stripe design will accentuate his smooth shape, whereas it wouldn't necessarily work on a female model.

Note that the thighs on these wetsuit pants swell out farther than the hips. On a male figure, the hips are narrower than a female's, and the thighs larger.

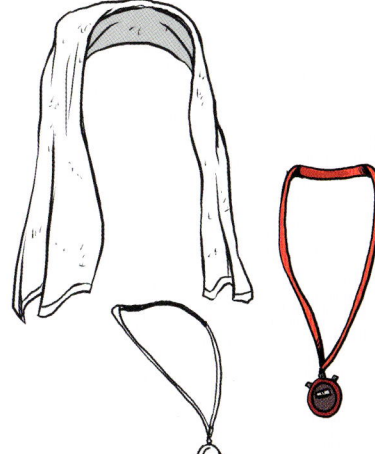

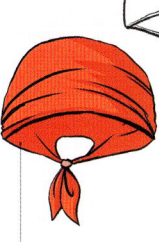

Whistles, stopwatches, and sweat towels are great accessories for any sports model. And they give something to wear around the neck. Straps can be personalized.

A pulled material bandana follows the same rules as a ponytail—show that the material is being pulled to a point behind the head by adding crease lines that follow the curve around to the knot.

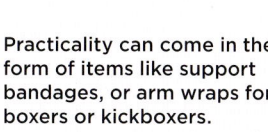

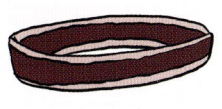

Practicality can come in the form of items like support bandages, or arm wraps for boxers or kickboxers.

For flippers, draw a shape that would fit over the model's foot, and then add a generous length, tapering outward.

SPORTSWEAR | 137

BON CHIC BON GENRE

BON CHIC BON GENRE (ALSO KNOWN AS BCBG) IS THE NAME OF A **FRENCH STREET FASHION** THAT TRANSLATES AS "GOOD STYLE, GOOD ATTITUDE." IT IS A FASHION THAT ORIGINATED WITHIN THE WELL-EDUCATED, UPPER CLASSES OF FRANCE AND, AS A RESULT, COMBINES **CURRENT FASHION TRENDS WITH AN AIR OF ARISTOCRATIC CLASS**. IT SHARES SIMILARITIES WITH PREPPY FASHION (SEE PAGES 46–49) IN THAT IT COMBINES ELEGANT BLOUSES, DRESSES, AND COATS WITH OTHER, MORE CASUAL ACCESSORIES, SUCH AS HATS AND CARDIGANS, FOR A **STYLISH**, YET **WELL-TAILORED LOOK**.

1 The average BCBG wearer is likely to be one confident, classy lady, so when drawing a model to show off these high-class clothes, make sure that she's got all the poise that she needs to make her look good. By having a strong, outwardly curving spine and holding her shoulders back, your model will exude an air of confidence and self-assuredness.

2 Draw your model's body around the rough skeleton. BCBGs are slender, classy, elegant ladies—don't forget a hand on the hips to give her added character.

3 BCBG combines elegant styles with casual, relaxed, and readily available clothing. This outfit shows off an elegant, ruffled blouse and high-waisted crop pants with a cardigan and a pair of flat loafers: imagine a short, summer's day walk or a boat trip down the Seine.

4 At this point of your sketching, details are the most important way to show off the cut of your clothes, and to make clear from which fabrics they are made. For example, drawing in the flat-felled seam of the pants shows that they're made of denim, and the ribbing along the cuff of the cardigan shows that it is woolen. Adding plenty of folds and creases in the blouse also expresses the idea that it is a thin, lightweight fabric.

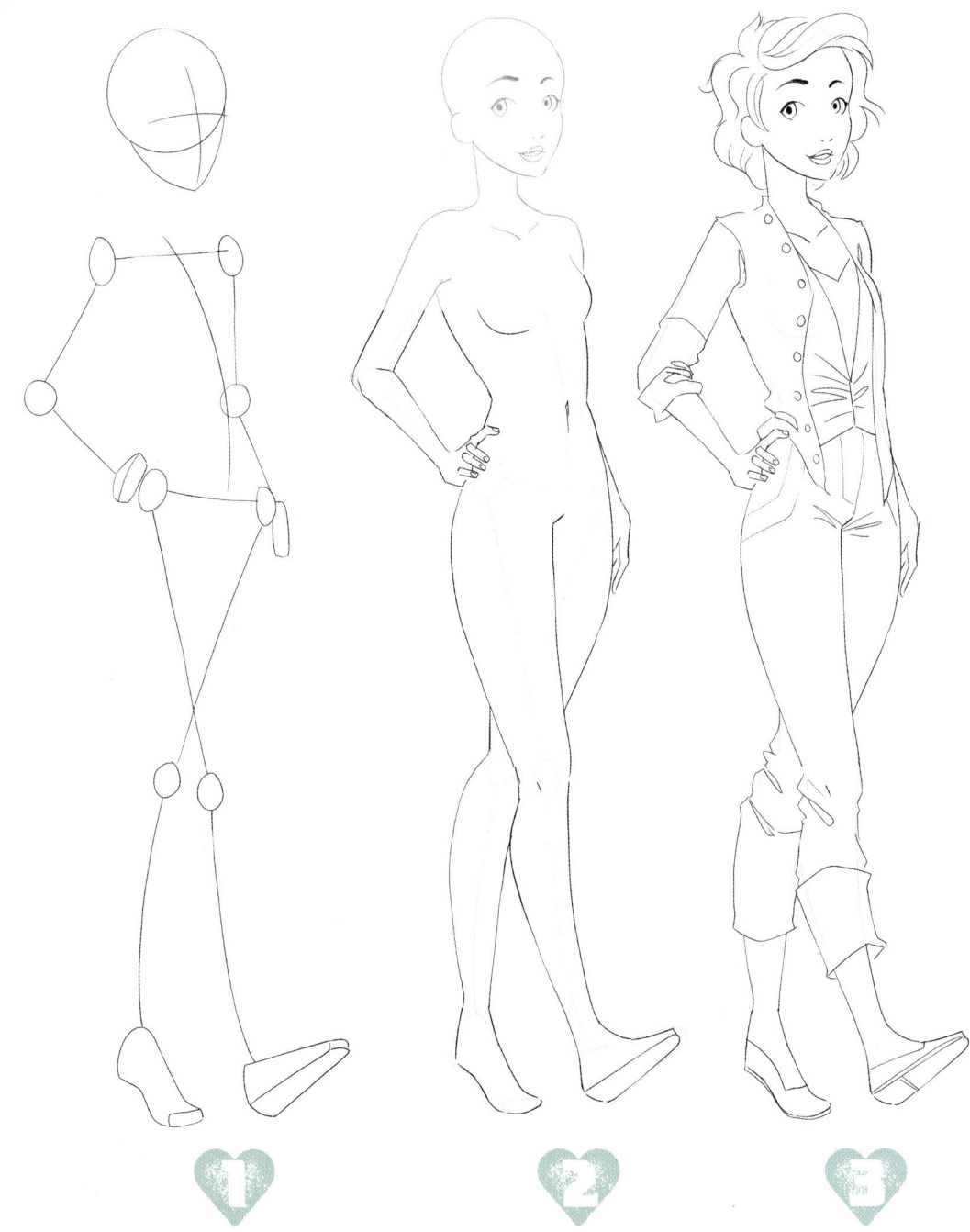

BON CHIC BON GENRE | **139**

5 Keeping in mind your color scheme, take a little while to look at your model and work out which colors suit which areas of the outfit best. Using a neutral brown for the cardigan keeps the outfit from looking too garish, whereas small sections of the lighter blue in the blouse and shoes make the whole look more eye-catching.

6 Adding a light source and subsequent shading helps define the folds and shape of your garment. For example, here it helps to emphasize the ruched detailing of the blouse, as well as giving definition to the soft, natural waves of the model's hairstyle, which has been chosen to complement the outfit. Though the model also has dark, lipstick, the rest of her makeup is kept natural; a touch of soft, pink blush reflects the understated yet feminine look of the style.

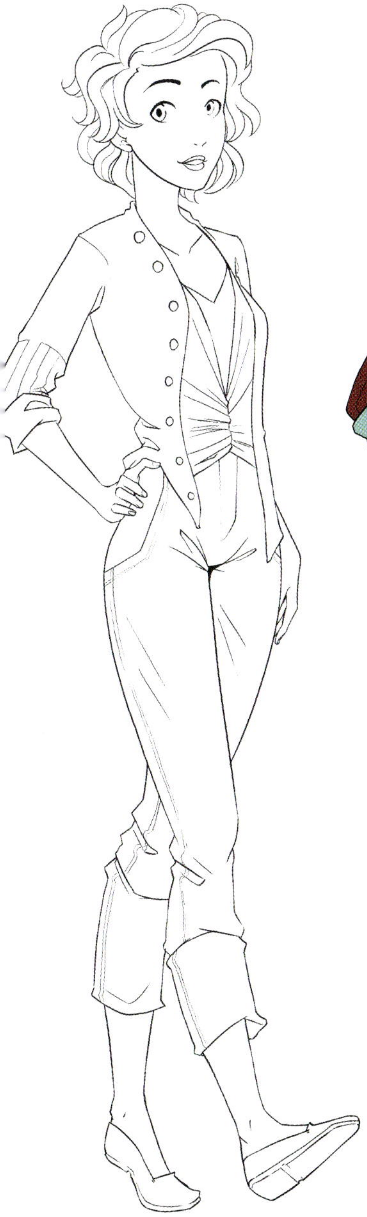

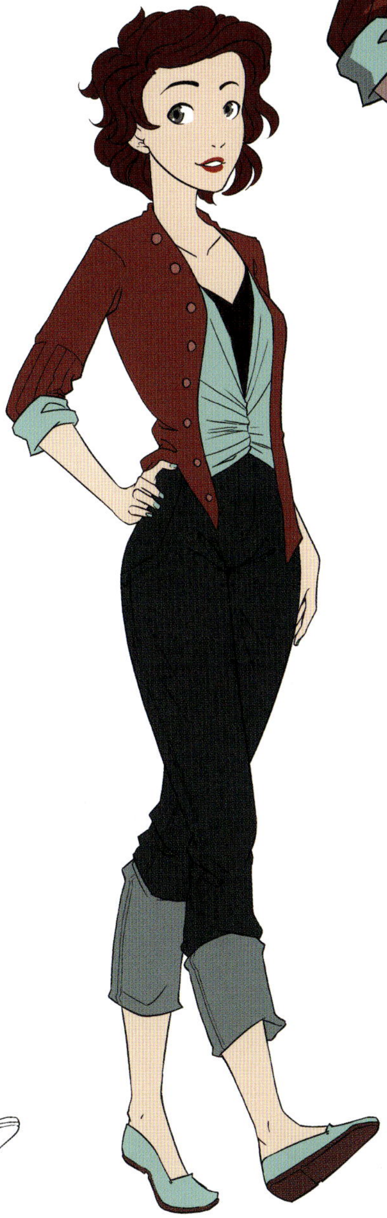

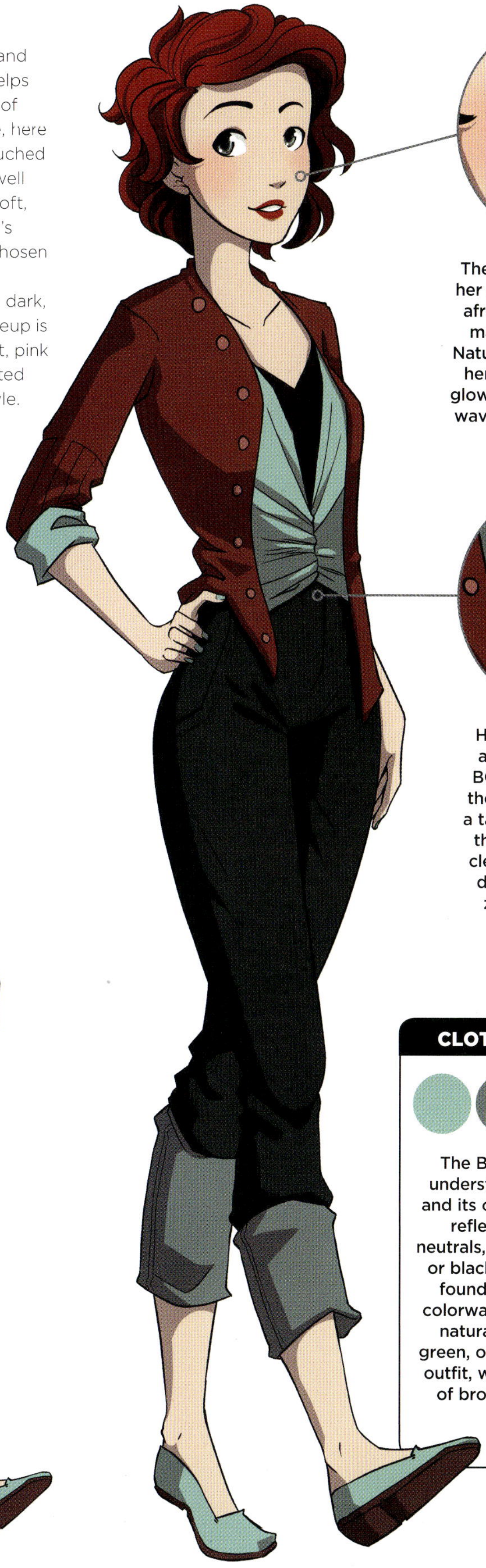

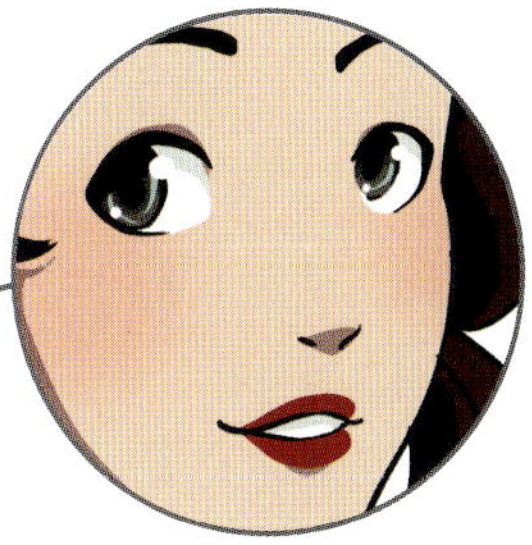

The BCBG girl is aware of her natural beauty, but not afraid to accentuate it to make herself stand out. Natural-colored blush gives her skin a healthy, active glow, and lipstick and short, wavy hair keep her looking fun and outgoing.

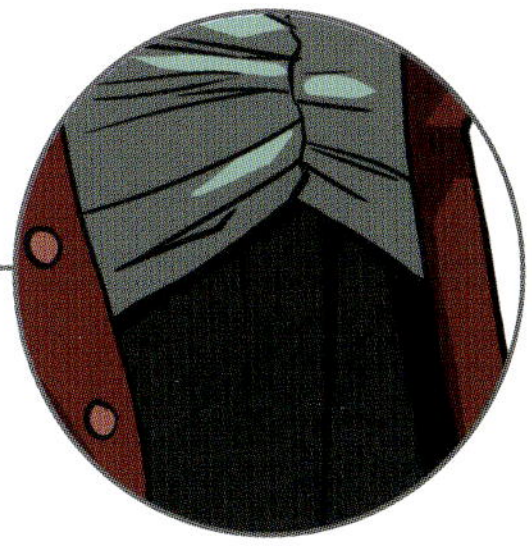

High-waisted pants are a popular staple in the BCBG look. Not only do they help give the model a tall, sleek silhouette, but they keep the waistline clear of any distracting details, such as belts, zippers, or buttons.

CLOTHING PALETTE

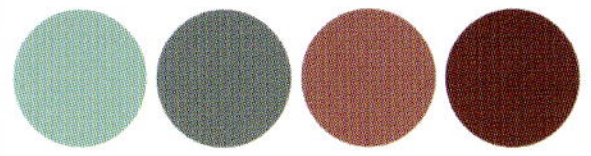

The BCBG look is about understated, elegant style, and its color palettes should reflect this. A base of neutrals, such as brown, gray, or black and white act as a foundation for a second colorway such as pastels, or naturals like dusky pink, green, or light orange. In this outfit, we'll be using shades of brown and variants of pastel blue.

140 | THE COLLECTIONS

One of the great features of the bon chic bon genre style is that it has a versatile range of looks. From casual, on-the-street outfits (such as that on page 139) to eveningwear and office clothing, different combinations of heels, shirts, coats, and hats create a plethora of looks to flesh out your BCBG collection.

Much of the modern BCBG style is inspired by clothing cuts and hairstyles from the early 1900s, and in fact it was the BCBG fashion movement that inspired many fashion designers of that period, such as Coco Chanel and Gucci. A short, tightly curled hairstyle adds a touch of vintage class to an outfit.

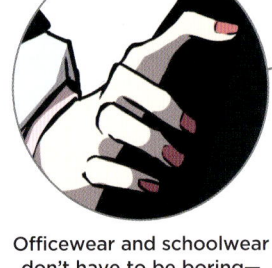

Officewear and schoolwear don't have to be boring—at least not when you're in Paris! Using accessories in the right place can stop any outfit from looking too dull. In this look, bright reds on the model's nails and in the belt make a bold statement.

Bold, straight stripes on the outside of a coat or the inside of an arm give the illusion of slimness, making an outfit appear elegant and elongated. This effect can even be replicated on the insides of pants or shoes.

Neckties aren't the only way to adorn a shirt or a blouse. Try replacing the classic necktie with a bow—not just a bow tie, but a ribbon tied in a bowknot. A silk, velvet, or satin bow will add interest and class to any outfit.

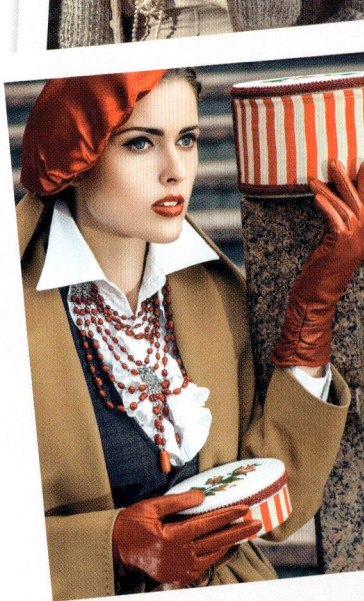

Long leather gloves, bold makeup, stylish headgear—all the essential elements are present to add that required panache.

CLOTHING AND ACCESSORIES

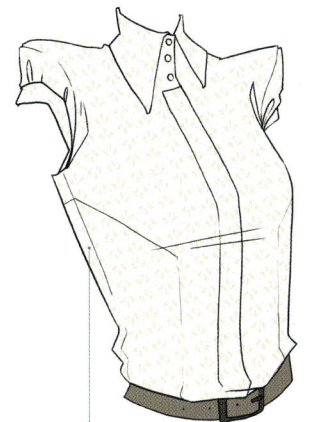
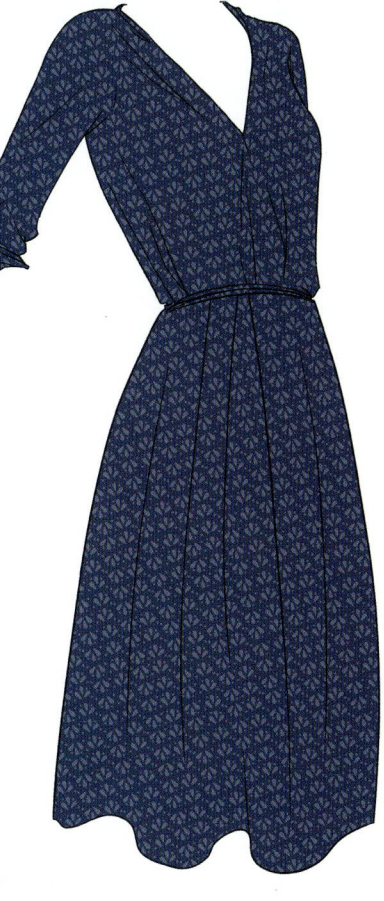
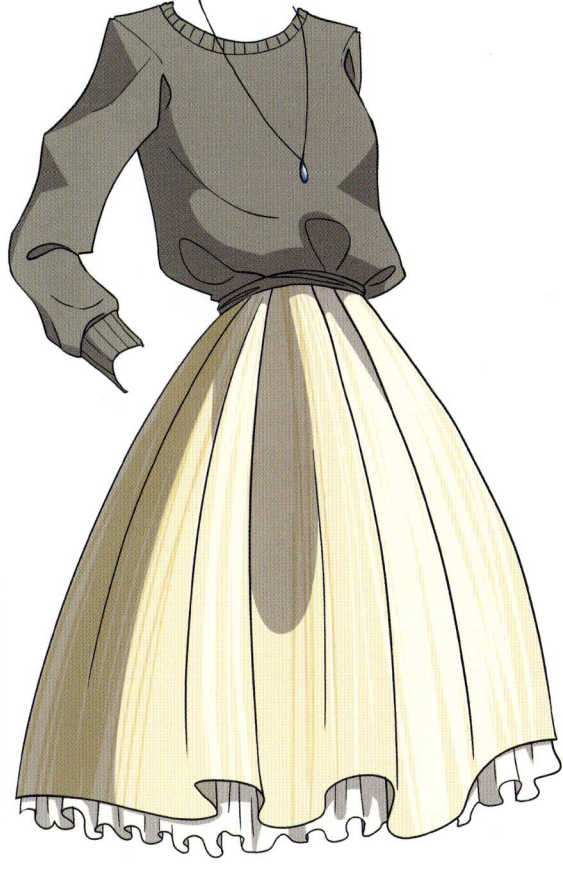

Along with an eye for acquiring good clothes, the BCBG girl knows just how to accessorize and wear them. A simple, patterned shirt goes well tucked into a plain leather belt, and even a loose dress can look stylish with a tie to pull in the waist and the sleeves folded back to the elbow. Pair a ruffled, tea-length dress with a comfortable woolen sweater for warm winter style.

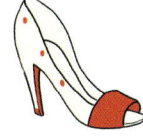
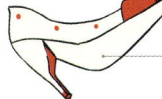
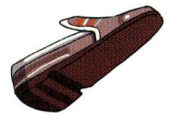
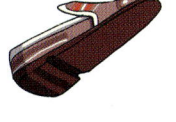
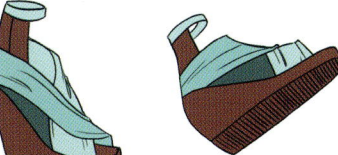
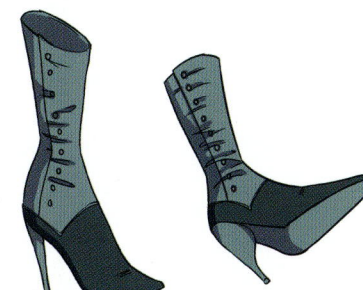

BCBG shoes not only need to be stylish, but practical too. Button-down boots, embroidered loafers, and classy heels are the perfect finishing touch for sashaying down the Parisian streets.

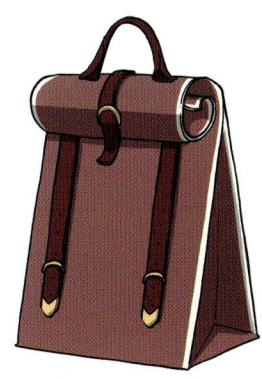

A leather (or faux leather) handbag is the perfect addition to a BCBG look. Whether in natural, undyed tones or with a splash of color to complement an outfit, the shape and style of a good bag can be just as important as the clothes.

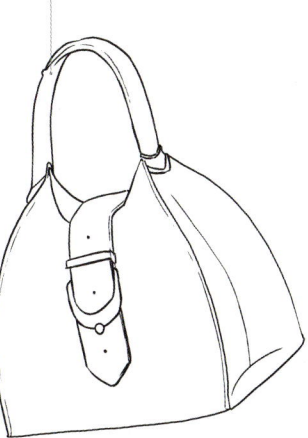
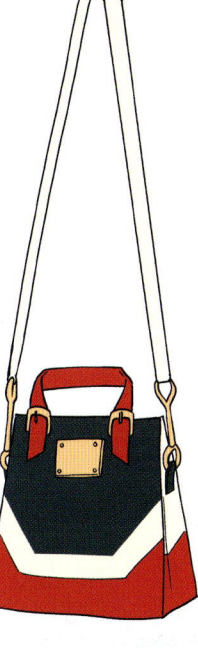

INDEX

A
A-line dresses 36
analogous colors 39
anatomy 14-15
Androgynous 122-125
ankle boots 37
Apocalypse Style 130-133
Argyle 30-31
asymmetric necklines 33
asymmetrical skirts 35

B
ballgown dresses 36
baseball caps 37
basque dresses 36
beanies 37
black skin tones 21
    dark cool tones 21
    dark warm tones 21
    warm tones 21
    yellow tones 21
blouse styles 32
boat necklines 33
Boho Chic 50-53
Bon Chic Bon Genre (BCBG) 138-141
boots 37

C
Chinese skin tones 20
classic garment styles 32-37
Classic Lolita 70-71
close-fitting clothes 24
    tight shirt 25
clothing 13
    basic folds 24
    movement 26-27
    pants crotch folds 25
    sleeves 24-25
color 38-39
color wheel 38
complementary colors 39
cowboy boots 37
cowl necklines 33
cropped pants 34
crowns 22
    back crowns 22
    multiple crowns 22
    side crowns 22
culottes 35
curly hair 22
Cyberpunk 102-105

D
denim 28
    creasing 28
    seams 28
Dolly Kei 96-97
double complementary colors 39
draped skirts 35
dress pants 34
dress styles 36
driver's caps 37

E
ear-flap knit caps 37
Egyptian skin tones 21
Emo and Scene 84-87
Empire-line dresses 36

F
fabrics 28
    denim 28
    leather 28
    mixing fabrics 29
    textile patterns 30-31
    thin fabric 25
female anatomy 14
female hairstyles 23
    bangs and braid combination 23
    buoyant vintage bob 23
    high ponytail 23
    loose and natural 23
    pixie cut 23
    straight, schoolgirl bob 23
footwear 37

G
Gaelic skin tones 20
Ganguro 76-79
godet skirts 35
Gothic Fashion 66-69
Gothic Lolita 74-75

H
hair 13
    crowns 22
    curly hair 22
hairlines 22
    curved hairlines 22
    heart-shaped hairlines 22
    peaked hairlines 22
    typically male hairlines 22
hairstyles 22
    long hair, female 23
    long hair, male 23
    short hair, female 23
    short hair, male 23
halter necklines 33
handkerchief skirts 35
Harajuku Street Style 42-45
harem pants 34
hats 26-27, 37
heads 18-19
    front view 18-19
    profile 18-19
headwear 26-27, 37
heels, wearing 17
Hip-Hop 126-129
Hipster 80-83
Hollywood Glam 58-61
hoods 37
hotpants 35
houndstooth 30-31

I
illusion necklines 33

J
Japanese skin tones 20
jeans 25

K
keyhole necklines 33
Kimono Street Style 98-101
kitten heels 37
Korean skin tones 20

L
lace 29
    adding a trim 29
    drawing a lace trim 29
lantern skirts 35
leather 28
    aged leather 28
    natural creases 28
long shorts 35
loose-fitting clothes 24
loose shirt 25
lounge pants 34

M
male anatomy 15
male hairstyles 23
    crew cut with pushed-up bangs 23
    formal combed hair with side parting 23
    long ponytail 23
    loose, curly hair 23
    punk-rocker Mohawk 23
    spiky hair with side parting 23
mandarin necklines 33
Mary Janes 37
maxi skirts 34
Mediterranean skin tones 21
Melanesian skin tones 21

mermaid skirt dresses 36
Mesoamerican skin tones 21
Miami Beach 88-91
Military 114-117
Mongolian skin tones 20
monochrome colors 39
mules 37

N

necklines 33
newsboy caps 37

P

palazzo pants 35
pants 25, 27
    casual pants 25
    dress pants 25
    pants styles 34-35
    skinny jeans 25
paper-bag shorts 35
patent leather 28
pencil skirts 34
Peter Pan necklines 33
platforms 37
pleated skirts 26-27, 34
plunge necklines 33
Polish skin tones 20
posing 13, 16-17
posture 17
Preppy Style 46-49
primary colors 38
Punk Style 54-57

R

riding boots 37
ringlets 22
Rock Royalty 62-65
Romanian skin tones 20

S

Scandinavian skin tones 20
secondary colors 38
shirts 25
shoes 37
shorts 26-27
    shorts styles 35
skater skirts 34
skin tones 20-21
skinny pants 34
skirts 26
    front and back 27
    pleated skirts 26-27, 34
    skirt styles 34-35
sleeves 24-25
split complementary colors 39
Sportswear 134-137
stetsons 37
stilettos 37
strapless necklines 33
Sunday Loungewear 106-109
Sweet Lolita 72-73
sweetheart necklines 33

T

T-straps 37
tartans 30-31
tertiary colors 38
thigh-high boots 37
triad colors 39
trilby hats 37
turtleneck necklines 33

V

Vintage Collection 92-95

W

wedges 37
Wilderness Chic 110-113
Winter Knitwear 118-121

RESOURCES

FASHION BLOGS AND REFERENCES
- **Vogue trends:**
  www.vogue.com/fashion/trends
- **She Wears Fashion:**
  www.shewearsfashion.com
- **Street Peeper:**
  www.streetpeeper.com
- **Le 21 Eme:**
  www.le21eme.com
- **Altamira NYC:**
  www.altamiranyc.com
- **The Sartorialist:**
  www.thesartorialist.com

SOFTWARE AND HARDWARE
- **Photoshop, Illustrator, Flash:**
  www.adobe.com
- **Painter:**
  www.corel.com
- **Graphics tablets:**
  www.wacom.com

TRADITIONAL ART SUPPLIES
- **Copic:**
  www.copicmarker.com
- **Deleter:**
  www.deleter.com

ONLINE ART GALLERIES
- **Deviantart:**
  www.deviantart.com
- **Pixiv:**
  www.pixiv.net
- **Society 6:**
  www.society6.com

BLOG AND WEBSITE HOSTING
- **Livejournal:**
  www.livejournal.com
- **Wordpress:**
  www.wordpress.com
- **Tumblr:**
  www.tumblr.com

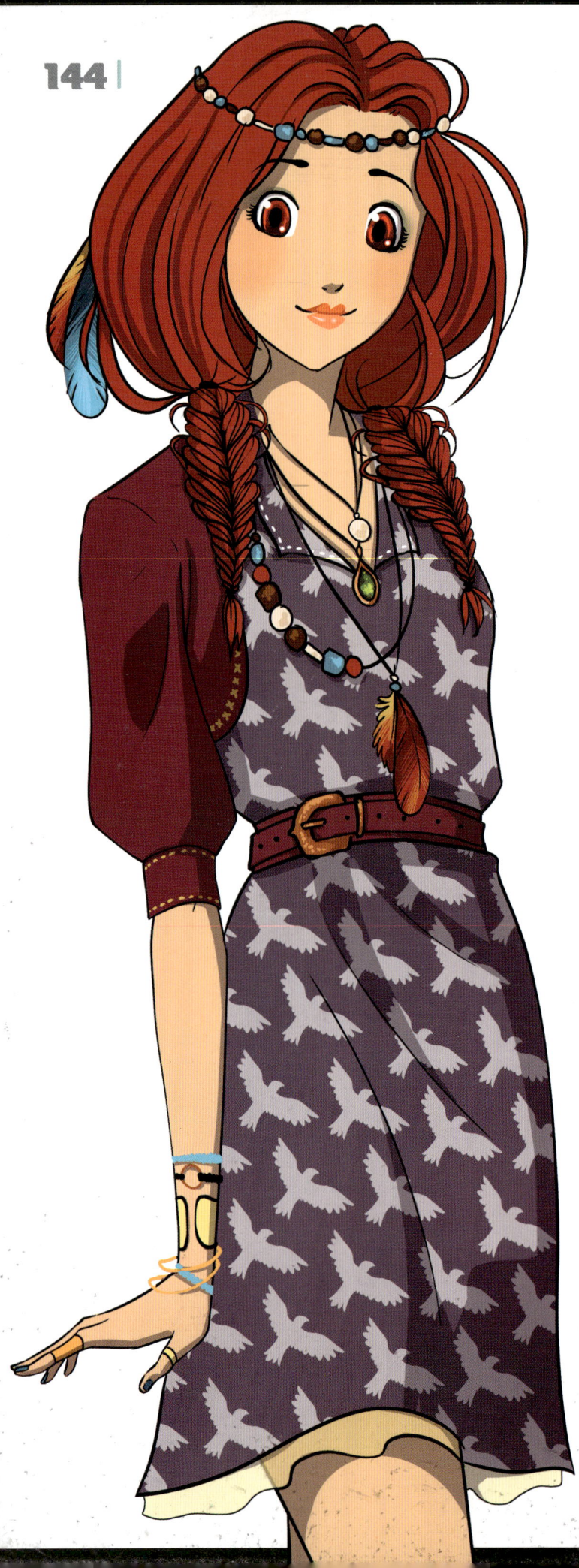

CREDITS

Quarto would like to thank the following for supplying images for inclusion in this book:

- Anchiy, Shutterstock.com, p.125cr
- Ayakovlevcom, Shutterstock.com, p.137tl
- Chaoss, Shutterstock.com, p.69cl
- Elisanth, Shutterstock.com, p.69tl
- Gladkov, Viktor, Shutterstock.com, p.53tr
- Gromovataya, Shutterstock.com, p.121
- Kharichkina, Elena, Shutterstock.com, p.53tl
- KPG_Payless, Shutterstock.com, p.73tr
- lightpoet, Shutterstock.com, p.121cr
- Maridav, Shutterstock.com, p.137tr
- Photocreative, Shutterstock.com, p.125tr
- Sherstobitov, Alexander, Shutterstock.com, p.65cr

All step-by-step and other images are the copyright of Quarto Publishing plc. While every effort has been made to credit contributors, Quarto would like to apologize should there have been any omissions or errors, and would be pleased to make the appropriate correction for future editions of the book.